LOVE
and FAULTS

LOVE
and FAULTS

Personalities Who Have Changed
the History of Tennis in My Lifetime

BY **TED TINLING**
with **ROD HUMPHRIES**

CROWN PUBLISHERS, INC., NEW YORK

FOR

Gladys Heldman and Joseph F. Cullman 3rd,
who, in changing the face of tennis, also changed my life

Grateful acknowledgments

To Bonnie Stahl, vice-president, Ruder and Finn, New York City, for invaluable
    guidance on American semantics
To the United States Tennis Association, for access to the USTA library
To DD and John Eisenberg, for the provision of very helpful material
To William J. Clothier, Jr., for access to his extensive tennis library
To Lynne Humphries, for hundreds of hours of transcription
To the *New Statesman*, for *Sagittarius*'s satirical lines
To Evelyn Dewhurst, Suzanne Lenglen's companion and opponent during their
    exhibition tour of Great Britain in 1927, for many interesting recollections of
    Lenglen
To Crown Executive Editor Lawrence Freundlich, for editorial guidance and assistance
Particularly to Rod Humphries for his generous patience in recording this story.

Author's Note: During the past five years outstanding progress has been made in the stabilization of
worldwide tennis administration. The criticisms made in *Love and Faults* of national and international establishments have, therefore, been outdated and should not be taken as applicable to any
person or persons holding office in today's structure.

©*1979 by Ted Tinling and Rod Humphries*

Printed in the United States of America

Published simultaneously in Canada by General Publishing Company Limited

Designed by Ruth Kolbert Smerechniak

Library of Congress Cataloging in Publication Data
Tinling, Ted
    Love and faults.

    1. Tennis players—Biography.   I. Humphries, Rod,
joint author.   II. Title.
GV994.A1T48   1979   796.34'2'0922 [B]   78-23276
ISBN 0-517-53305-7

Contents

[1]

Kingdom in the Sun

WHAT DO YOU DO WHEN A KING SPITS ON YOU?

This was the awkward question that confronted me at a gala dinner on the French Riviera in the 1920s. In those days the King of Sweden, eighty-year-old Gustav V, was a Riviera habitué. The Riviera meant gala dinners and tennis. Even at eighty, he was a devotee of both.

My neighbor that night was Edna May, the beautiful American star who had been the original Belle in *The Belle of New York*. Beyond her, to her right, was the king.

King Gustav still had his front teeth, but with large gaps on each side, so the trick, when he addressed you, was to stand squarely in front of him.

From the flanks at this dinner, I was in the full line of fire and when a large cube of meat landed on the lapel of my tuxedo, I was uncertain as to the correct course of action.

Edna May, being the perfect hostess, glanced quickly behind her. Meanwhile, the king leaned across Edna May, very purposefully removing the offending scrap, spittle and all, with his silk handkerchief. Carefully folding the handkerchief with the meat inside, he put it back into his breast pocket.

Not a word was said by anyone during this incident, but even the determined silence by the other guests taught me an early lesson in royal emergencies. Whatever you may think correct, a king will do it his way.

For the high-life seekers of the '20s, whether they were kings or commoners, the French Riviera provided a wonderful and apparently unending honeymoon. The sheer physical beauty of that magic coastline, beginning at Cannes and ending forty miles to the east at the Italian frontier, has never failed to cast an extraordinary, magnetic spell.

Two thousand years ago the Romans aptly named this strip the Azure Coast, and they called the bay that frames the proud city of Nice the Bay of Angels. Today's playground resorts of Cannes, Nice, Monaco, Monte Carlo, and Menton still shimmer at the base of the Maritime Alps like glittering jewels in the hot haze of the day or the particularly intense blue of Mediterranean nights.

Along the countless promontories and inlets of this coastline, dark cypresses and parasol pines blend almost imperceptibly into the edges of the royal blue water. In places, towering cliffs rise directly out of the sea to a height of over 3,000 feet, giving the whole seaboard a natural shield against the rain clouds that come traditionally from the north.

The parched lower levels of these cliffs are covered with an effusion of drab olive and locust trees. The English, more accustomed to fresh northern greenery, are often disappointed at their first sight of the Riviera, but it does not take long before its muted tapestry captures everyone with its own particular beauty.

Behind Nice is a stark hillside. Scorched by centuries of burning sun to a bald and arid dome, it gave Mussorgsky the inspiration for his famous orchestral piece *Night on Bald Mountain*.

Further along the coast the olives and cypresses shade into a more lush and exotic mixture. Tall date-palms tangle with acres of wild figs. Aloes and prickly pear make protective hedges around profusions of tuberoses, freesias, and mimosa. From first spring through late summer the scents of blossom and overripe fruit mingle to give off a heady fragrance that is the essence of Provence.

Queen Victoria, seeking refuge from the London fogs, was the first of the European monarchs to journey by horse carriage to this

o

"fragrant haven," as she described it in her private letters. Although invariably surrounded by her German relatives and her court ladies, a host of foreign ambassadors, anxious to report her every innovative movement to their own masters, closely followed her royal progress to the sunshine.

With Queen Victoria's presence acting like a magnet to the other royal courts of Europe, elaborate palaces and villas were built in exotically laid-out gardens. Eventually there was hardly a crowned head nor a royal courtier who did not spend his winter and spring days established in this sybaritic paradise.

Queen Victoria's middle and old age was the heyday of such French masters as Mistral, Cézanne, and van Gogh. Mistral gives a wonderfully impressionist word picture of Provence. The shimmering light of southern France inspired Cézanne and van Gogh to change the whole course of modern painting.

Lawn Tennis took its grasp of England in that same era, but the rich English found their garden lawns survived only a few summer months. They were deprived of their novel pastime by the cold and wet of the English winters. Although there were probably more indoor facilities in London then than there are today, they succumbed readily to the pleasanter prospect of chasing tennis balls under Mediterranean skies.

The first tennis courts in France were accordingly laid out by the English in the 1880s, amid the eucalyptus trees, the palms, and the flower beds of the Beau Site Hotel in Cannes. The name was appropriate because the beautiful gardens and the tennis courts remained there, unchanged for sixty years, from the days of the Renshaws, tennis's earliest idols, until World War II.

From the 1880s on there was an annual migration to the South of France of tennis players from America and almost every country in Europe. Every famous name in the game's history is inscribed somewhere on the rolls of honor of the clubs that still survive there. The records show that on the old Monaco courts the Doherty brothers won many early championships, and in Nice, there are still records, salvaged from the old club, of the first Central European masters of the game.

The settings were all extraordinarily beautiful because the courts everywhere were sited in a natural milieu of palms, oleanders, frangipanis, and mimosa, with the ubiquitous bougainvillea often climbing up the backstops. The surroundings were as typical of Provence as the gum-tree creeks are of Australia and the bayous of old colonial American plantations.

In the early part of this century palatial hotels, the first in Europe to include three- or four-hundred rooms, were built in strategic viewpoints in all the main Riviera centers. These were invariably crammed from Christmas through Easter with the complete *Almanach de Gotha*.

Also in those early days, Monaco, the tiny independent enclave in southern France now hereditarily ruled by Prince Rainier and Princess Grace, saw the commercial possibilities of organized gambling. The gilded enthusiasts were already there and searching for additional excitements.

Eventually, with the aid of François Blanc, who had already made Hamburg the gambling center of northern Europe, an ornate Casino was built on the rocky plateau neighboring Monaco. This plateau was dedicated with great ceremony on June 1, 1866, by the reigning prince Charles III, and given the name Monte Carlo.

In turn, Cannes and Nice decided that if they did not follow suit they would be losing out. So, piece by piece, this whole coastline was linked into the most luxurious and cosmopolitan playground ever recorded in history.

And it was there, on this coastline, surrounded by beauty and immersed in the crazy luxury-age of jazz and the Charleston, that I spent my formative years.

[2]

Thursday's Child

THE ENGLISH CHANNEL DIVIDES NORTHERN FRANCE FROM SOUTH-ern England. From its widest expanse, which stretches between Brittany and Cornwall, it narrows progressively eastward, squeezing its way through the Strait of Dover to the North Sea. The English Channel seldom smiles. Most times it seems an angry, frustrated strip of water, gray, choppy, and belligerent.

On the English south coast, sleepy fishing villages, dreaming of past glories, alternate with neat little towns and fussy ports, invaded daily by hordes of tourists who come on excursion steamers from France and Belgium.

Seventy miles inland, London has a firm hand on the life-styles of these coastal communities, which cluster like balloons on different lengths of string, their bright color or drabness varying with their different distances from the capital.

Brighton, the closest of these coastal towns, is only fifty miles from Piccadilly and has traditionally allowed London revelers and London's theaterland to commute daily back and forth to the seaside. Bournemouth, one hundred and twenty miles distant, adopts a more leisurely routine of biweekly visits. Here, too, are the picturesque White Cliffs of Dover and pasturelands of Romney Marsh (which have colonized the world with their highly prized breed of sheep.) And close by are the artists' dream villages of Wilchelsea and Rye, all white-painted clapboard and olde Englishe pubs, in spring, dripping with wistaria.

On fine days the coast of France, on the mainland of Europe, may appear in a haze on the horizon, reminding one that for 1,900 years until the blitz, the Channel made England an island fortress against the turbulence of Europe.

"The British Riviera," as the advertisements call it, extends westward from Dover to Southampton. Between lies the respected, and respectable, township of Eastbourne, less than ten miles from Pevensey Bay where William the Conqueror landed from Normandy in 1066. I remember Eastbourne as a windy place with the salt tang of fish in the cold air.

I should remember it well because I was born there on Thursday, June 23, 1910.

My father was a well-to-do certified public accountant. By Victorian standards, my mother had traveled extensively and we had an impressive and comfortable home. My mother was enthusiastic about the steam-heat systems she had seen in Sweden and had steam heat installed, making ours the first house in all southern England to enjoy this novelty. From romantic journeys to Italy, she brought back seedlings and planted a driveway of the flowering chestnut trees that give parts of Tuscany their ambiance.

My parents had good, solid Victorian first names: my father, James Alexander, my mother, Florence Elizabeth.

Our establishment was uncompromisingly middle class. In addition to my governess, there was a parlormaid, housemaid, "Cook," with her own kitchen maid, one man-servant, and a chauffeur. Being independent and humanitarian, my mother never encumbered herself with a personal lady's maid.

In the proper traditions of pre–World War I England, my child life, except for a brief time on Sundays, was controlled exclusively by my governess, Miss Pearce.

All my meals were served in the nursery, presided over by Miss Pearce. But on Sundays, when my parents took tea in the drawing room, Miss Pearce would take me to join them.

o

The Sunday tea ritual was a feast of delicate sandwiches and frosted cakes. But in Edwardian upbringing there was the stern discipline of eating four pieces of buttered bread before being allowed any cake. I remember quite a few occasions when I failed to reach the target of the eclairs or cream slices.

I was the spoiled child of the family because my elder brother, Collingwood, ten years older than I, was always away at his school, college or university. My second brother, Banastre, seven years my senior, was usually arriving at the same institutions just as my first brother was moving on.

I was born with a chronic chest problem, which the doctors described as bronchial asthma. As an annual routine I would be put to bed with the first wheezy nose cold of October and most times remained there until the following April.

Throughout, I was ceremoniously swathed in layers of lambs' wool. Frequently, I had dime-sized hives because it was not known in those days that one could be allergic to wool. The chest-rubbing routine with pungent camphorated oil still haunts my nightmares.

World War I was declared a few months after my fourth birthday. By then, my mother had taken it into her head to move us all to Pevensey Bay and in the summers of World War I I spent many long hours with Miss Pearce on the very beaches where William of Normandy began his approach to the Battle of Hastings. Battle, where the English were conquered for the only time in history, was a favorite picnicking spot for my governess. When it did not rain on Wednesdays, we invariably made the short journey by train and lunched on the grass among the ruins of Battle Abbey.

From 1915 to 1918 bombardments on the Western Front boomed or rumbled night and day across the sea, according to the direction of the wind. On the beach with my governess, I was already familiar in early childhood with bright explosions on the horizon, signifying the sinking of a ship in the Channel. Afterwards the high waterline would be cluttered for days with an endless assortment of goods, from cases of canned fruit to crates of ammunition that floated in on the tide.

The township of Eastbourne surrounds a picturesque, typically English, green woodland area known as Devonshire Park. The park accommodates twenty-plus tennis courts and has been a major stronghold of the British tennis calendar, having staged Britain's largest tournament annually since 1894.

Gentleman stars of the Edwardian era played the Eastbourne tournament as a matter of course. My mother was a regular spectator for a decade before I was born.

Probably the first tennis story I ever heard derived from my mother, reading in the newspaper, that Papa Lenglen had refused to bring Suzanne to Eastbourne because he was not satisfied with the terms offered. In tennis, the word "terms" had a horrendous significance in those amateur days.

After the Armistice of World War I my parents took my two brothers and me on a tour of the Flanders battlefields. "Glory" had been the feeling of millions of young bloods, who went, cheering, to their death for King and Country before 1918. My parents were intent on impressing us that there was no glory in war.

Later we settled for a while in Switzerland in an effort to resolve my chest problem. But my breathing never came to terms with cold air and it was then decided we should experiment with the winter sunshine of the South of France.

First we migrated *en famille* to one of the palatial hotels in Cimiez, behind Nice. Then, when my father's postwar finances showed signs of failing, we were forced to separate, my mother renting an apartment where I lived with her until a few months before her death.

In those teenage years I found it difficult to know what to believe: difficult to know right from wrong. My father was a God-fearing Victorian, the son of a clergyman and a staunch believer in the "Vengeance-of-Heaven" gospel. My mother was a progressive freethinker, always exploring the most newly conceived cults. In her youth she had been an ardent follower of Madame Blavatsky[1] and Annie Besant,[2] and later, of Rudolf Steiner.[3]

Meanwhile our friends, the English and American leisured classes, took off on the wild joyride of the '20s. The world turned upside down, and many of the sacred beliefs we were taught at my Catholic day school were tossed recklessly to the wind by the grownups.

Adolescence hit me just when Hollywood scenes were spilling into

1. Helena Petrovna Blavatsky (1831–91). Russian-born founder of the Theosophical Society (New York, 1875). Its aims were (a) to form a nucleus of universal brotherhood without distinction of race, color, creed or sex; (b) to promote study of comparative religion, philosophy, and science; and (c) to investigate the unexplained laws of nature and powers latent in man. Her mother, Russian novelist Elena Hahn, was among the first ever to advocate the emancipation of women (circa 1850).
2. Annie Besant (1847–1933). Originally atheist, British social reformer, strike leader, union organizer. First prominent English woman to advocate birth control. Converted to Fabian Socialism by George Bernard Shaw (1885). Suddenly reoriented by Blavatsky doctrines to Theosophy and became International President of the Theosophical Society in 1907.
3. Rudolf Steiner (1861–1925). Austrian philosopher and artist. At one time associated with the Theosophical Society. Later founded the independent Anthroposophical Society, another philosophic group dealing in spiritual science through enhanced consciousness (Dornach, Switzerland, 1913).

o

everyday life. The rich and famous were finding, on the sun-drenched Mediterranean, whatever stimulus they needed to recover from the hangovers of war.

Suddenly saxophones, cocktails, and shiny silk-stockinged legs became the new religion. Cole Porter and the Model T Ford were the new high-priests. Josephine Baker and Mistinguett became Queens of Paris overnight.

Then, of course, there was Tennis.

By the '20s the earlier aristocratic game had already taken its first downward steps toward being the plaything of the well-to-do middle classes. But from Christmas through Easter, the Riviera remained the in place for the stars and all the rich who surrounded them.

Tennis, dancing, and gambling were the catalysts of the high-fashion winter calendar, and Suzanne Lenglen, the unquestioned Queen of Art Deco, was the Pied Piper who had only to appear on a peal of laughter to have crowds flocking to see her play tennis between the cocktail hour and the thé-dansants.

"Prime time" for Suzanne's matches was always arranged to coincide with these rituals. Her matches were invariably concluded in forty-five minutes and everyone would then head for the hotel bars only to reappear at 4 p.m., rebeautified and regarbed for tea and dancing at the casinos. After that the women would ride back to their hotels for a Mah-Jongg session while the men gambled until it was time to change to their white-vested tuxedos for the gala dinners.

Every nationality and every type of person met up at the casinos. There were kings, famous financiers, demimondaines with their lovers, crooks, Hollywood silent stars, and the aristocracy of half-a-dozen countries, all mixed in with the old crones who needed twelve hours of daily good luck at the tables for the price of their hotel bills.

Many of the elegant women preferred to show off their Paris creations and their jewels while dancing rather than standing behind their husbands or lovers in the gaming rooms.

At the back tables round the dance floors, the good-looking professional gigolos sat alone, perusing the scene with unfailing instinct. For them, protocol involved the ultimate in formality, bowing low to the husband of any obviously married couple and saying, "May I have permission to invite Madame to dance?"

Following the nightly gala dinners, there would often be fireworks displays to amuse the bejeweled women while some of the richest men in the world puffed at their cigars. A second migration to the gaming tables would take place about 11:30, when millions of francs would change hands until sunrise. Then the whole round would begin again with mid-morning champagne and Suzanne's daily match.

I became a part of this now-extinct life-style through my infatuation with tennis. As a kid, I had had the usual condescending games with my elder brothers.

Then I received a gift subscription enabling me to become a schoolboy member of the Nice Tennis Club. Years later I was delighted to learn that Suzanne Lenglen had begun her tennis in the same way, with a school membership at the same club.

At thirteen I lived, and would gladly have died, for tennis. Schoolboy members were allowed to play only in out-of-school hours, which meant on Thursday and Sunday afternoons. To this day, I still recall the agonizing difference in enduring the three blank days from Sunday to Thursday and the two more blank days between Thursday and Sunday. Every Thursday and Sunday, on the stroke of midday, I was at the Nice Club, either waiting for one of my classmates to arrive, or just standing around goofing.

The Nice Club was Suzanne's personal empire and many times I waited for her appearance just to gape at the sight of her. I think now that I already had an affinity with fabrics, color, and design; certainly the glamor consciousness and the panache she projected already had an inborn fascination for me.

Ever since childhood my mother had read me accounts of the great tennis personalities like Tilden and Patterson, and of course, Lenglen.

As some boys collect photographs of film stars, or nowadays rock idols, I would adorn my bedroom wall with pictures of tennis greats. Actually living in the same city, playing in the same tennis club as the Empress herself, was very heady stuff in my teens.

Even now I can sense the excitement and electricity Suzanne generated in me the first time I saw her play. She had a special joy and abandon just from hitting the ball, with her perfect coordination making the opportunity for her ballet leaps and a projection that suggested complete sexual fulfillment from her own flowing movements.

At the time I was one of the youngest rookies of the club and I was soon to sympathize with the slaves of ancient Egypt for whom a mere glimpse of Cleopatra became a compulsive and rewarding ritual.

Destiny finally put it all together in '24. Lenglen was ready and waiting to make her entrance to the center court. But no one had thought to arrange an umpire ahead of time.

January 4 was the moment of confrontation when I was unsuspectingly recruited as a tennis umpire, five months before my fourteenth birthday. I was well and truly baptized by fire, as my first-ever experience of officiating in tennis was to call a match for the Incomparable

o

Lenglen herself. I was to earn my living in tennis administration on the Riviera for the following eight years.

On that fateful day I was just standing around hoping for a single glance from Suzanne as she passed through the exotic, flower-lined setting of the Nice club, when a voice said, "Have you ever called a match?"

I felt an immediate electric tremor as I spun round to find myself face-to-face with the Empress herself. I had hardly noticed the speaker had been Mrs. Wollaston Richards, the well-meaning but ineffectual British director of the tournament.

"I have never umpired," I told Mrs. Richards, my gaze still riveted on Suzanne. Before I could say another word, Mrs. Richards asked Suzanne, "Would you mind this young man calling your match?"

Awaiting her reply, I somehow knew the years ahead would be affected. At that moment I was already convinced that if Suzanne rejected me the whole course of my future would be different.

Instead, Suzanne flashed a radiant smile and said, *"Mais avec plaisir*, I would be delighted!" This had to be on a Thursday because funny things, like being born, always happen to me on Thursdays.

Thereafter I was incorporated straightaway into Suzanne's close entourage, which consisted of Papa and Mama Lenglen backed by the handsome escorts with whom Suzanne invariably made her entrances, and most often on a contrived peal of laughter.

The escorts were dismissed to front-row seats in the stands for the duration of the match while Papa and Mama Lenglen sat on a court-side bench beneath the umpire's chair. On Mama's lap, perched rather belligerently on a rug, was her pet Belgian Griffon, Gyp.

As Suzanne removed her luxurious winter coat, revealing a brilliantly colored cardigan over a white silk pleated dress, I stood hypnotized until I realized I should already be climbing the steps of the umpire's chair. Suzanne's opponent of the day was quite capable of rallying with her, but, like me, was overawed by the occasion.

Naturally I had never before experienced any situation like this. Papa and Mama Lenglen chattered incessantly on the bench below me. At that age I spoke better French than English and my thoughts wandered repeatedly as I overheard, fascinated, their running commentary on Suzanne's every movement.

"She's not arching her back on her serve today," from Papa Lenglen.

"I liked last year's cardigans without sleeves much better," from Mama.

With Gyp yapping with every rising intonation of the Lenglens'

o

Thursday's Child 11

voices, it was probably excusable that I became distracted.

The match had started when I realized I had not marked the umpire's blank and did not remember the score. Now, more than fifty years later, I still recall the stage fright and apprehension I felt, with beads of frozen perspiration falling inside my shirt.

Fortunately, the club's head ball-boy, Victor, who was also the friendly assistant pro, had been keeping an eye on the whole proceedings. Realizing my problem, he maneuvered himself beside my chair. This gave me the chance to ask his help. He prompted me, and I was saved.

Suzanne was very friendly after the match and introduced me to her parents with the customary French formality of the era.

The next day Mrs Richards told me Papa Lenglen had suggested that I call all Suzanne's matches. The organizers, accustomed to being scared to death by Suzanne's tantrums, were greatly relieved at this prospect.

There is always one lad in every stable who, by some unaccountable bond of telepathic sympathy, can hold the bridle of the star runner in peace and calm.

For two teenage years I was that "stableboy" to the greatest tennis star ever known.

Suddenly the old nursery rhyme became appropriate:

> Monday's child is fair of face,
> Tuesday's child is full of grace,
> Wednesday's child is full of woe,
> Thursday's child has far to go . . .

[3]

La Petite Suzanne

FROM 1919 TO 1926 ALL EUROPE, AS WELL AS THE LOTUSLAND
of the Riviera, belonged to Lenglen. She was the Southern Empress,
as unique herself as the capital cities of Europe and the sun-drenched
coastline over which she reigned supreme.

"Lenglen," wrote Grantland Rice at the time, "is not set up as any
female beauty, but she is beautiful as an athlete when the flaming
colors she wears begin to move, a red or orange lightness blown in the
wind." In a contemporary observation, Wallis Merrihew, editor of
the magazine *American Lawn Tennis*, said, "She seems to move *over*
the court not *on* it, as if she had winged feet."

Suzanne spent her youthful years in Nice and she remained faithful
to Nice when she became a star. The city recognized her loyalty by
giving the Lenglen family use of the Villa Ariem, a comfortable
residence in the heart of the exiled Russian community, and directly
facing the gates of the Nice Tennis Club.

The original Nice Club consisted of two courts in the Place Mozart, a tree-lined square in the town center. Suzanne's extraordinary attractions outdated this overnight when she first won at Wimbledon. For once, those in authority had the good sense to recognize this by planning twenty new courts on a beautiful hillside site. From the present clubhouse, built in 1921, the view of the city below and the grand sweep of the blue Mediterranean is reminiscent of the set good opera-houses use for the first act of *Madame Butterfly!*

The Parc Imperial, the name given to the club area by its expatriate Russian neighbors in remembrance of their past glories, contains one of the few Riviera clubs that are not located on the grounds of some luxury hotel. Until the present Monte Carlo club materialized in 1928, I do not believe there was a tennis club anywhere in the world where the natural beauty of the surroundings was as effectively blended with functional efficiency as in Nice.

The Nice clubhouse is a traditional Provençal "Maas," all flat-roofed pink stucco and white marble.

During Suzanne's reign there was usually a long row of terra-cotta Roman vases—separating the clubhouse from the main courts—which overflowed in early spring with torrents of bright pink geraniums. In late March these would be replaced with banks of sweet peas. Later there would be tall hedges of pink roses. The courts themselves were the same shade of terra-cotta as the rocks of the coastline. Bill Caudery, the first of the present club's secretaries, had the artistic taste to have all the court backstops painted the darkest of dark green, matching the surrounding cypresses.

Into this setting, almost daily from October through March, Suzanne would appear like some exotic bird of paradise. During the pre-Christmas months she would practice for hours on end, sometimes inviting the three Burke brothers from Cannes to play doubles with her. After Christmas the round of tournaments, which continued till Easter, would claim all her energy.

Somehow her star personality and the stage colorings of the settings combined to make her matches into gala appearances. Rich hostesses might have taken a party of guests to see Pavlova dance the previous night in Monte Carlo; they may have been to hear Galli-Curci in Cannes, or on an extravagant spending spree at Chanel's, but everybody would head for the midday tennis to see Suzanne play. She was the ultimate "diva" of sport, and she contrived to bring a taste of highly sophisticated theater to a world previously centered only on a leisurely pastime.

Suzanne was born at Compiègne, in northern France, on May 24,

1899. Papa Lenglen had been a pioneer racing bicyclist during the sudden Victorian fascination for speed, when ice-skating and bicycling first made possible for everybody the excitement of fast independent movement without the aid and expense of a horse.

Six-day bicycle races became a major attraction of the '80s and '90s, and the competitors, coming for the most part from a proletariat background, were professionals. They were not hypocritically shy like the gentlemen sportsmen, but proud of their moneymaking aptitute.

So Papa Lenglen generated early on a fixed and unbreakable habit of going after the main prize. On the other hand, if he could not win, he thought it more practical to conserve his energies by giving up the fight.

In the French language, to give up is to "abandon." The few times in Suzanne's life when her eventual victory may have been in question from whatever circumstance, Papa Lenglen, from years of practical French logic and uninhibited by any upper-class sporting code, would command his daughter, from the courtside or the stands, "Abandonne."

The introduction of this attitude to the Edwardian code of ethics, which was still law to many of Suzanne's opponents, gave her critics a head start for the repeated accusations of quitter that she endured to the bitter end of her amateur career.

From Suzanne's earliest childhood Papa Lenglen was determined to find, in his only offspring, the world supremacy that eluded his own performances. In Suzanne, destiny gave him the material to fulfill this ambition to the ultimate degree. From Suzanne's nursery days, the only question in Papa Lenglen's mind was at which sport she could excel the most easily.

As a growing child, Suzanne's natural effervescence and grace were such that when the Lenglens moved to the Riviera, strollers on the Promenade des Anglais, the seafront of Nice, would stop to admire her as she tossed and caught her toy diabolo on a string. Her capacity to entrance an audience, even at the age of eight or nine, was such that the visitors would inquire of the Lenglens what time Suzanne was likely to be there the next day.

Suzanne's immediate predecessor as champion of France and the last player to inflict a fair-and-square singles defeat on Suzanne in her whole life, was a very beautiful French girl, Marguerite Broquedis. Were Suzanne alive today, Madame Broquedis would be her senior by six years. She lives out her seniority with expectable grace in Orléans, the French city that has a centuries-old familiarity with heroines from its associations with the original Maid of Orléans, Joan of Arc.

Madame Broquedis was a Riviera habituée, and in my teens was still ranked annually among the world's first-ten players. Our lives went different ways and we had not met for fifty years, but I was anxious to obtain her memories of the beginnings of French tennis as well as her recollections of Suzanne Lenglen. For this purpose, I went from the '77 Wimbledon Centennial to visit with her in her French home.

Madame Broquedis told me how she had played her earliest tennis in Paris in a virtual fairground, appropriately named the Galerie des Machines. The novelty of tennis courts had been seized upon by the promoters, and two dusty courts were sited between the Big Wheel and the Roller Coaster, surrounded by a track on which bicycle races regularly took place. This was an established birth pattern of early French tennis that logically linked Papa Lenglen's philosophies, his experiences, and his ambitions.

The Racing Club de France, still one of the two top tennis spots in Paris, was established with just three sandy courts. This was at the turn of the century, about the time of Madame Broquedis's migration there with her parents from her native Pau, in the Pyrenees.

Madame Broquedis told me that, as a young girl, she would sit for hours on a Racing Club bench with her mother as chaperone, waiting for an invitation to play with the better players. The routine in those early days was to provide one set of balls on each of the three courts on opening day (which would probably be in April), and the same balls would remain there all summer, as they were considered adequate for everyone's use until the club's winter closing six months later.

Historically, most of the steps taken toward women's tennis evolution, which Suzanne took a decade later with such dazzling brilliance, were first traced by Marguerite Broquedis. The first public disdaining of corsets and bras by a woman, the first published tennis-fashion columns in magazines, the first thoughts of special hairstyles for tennis, the first Olympic Gold Medal won for France by a woman, even the first suggestion that women's tennis should be beautiful, all derived from Madame Broquedis, and were given the added authority of her outstanding personal beauty.

Charles (Papa) Lenglen inherited from his father a local horse-bus network with the convenient addition of several hundred horses. In fact, I well recall some elderly English critics of his tennis concepts referring bitterly to him as "nothing, really, but a horse-dealer."

Once tennis was decided on for Suzanne's future, she was given an extra-light racquet when she was ten years old.

o

After the family's move to the Riviera, a strict schedule of training was set up in the Place Mozart with a swarthy young local professional called Negro. Long sessions against a backboard were also arranged under the guidance of Negro, and the ever-watchful eye of Papa. In addition, Suzanne was enrolled in a ballet class, and in all these activities, her laughing eyes and natural ebullience seemed to find some sort of joyous fulfillment.

Meanwhile Papa Lenglen was augmenting his income by helping out with the club's secretarial needs, and on Suzanne's twelfth birthday, he gave her an adult-sized racquet, asking her to promise that with it she would one day become champion of the world. He had only three years to wait. By then the migration of tennis enthusiasts to the Riviera had been in full swing for two decades, and Papa Lenglen was never backward in asking the best players to play with his daughter. The evening hours of pitting her ever-increasing skill against much older male opponents became the daily reward for the tedious sessions of metronome rallying with Negro. "Voulez vous jouer avec ma fille?" (Will you play with my daughter?), became a familiar parrot cry from Papa Lenglen, but it was never resented because everyone loved Suzanne's spontaneous gaiety and marveled at the little girl's ability.

Events arranged for the top players of the pre–World War I era were always played on a handicap basis. The current code of sportsmanship demanded that everyone should start with an equal chance, so if one player was better than another, he was automatically "weighted" in order to give his weaker opponent a good game.

One of my early privileges from being a member of the Nice Club was to have access to the secretary's desk, this by virtue of being Suzanne's stableboy. The records of all the earliest tournaments were kept there, and from these handwritten pages one could trace Suzanne's extraordinary progress, the amazing speed with which her handicap went down and down in the years leading to 1914.

The previous year, two visiting personalities, both destined to play a leading part in Suzanne's life, arrived on the Riviera: Elizabeth Ryan and Count "Ludi" Salm. The familiar invitation: "Voulez vous jouer avec ma fille?" was readily accepted by both, and in 1914 Suzanne not only won the World Singles title in Paris, but also the World Doubles with Elizabeth Ryan and was the mixed finalist with Count Salm. From that moment on, the doubles team of Elizabeth and Suzanne lost only one set in seven years, while winning Wimbledon six times together, the World Championships in 1914 and 1923, and uncountable lesser doubles titles all over Europe.

The interruption of World War I had a remarkable effect on

o

Suzanne's tennis. She had experienced her last-ever straight singles defeat to Marguerite Broquedis in April, 1914. Two weeks later she became the World Singles and Doubles champion within days of her fifteenth birthday.

After these Paris triumphs there was great disappointment in England that Papa refused all invitations to the unfamiliar grass courts of Wimbledon. He was much too shrewd a planner to fall for that temptation, whatever the prestige attached, and Suzanne was quickly sent back to work for long hours each day in the Place Mozart.

"You have won two World titles," Papa told her rather harshly. "That is nothing, you must win them all."

So certain areas of the practice court were designated, and Negro was instructed to see that she placed the ball in those areas two or three hundred times in succession. Her ballet training was also intensified.

In the last years of World War I the French Riviera was offered by the French as a convalescent area for the American forces who had fought on the Western Front.

I recall that among these were at least two top-ranking American tennis players. This was fortunate again for Suzanne, as Elizabeth Ryan, although a Californian, was absent, generously working with the British, and Count Salm was away on a very different crusade than that followed by his illustrious ancestors.

"Will you play with my daughter?" must have been specially translated for the convalescent Americans, as Papa Lenglen resolutely refused to speak any English, although he understood it perfectly.

In my time on the Riviera, Father Lenglen had already retired from business and would spend hours, when Suzanne was not playing, watching us juniors and reproving us severely for any casual stroke or signs of frivolity. He was a tall, gaunt man with already bent shoulders and a penetrating gaze through very thick glasses. He always wore a hat and was usually muffled to the ears in a heavy coat, which gave him a slightly sinister appearance.

Mama Lenglen was the mother hen, fat, cheerful, and dumpy, and always fussing about something related to Suzanne. Suzanne often referred to her as "ma poule."

Nature had played a remarkably apt trick on Mama Lenglen, for she had such an acute astigmatism that both eyes looked outward in opposite directions, saving her the need to turn her head when following Suzanne's shots during the million hours she spent clucking over her daughter from the sidelines.

Father Lenglen always encouraged us to use table-tennis scoring

o

for tennis, because this gives added importance to every stroke. He never believed in the traditional tennis scoring because, as it still stands, it is possible to win fewer points than one's opponent, yet still win the match. On principle, he found this quite intolerable.

Immediately after the 1918 Armistice, the American forces on the Riviera decided on one last monster tennis spree.

Listening to some of the ranking Americans involved, Papa Lenglen and Suzanne heard irresistible whispers about the reopening of Wimbledon and Papa decided this was at last the time for Suzanne to take the plunge. The boldness of taking an already highly strung, twenty-year-old with an almost legendary, but unproven reputation, to Wimbledon with all its starch and inhibitions, should never be underestimated.

Elizabeth Ryan recalls that at that time the women's locker rooms in England habitually provided a rail before the fire on which players could dry their mandatory steel-boned corsets. "It was never a pretty sight," says Miss Ryan, "for most of them were blood-stained."

Unfortunately I never questioned Suzanne about her memories of her initial trip to England, but no one could have failed to be impressed by the purposeful severity of Mrs Dorothea Lambert Chambers, six times Wimbledon champion, her stance, her predatory shoulders, and the determination illustrated in her every action and incisive comment.

On her arrival in London, Suzanne lost no time at all in making her mark, for after her very first practice-session, most of London's society was agog with controversy about her calf-length cotton "frocks," and the audacity of her girlish silhouette so "brazenly" revealed. Quite a large section of the British public initially condemned her as "indecent," and only a small minority doubted that Mrs. Chambers would deal summarily with this French hussy.

Suzanne's capacity to adapt to grass within a few hours of her first sight of it amazed everyone, particularly her first four opponents whom she swept unceremoniously aside, apparently oblivious to the fact that they were themselves world-class players.

Yet in spite of these encouraging beginnings, there still remained the forbidding obstacle of Mrs. Chambers, solidly entrenched in the psychological fortress of twelve-years unquestioned supremacy. London's society chatter became crystallized into a single question: Could Suzanne *possibly* beat Mrs. Chambers?

By some demanding fate, Suzanne was called upon to play the two greatest matches of her life at the extremities of her career: the first at the very beginning of her stardom, the second at the very end.

In 1919, she responded marvelously to London's question and to Papa's critics by defeating Mrs. Chambers after having been twice at match-point down. When at times Suzanne seemed near to collapse, Papa threw her cognac-soaked sugar lumps from his seat in the stands. When Mrs. Chambers led Suzanne in the deciding set, his imperious gestures ordered her to move forward and attack from the net.

Under an unusually broiling sun, with the King and Queen of England leading the cheering thousands, Suzanne survived and overcame Mrs. Chambers's merciless driving to finish victorious in what was regarded as one of the greatest upsets in the record books.

After her victory Suzanne began her champion's life as she ultimately pursued it—by making her own rules and receiving her ecstatic admirers in her bath!

In life, Mrs. Chambers adamantly refused to disclose her age. Her death revealed that on the day of this great match, she was only two months short of being forty-one years old. Suzanne had celebrated her twentieth birthday a few weeks previously, so it is doubtful which of the two opponents was the most gallant: the victor or the defeated.

After the match Mrs. Chambers, with the greatest of generosity, said she had never played better, but years later she told me she considered the outcome of this match to have been a tragedy for them both. Her own case was obvious. She was twice deprived, by a single stroke, of an eighth Wimbledon Singles title, the all-time record achieved only by Helen Wills twenty years later. As for Suzanne, Mrs. Chambers considered this particular victory to have given her the taste of invincibility and a subsequent compulsion for it, which brought endless sacrifices and unnatural unhappiness, out of all proportion to the rewards of her fame.

Suzanne's 1919 triumph caused shock waves and a tide of adulation around the world. In the immediate postwar era women everywhere were longing for some release from the restrictions of the Edwardian decade. They worshipped Suzanne for daring to enact their secret dreams, men loved her for bringing them the ballet leaps, the intermittent glimpses of bare thigh, and the sexual connotations of her very visible silhouette, all of which they determinedly denied themselves in their own homes.

Punch magazine, London's keenest observer of contemporary modes and manners, announced: "Wimbledon is now a compulsion of the London season, and is packed for Suzanne alone."

This was the beginning of a seven-year period in Suzanne's life in which she blazed trails that were previously unthinkable and far beyond the realms of tennis.

○

After fifty years of reflection all the experts unanimously agree that she gave to tennis an importance never previously attached to any sport. My own interpretation is that she created a blueprint of tennis patterns that will still be valid in the year 2000.

But there were to be temporary eclipses, of course. The storm clouds gathered when her father's health began to fail. And in less than twenty years a terminal illness would afflict Suzanne herself.

In 1920 she returned to England with the new "bobbed" hairstyle; to keep her hair attractively in place, she conceived what was soon to become the famous "Lenglen bandeau," two yards of brightly colored silk chiffon, tightly swathed around her head. Within weeks the Lenglen bandeau was copied by a million women, and for the next six years there was not a tennis girl who did not attempt some imitation of the Lenglen look.

That same year Big Bill Tilden went to Europe from Philadelphia. Both he and Suzanne won the Wimbledon singles titles in '20, but from then on he decided to consider himself her rival, if not her superior, as a world star personality.

Mrs. Molla Mallory was also present and was fated to play a historic role in Suzanne's destiny.

Mrs. Mallory was not then making her Wimbledon début, because she had already played there, inauspiciously, in 1909, when working in London as a masseuse. Originally a Norwegian, she had emigrated to America in December, 1914, and in the interim had won the U.S. National Championships five times and had become the tennis heroine of her adopted country.

One can be sure that Papa Lenglen, knowing of Molla's reputation in America, made his customary reconnaissance of her game, but on that occasion she was summarily dismissed by Mrs. Chambers, whom Suzanne had already beaten, so he had no cause for concern.

In the spring of '21 Tilden and Mrs. Mallory went to Paris and Molla put Suzanne to the test. Suzanne had a difficult match with her, and at one point it even seemed she might give up the fight. But Papa rose dramatically in the stands and commanded Suzanne to go on and win, which she did. "Just wait till I get her on grass," was Molla's immediate comment to Bill Tilden at courtside, and well within Suzanne's hearing.

There are pictures for public consumption, in which Suzanne and Tilden appear to be on amicable terms, but this sharp challenge of Molla's was the spoken declaration of a feud that was inevitable between them, with Tilden firmly declared as Molla's ally.

In stage terms, Molla's position was that of an ambitious second lead, needling the established top name in the business. Appropriately, it was petty, one-sided, and often bitchy, and Suzanne was then still able to disdain the whole situation. Logically, in their relative positions, Suzanne and Mrs. Mallory were destined to clash, but the intrusion of Tilden's partisan emotions made the rivalry much more explosive.

Tilden appears to have developed a compulsive hatred of Suzanne from the moment of his first Wimbledon success. Whether his championing of Mrs. Mallory was due to plain, primitive jealousy of the adulation Suzanne commanded, or to some odd sense of patriotism in favor of the Americanized Molla, may never be understood. At all events, the seeds were well sown for the dramatic circumstances that led, a few months later, to the one really bitter setback. Suzanne ever experienced on the courts.

[4]

La Grande Suzanne

IN THE CONTEXT OF WOMEN'S TENNIS, TRANSATLANTIC TRAFFIC
had been one-way since the beginning. Several American ladies had
tried their luck at Wimbledon, May Sutton with spectacular success
in 1905 and 1907, but no European woman of standing, other than
Molla Mallory, had ever challenged an American on her home soil.

Soon after Suzanne's first Wimbledon win in '19, she received a
letter from Wallis Merrihew, asking when she was coming to the
United States. "I have no plans for doing so," she replied, *"because
my tennis is only a pastime."*

Suzanne's close friend Pierre Albarran has written in his memoirs
of a marked change in Suzanne's character that seemed to occur after
her second Wimbledon win in '20 when she was worshipped by British
men and hailed by British women as their liberating heroine.

Her attitude certainly appears to have somersaulted dramatically

○
23

as, from then on, her "pastime" became a compulsion. Suddenly she was determined on an American visit to conquer the New World as she had now conquered the Old.

The opportunity came in the late summer of '21, when Anne Morgan, whose father had been one of the pioneers of American tennis, invited Suzanne to play a series of exhibition games in the States for the benefit of French areas that had been devastated by World War I.

The proposed trip, and Suzanne's determination to accept the Morgan invitation, led to the fiercest of disagreements within the Lenglen household. Papa Lenglen had always refused to go on any long boat journey and one great objection was that Suzanne would be separated from Papa on an important occasion for the first time in her life.

Tennis politics then played, for once, into Suzanne's hands.

For the previous seven years the all-European International Federation had been frantically wooing the American tennis administrators to join with them. They wanted to consolidate a truly world-powerful organization, but for reasons of their own, the Americans were still refusing to play ball.

In '21 the French felt that the participation of their very own Suzanne in the forthcoming American national championships could greatly improve their chances of success. But Papa Lenglen adamantly refused to agree to Suzanne's participation on the grounds that she was not being prepared. He had acted on this belief when he refused to let her participate at Wimbledon before World War I. In his view, exhibition games were quite a different matter.

Being twenty-two years old at the time, Suzanne may well have thought the moment had come when her Trilby-Svengali relationship with Papa should end. Decades later Maureen Connolly had a similar experience when she decided, overnight, to split with "Teach" Tennant; later still, history was repeated when Evonne Goolagong split with Vic Edwards.

There was also a reason the American authorities wanted Suzanne in their championships. The women's U.S. national title had been fought out for thirty-three successive years in Philadelphia. That year the event was captured for the first time by Forest Hills. The New York authorities decided to celebrate the occasion by assembling the most impressive possible parade of champions, past and present.

Anne Morgan always accepted that Suzanne would play only in exhibitions, but Suzanne clearly saw wider horizons ahead of her, in defiance of Papa. She had beaten Molla Mallory in Europe. She had

o

also seen Molla decisively beaten by players whom she herself could beat with the utmost ease. Suzanne felt it her right to beat Molla's record as the only European to become the American national champion.

Papa Lenglen's agreement to the journey was extracted only on the absolute condition that Suzanne would not compete in the national championships at Forest Hills. The French Federation was informed, but it seems the message was never transmitted to the right people. Possibly, this was an intentional omission. In the final arrangement, Suzanne was to be accompanied by the vice-president of the French Federation, M. A. R. de Johannis, Mme de Johannis, and Mama Lenglen. For the first time in such circumstances, Papa Lenglen would not be along.

Billie Jean King would say nowadays there were "bad vibes" around the whole project.

To begin with, soon after Suzanne won her third Wimbledon in July, she contracted a summer cold that developed into bronchitis.

Her departure for America was postponed twice. Each time Anne Morgan patiently rearranged the exhibition schedule. Then the ship, *Paris*, which was due to sail from Le Havre with the Lenglen party on board, was delayed for two days by bad weather. As the gangways were eventually pulled up, Papa Lenglen yelled to Suzanne from the dockside: "Whatever else, do *not* play the championships."

The Forest Hills Championships were scheduled to begin on Monday, August 12. Suzanne docked in New York on the previous Friday, August 9. Mama Lenglen claimed later she did not think this mattered as, in her understanding, Suzanne had no official commitments until the championships finished.

It seems likely that for their own different reasons, Suzanne and de Johannis plotted privately that she would play the Championships, because, on arrival, Suzanne "discovered" she had been officially entered. In addition, the draw had already been made, making it diplomatically impossible for her to withdraw. From three thousand miles away, Papa never had a chance to enforce his advice.

The draw itself had a fatalistic quality. Seeding, or the separation of the top players from one another in the preliminary stages, was not in force in those days, and by another stroke of perverse chance, no fewer than eight of the top-ranking players came out of the hat in the same half as Suzanne.

Then came the rain that prevented Suzanne from even going to practice on the courts on either the Saturday or Sunday. Finally, her first-round match, against Eleanor Goss, the fifth ranking American, had to be postponed from Monday until Tuesday to allow Suzanne a few hours for her first warmup since landing.

Tuesday, the thirteenth of August, 1921, must have combined some of the worst vibes of Suzanne's life.

First, Miss Goss called to say she was sick and could not appear. Then the committee, seeing the chance of making up the day lost by rain, scheduled Suzanne's second-round match against Molla Mallory. Eventually, late in the afternoon and before 8,000 expectant spectators, Molla played the game of her life and humiliated Suzanne to an ignominious retirement in the middle of a match she was clearly going to lose anyway.

After a shaky start Suzanne began coughing conspicuously. She was mentally unprepared and physically unfit for Molla's unexpected onslaught. This time Papa's command "Abandonne" was not forthcoming. It would have seemed totally appropriate to Suzanne in the circumstances, so she made the decision herself.

As Suzanne left the court sobbing, supported by de Johannis, the match umpire, Edward C. Conlin, and the referee, J. M. Jennings, hissing was heard from several sections of the crowd, and the national press coined the bitterly appropriate barb Cough and Quit.

Suzanne never again wore the peacock-blue bandeau she had chosen for that match.

Tilden proudly proclaimed the hatred he had for Suzanne, boasting how he had kept Molla in an armchair for sixty minutes before the match, and during this time had brainwashed her with comments about Suzanne calculated to inflame Mrs. Mallory.

Suzanne's own intimate thoughts are described in one of her close friend Coco Gentien's most treasured possessions: a penciled note from her bed on the day after the match. "I am dreadfully unhappy," she confided. "America thinks of me as a monster and I am afraid of Papa. If only I had accepted his advice! As always, he was quite right."

Molla went on to win her sixth National title, although the earlier great names of May Sutton Bundy and Mary K. Browne had been specially invited to come out of semiretirement in California to take part. It was then seventeen years since May Sutton Bundy had last played the national championships, and six years since Mary K. Browne had given up tennis for golf, but it was decided to stage a full guard of honor to celebrate both Suzanne's visit and Forest Hill's new ascendancy over Philadelphia.

But with highly competitive star personalities, situations such as this may well serve as soul-searching motivations for later retribution. When Evonne Goolagong beat Chris Evert in '76, depriving her of her fourth Virginia Slims championship crown, Chris spent the following weeks in intense mental preparation, enabling her to revenge herself fully by beating Evonne in the subsequent Wimbledon final, the first time she had ever beaten Evonne on grass.

Suzanne probably felt the urge to stick pins in Molla Mallory's effigy every night in the first six months of '22.

When their rematch became inevitable, in the '22 Wimbledon final, such was the surrounding climate that Molla's husband bet $10,000 on his wife's renewed victory, and Mike Myrick, on behalf of the American authorities, felt himself obliged to issue a formal statement denying the derogatory remarks about Suzanne that were being attributed daily to his close friend Mrs. Mallory.

In the eventual match, Suzanne took exactly twenty-seven minutes to revenge herself with a 6–2, 6–0 victory .

Suzanne met Molla again six months later in Nice. There she took only twenty-six minutes to repeat the execution by 6–0, 6–0. The umpire's blank for the match is still framed on the wall of the Nice Club, whose members were justifiably proud of their Empress's achievement.

One of the most beautiful girls in the world watched Molla's humiliation of Suzanne at Forest Hills in '21. Hours later she won the Junior National Title. This was Helen Wills.

In '22–'23 Helen climbed the ladder of tennis fame very quickly, and in late '23 she was already considered good enough to lead the American women's team—ahead of Mrs. Mallory—in the first-ever international match between English and American women. Wimbledon in '24 was the occasion of Helen Wills's first trip to Europe, and the fact she had been so recently rated above Mrs. Mallory gave rise to the usual sensational speculations about her meeting with Lenglen.

In April '24 Suzanne contracted jaundice during a visit to Spain with Alain Gerbault. Wimbledon was to begin on June 23, yet her doctors refused her permission to pick up a racquet before June 5. All went well in the first week of Wimbledon when she scored three successive 6–0, 6–0 victories in the opening rounds. This in itself was a record, but her very short convalescence medically validated her subsequent claim that she was still unfit and should never have entered an event as demanding as Wimbledon.

At the start of the second week, Elizabeth Ryan, playing the game of her life, came within six points of beating Suzanne. A questionable line call, given the other way, would have put her even closer. The set lost to Miss Ryan in this match was one of only three sets Suzanne lost in singles in the seven years of her star reign.

The shock, and the effort of survival, proved too much for her nerves, and once again she decided to abandon the whole tournament.

Her emotional resources may have been exhausted, but her physical reserves were still sufficiently intact for her to ask Miss Ryan to go shopping with her the next day, adding insult to injury and certainly giving renewed fuel to her critics.

Needless to say, the critics lost no time in accusing Suzanne of running scared from her first risk of a meeting with Helen Wills. It was a complete replay of the "Cough and Quit" episode three years earlier, they said. The "aftermath of jaundice" was the reason quoted in the formal club bulletins. Then Papa Lenglen himself went on record saying, "Next year my daughter will play better than ever." This unusual intervention proved, I think, his remarkable understanding of Suzanne's nature, his mastery of what is now known as public relations, and the confidence he had in his own extraordinary influence on his daughter's game.

The year '25 was to become the very zenith of Suzanne's life. She won the French Championships with the loss of only seven games, and won six rounds of Wimbledon with the total loss of five games. Her opposition included at least three players, Diddie Vlasto, Kitty McKane, and Elizabeth Ryan, who would certainly win some of today's $100,000 tournaments, yet Suzanne's financial rewards from these triumphs totaled just two weeks' hospitality, a medal, and less than one hundred dollars in nonnegotiable prize vouchers.

My association with Suzanne started at the beginning of '24. After calling the first few of her matches and overcoming my stage fright, I became accustomed to Papa and Mama Lenglen's constant arguments on the courtside bench by my chair. These concerned Suzanne's every action, and at first were disconcerting as the yapping of Mama's lapdog, Gyp, always grew in intensity when they themselves raised their voices.

But the Lenglen parents were unfailingly fair to me, Papa always asking immediately if I was sure of my call when either of them thought I had made a mistake.

Never, in all the 104 matches I called for her, did Suzanne say a cross word to me. When she changed ends, she frequently took a nip of cognac from a silver flask that was kept either in the pocket of her usually lavish fur coat, or on Mama's lap on the rug beside Gyp.

Once, when I made an obviously bad call, she waved her flask at me and said laughingly, "When you're older, we can share this and you will see better."

o

In '25 she taught me the lesson of my life in the essential need for common sense and tact in handling the great stars. As usual, she had just won the singles final in Nice and had gone off to the Villa Ariem to change her ensemble. I never recall meeting anyone who saw her play two successive matches in the same colored bandeau and cardigan. To her this would have been a letdown to her public.

Her next opponents on that particular day were probably the world's best mixed-doubles pair at that time: Randolph Lycett and Elizabeth Ryan. We all waited patiently for Suzanne's return— "reentry on stage" would be a better description in her case. However, Lycett had reservations for an overnight berth on the Blue Train to Paris within a few hours, and he told me to go fetch her. Somehow I fell for that one, and it is no alibi to remember now that I was only fourteen. Knowing Suzanne, I should have known better, even then.

I reached the tall iron gates of the Villa Ariem at the exact moment that Suzanne opened them from the inside. She was radiant in the flaming orange bandeau and cardigan that had impressed Grantland Rice. "I came to fetch you, Mademoiselle," I said, very mistakenly. Her expression turned instantly from sunshine to thunder. "Fetch *me?*" she said. "Let them wait."

I knew that even in that lightning flash of temperament she would not slam the iron gates in my face, but she turned and disappeared inside the Villa. Ten minutes later she emerged laughing apologetically, but Lycett was so incensed at the delay that he hardly hit one good shot, giving poor Miss Ryan no chance to exercise her wonderful expertise in mixed-doubles.

After four years at the top, Suzanne's flare-ups became more frequent and more distressing to her friends. There were also times when she was found retching over the locker-room basin before playing and having wild hysterical outbursts after losing two games in a match. One should remember, of course, that when Suzanne lost two games in singles it made world-headline news.

Suzanne's first flowering in 1919 coincided exactly with women's postwar emancipation. For two thousand years fashion had not shown even the calf of a woman's leg. Suzanne's revealing little "frocks" worn, as the British said, "brazenly," without underpinnings, exactly symbolized the new freedoms. The hypnotic spell cast by her enormous popularity beckoned thousands of previously timid women toward the new liberties they had longed for.

All this caused the press to start asking questions about what made Suzanne's magnetism so compelling and what were the secrets of her life off the courts.

It is now generally accepted that her personal circle was purposely

o

restricted to a few intimate and presumably "safe" young male admirers.

These included, primarily, two contrasting young men. The first, Pierre Albarran, a brilliant brain, one of the world's leading cardplayers, and an accomplished tennis player, was at one time on the verge of marriage to her. It seems that only her first Wimbledon success and the new horizons it offered caused her a change of heart. The second, Alain Gerbault, also an accomplished tennis player, was later to become the lone Atlantic sailor of "Firecrest" fame. Gerbault subsequently developed such a compulsion for heroic withdrawal from life that he could appropriately have been called the "Lawrence of Arabia" of tennis.

Later these two young men were joined in Suzanne's affections by a delightful socialite playboy, Coco Gentien. Gentien's place in Suzanne's inner circle lasted until her death, but meanwhile Albarran, who won no fewer than seventeen successive mixed doubles events with Suzanne, was shocked into detailing how much celebrity and fame had changed not only Suzanne's character but her physical appearance.

In one sense at least, this was obviously true, because year by year she developed her star status to the point of transforming herself physically and dresswise from the ugly duckling of her beginnings to the bird of paradise she became.

But whatever else, a talented and delightful girl is expected to have her romances. One strong infatuation between Suzanne and Gerald Patterson, her co-hero of 1919 Wimbledon, was widely presumed, but some searching questions remained unanswered.

Her close friendships with Gerbault and Gentien appear, in retrospect, to have been the memorable, joie-de-vivre experiences of three delightful and sophisticated young people linked by a common love of tennis. Her teenage romance with Albarran was probably as close as she ever came to a true love affair until she left the competitive tennis scene in '26.

On another plane, Suzanne's entourage included a selection of highly influential people, notably Lady Wavertree and Lady Crosfield from London's socialite set, and Lady Wavertree's paramour, the Honorable F. M. B. Fisher.

"There's a Len-Glen Trail a'Winding," the waiting lines outside Wimbledon sang to pass the time, parodying the "Long, Long Trail," a wartime hit the British soldiers sang on their marches to and from the Flanders trenches.

But under the amateur tennis rules of the '20s, not even Suzanne's immense box-office attractions were allowed to bring her a legitimate

o

income. Even the most modest endorsements had to be secret in those days, and for the most part, were not worth having anyway. Her parents were what the French call *"petits rentiers,"* which means those who derive an unearned income from a pension or from modest capital investments.

Yet for ambitious hostesses, Suzanne was the ultimate catch in any European capital. There is no doubt that she and Sophie Wavertree had a far deeper mutual affection than this implies, but it was also true that Sophie's constant companion, "F. M. B.," as he was always called, was the managing director of one of Europe's most progressive sporting-goods manufacturers. With the best goodwill in the world, Lady Wavertree's close friendship with Suzanne, as with many other top tennis stars, could never, therefore, be entirely divorced from the commercial interests of "F. M. B."

Both Lady Wavertree and Lady Crosfield had sumptuous London properties where tennis stars could enjoy London's hospitality at its most glamorous. Lady Wavertree also had a beautiful home by the lake in Aix-les-Bains, a favorite French summer resort at that time.

In earlier days the English king Edward VII had been a regular visitor to Lady Wavertree's London mansion. The annual socialite mixed doubles in Lady Crosfield's gardens were always a gathering of cosmopolitan royalty. The event was won in '22, for example, by the Duke of York, later to become George VI, King of England.

Kings, princes, the most influential names of the British peerage, butlers, footmen, painted ceilings, champagne and roses every day . . . such was the scene London presented to Suzanne in the years of her triumphs. Yet she invariably returned with relief to her beloved Nice and to the companionship of her tennis buddies.

Some say the tremendous exertions and the constant invincibility demanded of her by Papa Lenglen eventually reduced her to a frail, nervous wreck. Others think that early repressions by both her parents, who felt any normal life might impair her performance, were the real cause. At the time of my Riviera association with her, she seemed to spend her whole life on her toes, unable ever to relax.

After a close friendship during the fifteen years which preceded her death, my feeling is that from childhood on, she became slowly, but inextricably, caught in a spotlit destiny she could never have anticipated, nor have been mentally prepared for in the short years available. Papa Lenglen drove her relentlessly toward the goal of absolute supremacy, which was compulsive to both their egos. To maintain this, Suzanne began very early to deprive herself of all the joys of a normal existence.

Eventually, some compulsion seemed to develop in her that might

o

be compared to the renunciations of a person taking the veil. By the fourth year of her stardom, and probably exacerbated by the Mallory debacle in America, she was confronted by the realization that to stay in the life she had come to adore, and retain the public's adulation she now depended on, would involve the total sacrifice of all natural life.

She was not yet twenty-five when I first saw her almost daily from close quarters, but the transformation, which had shocked Pierre Albarran, was fast taking place.

Her face and expression had already the traces of deep emotional experiences far beyond the normal for her true age. After her jaundice in Spain and the abandoning of the '24 Wimbledon, it seemed as if the sleek escorts were in danger of becoming mere stage props, and the habitual peals of laughter just a façade for the fans.

In '25, she reached a stage where to lose two successive points in any game automatically implied to her that she was sick. If she missed one shot, Mama, of course, would immediately say, "What is the matter?"

Nevertheless, all this resulted in the tennis miracles she performed in the summer of '25, probably the true summer of this marvelously glittering but artificial period in her life. Papa predicted it, and between them, they made his prediction a reality.

After the '25 Wimbledon she made a Grand Tour of Europe. She was welcomed and feted in half-a-dozen palaces with an uninhibited enthusiasm, which monarchs themselves seldom experience.

Yet the following year was still to provide the most triumphant—and tragic—climax to everything that had gone before.

[5]

The Bandeau and the Eyeshade (1)

FOR A HUNDRED YEARS THE NAMES RITZ AND CARLTON HAVE BEEN synonymous with everything that is luxurious and grand in hotel life. The Carlton Hotel in Cannes is no exception, but by some quirk of fate, it reached an unlikely summit of its fame on February 16, 1926. On this Tuesday, the small, rather inconspicuous tennis club, which faces a side-street entrance of the Carlton and shares its famous name, staged one of the most dramatic encounters ever seen in the history of tennis.

The simple program was content to announce in French:

à 11 heures:
* *Mlle Suzanne LENGLEN*   c   *Miss Helen WILLS* *
France   Etats-Unis

Al Laney, an immortal of American sports-reporting, described it more fully:

> This was the meeting of two girls, one French, the other American, in an otherwise unimportant tournament on the French Riviera. Only a girls' tennis match, but it was blown up into a titanic struggle such as the world had never seen before. By the time it came off, it was of world-wide interest and never again in the history of sport was such an event allowed to be played in such ridiculous and fantastic circumstances. It could have filled Yankee Stadium as it turned out.

There were two closely intertwined aspects of this extraordinary saga: the tennis, of course, but also the way this particular event lit up, like a klieg light, the insidious innovations of a sport that was beginning to transform itself into a spectacle.

After World War I tennis was ceasing to be the prerogative of the rich. The natural habitués of the palace hotels were finding, with sometimes painful surprise, that their dining-room neighbors could now be just tennis-playing people who were obvious newcomers to this luxury life-style. The "doggy" British set even questioned quite bluntly how they got there without being better "house-trained."

For three years Papa Lenglen's immediate response to any tournament invitation involving Suzanne was already "What is the proposition?" The implications of this question were endless, and his inquiry became increasingly logical as more and more spectators wanted to pay more and more money to see his daughter perform.

Suzanne's Grand Tour of the royal palaces of Europe a few months previously led to the initial questions as to how she maintained her exotic plumage and her luxurious modes of travel. At the summit of the men's game, Tilden's extravagances were also posing some searching questions back home in America. For the first time the financial aspects of star tennis began to assume worldwide public interest.

Since '23 Helen Wills, now twenty years old, had climbed the top rungs of the tennis ladder by several victories over Molla Mallory, by coming to within a few points of winning the '24 Wimbledon after Suzanne's withdrawal, and by winning the American championships three years in succession, in '23, '24, and '25.

In announcing that she would play the Riviera spring circuit in '26, her instinct must have told her the time had come to challenge Suzanne's reign and that she was ready to do so on Suzanne's own territory. Henceforth, a showdown somewhere along the Lenglen coast was inevitable.

o

Probably, from San Francisco six thousand miles away, Helen Wills and her mother, being quiet, dignified people, had no opportunity to appreciate the absolute pride of place Suzanne occupied in French national prestige. Had they done so they might have foreseen the worldwide interest Helen's invasion of the Riviera would arouse.

In the minds of sports editors, memories of Lenglen's "cough and quit" incident in '21 made this new encounter, between the French Empress of tennis and the American successor to Molla Mallory, potentially big news, and they sent countless hard-nosed journalists who had never previously seen a tennis match, hot-foot to the South of France.

On January 15, 1926, Helen Wills, accompanied by her mother and fifteen unstrung tennis racquets, arrived at Le Havre in France on a liner called the *De Grasse*. Somewhat to their astonishment, the two ladies were met on their arrival in Paris by the president of the French Tennis Federation, Pierre Gillou, accompanied by Jean Borotra and an unusually large muster of sensation-seeking journalists.

Later they boarded the Blue Train for Cannes, and on arrival, were again surprised by another welcoming crowd. Among these was Charles Aeschliman, probably the best player Switzerland ever produced. He had been married to a delightful American girl, Lesley Bancroft, at one time ranked No. 2 in this country ahead of Helen Wills herself. This apparently gave him the feeling he should have a part in the arrangements for the Wills's visit. No one could have foreseen that he would soon play the most controversial of all roles at the climax of the forthcoming drama.

Helen told the welcoming party she planned a nine-week schedule of singles and doubles on the Riviera, beginning with the Metropole tournament in Cannes. She said she intended to play every week; so the burning question was which week would the Empress Lenglen submit herself in singles to the Wills challenge.

They had never played against each other so their first meeting would be interesting, even in doubles. But what all the newsmen in the world were waiting for was their first face-to-face confrontation in singles.

In the first week of Helen's schedule, she won the singles of the Hotel Metropole event, but was disappointed to find Suzanne had entered only in doubles.

The Lenglen parents, however, wasted no time in making a microscopic inspection of the newcomer's form. They sat, wrapped in rugs in the honor seats. These overlooked the Metropole courts from a high escarpment, and Helen recalls that while playing below she felt very self-conscious under the combined scrutiny of the Lenglen trio.

Helen scheduled her first tournament immediately on arrival to accustom herself to the slow, French clay surface and was far from showing the peak form she reached three weeks later.

Conversely, Suzanne, determined to impress Helen to the utmost, put on one of her most dazzling displays and lost only seven games in winning the eight matches of the two doubles events partnered by Diddie Vlasto and Toto Brugnon.

Meanwhile, all types of writers from tough newsmen to best-selling authors, were swarming to the Riviera to a point where regular sports-aces like Al Laney could not find a room in an appropriate hotel.

Blasco Ibáñez, famous Spanish author of *The Four Horsemen of the Apocalypse*, was commissioned by a South American newspaper to report the anticipated Lenglen-Wills singles match for today's equivalent of $15,000, although he had never seen a tennis game in his life.

This kind of atmosphere was one previously only associated with million-dollar prizefights. It was the era when men like Tex Rickard were injecting a measure of ballyhoo never previously conceived in a sport. Within months, Jack Dempsey would square off with Gene Tunney before 135,000 fans, paying an unbelievable $2 million at the box office of the Philadelphia Stadium. The names of Babe Ruth and Bobby Jones strode the sports pages like colossi. Al Capone made daily headlines.

Yet on the faraway Riviera, two girls were attracting as much, if not more attention to what would normally have been "just a tennis match," and with its actual venue still undecided.

The second week of Helen's visit coincided with the Gallia tournament. That week Papa Lenglen became ill and was unable to attend. The significance of this fact did not emerge until later because, as it turned out, he never again saw Helen Wills play singles. I always thought his appraisal of her at the Metropole before she had found her land legs after six days on the Atlantic, gave him an inaccurate picture of her true potential.

Moreover, Suzanne announced that because of Papa's illness she would not play any events at the Gallia, which meant that her own appraisal of Helen Wills in singles was also confined to Helen's first performances at the Metropole.

The announcement of Suzanne's nonparticipation at the Gallia tournament became a signal for the impatient newsmen to start saying this was a deliberate cop-out from a possible final against Helen Wills.

o

Suzanne's "aftermath of jaundice" had caused her to pull out of Helen Wills's first Wimbledon and also the '24 Olympics. These were their only previous opportunities of meeting. The old accusation of "quitter" was quickly revived and the specter of Molla Mallory loomed in almost every tennis report from the Riviera.

The tournament in Helen's third week was in Nice. Suzanne responded sharply to the bad press image she was getting by entering the singles before Helen even had time to do so. But now it was Helen's turn to play catch-as-catch-can.

On arrival Helen had said she would play every week. Her entry blank for Nice was received, but at the last moment she said she intended to play doubles only. The tournament director, George Simond, inquisitioned by all the reporters, said that Charles Aeschliman, in entering the mixed doubles with Helen Wills, had also listed her in the singles. But George conceded that this may have been without Helen's authority.

The reason Helen did not play the Nice singles when it was known that Suzanne would play, is still only partly answered in her own statement that said, "I may *or may not* have entered." In her memoirs she adds, significantly, that she may *also* have thought, Why play Suzanne on the one court she knows best in the whole world? The likely answer seems to be in her additional thoughts.

From the journalists' point of view, the Nice week was a near fiasco. By entering the singles before she knew that Helen was not playing the Nice singles event. Suzanne refuted all the "quitter" accusations and successfully spoiled their stories.

Suzanne, too, went to great lengths to disprove theories that she was antagonistic toward Helen. Helen stayed in her Cannes hotel during the Nice week but drove to Nice for the doubles. On her arrival, Suzanne was seen to wave gaily to Helen from the Villa Ariem, across the street from the club.

Later she went to the club to greet Helen personally, playing to perfection the role of gracious Empress receiving an honored guest in her own palace. Suzanne and Helen met together on the flat terrace roof of the Nice club and many picture captions described this as their "first social meeting." This was obviously inaccurate, as they had been at the '24 Wimbledon simultaneously in the week before Suzanne pulled out, and also met off court at the Metropole during Helen's Riviera debut.

The atmosphere of this waiting game built to fever pitch during the week of the Nice tournament. The whole world was now asking whether the showdown might come the next week at the Carlton in

Cannes. Helen Wills signified early on that she would play singles there, but Suzanne gave no hint of her intentions.

Researchers discovered that she had not played the Carlton singles for the past three years, though she had won the second tournament of her life there at the age of fourteen.

Tex Rickard could not have planned a better promotional buildup. Meanwhile, more than two hundred frustrated journalists drowned their anger daily in bars the whole length of the Riviera. And the world waited.

Some small consolation was derived in Nice from the possibility that Suzanne and Helen might find themselves on opposite sides of the net for the first time in the mixed doubles final. Suzanne was again in dazzling form, winning five rounds of singles with identical scores of 6–0, 6–0. Sixty games won to none lost must have impressed Helen Wills.

Helen Wills won the ladies' doubles in which Suzanne did not play. But at last they met in the mixed final. Suzanne and her partner, the Italian Hubert de Morpurgo, inflicted a crushing defeat on Helen Wills and Charles Aeschliman and I had the privilege of umpiring the match.

The crowd of newsmen were frantically calling their editors for instructions. They had no story and still did not know if and when they would get one. Should they stay or go? It was even thought for a time that Suzanne and Helen would never play each other in singles. But since Suzanne's unparalleled triumphs of '25 she had been considering several professional offers for exhibition tours of the United States, so it was obvious she must play—and beat—Helen somewhere if she was to push up the pro offers.

Two dominant personalities in this complex situation were Lady Wavertree and F. M. B. Fisher. The Riviera had been the natural winter habitat of this pair and it was more than coincidental that their presence greatly enhanced the promotion of Dunlop tournaments and the adoption of the Dunlop brand of balls. Moreover, Suzanne was Sophie Wavertree's close personal friend. Another relevant fact was that the Carlton Club was the private enterprise of the three Burke brothers, Suzanne's lifelong sparring partners and friends. Still another consideration was that all three Burkes, Albert, Tommy, and Edmond, were also friends of the Dunlop executive.

Toward the end of the Nice week, George Simond at long last announced that both Lenglen and Wills had entered the Carlton Club singles.

From that moment on, the Dunlop people were publicly involved and this placed "F. M. B." in the spotlight of full center-stage.

o

Many of the newsmen sent to the Riviera were being initiated in the brittle veneer of the tennis scene and thought it clever to demand answers to basic money questions that had been tactfully, and purposely, avoided in the past.

John Tunis, a tough, ace reporter for Wallis Merrihew's *American Lawn Tennis*, and also a good player who had access to the Riviera locker rooms, was already terrifying many of the stars with his bloodhound professionalism.

"How can you afford to live here?" Tunis asked the perennial English finalist Phyllis Satterthwaite, who was, in fact, on the payroll of an important chain of Riviera palace hotels. The circumstances surrounding the Lenglen-Wills confrontation seemed likely to present the greatest stimulus for his probing character.

With Tunis leading the pack, the journalists immediately attacked Fisher in strength. Every awkward question conceivable was asked about the finances of the match.

Tunis had done his homework with great care. He calculated the gross receipts would approximate half-a-million francs, the equivalent of almost $200,000 at the time. He was prepared to allow 350,000 francs (almost $140,000) for expenses and taxes, already a generous calculation. But these were "amateur" days according to the establishment, and Tunis wanted to know "what the hell" was going to happen to the balance of the money.

"F. M. B." was big, fat, and jovial, with a broad face, a strong handshake, and a slap on the back for most people. He originated from a well-known sporting family in New Zealand, but had adopted an authentic English manner and behind the joviality was a feeling there would be no holds barred in any business arguments.

It was typical of his character that he arranged for these awkward press questions to be asked in the same Carlton Hotel suite in which the Prime Ministers of Great Britain and France, Lloyd George and Aristide Briand, had argued for days at the International Cannes Conference in '21. He also conducted the press conference from the same chair that Lloyd George had used.

So the whole question of under-the-table payments to "amateur" stars, and the then dirty word "shamateurism," was first publicly aired in the discussions about the Lenglen-Wills match. The arguments were reported in newspapers across the world. Was Suzanne making a personal profit out of the match? And what was to be Helen Wills's benefit? Were the Burke brothers and the Dunlop company, by virtue of providing a few dozen balls, going to make it rich at the expense of two girls?

There was also a long argument about the newsreel rights. Finally, both Suzanne's and Helen's advisers agreed the whole world should have the opportunity of seeing the match and the Burkes were told they could not sell the sole newsreel rights to any one company.

Tilden was shortly to be suspended by the American tennis authorities for having a "writing arrangement" with the newspapers, but no one seems to have been unduly bothered that Helen Wills had a contract to report for the American International News Service and was, consequently, already on their payroll.

Two of the questions "F. M. B." carefully sidetracked at the press conference were the means by which Helen and her mother had recently moved into luxury accommodation at the Carlton Hotel and how Helen, meanwhile, had been outfitted by a leading Paris couturier with a wardrobe said to have cost 25,000 francs (about $2,000).

Father Lenglen, having got up too soon from his illness in order to see Suzanne's matches in Nice, was again sick at home. From the Villa Ariem, however, he told George Simond there must be no Americans officiating when his daughter played Helen Wills. The American press (without involving the Willses because this was not their way) made a public demand that there should be no Frenchmen either.

At that time I had in two years called 104 of Suzanne's matches. The question of my umpiring this match was very tactfully broached by my boss, George Simond, immediately after Helen's arrival in France. I was only fifteen and he foresaw that the eventual clash of these two stars would be of such importance that my age would preclude me from the all-important role of umpire.

Very sensibly, he also said that if any questionable incident should arise, my close association with Suzanne would immediately be raised and could create embarrassments for all concerned. For sixty minutes I was heartbroken. But then a great sense of relief set in. In retrospect, and since the full drama has become history, I have been very glad of Simond's decision.

Some years after women were first allowed to take part in the early Wimbledon championships, Commander George Hillyard, then the Wimbledon secretary, decided he would convey to the ladies' singles what he considered the honor of having the club secretary umpire their final. This set up a long precedent by which he umpired all the Wimbledon ladies' singles finals for over thirty years and many other important women's finals in Europe.

As a player Hillyard won an Olympic Gold Medal for Britain in 1908 and, by strange coincidence, finished his playing career winning the

o

handicap mixed, at well over sixty years of age, in the Gallia tournament while Helen was playing there in the second week of her Riviera visit.

So it was not only inevitable, but a natural choice for George Simond to ask Hillyard to take charge of the Lenglen-Wills match. Simond was also faced with finding a crew of linesmen who were all British or, at least, of non-French and non-American nationality. I was British, but again Simond took into account my close association with Suzanne and we agreed that I should not be included.

The importance of the event made Simond feel that staunch supporters of tennis, well-known people who had been faithful to the Riviera tournaments, should be rewarded by involvement in this historic event.

A rather strange cast of characters therefore became line judges for this match. Some of these were to play, as is usual in climactic events, unsuspecting but leading parts.

The first of these was Lord Charles Hope, a brother of the Viceroy of India, who made the most controversial call of the match. The second most controversial call was made by Cyril Tolley, one of England's top golfers. Another line judge was Sir Francis Towle, president of the hotel chain that employed Phyllis Satterthwaite and in whose gardens many of the top Riviera tournaments were staged.

Among the remainder were Victor Cazalet, a famous English horse trainer whose family had been involved in tennis for years. A German, a Russian, and four others whose names I have forgotten, were involved only in routine calls. No foot-fault judge was considered necessary.

Riviera tournaments began every Monday morning and, supposedly, finished with the finals the following Sunday afternoon. But on this occasion, the heavens opened at midday on the first day and the rain did not stop until Thursday night. All the handicap events were canceled. The tournament proper did not get under way until Friday, when the real countdown began. The four days of waiting to meet Helen Wills's challenge must have imposed an almost unbearable strain on Suzanne's nerves.

The early rounds were foregone conclusions, and in spite of the delay, Suzanne seemed calm, especially in one photograph I took of her myself on February 12, four days before the big match. After that the strain began to show outwardly in her appearance.

The final, instead of taking place on the usual Sunday, could not be played until Tuesday, and by Saturday night Suzanne had only reached the last eight.

Suzanne's favorite Nice club, and almost every other Riviera club or casino, held a thé-dansant on Saturday afternoons. I can still see Suzanne returning from Cannes on this particular day looking drawn and deathly pale.

I remember her standing by the bar of the club with only a ghost of her customary public smile, even this made with an effort. She also had the dry, tickle cough that normally only came on when she was tensed up on court.

Everyone around me commented on how ill she looked. One of her close friends even whispered to me, "She looks to me like she's not going to play that match." This was just three days before the final.

On February 15, the day of the semis, the two Greek cousins Helen Contostavlos and Diddie Vlasto played Suzanne and Helen Wills respectively.

Even in Suzanne's obvious state of high tension, Contostavlos was unable to take more than two games from her. Helen's comparable domination was demonstrated against Diddie Vlasto. Diddie had been champion of France in '24, the year of Suzanne's jaundice, and in that year was runner-up for France against Helen Wills in the Paris Olympics. On this day in Cannes Vlasto was lucky to take five games from Helen Wills. Suzanne and Helen Wills were head-and-shoulders better than any other girls in the world.

So February 16, the day of the "all-time" confrontation, came at last.

One of the distinctive features of the Riviera is that a heavy spell of rain nearly always lasts for four days. It is a sort of purging of the whole coast, and afterwards the scene looks even more beautiful than before.

This Tuesday was one of those peerless days that seem, in one's memory, only associated with the French Riviera and Lenglen.

[6]

The Bandeau and
the Eyeshade (2)

THE SIX COURTS OF THE CARLTON CLUB WERE SANDWICHED INTO A
small square of ground beside the Carlton Hotel. There was an arena
court with a permanent stand down one side that could accommodate
about fifteen hundred spectators. Behind this was a garage with a
sharply pointed tin roof. The Carlton Hotel towered over one end of
the arena court, while at the opposite end was a street edged with
small villas. These were all roofed with red tiles. Growing astride the
street and the backstop of the court by the little villas, was a tall
eucalyptus tree.

In those days Riviera finals usually drew five or six hundred spectators, maybe a couple of thousand when Suzanne played in singles.
The unprecedented interest in the match against Helen Wills meant
the seating accommodation around the Carlton arena court had to be
doubled. A temporary stand for two thousand more people was hur-

riedly erected on what was normally the second court. How well I remember the carpenters still hammering long after the start of the match. We sat there and the temporary structure rocked alarmingly.

As I was not to take an official part in the match Simond said to me, "Enter the tournament and you will then have a competitor's pass." My mother rarely went to tournaments outside Nice, but she, too, was caught up in the wild enthusiasm of the occasion and also took Simond's advice.

I took the train from Nice with my mother in time to reach the Carlton by 10 a.m., a good hour before the appointed time of the match.

We were confronted with total chaos. Both streets beside the club were already jammed with jostling crowds trying to squeeze through a single gate where Albert Burke was attempting, in vain, to check the tickets and prevent a total invasion of the club.

Albert told me later that the waiting lines had been five abreast since early dawn, and dozens of the leading journalists, who had been waiting for weeks for this moment, seemed likely not to see it at all. One group of twenty tough writers switched tactics and formed a flying wedge, forcing an entry on the other side of the club, partly by pushing through the indignant crowd, and partly by demolishing the fence behind the unfinished stand.

This was one of the times in my life I was glad of being 6 feet 5 inches tall. With my mother right behind me and with some encouragement from Albert Burke, we managed to reach our seats on the temporary stand between the hammering carpenters.

By this time, about twenty people were precariously perched on the summit of the pointed roof of the garage opposite, and when they attempted the perilous maneuver of moving along to allow even more friends to join them, they received a loud ovation from everyone, glad to have some comic relief from the growing tensions.

About 10:30, there was a crash of tiles in the street of the small villas and two heads suddenly appeared through a hole in one of the roofs. Thereafter, this operation was repeated at about two-minute intervals until the sidewalk below was a sea of red tiledust and the roof of each villa looked like some cocktail-party centerpiece from which dark olives on toothpicks protrude from cubes of red cheese. As the minutes went by, the holes in the roof were progressively enlarged to allow arms with flags and handkerchiefs to wave to their neighbors and indicate their support for Suzanne.

The next invasion was of the tall eucalyptus tree. Some ten local boys climbed to the highest branches and were about to settle for their front-row view when a squad of police went after them. A pitched

o

battle took place in the branches until the police dismissed the original occupants. Then all six policemen decided to remain in the tree themselves to cheer their French heroine.

Another ovation greeted "F. M. B." Fisher when he walked onto the court, solemnly carrying three boxes of six Dunlop tennis balls as piously as any acolyte approaching an altar. As I recall, he was then joined on the courtside bench by the faithful Lady Wavertree and Charles Aeschliman.

The most expensive reserved seats, costing $12 compared to $3 for the best seats at Forest Hills at the time, were located immediately behind the umpire and the courtside benches.

At about 10:45, the front row began to fill with some of the world's best-known faces. There were the former King Manoel of Portugal, Grand Duke Michael of Russia, Prince George of Greece, the Rajah and Ranee of Pudukota, and among many other celebrities, the Duke of Westminster, whose family still owns half of London.

The tycoons were represented by Gordon Selfridge, Britain's answer to Marshall Field of Chicago, Selfridge escorted as usual that season by the Dolly Sisters, laden with diamonds, with everyone asking which was Rosie and which was Jenny.

The arrival of each celebrity was greeted with an ovation usually associated with a Hollywood first night. Helen Wills's mother sat alone, calm and dignified on the opposite side.

From beyond the barricades of the club, murmurs and shouts of the seething mass of people still outside the gate suddenly changed to loud cries of "Suzanne! Suzanne! Voilà Suzanne!" All the flags and handkerchiefs from the roofs across the street started to wave frantically like mechanical toys in a store display at Christmas.

To those who were outside the club as Suzanne's car inched through the still hopeful fans, she blew kisses right and left, and was obviously deeply moved by the fervor and patriotism of their greeting.

Helen's memoirs recount that the night before the match she dined on filet mignon, ice cream and cake, and also recalls that although the Carlton Hotel orchestra blared out the song of the hour, "Valencia," she very soon went to sleep.

Superstition always forms a large part in a game-player's thinking. In Suzanne's earlier years she would not play a match without a particular gold bangle worn on her left arm. Mrs. Mallory would never play without the triangle of diamonds that surrounded her monogram. As previously mentioned, Suzanne never again wore, at any time—day or night—the peacock blue color of the bandeau in which she defaulted to Mrs. Mallory.

In '26 her "lucky" ensemble was the delicate shrimp-colored ban-

o

The Bandeau and the Eyeshade (2)   45

deau and cardigan that she chose for this vital match.

A moment before 11 a.m., the two champions appeared. Suzanne's entrance was that of the complete prima donna with full war-paint, a long white coat with white fur collar and fur cuffs. Her confidence seemed to be unimpaired, and she acknowledged graciously the marvelous ovation she received.

Helen looked the clean, uninhibited all-American college girl in starched cotton, with the cerise cardigan she invariably wore, and the "Wills eyeshade."

Suzanne stood bowing and posing while Helen Wills, possibly out of some sense of respect, kept slightly behind the Empress. There was a battery of photographers already on the court, and the first pictures show Suzanne with her full-stage smile and in the ballet pose she always assumed on such occasions.

But the moment the razzmatazz died down, Suzanne's face changed. At last she was confronted with the moment of truth. Being the extraordinary professional she was, her whole image altered. It seemed as if the change transformed the outward façade to the revelation of the inner soul. Suddenly the circles under her eyes were much darker and her expression showed a degree of apprehension that was quite unnatural for her in normal circumstances.

There was still a great deal of noise from the crowd as well as continued hammering in the temporary stand. One official addressed the crowd asking for quiet in English and in French. He received a public brush-off for his trouble. There were too many Frenchmen new to tennis, and more importantly, they had come to applaud their heroine, La Grande Suzanne.

Eventually, the Empress herself spoke. "*Un peu de silence, s'il vous plaît.*" Later she repeated this on a more pleading note and finally reproved her subjects harshly for not acceding to her requests.

Tommy Burke spent many hours of his later life recalling the famous eighty minutes he spent next to Mama Lenglen during the match.

It seems Mama Lenglen also had totally misread Helen's real ability and repeatedly reproved Suzanne for not winning more easily. How different things would have been for Suzanne had Papa Lenglen been able to observe Helen Wills's improvement in the past weeks and had been present with his hypnotic influence over his daughter.

Papa's absence must also have told heavily on Mama Lenglen. It is said the frayed nerves of both mother and daughter gave rise to a bitter argument that endured late into the night before the match. Tommy Burke recalls that he repeatedly implored Mama Lenglen to calm herself as her nervous state was communicating to Suzanne at each change of ends.

The first set took about twenty-five minutes, and I think the score of 6–3 to Suzanne was predictable from the girls' form on the day. What came as a shock was the second set, when Helen managed to speed up her shots, and on two or three occasions, Suzanne seemed close to physical collapse.

There were several crisis points in that second set, the first when Suzanne trailed 1–3. Then it appeared that Helen "let her off the hook" by changing from an attacking strategy to an attempt to slow down the pace.

The many instructional manuals written by Suzanne all put great emphasis on the importance of winning the seventh game of any set. She always referred to this as the "gateway to victory." So she must have been deeply discouraged to lose the vital seventh game after a struggle that involved fourteen points.

After this it became increasingly apparent that Suzanne would face almost certain defeat if forced to a third set because her strength was ebbing fast. She was having spasms of the famous dry, tickle cough, and was also clutching sporadically at her heart between points.

Suzanne's silver flask of cognac was never more in evidence than in this match. During the first set she took liberal sips during each change of ends. In the second set she took swigs between every game. I wondered what Helen Wills thought of this procedure, so far removed from anything she might do herself.

The next crisis occurred when Helen led 4–3 with Suzanne at 30–all on her own serve. Suzanne hit a shot to Helen's forehand line that Helen clearly thought was out.

As the umpire called "40–30," Helen asked the linesman, Cyril Tolley, "How did you call that?" When he told her he had called the shot "good" in Suzanne's favor, Helen exhibited probably the greatest degree of expression her "poker face" ever allowed in her career, an expression of total disgust.

If Cyril Tolley had given this ball out—as Helen obviously thought—she would have had a point for 5–3. With Suzanne clearly at the end of her resources, this advantage could have changed the whole outcome.

The last, the most contentious, and the most dramatic moment of all came when Suzanne finally reached 6–5, 40–15, match point on her service.

Helen, who had resumed her hard-hitting tactics, hit a blazing cross-court forehand, which landed either just on the sideline in front of Suzanne, or just in the alley, as I myself thought.

There was a cry of "out." Suzanne threw the two spare balls from her left hand into the air, then ran to the net to shake hands. Helen accepted Suzanne's hand rather ruefully, and Commander Hillyard announced, "Game, set, and match." Although the match took place in France, his calls were in English throughout.

With the invasion of photographers about to take place, and an accompanying army of bellmen and delivery boys carrying floral tributes for the heroine, I recall seeing Charles Aeschliman go toward the foot of the umpire's chair as if to take control, once again, of the situation.

He would soon have had to move in order to allow Hillyard to leave the chair, but while still standing at the base of the steps, he noticed the side-linesman, Lord Charles Hope, making a semaphore with his arms as he came across the court toward George Hillyard. I played Aeschliman many times in my life, and always felt that he had an exaggerated sense of the dramatic, which many other players considered an ego trip. He was an extremely imposing figure of a man, outstandingly good-looking with the rugged aura of a Swiss Alpine guide.

Aeschliman, from the foot of the umpire's chair, then made what was probably one of the most incredible utterances ever made on a tennis court. "*Attention, le match n'est past terminé,*" he said in French. The nearest equivalent to this in English would be, "Just a moment, the match is not over."

Lord Charles Hope had made Aeschliman understand he had not called Helen's shot out. He had seen the ball "good," and the cry of "out" had come from the crowd behind where he was sitting.

By this time Suzanne had sunk onto the courtside bench, and was already disappearing behind six-foot floral tributes and an army of photographers and bellmen.

Hearing Aeschliman's statement, Suzanne tensed and her face framed the largest question mark in the world. "*Alors il faut continuer?*" she asked blankly. Again, the sense of this can be expressed only in English as "Then, must we go on?"

Hillyard, taking his cue either from Charles Hope's frantic gestures or Aeschliman's incredible statement, or both, resumed his seat. To everyone's amazement he announced that Helen's shot had been good and the match would continue at 40–30.

Aeschliman's intervention must remain one of the most incredible in the game's history, particularly coming from an international player who would be—or should have been—immediately conscious of the implications of his action.

Hillyard, being over sixty and a Victorian gentleman, was probably too taken aback to react as he might.

In fact, the match had positively and formally ended. Helen had accepted the umpire's announcement, right or wrong, and the players had shaken hands. There was no reason on earth why Hillyard could not have told this to Charles Hope, and particularly to Charles Aeschliman, and left things as they were.

There cannot be a player today who would not claim that such a point should at least be replayed.

Suzanne, instead, after her initial amazement, removed her coat. Looking straight ahead and without a word or a gesture, she went back to serve at 40–30 from the left court.

She lost the point, lost the game, and was in obvious danger of losing the set, which in everybody's observation would have meant losing the match because she was so close to total collapse. But she fought back and, a good ten minutes after having thought she had won the first time, she stood at match point again, with the scores at 7–6, 40–15.

Double fault!

In all Suzanne's years of supremacy, she was known to have served only six double faults. Then the game went to deuce and it was almost unbelievable that after such traumatic setbacks, she was able to win the match for the second time, with two blazing winners. The final score was 6–3, 8–6.

Once again, all was total chaos on the court. This time Suzanne collapsed sobbing on the bench. Blinded with tears, she avoided the hundred hands preferred in congratulation. Even the immense floral tributes seemed unnoticed until, as she recovered, a French army officer offered the miraculous compliment that she had really won "two matches in one morning." This brought a faint smile to her lips, and she even managed to pull a rose from one of the bouquets and pin it to his tunic.

By then the area was so surrounded with a clogging mass of photographers and admirers, Helen hardly had room to raise her arms to put on the cerise cardigan.

On Helen's first day in Cannes, she had noticed a good-looking young man with his mother, but at the time they had not spoken. Standing alone now and ignored behind the hysterical throng and the banks of flowers that surrounded Suzanne, Helen was surprised to see the young man leap the barrier, force his way to her side, and say, "You played awfully well."

This was Freddie Moody, and on January 28, 1929, *Time* magazine announced Helen Wills's engagement to Frederick Shander Moody, Jr., stockbroker of San Francisco.

It had been arranged that the winner's cup be presented by either Mama Lenglen or Mrs. Wills, according to who won. This was, of course, impossible in the circumstances. There was no presentation and for many minutes, Suzanne remained prostrate amid the floral tributes and the outpourings of admiration.

Helen left the court alone and unnoticed; nobody even seemed to care that she had gone.

Suzanne was assisted from the court. She was taken to the small wooden clubhouse that revealed, when unlocked, a scene of wild disorder, because the thousands of francs in paper money that had been taken at the gate had yet to be counted and checked.

Once in private, Suzanne's nerves finally gave way, and her friends recount a bout of terrible hysterics in which Suzanne lay on the floor screaming and clutching fists full of notes. It has often occurred to me that the sight of the piles of money, when she was making so much for everybody else and so little for herself, may have unconsciously set off these hysterics.

Eventually Suzanne reached the suite allocated to her in the Carlton. But there was still no peace for her because her private room was invaded by Ferdy Tuohy of the *New York Times*. A more outstanding contradiction between forceful reporting and the ultimate in cruel bad taste has yet to be imagined!

Needless to say, Suzanne upbraided him in a torrent of hysterical French, fenced all his questions, and told him with angry bravado, that she was still Empress of the Courts and intended to remain so for a long time to come.

Meanwhile, the crowds below her sixth-floor Carlton suite were shouting and calling for her to appear. This, she was quite unable to do, and all the victory celebrations that had been planned for that evening were firmly canceled by Mama Lenglen.

It is perhaps difficult to recall that these were days before immediately relayed radio news of events, and that Mama Lenglen had to telephone the result to Papa's bedside. Hopefully, she did not tell him, as she had told Suzanne at the moment of her greatest triumph, *"Mon dieu, how badly you played!"*

Recounting her feelings later to her friends at the Nice Club, Suzanne said of the match:

"I never tried to impose my game."

"I never tried to win points."

o

"I contented myself with returning the ball the best I could."

"I did not deserve the applause or the flowers that I received because I was ashamed of my performance."

Helen's comment was, "There will be other tennis matches, other years." This was essentially the remark of a young aspirant at the sunrise of her career. She could not know that she would never again meet Suzanne in singles.

That afternoon Helen was to lose once more in doubles to Suzanne.

Suzanne had changed to a brand-new bandeau-and-cardigan ensemble in rose pink, but she was so exhausted that she was almost carried through the match by her partner, Diddie Vlasto.

After the match, Helen shook hands with Diddie but appeared to ignore Suzanne altogether.

Between 1914 and 1938 Suzanne's and Helen's careers as Queens of Tennis overlapped for three years from '24 to '26. Everyone expected that in these years they would meet many times. Extraordinary sets of circumstances, which could have been decreed only by destiny, allowed them only three meetings in which Suzanne won all three—one in singles, one in doubles, and their first-ever clash in mixed doubles in Nice.

Later that evening, with the victory celebrations all canceled, Suzanne withdrew to the lone company of her most intimate confidant, Coco Gentien. Coco recalls that they dined at a restaurant near the old Nice port. During the evening some guests at a neighboring table, recognizing Suzanne, commented proudly, "Our Suzanne is still Queen."

It was tragic that Suzanne should overhear this remark for the moment seemed to reveal her innermost soul. She whispered almost inaudibly, as she looked into the far recesses of the restaurant, "Yes, but not for much longer now."

So ended February 16, 1926. Helen Wills a more gallant loser than anybody predicted possible; Suzanne, for a short while, still the Empress, not only of her Riviera coastline, but now of Europe and the Whole World.

Most of the tennis community of my time agreed that John Tunis, a first-class tennis player and first-class reporter, had an acid pen, which was reflected in his almost daily comments about all of us.

Tunis and I disagreed on many aspects of tennis, but on one point we agreed completely: his assessment of Suzanne's silent resumption of play after having already been awarded the most important match of her life.

"Never in her long and luminous career," Tunis reported, "did Suzanne so justify her claim to greatness as she did at this moment."

The party was also over for the world corps of journalists.

Most headed back by train to Paris or Le Havre, but two enterprising companies decided to outdo their rivals by chartering the still-novel airplane to rush photographs back to London.

The first plane developed engine trouble and was forced to land in the Durance Valley and the second came down shortly afterwards near Lyon. Meanwhile, the train carrying most of the other newsmen crawled northward and passed the stranded and humbled pioneers.

One British newspaper summed up succinctly, in bold headlines, the ending of this four-week episode, unique in sports history: "The Universe Can Now Go On As Before."

AUTHOR'S NOTE: As my age at the time of the match precluded me from my usual position as Suzanne's umpire, I took an umpire's blank with me to the stands. My own record of the points score is below:

First Set

	1	2	3	4	5	6	7	8	9			
Lenglen	4	2	3	4	4	4	1	4	4		= 30	6
Wills	0	4	5	0	0	2	4	1	1		= 17	3

Second Set

	1	2	3	4	5	6	7	8	9	10	11	12	13	14			
Lenglen	0	5	2	1	4	4	6	4	3	4	4	3	6	6		= 52	8
Wills	4	3	4	4	1	1	8	2	5	0	2	5	4	4		= 47	6

	IN NET	OUT
Lenglen	13	30
Wills	31	32

[7]

Wimbledon's
Classic Tragedy

FOR SUZANNE LENGLEN, WIMBLEDON'S FIFTIETH JUBILEE IN '26 had every ingredient of a Greek tragedy.

Those interested in the dynamics of Greek tragedies, may recall that their customary format features a Hero or Heroine of brilliant achievement, a Messenger of Destiny, a Chorus, who describe and elaborate on the action, and finally, an inborn and self-destructive flaw in the Main Character.

Heavy significance is also attached to Auguries, Omens, and Fates.

Suzanne's experiences at her last Wimbledon could well have inspired the classic writers of the fifth century B.C. Like the Greek theaters of old, the open stage of Wimbledon provided a backdrop that early Greek audiences would have approved.

Suzanne, at the beginning of the '26 Wimbledon, was certainly a heroine of unmatched achievement. The previous year she had won

○

Wimbledon with the loss of only five games in the whole singles championship. She had also won the doubles and mixed, Wimbledon's "Triple," for the third time in her life, an achievement unsurpassed to this day. She had beaten Helen Wills, her only possible rival, in Cannes, and two weeks before Wimbledon, won the French championships for the sixth time, literally demolishing the past American champion, Mary K. Browne, in the final.

But the Auguries, essential to Greek plays, had already made their appearance on the stage of Suzanne's life. There were five.

The first recalled the traumas of the Cannes meeting with Helen Wills. This match foreshadowed, for the first time, the possibility that Suzanne's world supremacy in singles might be coming to an end.

The second revealed a more complex situation, which implied the possibility that her supremacy in doubles might also be over. In all her Wimbledon years, Suzanne's partner had been the Californian Elizabeth Ryan. At the start of the '26 Wimbledon they had never been beaten together in an open event, and at Wimbledon alone their record stood at thirty-one wins without the loss of a set.

However, the French Federation had been itching for years to force Suzanne to forsake Elizabeth Ryan for a partner of her own French nationality. There was only one woman player in France even remotely capable of partnering Suzanne at international level. This was Diddie Vlasto, a confirmed base-line driver, and a stark contrast to Miss Ryan, the world's greatest volleyer.

From Miss Ryan's side the proposed breakup was also extraordinary, although she had expected some sort of situation comparable to Suzanne's. Since '24 the American authorities had been making similar demands about her partnering an American. Molla Mallory, in particular, had been vociferous in questioning Miss Ryan's qualifications to represent the United States so long as she persistently partnered Suzanne at Wimbledon. Personal and official jealousies played a major part in all aspects of these devious maneuvers.

The third Augury spoke of money. For nearly a year the American impresario "Cash and Carry" Pyle had been trying in vain to assemble a tennis "circus" of which Suzanne would be the undoubted star. And there were several other proposals.

For Suzanne, the question of which offer to accept, and when to accept it, had become a daily poker-game with the whole family's future at stake. The "amateur" rules of her era precluded her from accruing any substantial rewards for her skill. The Lenglen's finances were often thought to be insecure and now Papa was seriously ill.

The fourth Augury appeared when the French Federation made a very unwelcome proposal. This suggested a completely new event, an international match between French and American women. It was to be played at the end of May. The heart of the affair was that it would involve Suzanne inescapably in a rematch with Helen Wills.

She had risked her all the first time, and won. This time she had everything to lose. There would be no title at stake, no money could be mentioned. It would be "just another match," yet one involving immense effort and risks to her future for no appreciable reward.

The proposal clearly found its way into Suzanne's trash can, for, simultaneously, she was accused by her Federation of having "emotional caprices." The match never materialized, but she had provided fresh grounds for French Federation anger at her willful disregard for their wishes.

The fifth Augury caught Suzanne in a trap. During Wimbledon's '26 preparations it was announced that because of this special occasion all overseas players would be invited to the Jubilee Championships as Wimbledon's guests.

Less publicized was that this gesture would replace the usual arrangement by which Wimbledon allocated official monetary "grants" to foreign associations, a proportion of which filtered down to the players.

This change in arrangements touched Suzanne very closely. In past years she had assumed a fair share of the French allocation. Under the "Jubilee Guest" system, she would become a two-time loser. There would be no Wimbledon money to distribute and since she had a standing invitation to be Lady Wavertree's houseguest, she would lose out again by not availing herself of the alternative hospitality.

Any allowable funds for Suzanne would thus have to come from the French Federation itself, and this gave her Paris antagonists their long-awaited leverage. At last they were able to say to Suzanne, "A French partner. Or else!"

The agonizing decision she had to make was the breakup of her partnership with Miss Ryan. It was unlikely she would win the Wimbledon doubles with anyone else while Elizabeth Ryan was still in the field. And this proved true.

Meanwhile, on the Riviera, Helen Wills was finding plenty of consolation for the loss of her first Lenglen challenge with a full round of socialite activities, now always escorted by young Freddie Moody.

After the nerve-wracking exhaustions of the Carlton match, and with five nagging problems unresolved, Suzanne retired to Italy for some rest. A communiqué announced ironically that she had gone there to "prepare for an ever-more brilliant success in Paris and Wimbledon."

The brilliance she expected was reflected in a Royal Command to attend an official evening function being given by King George V and Queen Mary at Buckingham Palace in July. Suzanne's formal presentation at the Court of St. James's was to be the crowning glory of her personal achievements. She had ordered a special Paris creation for the occasion, but it was really her future and the Helen Wills problem that occupied her attention.

By May, after a long rest in the Italian sunshine, she seemed confident she could beat Helen Wills in the French championships and again at Wimbledon, so perhaps things would work out.

She had not taken the Omens into account.

Eventually the French Championships began on June 2. Suzanne was expecting to meet Helen Wills in the final. The Auguries and Omens remained offstage until June 4, but then Helen Wills was rushed by ambulance to the American Hospital in Paris. A few hours later she needed surgery for acute appendicitis.

No doubt with bitter memories of the Mallory incident, Suzanne's first reaction was to say in an acid press-release, "I am sure France will be as sympathetic to Miss Wills as America was to me when I was ill in a foreign country."

Though by now she thought she would beat Helen Wills anyway, Suzanne would have been less than the star she was if she had not felt a sense of relief on hearing of Helen's illness. Henceforth, she would be spared the effort and risk of the actual matches, not only in Paris but also at Wimbledon.

With the dawning of this realization, Suzanne quickly made amends for her spontaneous bitter comment by being the first of Helen's visitors and surrounding her hospital bed with bouquets of flowers.

The first act in Greek classics often ends with a Chorus elaborating on the unsurpassed achievements and dazzling feats of the heroine. Such was the case with Suzanne in the days surrounding the '26 Paris final.

With the announcement of Helen Wills's removal from the immediate scene, Suzanne seemed suddenly in a state of euphoria and inspired to play the best tennis of her life. She won the French Championships more easily than ever before. Mary K. Browne, congratulating her after being able to win only a handful of points in the final, told Suzanne in utter frustration, "You're just too damn good!"

o

56   *Love & Faults*

But moving to the next act, which was Wimbledon in June, the tone of the Chorus changed abruptly. It foreshadowed impending storms, though the far-reaching effects of these were not yet revealed.

The first storm involved Suzanne in a minor arm injury, and on her arrival in London she was already nervy and saying she needed to see a doctor.

The next storm broke when the Wimbledon draw was announced. With every player's name tossed in the hat in those days, the Messenger of Destiny made his first speech in announcing that not only had Suzanne drawn the Paris finalist, Mary K. Browne, in her first-round singles, but the artificially formed teams of Lenglen-Diddie Vlasto and Ryan-Mary Browne would meet in their first match in the doubles.

Fates, Omens, and Auguries were all on stage at this point. The draw Fate decreed was close to being unbelievable. Neither Suzanne nor Elizabeth had ever lost a doubles match at Wimbledon. Now one of them must inescapably lose in the very first round.

In *Wimbledon Story*, Norah Cleather, who spent twenty-five years at the heart of Wimbledon's organization, writes of Suzanne's indignation on hearing of the draw. *"C'est incroyable!"* (It is unbelievable). "How could they be so tactless," Suzanne said of the organizers.

Twenty-one years after this "tactless" contention I was invited to be the director of Britain's National Covered-Courts Championships. The draw was formal and public so I was amazed when the names of two sisters were drawn from the hat to play each other and the secretary of the official organizing committee said, "We can't have that. Put one back in the hat."

The question of whether this same action would have been advisable, whether it could or should have been taken to avert the inevitable crisis in '26, will be debatable whenever Lenglen's tragic exit from Wimbledon is discussed.

But in '26 the draw, as Fate ordained it, was imposed in its original form, and only one last day of public acclaim remained for Suzanne.

On the first Monday of the Jubilee Championships, the King and Queen of England presented commemorative gold medals to every past and current champion of Wimbledon's fifty years. Nine of the twelve lady champions from the whole history of tennis were still alive and made their curtsy to the royal couple, but on that afternoon everyone agreed that Suzanne received by far the greatest ovation from the big crowd.

One wonders how the Greek writers would have made it known to their audience that, after seven years of adulation, this was the last time Suzanne would find favor with the fickle British public, that she

o

had already played her last Wimbledon final the previous year.

Following the ceremony, a one-set exhibition doubles match was arranged in which Suzanne and Elizabeth Ryan opposed Kitty McKane-Godfree and the Dutch champion, Kea Bouman. This was the first and only time in the history of championship tennis that Suzanne and Elizabeth were beaten. It was also the last time they were ever teamed together on court as partners.

In the state of tension Suzanne reached, because of the fateful pairings of the draw, the pain in her tennis arm, and the unaccustomed absence of Papa, this first defeat, although only a one-set exhibition match, assumed an altogether out-of-proportion effect on her morale.

To the connoisseurs it was another Omen. Still another appeared when Suzanne lost five games to Mary K. Browne in her first-round single the next day, the same total she had lost in the entire Wimbledon singles championship the previous year.

Wednesday, the third day of Wimbledon, was the day of the doubles with her young partner Diddie Vlasto against Elizabeth Ryan and Mary K. Browne.

Realizing she would have to exert every ounce of her strength and skill if she were to pull Diddie through this match, she made a point of asking the Tournament Director, F. R. Burrow, about the schedule to be sure she would not be required to play a previous match on the same day.

On leaving the club on Tuesday evening, she also confirmed that the doubles was scheduled for the center court around 4:30 on Wednesday. Suzanne was not told, however, that Burrow's Wednesday schedule was not yet made final and nothing whatever was said to her about playing two matches.

Eventually, about 7 p.m., Burrow's final schedule was distributed to the press and dispatched, as a nightly procedure, to the royal residences of London, which included Buckingham Palace.

But meanwhile, after Suzanne's departure, Burrow performed the act that became the main single factor in the ending of her amateur career and her exit from Wimbledon. He added to his final schedule the additional match Suzanne had particularly asked not to play. This was a second-round single against the champion of Ceylon, Mrs. Evelyn Dewhurst. Burrow's excuse for his disregard of Suzanne's expressed wish was, "This was an unimportant match and should not have bothered Suzanne at all."

Theories have differed for fifty years as to whether or when Suzanne became aware of this addition. Burrow's final schedule was published in most, but not all, the London newspapers the next morning. But it is still agreed by all the members of the French team that Suzanne never read the newspapers during Wimbledon.

Here again the name of Commander George Hillyard appears in Suzanne's life, and again at a peak moment affecting her whole future.

George Hillyard had been succeeded as Wimbledon secretary the previous year by Dudley Larcombe. In all the years of Hillyard's secretaryship, he made a point of Victorian courtesy by informing the Empress of Tennis each evening of her following day's program. This Tuesday evening in '26 there was no communication between Hillyard and Suzanne.

For some years the gap in communications was attributed to the change of command in the secretary's office and the possibility that Hillyard no longer felt himself responsible to Suzanne.

Sometime later it appeared that a deep rift had arisen between Suzanne and Hillyard because of Hillyard's conduct in the vital last games of the Lenglen-Wills match in Cannes. Suzanne believed that in forcing her to resume the match against Helen after he had already declared Suzanne the winner, Hillyard put her entire future recklessly in jeopardy and she never forgave him. In her mind Charles Hope and Charles Aeschliman were bracketed in that same extraordinary incident and it is said she never again spoke to any one of the three.

On the night before the contentious first-round doubles, Suzanne dined quietly with friends in London. Her enemies have suggested she already knew about Burrow's addition to the schedule at that time. Yet she made a date with her doctor for noon the following day.

To my personal knowledge Suzanne was always extremely punctilious about her match timings. Every match was a stage entrance to her and needed the fullest preparation, so she certainly would not have made this midday date had she really believed she had to be at Wimbledon early the same afternoon.

At 11:30 on Wednesday morning, Diddie Vlasto played the classic role of Messenger when she read the newspapers and told Suzanne she was scheduled to appear in the single she had asked not to play. Moreover, this was listed for two o'clock. There were no hysterics, but the resentment of an Empress, hearing that her express wishes had been disregarded, can easily be imagined.

It has been said that with her doctor's appointment still thirty minutes away, Suzanne had time to contact Burrow personally. Instead, from a mixture of haste, disbelief, and probably some anger, she asked her teammate Toto Brugnon to reach Burrow and explain she would not be there for the single, but would arrive, as arranged, in good time for the 4:30 double.

Throughout the rest of his career, Burrow refused to accept that he ever received Suzanne's message, though this was allegedly transmitted by Toto Brugnon to his office.

Burrow had directed the Wimbledon championships for seven years. Just as it would not have occurred to Suzanne that her personal request would not be respected, it would not have occurred to Burrow that his schedule would be questioned.

Knowing Suzanne and Wimbledon as I did, I think that if the routine we subsequently set up had been followed in '26, Suzanne would have been informed by 11 a.m. of Queen Mary's intention to be present as early as 3 p.m.

Had this been done, I feel certain Suzanne would have canceled the date with her doctor, would have agreed to play the unwanted single, and then, possibly, have requested a postponement of the doubles. All this would have been a sensible and reasonable course of action, particularly as Suzanne was due to make her formal curtsy at Buckingham Palace two weeks later.

Burrow's late addition to the schedule and deliberate disregard for Suzanne's particular request were the keys to the whole tragedy to come. A fundamental clash of personalities combined with a total breakdown of vital communications.

On Wednesday at 3 p.m., Queen Mary came to see Suzanne, but Suzanne did not arrive until 3:30.

All the officials were summoned to a meeting, and the only temporary solution they could reach was that the empty center court should be rolled in an attempt to make it appear the break in the schedule was routine necessity. Eventually, the court was rolled for twenty minutes under Queen Mary's hopefully unsuspecting gaze.

By this time almost the whole Wimbledon Committee was assembled on the doorway looking toward the gates for Suzanne's car.

Although Suzanne did not know her message to Burrow had served no purpose, she must have gone to Wimbledon prepared for a showdown with him. To say she stepped from her car into a wasps' nest would be an understatement. Recriminations flew in all directions to such effect that after fifteen minutes of public haranguing, she ran sobbing to the locker room.

In those days, one of the cubicles in the ladies' locker room was reserved with the words "The Lady Champion" on the door. Locked firmly in the star cubicle, Suzanne refused all entreaties by Diddie

Vlasto. Meanwhile Queen Mary was still watching a perfectly rolled but empty court.

Discussing this whole episode with Jean Borotra at the Wimbledon Centennial fifty years later, Jean said it was at that moment he arrived at Wimbledon. He told me that as captain of the French team he was immediately pounced on by numerous angry committee members who implored him to use his influence with Suzanne in the hope she might still appear.

Even in his account of this tragic confusion, Jean's unquenchable Gallic humor somehow managed to inject some comic relief. He said that going upstairs to the ladies' locker room, he was given a towel to put over his head in deference to the other girls' modesty. A game of Blind Man's Bluff ensued with Diddie Vlasto guiding him by the finger to Suzanne's locked door.

Unfortunately, even Jean's unique powers of persuasion had no effect whatever. Suzanne had become hysterical. There was no longer any question of her playing anything at all, singles, doubles, or whatever else.

Borotra then offered to be the spokesman who would make the corporate apologies of the French team to Queen Mary. He did this in the Royal Box, telling Queen Mary that Suzanne had suffered a sudden indisposition.

Burrow, of course, wanted to default Suzanne from the doubles and proposed to do so. However, Elizabeth Ryan, supported by Mary K. Browne, adamantly refused to accept the default. After a long argument the committee bowed to the pressure of Suzanne's opponents and agreed to postpone both her matches.

On Thursday it was thundery and wet, but in spite of all that had gone before Suzanne achieved one last victory over Burrow. Priority was given to her vital doubles match, and the single against Mrs. Dewhurst was again postponed.

Suzanne and Diddie Vlasto appeared for their fateful center-court doubles in defiant battle regalia, Suzanne complete with yards-long chiffon scarf and flowered corsage pinned to her furs. Even more than the rest of the tennis world, Diddie affected a replica of Suzanne's outfits. This time both French girls carried identical silver flasks of cognac to fortify them in the coming struggle.

For a short time the Auguries seemed propitious to the French pair. They won the first set, and after an intervening thunderstorm, reached 5–2, with double match-point on Miss Ryan's service.

In the early part of the match, Mary K. Browne had been badly beset with nerves and was outstandingly the worst of the four players, but during the thunderstorm break, Miss Ryan was able to restore her partner's confidence to such effect the American pair won the second set and eventually the whole match.

It was an incredible situation for Suzanne to lose any match, least of all a first round and from such a commanding lead. The result, which itself had arisen from amazing circumstances, was a last and bitter twist of fate in Suzanne's and Elizabeth's twelve-year relationship.

Meanwhile, on her way to the locker room, Suzanne stood back respectfully for Queen Mary's exit from the club. For years, Queen Mary had been very cordial to Suzanne and one of Suzanne's greatest prides was the friendliness shown her by both Queen Mary and King George V since the day of her first Wimbledon victory in '19.

On this occasion in '26, passing within handshake distance of Suzanne, Queen Mary appeared not to notice her. This was quickly interpreted by her detractors as a deliberate royal snub.

The press "Chorus," fulfilling its classic role of elaboration, publicly disgraced Suzanne in all the newspapers the following day. It was even reported that Suzanne had deliberately kept the queen waiting to show that she recognized no peers in the world of women.

Against Evelyn Dewhurst on the grandstand court Suzanne lost four games — the last Augury — and forthwith complained of being ill as well as having pain in her right arm.

When Suzanne returned to the center court on Saturday for a mixed doubles with Jean Borotra, she received a hostile reception for the first time in her life. She had "insulted" the English queen, and her myriad fans turned against her in an hour.

The situation was marginally salvaged by Jean Borotra's sensitivity to the unpleasant atmosphere. Once again his inspired Gallic charm provided some measure of clowning relief when he deliberately served half-a-dozen wild services yards outside the court, gesticulating in mock despair, at the start of the proceedings.

But on Monday, the Messenger announced the final lines. Suzanne would withdraw from all events at Wimbledon, she would excuse herself from being formally presented at Buckingham Palace and would return to Paris at once.

Molla Mallory, finding her possible path to the final unexpectedly cleared by Suzanne's withdrawal, must have derived some cynical pleasure from the whole play.

As is often the case, history was corrected many years later in an unusual way. Norah Cleather was asked by one of the palace equerries to send a copy of her book *Wimbledon Story* to Queen Mary.

o

Later, Norah received a letter from the queen, thanking her for her gift. However, the queen also conveyed her sorrow at reading, in the account of the Lenglen incident, that she had allegedly snubbed Suzanne. Queen Mary emphasized that the day following Suzanne's indisposition she had, in fact, commanded the French Ambassadress in London, Madame de Fleuriau, to inquire about Suzanne's health on her behalf.

It became clear, once again, that a complete communications breakdown had occurred, but this time the reason was no mystery.

During Suzanne's many visits to Sophie Wavertree's London mansion, Mme de Fleuriau made no attempt to disguise her antagonism toward Suzanne. She considered her socially inferior and deeply resented the enormous popularity that made Suzanne France's "First Lady" in London, a position Mme de Fleuriau considered should be reserved for her personally.

This was the opportunity for Mme de Fleuriau to give full rein to her personal dislike.

Instead of placing emphasis on the press blowup of the alleged snub to the queen, the Ambassadress should more correctly have complied with Queen Mary's command to convey her personal sympathy to Suzanne. Had she done so, she might have discovered, in the ensuing diplomatic proceedings, that Suzanne was still welcome at Buckingham Palace. Instead, she told her abruptly she had become persona non grata and advised her to go home.

This was the final blow to Suzanne's reign in Britain.

To Mme de Fleuriau fell the role of the last Fate to appear in this long cast. Suzanne's susceptibility to high-tension hysterics at the great climaxes of her career was the inborn and self-destructive flaw required of all classic Heroines.

In retrospect, Burrow's conduct seemed to have stemmed from his dedication to an outdated concept of sporting ethics. The players of his day often found him something of an autocrat. I had one or two sharp brushes with him myself on the circuit. His thinking certainly derived from the pre–World War I era before there were empresses to make tennis into the big-money spectacle it was destined to become.

Burrow's published account of these two stormy weeks begin with pages of unmitigated praise for Suzanne. He speaks of her uniqueness, of her supremacy, and her contribution to Wimbledon in the most glowing terms—only to contradict this whole picture in one short statement, "No one should expect me to give priority to the wishes of any one player."

As early as '20 London's infallible monitor of society, *Punch* magazine, was saying, "Wimbledon is packed for Suzanne alone." In the intervening years it was unanimously agreed she gave an importance to tennis never previously attached to any sport. In so doing she brought millions in cash and a wonderful flowering to Wimbledon. Even Wallis Myers, who disliked Suzanne, wrote that she was the "Lodestar around which all tennis revolved."

In the world that Suzanne had done so much to build, her supremacy had been absolute. Yet Wimbledon, itself made great by Lenglen, delivered the final blow against her.

Papa Lenglen's comments are best left to the imagination. But Suzanne's life history proved that in the absence of his domination over her, things invariably went wrong.

In late July '26 Suzanne decided to accept "Cash and Carry" Pyle's offer to embark on an exhibition tour of America. Thus she became the first world-star to do so.

With this step she was taking a leap into the unknown. At that time professional sports performers were regarded as tradesmen; many of them came from a background of manual work. Because of this, French reporters made a strong point of saying that Suzanne was not denigrating herself but uplifting the world of sport.

One last problem was to find opponents brave enough to follow her example. Suzanne was joined by Frenchman Paul Feret and Howard ("Howdy") Kinsey, the American Wimbledon finalist of that same year. Mary K. Browne and Vincent Richards were persuaded to do so on pure grounds of finance. On joining Suzanne, Vincent Richards had the honesty to say, "I need to sign to maintain my wife and kids."

Suzanne, now without the need to win at all costs, and with the family finances more secure, could turn her thoughts to a more natural existence. Henceforth at least men and sex could play a part in her new life.

Asked by reporters about her future plans as a professional, the secret of her years of sacrifice came out at last.

"First let me live a little!" she cried out.

[8]

Love and Faults (1)

BILL TILDEN DIED ON JUNE 5, 1953, AFTER SERVING TWO PRISON sentences related to homosexuality. "Contributing to the delinquency of a minor" was the official charge.

Both times he was sentenced to a year in prison; the first after pleading guilty to interfering with a fourteen-year-old boy while allowing him to drive Tilden's car in Los Angeles shortly after World War II. The second, again in his car, for interfering with a sixteen-year-old hitchhiker in the same city three years later.

Before receiving his first prison sentence Tilden told the judge he had not been involved with boys from the time he left college until recent years, when a car accident "frayed his nerves."

To me, Tilden seemed obviously attracted by blond "young hopefuls" in tennis, right down to ball boys and the like. In my job as tennis organizer of many tournaments in which Tilden took part, it was impossible, from close quarters, to overlook the situation. When Tilden toured the Riviera in '30, there were incidents that surprise me to this day in their blatantness.

The thread of Tilden's associations with young boys was to weave through his entire life and began, in tennis at least, with his "protégé," the blond, budding star Vincent Richards.

They won the American national doubles title together in the last year of World War I. Tilden was twenty-five at the time and the boy, Richards, only fifteen. Later he was to develop another protégé, Arnold Jones. After that still another "young hopeful," Wilbur Coen, who was called "Junior."

A great deal has been written about Tilden's friendships with young boys, but since in the '20s the word "homosexual" was never referred to and the word "gay" had not yet assumed its present associations, it is not clear what "friendships" implied in the minds of the writers.

Also, what must be remembered is the "Upstairs-Downstairs" codes of behavior of that era. While those in the "Downstairs" stratum could be criticized for almost anything they did, those "Upstairs" had the prerogative of indulging their eccentricities to the utmost.

Tilden was automatically in the "Upstairs" category, not only from his standing in tennis but also from his Philadelphia background of respected, well-to-do parents.

So any early homosexual leanings Big Bill may have had did not arouse the comment they did in later years when everyone became more interested in possible scandals about famous people.

The compensating factor Tilden offered his "young hopefuls" was the patronage of his outstanding personality plus his enormous technical knowledge. And one must not forget the exciting status a young guy could derive from these factors.

In any case, no one in Philadelphia recalls any suggestion that Tilden was actually an influence of evil.

On the tennis courts there was no denying Tilden was a genius. What has been forgotten with the passing years is that Big Bill was *a genius of his own making*.

Big Bill always had a big serve, but he realized in his teens that his service alone would not make him a champion. His ideal was to be a baseliner and a volleyer; in fact the all-court master he became. "Everyone, including my friends, told me I was foolish," Tilden said in an interview. "They said I couldn't have everything, but I was pig-headed enough not to believe them and kept at it."

o

So Bill worked and worked at his game and by 1918 was ranked in America's top ten. By then he was already twenty-five. As late as 1919 he was still not preeminent in this country, because although he had twice reached the last round of the national singles championships, he failed to win a set in either final.

As a result, he spent the entire winter of '19 hitting thousands of backhands in an indoor court belonging to a millionaire friend, Jed Jones, of Providence, Rhode Island. This was one of the few indoor facilities in this country at the time and Tilden was supposed to sell insurance for Mr. Jones's company, The Equitable, in return for his keep. Tilden's sparring partner each day was Jed Jones's son Arnold, the national Boy Champion of that same year.

The arrangement worked out well, because Big Bill put the finishing touches to his game during that winter. Thereafter he became the ultimate tennis craftsman, the only player I ever saw who could use three complete tennis styles, flat, top spin, and slice, to destroy an opponent.

But while his game was improving, Bill Bill's personality was far from popular in America. His natural arrogance and the air of superiority he projected were too different from the Philadelphia gentlemanly image to be understood. Tilden had undoubted charisma that ordinary mortals had not seen outside the great silent movie stars who seldom emerged from Hollywood. Hollywood and Philadelphia were different worlds. Germantown and the Philadelphia Cricket Club could not take both worlds in one stride.

Bill Clothier, of the Philadelphia Clothiers, whose father, Bill senior, was a member of the successful first-ever American Davis Cup team to campaign in Europe, confirms that Tilden was never accepted as a "good guy," even in his home city. He recalls that Bill senior always considered Tilden a "nut who had strange ideas," despite his great talents at tennis.

William T. Tilden was born in Germantown, Pennsylvania, on February 10, 1893. Twenty-one months later, on November 2, 1894, William M. Johnston was born in San Francisco.

For more than a decade they were rivals, partners, friends, and were eventually to be opponents six times in the finals of the American national singles.

With both players inevitably being called "Bill," some extra distinction had to be found. At 6 feet 1½ inches Tilden was "Big." Johnston, at 5 feet 7 inches was "Little." Both came to national prominence almost simultaneously. In 1913 Little Bill won the first of seven Pacific Coast championships as well as the singles at Longwood. That same year the American singles title holder, Mary K. Browne, was asked to partner a promising young Philadelphian in the National Mixed Doubles Championships. "He is not that good, but he has a big serve," she was told. This was Big Bill and they won. "The establishment certainly figured Mary pulled me through that tournament," Big Bill said later. "Because in spite of being National Mixed Doubles Champion they still ranked me somewhere between fifty and five hundred the next year."

From then on Little Bill stole a march on Big Bill. Little Bill won the National Singles Championships in '15. Big Bill did not even compete at Forest Hills until the following year and did not win his first National Singles title until '20.

Their face-to-face confrontations began in '19. Strangely, Tilden won their first meeting, but for the next eighteen months Johnston won all their clashes when it really mattered.

In '20 Johnston and Tilden were ranked Nos. 1 and 2 respectively in this country and in consequence were sent to regain the Davis Cup from Australia in New Zealand.

On the way they made their joint debuts at Wimbledon, and London was to see the first real flowering of Big Bill's career.

In the United States everybody loved Little Bill. Tilden was a very late bloomer, whereas Johnston came to prominence much younger, and in so doing, assumed the image of a contemporary gentleman sportsman of pre–First War vintage. Al Laney has described Tilden as "arrogant, quarrelsome and unreasonable." The dissimilarity of their temperaments was unfavorable to Big Bill and contributed conspicuously to the American public's affection for Johnston, in strong contrast to their dislike of Tilden.

At Wimbledon the whole concept was reversed overnight.

When Tilden hit London, staid old Wimbledon was still recovering from the shell shock of Lenglen the previous year. To the English he was a romantic, Hollywood-style figure with the rangy stride of a hero from some early western. The English were fascinated by a man who some genuinely thought was a cowboy. Tilden's coat-hanger shoulders, the arrogant grace of his long legs, even his "woolly bear" pullovers, were things the English had never seen except in silent movies.

By comparison with Tilden, the English found Johnston uninspiring and dull. Despite beating Tilden in the final of London's Queen's Club on the eve of Wimbledon in '20, and actually going on to win Wimbledon in '23, Little Bill, as a personality, never really had a chance. England was worshipping Suzanne and Big Bill.

o

At their first Wimbledon in '20, both Big and Little Bill found themselves in the same section of the draw and scheduled to meet in the third round. However, Johnston's wife became sick and he was so distraught he unexpectedly lost, leaving a relatively easy path to the final for Tilden.

For Big Bill this was curtain up on a decade of dazzling world stardom.

In his first Wimbledon final, Tilden had to challenge the rugged Australian Gerald Patterson. Patterson was a man who looked as if he had come straight from the Madison Square Garden prize ring. On the center court Patterson was the boxer and Tilden the fencer. Tilden used his racquet as a rapier and in a short time parried his way to the Wimbledon championship.

At twenty-seven, an age when many players are already past their best, Big Bill was only at the start of a period of tennis glory.

Once again Wimbledon fervor exploded overnight. Big Bill was a hero who brought a new connotation of showmanship to men's tennis. The Dohertys had won everyone's hearts at the turn of the century with their sporting chivalry. Tilden commanded people to admire him through the challenge of his personality. He was a frustrated actor who used the tennis court for his stage and the English loved every moment of his act. After Wimbledon, the two Bills traveled to New Zealand to capture the Davis Cup from Down Under and retain it in the United States for the next six years.

But on returning home, Tilden discovered that despite his Wimbledon and Davis Cup successes, and despite the adulation the English had given him, the American public still preferred Little Bill. The previous year Tilden had lost to Johnston in the Forest Hills final, winning only eleven games. Little Bill was still not only the American national champion but close to everyone's heart because of his purist, sporting demeanor. His many American fans were still unable to understand Johnston's loss at Wimbledon and were certain the record would be put straight if he and Tilden were to meet again at the forthcoming championship.

Ten thousand fans packed the old wooden stands at Forest Hills for the showdown. The Irish tenor John McCormack bet $10 on Big Bill to win, but nearly everyone else felt Little Bill was a certainty.

The match had every possible element of drama. The two Bills split the first two sets 6–1, 1–6, and split the third and fourth sets 7–5, 5–7—after four sets a dead tie, although at one point Tilden had been only two points away from winning.

At that moment the incident took place in which a plane taking aerial photographs of the match crashed and both occupants were killed within two hundred feet of the spectators.

The impact of the crash was such that Tilden felt the ground tremor under his feet. The umpire even feared a panic, but both players agreed to carry on.

In that momentous final, Tilden served twenty outright aces and Johnston could never get control of the match.

At last Big Bill beat Little Bill in a major championship. He was now champion of America and Wimbledon and stood unchallenged at the summit of world tennis.

Alan J. Gould, of the Associated Press, wrote of that era: "Tilden had a formula for success, compounded out of the elements of his career of unprecedented triumph. It is the formula that has given Tilden the magic touch and made him Champion of Champions in a time of stirring competition. But there is no secret key to it, no short-cut to the final product, for its chief ingredients are sacrifice, concentration and an all-round game. There is a sacrifice of a most Spartan sort in the story of Tilden's early career."

Popular or unpopular, homosexual or not, there was no longer any denying Big Bill's supremacy as a tennis player.

In fact, from '20 on, he was not to lose another match in any significant tournament until '26, a record that has yet to be equaled.

○

[9]

Love and Faults (2)

FOR TILDEN THE SPRING OF '21 REPRESENTED THE SUNRISE OF A glorious era. He was champion of Wimbledon and Forest Hills but had not previously competed in the so-called World Championships on Hard-Courts, which were still played at Saint Cloud on the outskirts of Paris.

On May 12 Tilden set out with his friends, Jed and Arnold Jones, and sailed from New York to Cherbourg on the then fashionable *Mauretania*. Molla Mallory and her friend, the ninth-ranking American, Edith Sigourney, traveled separately, and they all met for a romantic spring amid the flowering chestnut trees of Paris.

At last Tilden enjoyed the rewards of his long years of hard work. The highest authorities of the French Tennis Federation treated him like some sort of god. Soon after their arrival Tilden introduced the Joneses to Suzanne at the Racing Club and thereafter there were ceremonial lunches each day at which the crowned heads of tennis, Lenglen and Tilden, were the subject of formal eulogies and were placed side-by-side in the honor seats on every occasion.

After five days at sea and two weeks in Paris the Americans were still complaining of not having found their land legs. Their practice matches were so much below form the whole party decided to drown their sorrows in a visit to the Folies Bergères. History records that Tilden was "reluctant" to go. Nevertheless, everyone was in much better form the next day.

On May 27, Suzanne was again Tilden's lunchtime neighbor, and with all the speeches and the hilarity she allowed herself to be drawn into a challenge set in singles with Tilden.

The French were so impressed by Tilden's presence they would only allow him to practice on their stadium court, a unique honor at Saint Cloud.

Suzanne and Tilden played their challenge set there, "amid a great furor." Not one to be upstaged, even by an Empress in her own country, Tilden inflicted an ignominious 6–0 defeat on Suzanne. On being asked the result in the locker room, Suzanne, always the star of stars, elusively replied, "Someone won 6–0, but I don't recall who it was."

In revenge, Suzanne immediately challenged Tilden to play the next day with his protégé, Arnold Jones, against her and Max Decugis. She realized it would be degrading for two men to lose to a mixed doubles pair. The rivalry between Suzanne and Tilden, which was to become so deeply antagonistic very soon afterwards, had already been set in motion and Suzanne assured her vindication by beating Tilden and Jones with a one-set 6–4 victory.

Suzanne's vindication turned out to be all the more impressive because Tilden and young Arnold fought their way through several internationally known doubles teams to reach the semifinals of the World Championships against the top French team of André Gobert and William Laurentz.

History was also made in other ways in this tournament for several far-reaching events had their origins in the idyllic setting of Saint Cloud. The beginning of Molla Mallory's bitter antagonism toward Suzanne was rooted in the first of their meetings when Suzanne beat her that week. On that same day René Lacoste first saw Tilden and vowed to himself that one day he would beat the great master.

Tilden beat the Belgian Jean Washer in the final. But with the social rounds and the strain of completing his triple victories of Wimbledon, Forest Hills, and Paris, he developed a serious attack of boils and spent two weeks recovering in hospital from the surgery that was necessary.

While the English were falling in love with Tilden and Americans were at last forced to show him the respect he thought he deserved, Tilden was becoming infatuated with yet another protégé.

This time it was an amusing twenty-one-year-old from South Africa. Brian Norton, or "Babe," as Tilden nicknamed him, with fair hair and an impish face, was originally just a raw South African boy. But he was a fine natural player and a born show-off. In these respects he was a miniature of Tilden himself.

Norton reveled in the fame and attention his tennis brought him, but his apparently romantic association with Tilden was the spark that really lit up his talent. For a few short years Tilden made him an international celebrity.

This relationship produced one of the most controversial matches ever seen at Wimbledon when Tilden defended his title against Norton in the '21 Challenge Round.

Tilden had still not recovered from his illness in Paris when he played Norton.

In accordance with the system before '22, Tilden, as current champion, had to sit around for two weeks waiting for a challenger to emerge from the "All-Comers" event, and this could not have helped his condition. Incidentally, he declared from the outset his challenger would be Norton.

Because of his physical condition, Tilden did not enter the Men's Doubles with either of his protégés, Norton or Jones, and only survived two rounds of Mixed Doubles with Molla Mallory. Thus, before the Challenge Round, Tilden played only three matches in four weeks and Wallis Merrihew recounts that he had still not "regained his wind" when the time came for the eventual confrontation with Norton.

The Wimbledon Tournament Director, F. R. Burrow, who had seen every Wimbledon since 1886, told me the public's behavior at that match was the most disgraceful he ever saw.

Norton won the first two sets and in desperation Tilden started to drop-shot. At one moment he played three untouchable drop shots in four points.

A section of the crowd began to voice its disapproval of Tilden's tactics and the situation reached boiling point when a spectator rose in his seat, shouting, "Play the game, Tilden!" Obviously he did not regard drop shots as playing the game. Arguments began among spectators of opposing philosophies and this section of the crowd was strongly admonished by the umpire.

At one stage, parts of the crowd were so anti-Tilden, Big Bill told the umpire that if the spectators could not be controlled, he would leave the court. Norton, jumping to the defense of his mentor, said that if anyone was going to retire from the match, it would be he.

Clearly Norton had a deep infatuation for Tilden, and it is widely accepted that Babe deliberately threw the next two sets. Wallis Merrihew concludes this in his report of the match. Wallis Myers makes the same observation. "Norton missed a great many shots because of his sympathy for Tilden's sufferings from the crowd," he said.

The throwing of whole sets amazed and disgusted the Wimbledon spectators who had never seen anything like this before in their gentlemanly game. Norton obviously felt his idol was being disgraced and their relationship could be destroyed as a result.

It has been suggested that Norton could never bring himself to defeat his idol. I do not subscribe to this theory because in the fifth set Norton returned to the attack and led 4–2 and 5–4, reaching match point twice.

The first match point produced one of the strangest incidents of all. Tilden chanced a daring drive to Norton's sideline. The ball looked to be sailing out but fell dead on the line. Tilden followed his shot to the net, but not, as Norton supposed, to volley. In reality, Tilden had resigned himself to the fact that his shot missed the line and was running forward to congratulate Babe. He had even transferred his racquet to his left hand.

If Norton had only realized! Instead, he tried a difficult passing shot and missed. Thus reprieved, Tilden made short work of the second match point with an ace and went on, in two quick games to retain his title. The final scores were 4–6, 1–6, 6–1, 6–0, 7–5.

Fifty-seven years have now elapsed since this unfathomed mystery, but by many accounts the match had a weird quality throughout. I know many connoisseurs who were present and all accept the fact that a deep, psychological, probably homosexual, relationship affected the result.

Merrihew described this last Wimbledon Challenge Round, which took place on July 2, 1921, saying, "It will always remain one of the great enigmas of tennis."

The year '21 was the last of many old traditions on which tennis had been raised: the last Wimbledon championships at Worple Road, the last Challenge Round, the final days of the vicarage-garden-party atmosphere.

In '19 the advent of Suzanne outdated Worple Road overnight and the ovations for Tilden the following year confirmed its legitimate

o

demise. Already Suzanne's startling debut caused five thousand applications for the five hundred bookable seats and the Wimbledon Committee decided forthwith to commission an architect to design a "Grand New Stadium" on a larger site.

By '21 the excitement of Lenglen plus Tilden overtaxed the Worple Road seating capacity of seven thousand to bursting point. The committee must have been relieved that the following year the new stadium would provide for seventeen thousand spectators on the center court alone.

Another feature of '21 was the deep rivalry that developed between Suzanne and Tilden.

Lenglen and Tilden both had the same strong drive for success, the same extraordinary instinct for showmanship, and the same reading of public taste.

They both had boundless technical knowledge of the game induced by determination to excel and an unbelievable capacity for practice.

Tilden actually invented strokes never previously conceived. To this day, his book *Match Play and the Spin of the Ball* remains the outstanding masterpiece of technical tennis analysis.

Meanwhile Suzanne became such a dominating figure that the world was automatically her stage. Everything she did was scrutinized in detail by the world press. She did not need to seek adulation. Tilden, however, had to draw attention to himself, and did.

I remember Tilden once becoming infuriated and stopping an entire match because he noticed a woman spectator repairing her makeup from her compact in the second row. This upset Big Bill mostly because she was not concentrating on him. The excuse for his anger was that the reflection from her mirror was distracting him.

Suzanne's pride of performance was also in direct contrast to Tilden in that she regarded it as the ultimate sin to miss a shot. Bill, in his prime, would throw a whole set for the sole purpose of showing spectators how he could demean his opponent at will.

When I played Tilden on the Riviera in '30 I took one game in the first set and three in the second. There is not the slightest doubt that if he wished to beat me 6-0, 6-0, he could have. I remember praying that his flat first serve would come in because there was a chance of blocking this back. His second serve kicked from well outside one's right foot to well over one's left ear, and even on soft clay courts many good players found this impossible to handle.

It was inevitable there should be clashes between Lenglen and Tilden. I do not believe Suzanne ever felt the same degree of antagonism toward Big Bill as he toward her. Possibly Tilden felt the enormous publicity given to Lenglen's bandeau upstaged the almost

o

equal publicity his "woolly bear" sweaters were attracting. Tennis clothing has always caused out-of-proportion emotions with the press and the spectators, and Bill seemed to dress for maximum effect.

From '21 on Tilden never passed up an opportunity to denigrate Suzanne in public or in conversation. At the same time he never missed the chance of backing Molla Mallory in her feud with Suzanne, culminating in his famous brainwashing session before her historic match against Suzanne at Forest Hills in '21.

One aspect in life that Suzanne and Tilden had in common was a special magnetism that caused other great personalities to want to watch them. Just as Suzanne's audiences invariably included kings, rajahs, and international tycoons, Tilden always attracted the queens of Broadway and Hollywood. Tallulah Bankhead was a great Tilden devotee. I remember during his Wimbledon semifinal against Lacoste in '28, Tallulah chewed a pink rose down to the thorns in sheer nervous excitement as Tilden lost in five sets.

In '21, after winning Wimbledon for the second time, Tilden came home and conducted his activities out of Philadelphia, confining all his tennis to America. At last he had established unanswerable proof that he had made the United States the summit of men's tennis and himself champion of the world. From Philadelphia he looked down and literally declared that if there were any aspiring Mohammads around they would have to come to the American Mountain.

The American Mountain remained impregnable for six years during which Tilden led the U.S. Davis Cup team to victory every year and won no fewer than forty-two consecutive matches himself in the U.S. National Singles.

He was the absolute monarch in what was the Golden Age of sports. On the courts he was the complete autocrat, and away from them he indulged a luxurious life-style that he considered appropriate to his status. From tournament organizers he demanded only the best in travel, hotel accommodation, and food, but they knew Tilden's name kept the turnstiles clicking merrily and most often obliged.

Bill maintained a permanent suite at New York's Algonquin Hotel, although he rarely spent more than a month there each year.

It was not unusual for him to allow his young protégés to run up sizable charge accounts, which Bill always paid. One German boy Tilden brought to the United States even had all his purchases from Madison Avenue shops delivered to the Algonquin and charged to Bill's account.

As Tilden strode his American domain many people wondered why he stayed here and did not go to Europe after the dazzling welcome he had received there. But Big Bill decided he could afford outside indulgences during the years of his tennis domination and spent his time—and his inheritance—in his beloved world of the American theater. He wrote, produced, and acted in his own plays and movies, which were usually disastrous productions invariably panned by the critics.

Naturally, Tilden's name as a world champion, coupled with his genuine love of the stage and screen, led him to the exclusive inner circle of many opera and Hollywood stars. John McCormack, Enrico Caruso, Charlie Chaplin, and Douglas Fairbanks, Sr., were among his good friends. There was definitely no name-dropping. For Tilden it was kings and queens across the board—a matter of league, stars on the same top level speaking the same language.

It was then the height of the Gatsby era, when to some the main philosophy of life was to laugh and have fun. If one could afford it, fun and laughter were the things that counted.

I remember Tilden telling me how he and the world famous tenor Caruso were delighted and surprised to meet at a European train terminal.

They embraced, of course, and Caruso said, "Why walk when we can ride?" Caruso then jumped aboard a pile of luggage on a porter's cart, dragging Tilden after him. The whole station came to a halt as they roller-coastered the length of the track, on their backs, their legs flailing the air and the voice of Caruso echoing through the vast dome of the terminal as he let forth his golden tones in some tremendous operatic aria.

Tilden took particular pride in having persuaded the world's most renowned violinist, Fritz Kreisler, to record a violin obbligato to John McCormack singing Rachmaninoff's "When Night Descends." At that time Kreisler enjoyed a much higher level of celebrity than McCormack and to have induced him to play a subordinate, accompanying role was a triumph for Tilden's particular bonhomie in getting these two together.

Tilden was also a good friend of another great violinist, Jascha Heifetz.

Tilden told me that at a concert in Paris he asked Heifetz to include one of his favorite pieces. Tilden thought, at best, Heifetz might play it among the encores, but instead, Heifetz unexpectedly substituted Tilden's request for one of the main items on the program. Tilden laughed as he told me how the whole audience was distracted by the ruffling of programs as everybody searched for the unlisted item. International celebrities have an infallible affinity for each other and Tilden was no exception.

Big Bill was fascinated by movie stars, and on a voyage to Europe in the late '20s he was delighted to find Pola Negri and her husband, Prince Mdivani, were fellow passengers. Bill arranged a bridge night with his teammate, George Lott, and the celebrated couple, but Tilden was so excited by the whole situation that he played like a beginner and lost $126 to the Prince and the actress.

George Lott recounts that as they left Pola Negri's stateroom, a starry-eyed Bill said, "Isn't she marvelous?"

Lott replied, "I'm only twenty-two, Mr. Tilden. I've seen quite a few beautiful women, but I have yet to see one worth $126 to look at." When Bill arranged a second game with the Mdivanis, Lott declined. "You might like the Hollywood glamor, Mr. Tilden, but tonight I am trying something a little less dangerous, like swimming alongside the ship for an hour or so."

Tilden did what pleased him and did it when he wanted to, trampling on tournament committees and officials in general. Above all, he incurred the wrath of the establishment which continually tried to make him toe its line.

But in America of the '20s "Tilden and Tennis," in that order, was the catchphrase always associated with the game.

Whether or not he was homosexual, whether or not he antagonized people with his abrasive manner, I have still to meet anyone of Tilden's era who would not rather watch him on court than any other player of his time.

Tennis writer John Olliff, who knew Tilden well and played him many times in Europe and in this country, wrote, "It is my belief that most people who do not like Bill are those who are jealous of him. And there are plenty of these."

I totally subscribe to Olliff's opinion, which I think applied equally to Suzanne Lenglen.

It is not difficult to see, therefore, that in both cases an almost running battle was conducted between these brilliant stars and their national associations on nearly every aspect of their tennis lives.

The dawning of professionalism in tennis after World War I brought an unprecedented set of problems because the majority of the leading administrators of the game were volunteers.

The very essence of the words volunteer and professional implies contradictions in schools of thought. Long before the revolutionary period in tennis in the late '60s, Tilden on the one hand and Lenglen on the other indulged in almost day-to-day confrontations with the USLTA and the French Federation. The professional postures already adopted by Tilden and Lenglen in the '20s, when both were theoretically amateurs, put the American and French establishments in a state of future shock.

Money, of course, was considered the villain of the piece by the administrators, but considered the just reward for their efforts by the stars. Tilden is said to have spurned outwardly the "taint" of monetary reward for playing tennis. However, he thoroughly enjoyed writing for the press as an ego trip and it seems that he did not refuse the considerable sums the newspapers offered to stars in those days. Lenglen naturally had her share, though she never considered it a fair share. The administrators, as volunteer protectors of the amateur code, considered both Tilden and Lenglen as something close to criminals for earning anything whatever from their tennis.

In *My Story*, written by Tilden five years before his death, he says, "I must own to a special dislike of amateur sports officials." One way and another the mutual recriminations between all concerned never let up until Suzanne and Big Bill decided to become "legitimate" professionals, Suzanne in '26, and Tilden in '30.

The incomparable Al Laney, commenting on Tilden's finances after his death wrote: "It is not generally known that Tilden was a wealthy man and that he ran through at least two substantial family fortunes and died with ten dollars in his pocket. And he probably made more money out of tennis than even the modern plutocrats of the professional exhibition racket."

As for Suzanne, she not only thought she should share the money she was generating in unprecedented amounts for the establishment but she also felt a deep sense of indignation that the establishment could not understand this and did not themselves suggest that she have a part of it.

In turn, the administrations were highly critical of Suzanne leaving the "amateur" ranks. They became terrified other top stars might follow her lead, but could never accept that it was their actions in the first place that forced her to become a professional.

In refuting the diehards' criticisms, Suzanne made a very pertinent point, "If tennis is an 'amateur' game, how is it one does not see an 'amateur' gallery where either at Wimbledon or Paris spectators could watch free of charge?" She also asked why stars like herself and Tilden were expected to perform "free of charge" while the establishment reaped the full benefit—even in trust—of packed galleries who paid high prices for their seats. Obviously this money was passed on to many tennis programs and projects, but those who earned it had no say in how their earnings were spent.

So Bill, arrogant and single-minded, fought the establishment continually through his amateur days in the '20s. Throughout this period he had a running feud with the "strong man" of the USLTA, Julian (Mike) Myrick, who had been trying unsuccessfully to gag him for years.

Myrick and Tilden were so polarized in their thinking they were constantly at each other's throats. The U.S. authorities were also scared that the original effete image of American men's tennis they had been at such pains to obliterate since its pioneer days, could be revived by the world's No. 1 player projecting a homosexual aura.

The bitter feud came to boiling point in '28. While I was watching Tallulah Bankhead nibble her pink rose down to the stem at Wimbledon, Tilden was reporting regularly for the American press on the tournament. On learning of Tilden's defiance of the rule that precluded players from writing about tournaments in which they were still competing, the U.S. authorities finally suspended him on the eve of the '28 Davis Cup semifinal against Italy, scheduled to take place in Paris. Beating Italy was considered a formality for the Americans, and it was the final round against France about which the controversy arose.

France, with its Four Musketeers—Brugnon, Borotra, Cochet, and Lacoste—ready to defend the Cup for the first time since toppling Tilden in Philadelphia the previous year, were shocked and amazed when Tilden's suspension was announced.

First, the French had just completed a new stadium in Paris and were relying on Tilden's box-office power to help pay for it. Second, they could not believe anyone in his right senses could be so uncommercial as to suspend their top star performer.

The French, on receiving absolute refusal to cooperate from the USLTA, appealed in the first place to their own Department of Foreign Affairs, the Quai d'Orsay. This meant, in effect, the controversy would soon reach the Secretary of State in Washington.

In the days following, the cables between Washington and the Quai d'Orsay resembled a ping-pong game. Eventually, the U.S. Ambassador in Paris, Myron T. Herrick, fortunately a sportsman himself, realized that though time was short, no real progress was being made. Through his personal efforts the case finally came to the President of the United States himself. This was no tempest in a teacup.

Herrick clearly advised that in the circumstances, Tilden's absence from the American team would seriously damage American/French diplomatic relations. This was not the first time a President of the United States felt obliged to intervene in Tilden's squabbles with the USLTA who were incapable of considering the country's international relations.

o

Tilden was unpopular at home and the American tennis establishment was never willing to admit that abroad Tilden was a fine ambassador of goodwill for his country.

In '21 USLTA president and tough guy, Mike Myrick, refused Tilden's conditions for going to Europe, but President Harding intervened personally and overruled Myrick.

In '28 on behalf of international relations again, President Coolidge put pressure on the USLTA, at the same time giving Ambassador Herrick an unofficial nod from the White House.

In an overseas country an ambassador, having consulted with his peers, can make the final recommendation on all matters relating to his own nationals. But it was finally Tilden who came up with the Solomon-like solution: "The ambassador himself should nominate Tilden to the team."

Herrick did an on-the-spot deal with Tilden to go ahead if he would take the consequences later.

Big Bill won the only match of the Challenge Round for the United States. The new stadium was packed to overflowing and the USLTA derived considerably more money from the box office than if Tilden had not appeared.

Meanwhile, within the small-time minds of the tennis establishment, rules were rules, discipline was discipline, and Tilden was suspended for the rest of the year.

By a curious twist of fate Lenglen and Tilden simultaneously created a new concept of tennis, attracting thousands of young players from areas never previously exposed to the game.

Just as curiously, the lights of both stars were dimmed within months of each other in '26, Lenglen's by her tragic exit from Wimbledon and Tilden's at New York's Seventh Regiment Armory, when he experienced his first-ever loss to Jean Borotra. On that day Borotra became the first European to dent the glory that was American tennis and Tilden.

Tilden was then thirty-four, and before the year's end two of the other Musketeers, René Lacoste and Henri Cochet, were to beat him in major American events. Lacoste beat him in a Davis Cup match for the first time and Cochet dethroned him in his own kingdom of the American singles championship.

In '26 three of the four Musketeers dominated the semifinals at Forest Hills and the final was all-French.

The coming of the Frenchmen was an ominous danger sign for Big Bill.

But it was to spark a new challenge.

[10]

Love and Faults (3)

AFTER SIX YEARS' ABSENCE, BILL TILDEN RETURNED TO WIMBLE-
don in 1927. This was also a red-letter year for me on three counts: It
was my first sight of Tilden; my first sight of Paris; and later my first
sight of Wimbledon.

I was invited to umpire at the French championships in May. This
led, unexpectedly, to my first Wimbledon job in June, which lasted
until the controversy over Gussy Moran's panties in '49.

In '26, after six years of absolute supremacy, the French challenge
spurred Big Bill to reemerge from the United States to campaign
again in Europe for his lost prestige.

For nearly a year his knee had been bothering him. This was
diagnosed as an injured cartilage and on several occasions he was
advised to have the offending object surgically removed. However, in
those days the success of cartilage surgery was notoriously questiona-

ble and Tilden was very loath to accept a risky interruption to his career.

Tilden was thirty-four when he decided to make his comeback. It is fascinating to compare Tilden's determination to reassert himself at this age with Billie Jean King's similar determination (which she called her recycling) at the same age in '78. Both had experienced a comparably unexpected series of defeats and in both cases their losses related to knee trouble.

Tilden's on-court character was a strange paradox. He would allow himself to become uncontrollably upset over some trivial irritation like a dog barking two courts away, or as we have seen, a woman powdering her nose in the court-side seats. But I do not recall his ever mentioning that a physical injury or even quite severe pain bothered him.

In '22 Big Bill suffered an infection in the middle finger of his right hand when he nicked it on a wire backstop during an exhibition in Bridgeton, New Jersey. Gangrene set in, and it was Bill himself who decided to try to save some of the finger even though in those days it could have proved fatal. Part of his finger was removed in the first operation but the infection flared again and a second operation was necessary. His finger was amputated to just above the second joint. Not once did Tilden complain and he was soon back in action, apparently unimpeded by the experience.

In '26 he played many of his matches with a damaged knee, but he never once used this as an alibi. Instead, he decided to set out on a tour of Europe with Frank Hunter. Hunter first gained notice as a young naval officer in exhibition matches for the Red Cross in London a few months before the Armistice of World War I. Hunter had a few sporadic major victories in the early '20s. He reached the singles final at Wimbledon in '23 and won a Gold Medal in doubles with Vincent Richards at the '24 Paris Olympics. He understood Tilden's eccentricities, and at his suggestion they paired together as a regular team in '27.

On their grand tour of Europe early that year, Tilden and Hunter had a long run of success, winning almost everything on their way to the French championships at Saint Cloud.

With Suzanne far away on her professional tour of the United States, my invitation to Saint Cloud was very welcome. It compensated greatly for the anticlimax of my first Riviera season without Lenglen.

In those days all America and all England were in love with Paris. They were the days of Harry's Bar . . . the days of Wagner's "Ring,"

sung for the first time in German at the Paris Opera since World War I
. . . the first tennis championship to which German players were
readmitted since '14 . . . and the days of the great transcontinental
trains: the Orient Express to Constantinople and the Trans-Siberian
to Vladivostok. Whether your fancy led you to champagne at
Maxim's until dawn, or to the flowering pink chestnuts of the Bois de
Boulogne, this was romantic stuff for visitors of any age.

I was determined to make my first trip from Nice to Paris on the
Blue Train. This luxury took a large bite of my youthful savings, and it
was a year before I could convince my father, although his fortunes
were well on the mend, that it was not an inexcusable extravagance.

My father had rented a small house in Passy so that my mother
could be close to her doctor. The house was on the right side of Paris
for the long journey to Saint Cloud and this made it easier for me to
accept the invitation to umpire at the championships.

Saint Cloud, on the fringes of a medieval hunting forest, was the
greatest possible contrast with the exotic aura of the South of France.
The Saint Cloud club, the Stade Français, had been laid at the turn of
the century and was styled after the original Worple Road Wimbledon. There were the same creaky wooden stands and the same tall,
aging trees, which, for all their beauty, cast disturbing shadows on
many of the courts.

But a new and faster pulse was already beating in French tennis.
The young "Musketeers," Borotra, Lacoste and Cochet, had already
beaten the great Tilden and successfully stormed the hitherto impregnable mountain of American Tennis.

The French authorities saw this in terms of the proverb Coming
Events Cast Their Shadows Before. More spectators than ever were
flocking to see their young national heroes, and already in '27 the
French had the commercial foresight to realize Saint Cloud was
doomed as inadequate for important international events.

However, the impression of my first major championships was one
of disappointment. I had not been forewarned of the leisurely, old-
fashioned atmosphere of Saint Cloud, the fact that only five courts
would be used because of the long shadows cast by the forest. I had
been used to the bustling activity of the Riviera tournaments where
literally, from dawn till dusk, we filled sometimes seven, sometimes
twenty courts, at forty-five-minute intervals in the short winter-
daylight hours.

Awaiting the doctors' daily verdicts on my mother, I was not able to
go to Saint Cloud every day. So my first sight of Tilden was in a very
erratic mixed doubles. In this, partnered by the Spanish star Lili de

○

Alvarez, he escaped defeat only when the South Africans, Pat Spence and Billie Tapscott, missed a sitter on one of their two match points. This was a disappointing anticlimax to the excitement I had anticipated. It never occurred to me that my first sight of my boyhood idol, Tilden, would be in barely surviving defeat.

Because most of the occupants of the Saint Cloud courtside boxes of those days were English or American, umpires who were bilingual were very much sought after and I was asked several times to umpire on the stadium court.

I had no means of knowing that, on the Thursday of the second week, I was being observed by a special visitor in the committee box. Coming off court, the assistant refereee Fifi Lefebure, told me that Dudley Larcombe from Wimbledon wished to see me. I had never before met Larcombe because I had not then been to Wimbledon. But on the way to the committee room where he was waiting, I felt an exhilarating sense of anticipation.

When I arrived, Larcombe was pacing the room and with the directness I came to know so well, he came straight to the point. "I hear you know all the players," he said. "Would you like to come and help us at Wimbledon?" I do not recall any preliminary greeting or introduction. That was his way.

He was a small man with a bullet head. I was only sixteen, but something about the gimlet quality of his blue eyes gave me immediate confidence and I accepted without a moment of hesitation. At that date in my life the long string of what would be fateful Thursdays had not accumulated enough for me to sense their deep portent for the future.

Major Larcombe told me the Wimbledon championships started on June 22 and he would expect to see me that morning.

He made no reference at all at that time to the disastrous Lenglen incident of the previous year. But he did mention that Wallis Myers had recommended me for a new Wimbledon post he was thinking of creating. I was so thrilled at the prospect of going to Wimbledon in any capacity that the matter of what I was supposed to do when I got there never occurred to me.

My early disappointment over Tilden at Saint Cloud was only emphasized in the final, when he failed by a hair's-breadth to achieve the first goal of his comeback in losing to Lacoste after holding two match points.

Tilden's loss cast a pall of gloom over the whole American colony in Paris. Harry's Bar was twice as packed as usual with American sportswriters drowning their sorrows, while at Maxim's chagrined

American hostesses were actually canceling their parties.

However, Wimbledon was still to come. The Wimbledon championships seemed up for grabs, but in London many of the English, as well as the American colony, remembered Tilden's glories of '20 and '21 and were keyed up for the return of the Master.

June 22, 1927, began my lifelong association with Wimbledon. I was going to be seventeen the next morning and I thought I cut a dashing, figure in my best navy blazer, white flannel pants, and the straw boater that was worn by all the aspiring beaux of that era.

I had to be there by 10 o'clock and went straight to Dudley Larcombe's office where I found him sitting behind his desk. Once again there were no formalities, not even "Please sit down." After all, I was there, I was not applying for a job, I already had one.

So I hung my straw boater on the office clothes-peg and his opening words were, "Don't think you are going to hang your hat there." I was taken aback, and rather embarrassed, but I suppose, in retrospect, he regarded it as an impertinence that I appeared to be setting up shop in his inner sanctum.

In that first year I was assigned to the tournament director's staff, doing odd jobs and filling gaps when linesmen were in short supply.

Evidently I did not blot my copybook for when I was invited to return to Wimbledon the following year, I found I was to fill the post that Larcombe already had in mind before he spoke to me in Paris.

The tally of countries represented at Wimbledon had doubled in a very few years. Larcombe felt that with so many new faces coming from countries that were new to tennis, his committee was losing the close touch with the players they had in earlier years.

It was not until I had worked for Larcombe for ten years that he took me completely into his confidence and revealed how deeply he had shared in the tragic Lenglen exit of 1926. He said he felt it was a lack of communications organization resulting from his own shortcomings and those of his committee. Apparently he had sworn to himself then that the situation would never again arise. He felt the need for a personal go-between on whom he could depend to report to him every complaint or grievance overseas players might have about the complexities of the Wimbledon championships. This was my primary task from '27 to '49.

My first Wimbledon, although made melancholy by the absence of Suzanne, will always remain vivid in my memory because of the unbelievable feat of my original friend in tennis, Henri Cochet. Cochet did what no other player has done at Wimbledon this century: he came back from two sets behind in all three of the last rounds to win the title.

o

Nowadays, one frequently hears that Evonne Goolagong has a "charmed life." Exactly the same was said a dozen times about Cochet. The real answer is that in both cases they have a unique capacity to produce some sort of magic when particular circumstances make the adrenalin flow faster.

Both Evonne's and Cochet's reactions to crises were more dramatic than other players' because, with things running normally, they both so easily appeared nonchalant, or even bored. In Evonne's case the term "walkabout," used to describe the Australian aborigines' habit of seeking solitude for periods of mental "dreamtime," is perhaps too easy an association with her origins. But Cochet had no such alibi.

In his quarter final in '27, Cochet first beat Frank Hunter, Tilden's partner and buddy, who seemed to have everything in hand when he led by two sets to love.

In the next match, the semifinal, Cochet was again two sets down and 1–5 as well. What followed remains the greatest Wimbledon enigma since the Norton affair. Cochet won seventeen consecutive points, and went on not only to win the set but the match.

Then in the final Borotra had six match points, and the question of whether or not he actually won one of these is yet another enigma.

On this particular match point, the players had a quick volleying exchange close to the net and half the people there, including Borotra, thought Cochet had spooned back one of his volleys with an illegal double-hit. Cochet's controversial volley was deemed good by the umpire, Mr. E. W. Timmis, whom I came to know very well. Unlike some, Timmis was a very fair and able umpire. But no one on earth could have envied him his decision. Not only that Wimbledon title but the whole sequence of tennis history would have been changed had he decided differently.

During the subsequent Wimbledon Ball speeches, Borotra made one of the most generous possible tributes, "The Roll of Wimbledon winners would not be complete without the name of Henri Cochet."

Borotra and Lacoste had already won the Singles title, Brugnon the doubles title for France, and it was this extraordinarily high degree of French national pride in each other that enabled them, two months later, to mount an unforgettable assault on Tilden and the citadel of American tennis.

[11]

One for All

"ALL FOR ONE AND ONE FOR ALL." A PHILOSOPHY BORN FROM a motto, or was it more likely a motto born from a philosophy? Either way, this was the heart, soul, and dedication of the four adventurous Gallic tennis characters, the French Musketeers.

Jacques ("Toto") Brugnon, Jean Borotra, Henri Cochet, and René Lacoste climbed individually, and side by side, to a summit of achievement unequaled by any one band of men before or after them in the world of tennis.

In their days, the most highly regarded tennis titles were the championships of France, Wimbledon, and America. Above all, the team event of the Davis Cup stood highest in prestige.

In 1922–'23 they won their own championships in Paris for the first time. In 1924–'25 they won the French championships and Wimbledon. In '26 they captured the French, Wimbledon, and American titles.

○

In their peak period of 1927–'28 France took every major tennis honor. The vertical red, white, and blue stripes of the Tricolor fluttered triumphantly over every championship court in the world, plus the Davis Cup.

Concurrently, their individual efforts were no less memorable than their team victories. In the period 1924–'32 the Musketeers collected no fewer than nineteen major titles among them.

In the Davis Cup team event, after chipping away at the might of Australia, then America, their additional corporate triumph was to hold the Davis Cup from '27 to '33.

They gave a golden era to France. Together with Suzanne, they created joint legends never to be forgotten in world sport, and their struggles with the mighty Tilden will forever remain classics of the game.

There is only one possible comparison to the legend of the Musketeers, the Australian teams of the '50s and '60s, so carefully selected and nurtured by their captain and coach Harry Hopman. But even the Australian teams, spread over a much larger stable and also a longer time period, fell at times to the challenge of the Americans.

Harry achieved a comparable degree of national unity that resulted in four winning spells. Four, three, four, and four years respectively, were the magic numbers. But whereas the Australian teams needed the master chef, Hopman, to select and blend the ingredients, the Frenchmen were contrasting and individual personalities drawn together only by the common cause that was France.

The phenomenon of the French quartet was the span of a decade in their ages and the fact that all four emerged from quite different social backgrounds. Brugnon and Lacoste were Parisian, Cochet was from the provinces, while Borotra was from the Basque country, an area of southwestern France where the people have a pride of heritage comparable to Wales's independence in Britain.

As a team, each one of the Four Musketeers made so essential, yet individual, a contribution that it is difficult to give pride of place to any particular one.

On reflection, it is probably logical to think first of the oldest. This was Brugnon, though, of the four, he made the least impact in singles.

Brugnon's amenable personality made him the cornerstone of the Musketeers' success. He was "Mr. Dependable" in this mix-and-match, a model team member, always ready and willing to help iron out any problems with his friends on the practice court, as well as advise or comfort them.

Cochet, the most successful major tournament winner of them all, said, "In the victories of the French team, Toto had a role that surpassed all he had already done with his racquet."

Brugnon was a master of doubles play, brilliant on the volley and remarkable on the return of serve. His only weakness was overhead, but he was able to cover this against most opponents with a high, round-arm "slap." Brugnon was the perfect foil for all his teammates in doubles, always encouraging whichever partner he might have, and apparently incapable of a moment of bad humor.

I remember calling a line for Toto when he played Gerald Patterson on Wimbledon's center court in '28. I infuriated Patterson by calling one of his cannonball services a fault when it was good. At the change of ends, he picked up a roll of adhesive tape from the umpire's chair and threw it at me. Brugnon was actually embarrassed for me. "I'm not going to dispute a present," he said with a smile. "But that is not the way to behave and I apologize for him."

It was the combination of Toto's many charming characteristics that made Papa Lenglen decide he would be the ideal mixed doubles partner for Suzanne and together they were never beaten. And it was through this partnership that I had the pleasure of becoming a close friend of Toto's.

French tennis had been spearheaded by Maurice Germot, Max Decugis, Marguerite Broquedis, and Suzanne. Between the original elders of the men's game and the Musketeers, came André Gobert and a Belgian, William Laurentz, who became a Parisian by adoption. It was perhaps natural that Brugnon, being the oldest of the Musketeers, was the first to emerge internationally, with either Gobert or Laurentz as his partner.

Toto was awarded his initial French laurels in the '20 Olympic games at Antwerp, then in a Davis Cup match against India in '21. The next year saw the emergence of Borotra and Cochet, followed in '23 by the "Crocodile," Lacoste.

Jean Borotra, a master showman, and a magnet of appeal in every country, could not have been more of a contrast to Brugnon. Charm was the mutual trait of all four Musketeers, but Borotra had his own unique expression that set him apart from his colleagues. He was an extrovert in both personality and tennis style.

Borotra did it his way. His effervescence on and off court was both astounding and exciting. The English loved all the things he represented in French chivalry, from his invariable hand-kissing to the unending flattery he bestowed on all.

Jean would always announce his arrival at Wimbledon by sending Norah Cleather, Dudley Larcombe's assistant, a gigantic basket of

o

Cannes, 1923. An extinct print of the Beau Site Hotel courts in Cannes, France, showing the surrounding palm and eucalyptus tree setting. Left to right: King Manoel of Portugal, Suzanne Lenglen (back to camera), Mrs. Geraldine Beamish, and King Gustav V of Sweden (back to camera). This was a game these same four played annually for five years on this same court.

Left to right: Fräulein Cilly Aussem (Germany), later to become Wimbledon Champion, 1931, "Mr. G.," King Gustav V of Sweden, Mrs. William Grogan, and Ted Tinling. Nice Tennis Club, 1928.

My parents, James Alexander and Florence Elizabeth Tinling, in their "going-away" outfits after their wedding, November 2, 1898.

Left to right: Jacques ("Toto") Brugnon and Mrs. Wollaston Richards, the "instrument of destiny" who changed Ted Tinling's life by suggesting he umpire for Suzanne Lenglen, and Ted Tinling. New Courts Club, Cannes, 1925.

Left to right: *George Simond, Ted Tinling's first "boss" as tournament director to the Riviera circuit and director of Le Touquet tennis; Mrs. Phyllis Satterthwaite, who played the longest-ever tennis rally in the world, and was a perennial Riviera winner; and Ted Tinling. New Courts Club, Cannes, 1927.*

Left to right: *Elizabeth Ryan, Suzanne Lenglen, aged 13, Miss O. Ranson, and Miss M. Stuart. Monte Carlo, 1913. This was the first time Elizabeth Ryan and Suzanne Lenglen ever played together. It was a handicap ladies' doubles event. They gave points to their opponents and lost 7–5 in the third set. They were never again beaten together throughout their playing careers.*

Mrs. Dorothea Lambert Chambers in play at Wimbledon, 1919.

Left: Suzanne Lenglen, aged 14, with Count Ludwig (Ludi) Salm, World Hard Court Championships mixed doubles finalists, St. Cloud, Paris, 1914. Courtesy USTA

Suzanne at Wimbledon, 1919, wearing the calf-length, short-sleeved "brazen" little frock with no petticoat that shocked everybody.

Beautiful Marguerite Broquedis (France), the first pinup girl in tennis history. She was called the "Goddess." She is shown here, at the age of 16, when she won her first French championship. Villa Primerose, Bordeaux, France, 1908.

Left: *Toto Brugnon with T.T. Gallia Club, Cannes, 1926.*

Two of the greatest stars tennis has ever known: Suzanne Lenglen and Bill Tilden in a very rare pose. Wimbledon, 1920. Courtesy USTA

On board the S.S. Paris on the way to America, 1921, to the Mallory disaster at Forest Hills. Left to right: Madame A. R. de Johannis, Mr. A. R. de Johannis, vice-president, French Tennis Federation, Suzanne Lenglen, and Mama Lenglen. Courtesy USTA

Wimbledon Ladies' Singles Final, 1922. Left: Mrs. Molla Mallory, with Suzanne Lenglen before the match. Suzanne won 6–2, 6–0, in 27 minutes. This was the great "revenge" match on which Mrs. Mallory's husband had bet $10,000 his wife would win.

Wimbledon, 1925. Suzanne puts silk and sex into tennis. No one had ever done either before.

Suzanne Lenglen after beating Helen Wills, Carlton Club, Cannes, February 16, 1926. The floral tributes are just beginning to arrive.
Courtesy USTA

e photo of Suzanne Lenglen taken by the *thor on February 12, 1926, four days before r match against Helen Wills. Carlton Club, nnes.* Copyright: Ted Tinling

Suzanne Lenglen (left) *with Helen Wills before their historic match. Carlton Club, Cannes, February 16, 1926.* Courtesy Mirropic

Wimbledon, 1926. Left to right: Suzanne Lenglen, Diddie Vlasto, Mary K. Browne, and Elizabeth Ryan, leaving center court after the historic women's double. Suzanne and partner had two match points. Elizabeth and partner won. Neither had ever previously lost a doubles match at Wimbledon as they had always played together and were never beaten. London News Agency photo

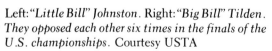

Left: *"Little Bill" Johnston.* Right: *"Big Bill" Tilden. They opposed each other six times in the finals of the U.S. championships.* Courtesy USTA

Gallia Club, Cannes, 1930. Left: T.T.
with Tilden. The picture was specially
taken to prove which one was the tallest.

Wimbledon, 1920. "Big Bill's"
"woolly bear" sweaters fascinated the English spectators.
Courtesy USTA

Wimbledon, 1921. Brian (Babe) Norton with Bill Tilden
after their Challenge Round "enigma" match. London
News Agency photo.

Wimbledon, 1928. "Big Bill's" wonderful grace is demonstrated in this backhand drive. Both feet are off the ground. Times of London photo

Hurlingham, London, 1960. Tilden's "Angel Child," Gloria Butler, daughter of Mr. & Mrs. George Pierce Butler, famous patrons of the Monte Carlo Club. George Butler donated the "Butler Trophy" there. London Daily Herald photo

Monteil's cartoon of the four French Musketeers preparing for their successful assault on the Davis Cup (Philadelphia, 1927). Left to right: Jean Borotra, René Lacoste, Henri Cochet, and Toto Brugnon. R. Monteil

1928. René Lacoste (France) with the ball machine that was originally his invention.

Wimbledon, 1927. Left: Jean Borotra with Henri Cochet before the controversial final that Cochet may have won with an illegal double hit. London News Agency photo

At the Wimbledon Centennial Medal presentation, 1977: Elizabeth Ryan represented all the past fifty-five women-doubles and mixed-doubles champions. She is shown here being congratulated by the 1976 ladies' singles champion, Chris Evert. Leroye Productions photo

Wimbledon, 1930. Elizabeth Ryan preparing her famous "chop" shot.

Wimbledon, 1935. Left: Helen Jacobs with Helen Wills Moody before the ladies' singles final. Two years previously Helen Jacobs had been the first woman to wear shorts at Wimbledon. Planet Agency photo

Helen Wills Moody in play at Wimbledon, 1935. Fox Photos

Fred Perry winning Wimbledon, 1934. London News Agency photo

Baron Gottfried von Cr paying his respects to Hit

Left: *Baron Gottfried von Cramm with "Mr. G.," King Gustav V of Sweden.*

crystallized fruit. A pioneer of air travel, he would wing into London accompanied by his secretary, Suzanne Duboy, and his faithful chauffeur/valet, Albert, setting up residence at the old Carlton Hotel.

Wimbledon was a continual whirl of engagements for Jean, and Mlle Duboy always had to be on hand to grapple with his personal business, shielding her boss from the admiring hostesses who deluged him with invitations for their parties and official functions.

He had an apparently endless succession of friends, business contacts, and followers, and it became a full-time job arranging tickets for even a fraction of them to see his matches. Norah Cleather spent countless hours with Mlle Duboy over Jean's ticket problems. "But Mees Clezair, M'sieu Borotra must 'ave ze tickettes, 'e 'as already promeesed zem." I was never quite sure which of the two girls had the final say in these discussions.

Typical of Borotra was his showering of gifts on those around him. Even after he lost to Cochet in the great '27 Wimbledon final, he sent Norah a gold trinket with the very sporting inscription: "From Your Most Troublesome Runner-Up."

The corporate chivalry of the Musketeers made the perfect complement to Norah's own charm. She happened to be a very beautiful woman, and the setting in her office, much of which was provided by the Musketeers, made a perfect backdrop to her beauty. Borotra's six-foot-high centerpiece of crystallized fruit was most often surrounded by yard-square boxes of chocolates put on the floor because they were too big for the tables. And I remember on one occasion counting no fewer than eighteen floral offerings that almost muffled the incessantly ringing telephones.

It was also a typical Borotra gesture that, as early as my second year at Wimbledon, he should present me with an autographed gold fountain pen.

Albert, after parking the much-traveled Hispano-Suiza car, was always in attendance, carrying an armful of racquets and the huge tennis kit complete with a hat-box full of Jean's traditional berets.

Habitually, he took six berets with him when he had a long match in view. Changing berets as he changed ends (and sometimes when he was not changing ends) was a danger signal for his opponents because it meant he was really getting down to business.

Then, in between matches at Wimbledon, the busy Basque would fly back to Paris for the inevitable important business meeting, returning the following day to excite the crowds all over again.

It was one such return trip to Paris that still rankles Pat Hughes, a Wimbledon doubles champion and a member of Britain's four winning Davis Cup teams in the '30s. Hughes played Borotra in the second round of the '28 Wimbledon, and because the Frenchman had his rush, cross-Channel trip scheduled for that evening, the match was played on a soaking-wet court. By rights it should not have been played at all on that wet day.

Halfway through, one of Borotra's cat-gut strings snapped with the damp. Borotra called to the ever-watchful Albert. "Pass me racquet Number Six B," he said. The gesture was typical of Borotra and still rankles Hughes to this day.

Borotra had a natural flair for tennis, with a flair for showmanship as well. He delighted the crowds, more often than not infuriating his opponents.

One such display of showmanship occurred in a Wimbledon doubles with Toto Brugnon in the early '30s. In this game Borotra chased a wide ball that most players would have ignored, and finished the stroke in the laps of two startled female spectators in the second row of the stands. He managed to get the ball back into play. Then, helped to his feet, found time to kiss the ladies' hands while Brugnon kept the rally going, miraculously, for three shots. Seemingly from nowhere, Borotra then swooped from the stands to smash away a winning volley. One can imagine the reaction of the pro-Borotra crowd! I saw the incident nearly fifty years ago, and still find it difficult to understand how he managed it. It was vintage Borotra at its best!

This kind of dramatic escapade always annoyed Tilden intensely and produced another of the bitter feuds of tennis. Tilden thought that he alone should be master of every stage. Tilden once declared that he never lost to anyone he hated, and he certainly hated Borotra's "antics," as he called them. He once described Borotra as "the greatest faker in tennis history."

One might suppose that Borotra and Suzanne would have been involved in a comparable clash of personalities. They did not share any great affection for each other, but because they were both French and Tilden despised them equally, they fought for France as a common cause. It was the Tricolor versus the Stars and Stripes. Fortunately for the Tricolor, Molla Mallory was never quite good enough to make her partnership with Tilden comparable to either Lenglen and Borotra or Lenglen and Brugnon.

When I visited Marguerite Broquedis in Orléans after the Wimbledon Centennial, she had some amusing memories of an amorous young Borotra. Marguerite was described to me as a "Goddess" by Borotra, and he led a long line of men always anxious for the opportunity of flirting with her.

○

At one reception she was sitting between Borotra and Brugnon and Jean was making under-the-table advances with his hands. Marguerite told me she got bored with his constant passes at lunchtime and told him to calm down. Borotra, of course, was only stimulated by the rebuff, so she told Brugnon to say nothing as she was going to play a trick. Marguerite moved slightly back. Pretending to use her compact as an excuse, she maneuvered her legs out of Borotra's reach and the groping Borotra then found himself stroking Brugnon's legs. Marguerite's still beautiful eyes laughed as she recalled the embarrassment she had caused him.

The effervescent smiles, the gallantry, and the hand-kissing routine made Borotra a hero in England. To the English he represented the actions, grace, and charm that English women rarely received from their own men.

However, underneath the extrovert behavior, beat the heart of a real competitor, a man who never recognized Papa Lenglen's philosophy of giving up in the face of defeat. It was his enormously competitive spirit that made it possible for him to become the first-ever Frenchman, not only to reach the final at Wimbledon, but win it.

Borotra's rather ungainly tennis style derived from the game of pelota (*pelote basque*), a native game of Basque origin. In pelota, players use a "chistera," a sort of banana-shaped glove made from wicker, to project the ball against a wall. This results in an awkward gesture from the backhand side and needs a sharp twist of the wrist, which looks very unnatural when performed with a tennis racquet. There certainly seemed to be a carry-over of pelota into Borotra's tennis. He chipped his forehand and stabbed at his backhand to such a degree that some people thought he used the same face of the racquet for both shots. This was not so, but his style was very different from his contemporaries', particularly in an era when the classic continental forehand was considered a basic hard-court technique.

However, Borotra's athleticism, his unique capacity to move laterally across the net (only comparable in my experience with Billie Jean King at her best) made Borotra almost impossible to pass. His knack of exploding from the starting blocks, enhanced by his already telescopic reach, fully justified the nickname the "Bounding Basque" that the English press was quick to give him. In French newspapers "Basque Bondissant" sounded equally appropriate and impressive.

Henri Cochet, from Lyon, was essentially the product of that industrial, hard-working city. He was the tough little "bantam-cock" of the four, a fighting mixture of aggressiveness and determination when the chips were down but with a dry wit that spilled over irresistibly whenever something unusual or incongruous caught his eye.

Henri's wit was based on keen observation and a sharply sarcastic mind, but his wisecracks were never delivered in a sarcastic way.

When I finished my first year as assistant director of the French championships in '28, I marked the occasion with a gold identity bracelet. Bracelets for men were a novelty in those days, and on mine I had engraved what I thought a natural souvenir of some very happy days. The inscription read: "Championships of France, 1928," and I often looked at my wrist with pride.

As soon as I began wearing it, Henri observed the inscription without any appearance of noticing it at all. Quite innocently he asked, with his usual dry grin, "Which event did you win in the French championships, Ted?" No sarcasm, no put-down, such things were unknown to him. He was a true "copain," which is the closest the French language gets to the word "buddy."

As a buddy, he was always prepared to help out if possible. I was running one of the late '20's Riviera tournaments in George Simond's absence and I hoped desperately for the status of Cochet's entry. However, with his forthcoming international schedule it seemed an impossibility. But when he understood how much his participation meant to me, he immediately agreed to rearrange his plans.

I remember one evening in that happy week when he even suggested we have a hit, and he concentrated on showing me the great tactical value of a cross-court forehand dink. I went around like a dog with six tails for the next two weeks thinking about my Cochet dink. I lost it all again because it had been learned too quickly. But in later years I did adapt it to my own game, and it served me a thousand times in doubles when I became a circuit player. For years I always remembered Henri whenever I heard my opponent bitching as the ball drifted sweetly across him into the right-court alley!

Cochet had that rare quality of being able to lift his game whenever a situation arose that triggered the necessary reflexes.

At Wimbledon in '28 I was filling in for an absent linesman on center court when Cochet was playing the semifinal singles against Christian Boussus. Boussus was heir apparent to the French Musketeers and was edging into world class. In this particular match Cochet had lost the second set and was well on the way to losing the third.

I had the outside line, the farthest removed from the umpire. This is a long way away at Wimbledon because of the unusual length of the runback. Cochet appeared totally bored with the whole proceeding, and at one point, ignoring the ballboys, he wandered aimlessly toward my corner to pick up some stray ball himself.

o

As he came toward me, I spoke to him in French. "Henri, you are a bore to take so long. I have seats for the theater tonight and really wanted to make it." His eyes lit up immediately. Some new and totally extraneous interest had appeared that was the signal to rub the Aladdin's lamp of his genius. "Ah," he said. "You want to go to the theater?" He lost only three more games and turned to me from the umpire's chair with the wry grin I knew so well. "Will you make it now?" he asked, as I ran off the court like a scalded cat.

Another time, I was calling a line for a Riviera mixed doubles final in which his partner was Diddie Vlasto. They had a long lead in the final set, but only managed to clinch it at 13–11 nearly an hour later. Leaving the court, I found myself beside Diddie, saying how unnecessary it had been for them to take so long.

"Henri is always the same," Diddie said. "For him it is the impossible which is the easiest. Sometimes the easiest is the impossible." Diddie obviously shared my feelings that the match could have been won much earlier had Henri made a few bread-and-butter shots at the crucial points instead of attempting his favorite miracles.

Even against top-class players, Henri's miracles derived from his amazing capacity on the half volley. Notoriously one of the most difficult shots in tennis, the half volley was a natural reflex to Cochet on both wings. With this approach he reached his favorite net position without making any visible attempt to get there. He probably had the world's finest overhead, and once installed at the net, it was pretty much curtains for any opponent other than a Tilden, Borotra, or Lacoste. Even Tilden went on record as saying, "Cochet plays a brand of tennis I shall never understand."

Henri had a very sharp eye for everything, including pretty girls. In mixed doubles he invariably partnered the prettiest of the good players in the tournament. Pretty girls were the only influence likely to subdue his determination to win. This is probably why Henri never won a mixed doubles title at Wimbledon and only two in Paris, in sharp contrast to Brugnon's seven.

The greatest contrast among the Four Musketeers was René Lacoste, a pale, studious, young man with soulful dark eyes, and a Semitic profile. He was the archetypal student of everything. Everything he did was pre-thought out and pre-planned to the utmost detail.

He was a frail teenager, and at fifteen his father told him to give up sport altogether. It is a testimony to Lacoste's extraordinary dedication that, by the age of twenty, he was the Wimbledon champion and at twenty-one was also champion of the United States.

From the outset, René knew in his heart that he had the makings of

o

One for All   95

world supremacy provided he was allowed enough time to study the mechanics and technique of tennis. Even the dimensions of different areas of the court always figured in his calculations and he would sit for hours taking copious notes on every player he was likely to meet in a match.

There was definitely something machinelike in his approach to the game. He was a dyed-in-the-wool baseliner, with the same abundant energy as Suzanne's to practice for long hours.

In fact, he gives credit to Suzanne for showing him the importance of "target grouping" his shots. One of my clearest memories of calling Suzanne's matches is of her ability to place three consecutive shots within an inch of each other, the marks being clearly visible on the red French clay courts.

Never satisfied he was getting enough practice, René was one of the first to conceive a ball machine against which he spent countless hours a day, working at whatever shot he thought needed strengthening or tuning, even after the longest matches. Tilden said he sometimes thought he was playing the ball machine and not Lacoste at all.

Then, after hours on the court, he would return home to practice his strokes in front of a full-length mirror. During a spell when he thought he had lost his service swing he saw a photograph of himself serving with a bent elbow. With his usual studiousness he traced the bent elbow. In practice in his bedroom he had been avoiding the chandelier. From then on his team captain, Pierre Gillou, always insisted on a room for Lacoste with no hanging lights.

In René's youth, and with this studious approach to the game, Tilden's unsurpassed knowledge made him Lacoste's idol, eventually the man to beat at all costs. From the day at Saint Cloud in '21 when Lacoste first set eyes on Tilden, to beat Big Bill became the all-consuming passion of Lacoste's youthful life.

It took him five years to achieve this. The year 1926 saw the first fatal piercing of Tilden's armor. Borotra had already thrown down the French glove by beating Tilden indoors, but Tilden had never previously lost to a Frenchman on an outdoor court.

Lacoste, who had been in poor health in the spring, took three months away from tennis, to the point of foregoing Wimbledon, to tune up for the assault on America, even though he was the defending Wimbledon champion at the time.

Very appropriately, the *New York Times*, reporting Lacoste's comments on the Lenglen-Wills match at that same period, described Lacoste as "a young man who bears the weight of his twenty-one years very much more seriously than does Miss Wills the burden of her twenty."

o

Tennis always came first and last with Lacoste. During most Wimbledons the French team would be Lady Wavertree's houseguests. However, Lacoste would separate himself as much as possible from the social round of her life. Wimbledon is a peak of the London season and the price he paid for being Sophie's guest was having to endure, on the way to Wimbledon in her car, an endless flow of socialite chatter, whereas his normal inclination before any match was for two hours' meditation or, at least, silence.

René was never an instinctive volleyer and rarely went in to volley unless forced to do so. I remember one telling point in his semifinal against Tilden at the '28 Wimbledon. He had made one of his rare forward sallies, probably because it was set point to him, but he had to take three bites at the cherry before being able to put the ball away. Each time he put the ball almost onto Tilden's racquet. Tilden told me he was so surprised himself that he could not manage to get the ball past Lacoste either. Eventually, out of sheer frustration, René let fly an almighty swat with both hands, falling flat on his back in the process. But he finally won the point and the set.

Lacoste's single-mindedness and his style of play made him the least flexible doubles player of the four Musketeers. He won one Wimbledon and two French Doubles titles, with the mercurial Borotra compensating for his inflexibility, but while Lacoste's teammates revered him as a singles player, Cochet and Brugnon considered themselves the crack team and never thought they should lose to him in doubles.

I have an amusing memory of the relationship between these outstanding characters. I was walking back to the locker room with Henri some hours after the second French Doubles title won by Lacoste and Borotra against Brugnon and Cochet. As Brugnon came toward us from the opposite direction and passed us, without a turn of the head or a change in expression, Brugnon's and Cochet's eyes met and they both said "Merde."

This single simultaneous utterance from them both illustrated their feelings about their loss more vividly than any argument or subsequent inquest could have done in hours.

It was in '23, in a Davis Cup match against Ireland in Dublin, that the famous Musketeers conducted the first of their memorable campaigns as a foursome. Brugnon,* the eldest, was a month past his twenty-eighth birthday and Lacoste, the youngest, was still a month short of being nineteen.

During the Wimbledon Centennial I was already engaged in

* Jacques ("Toto") Brugnon died in Paris, March 22, 1978, aged 82.

○

One for All 97

writing *Love and Faults*. Knowing full well the complexities of Jean Borotra's character, while at the same time remembering our half century of friendship, I asked him, "Jean, from your long years in tennis, what do you now regard as the ultimate highlight which gave you the most pleasure?"

With his normally instant reflexes, I was surprised when he took quite a few moments before replying, "Of course, winning Wimbledon and being the first Frenchman to do so."

Then he dipped deeper into his memory. Fifty-five years had passed since his Davis Cup debut and an expression of great nostalgia crossed his face. "I think the most treasured memory of all," he said, "is of the wonderful unity of spirit we evolved in the French team. In today's circumstances nothing comparable is even conceivable. Our winning the Davis Cup in Philadelphia was a crowning moment of national pride and emotion that has to be incomprehensible to those who never experienced it."

The team spirit and the crowning victory referred to by Jean derived from long-thought-out and preconcerted battle plans. The French boys had decided the beating of Tilden was the heart and soul of the affair. The Musketeers knew from previous experience that in the '27 Philadelphia Challenge Round they would need more than one hero to achieve their dream.

They knew Tilden would be called upon to play all three matches: two singles and the double. Tilden was then thirty-four, and the French plot was that by wearing him down in the first two days, they could conceivably deliver the fatal slingshot on the last day.

Little Bill Johnston had been called out of semiretirement because of Frank Hunter's previous failures against the Frenchmen and did not appear to pose any great threat. One falter by Tilden was all they needed for victory.

The French team was calm and deliberate in its preparation. Only the ultra-perfectionist Lacoste, complained, first of losing his backhand, then his forehand, then both together. His teammates knew him well. He would be ready when the moment of truth came.

A tennis colleague of mine, called de Monteil, produced a very witty book of caricatures of these widely different personalities on their crusade. His drawing depicts the true scene on the eve of the match: Cochet forever on his toes, Brugnon cleaning his pipe and calmly reminiscing, Lacoste furbishing his weapons (in this case his crocodile), and Borotra telephoning agitatedly (probably to Mlle Duboy).

In Philadelphia, chance gave them the draw they most hoped for:

o

Tilden against Cochet on the first day, a fresh team of Borotra and Brugnon to play Tilden and partner on the second day, and the one Tilden feared most, the imperturbable Lacoste, for the showdown on the last day.

In the opening match, Cochet played his preplanned part by running Tilden into the ground for four tough sets while Lacoste quickly disposed of Johnston in three.

Meanwhile Tilden was also being emotionally drained by his own selection committee being unable to make up their minds until five minutes before the doubles whether to pair Johnston or Hunter with Tilden. Eventually Hunter was chosen and Borotra-Brugnon further blunted Tilden's armor by keeping him on court for the full five sets. Rather tactlessly I mentioned this situation to one of the U.S. selection committee a few years later and his reply was, "You can't win a match when one of the team thinks he's God."

Big Bill, at loggerheads, again, with his own administrators, knew that he had to blast Lacoste off the court in quick sets if he were to survive the last singles. He played like a tornado in the opening set, but Lacoste, more than twelve years his junior, bided his time until Tilden had spent his all before moving in the for the coup de grace.

Lacoste won in four sets. Cochet also beat Johnston in four sets. Thus the French Musketeers became the first and only team reared on slow hard courts ever to capture the Davis Cup from a home nation reared on turf. Brugnon dropped his pipe, Cochet grinned quizzically as usual, Borotra became his "Bounding Basque" self again, while Lacoste, allowing himself one brief moment of celebration, left immediately for some more practice.

The record says there were only thirteen French patriots in the Philadelphia crowd of thirteen thousand. But these thirteen included Suzanne Lenglen. She had been an integral part of the technical scheming and thus finally repaid Tilden for Molla Mallory's victory over her in which he played such a psychological part in '26.

On May 20, 1927, Paris danced in the streets when Lindbergh landed after his historic first lone flight across the Atlantic. On September 10, 1927, Paris again danced in the streets, this time jubilant with its own national pride.

There was dancing in the streets a third time the following year. The USLTA did its best to hand the French the Davis Cup on its medallioned plinth by suspending its top player, Tilden, on the eve of the confrontation. This was not the first time Tilden controversies with the USLTA had reached the White House, and once again, as a result, Tilden was restored to the team at the last moment and at the personal instigation of the President.

He was supported only by Hunter and a newcomer, John Hennessy. His achievement in taking revenge on Lacoste was not enough and he succumbed to his old hex, Cochet, who led the French to their second victory.

That was the last Challenge Round for Lacoste. In his memoirs, Lacoste's close friend, Coco Gentien, recalls that almost immediately before the '29 match in Paris, Lacoste was hospitalized with pneumonia. The French team captain, Pierre Gillou, visiting his sickbed and offering some would-be consolation, said, "Don't worry, your place in the team will always be waiting for you when you recover." In reply, Lacoste, who had just turned twenty-five, delivered one of the greatest-ever shocks to the French Federation, probably to the tennis world at large, when he replied, "I shall not be back. I am giving up tennis!"

Lacoste was the ultimate in single-mindedness. He achieved the goal set for himself as a boy, after five years of preparation beating Tilden and winning the Davis Cup for France. Now his thoughts could stray to other things, his health, his business future, both of new concern as he had recently fallen in love. The beautiful golf champion Simone Thion de la Chaume became his wife. It then took a great deal of persuasion for him to accept the captaincy of later Davis Cup teams.

With Lacoste in retirement, the Royal Flush of French Tennis was broken. Without Lacoste they needed the advantage of their home clay courts to retain the Cup until '33, when the British team of Fred Perry and "Bunny" Austin ended France's fourteen-year period of glory, which Suzanne had initiated.

[12]

Love and Faults (4)

BILL TILDEN WENT THROUGH 1927 WITHOUT A VICTORY IN ANY OF the world's major tournaments. Except for winning his seventh U.S. National Singles in '29, those last years of the '20s must have been a heavy disappointment for him in terms of a top-level comeback.

In '30, within days of his thirty-seventh birthday, any lesser mortal could have been excused for giving up hope. But this was not Big Bill's way. There was to be one more try, and even this started inauspiciously with two covered-court defeats by Borotra in Paris at Christmas, '29.

Billie Jean King's famous theory of "vibes" may have played a part in what then occurred. If so, they changed very much for the better for Tilden with the coming of the new year, for in the next six months Tilden was to lose only two singles matches.

Once he had recovered from his rage over his double loss to Borotra

o

in Paris, Tilden seemed to blossom under the blue skies of the French Riviera, just as Suzanne had done.

His protégé on this occasion was Junior Coen whom Tilden had selected, at the age of fifteen, for a Davis Cup tie against China, making him the youngest American ever to play in this international team event.

It was an echo of the past for me to see Tilden showing off in the sun, just like Suzanne, when I served my apprenticeship umpiring for her on the same center courts.

Now I had three years' experience as assistant director to George Simond on the Riviera circuit. So for the best part of three months I saw Tilden every day as we shuttled from one famous resort to another along the coastline and back.

The South of France opened up a whole new life for Tilden. He had never been there and he found a new doting audience ready and waiting to listen whenever he wanted to hold court, which was from early morning until well into the night.

The Mediterranean could not have been farther removed from the effects of the Great Depression in the United States and Bill obviously felt revitalized by the attention he received that winter on the Riviera.

We lived in the same hotels week after week and Tilden loved nothing more than to sit around a tennis club all day holding the stage or playing his beloved bridge game. As soon as play began at nine he would be there most days, laughing and joking with all of us. So I got to know him very well on a casual basis.

Bill recognized instinctively that I was not critical of him, that I always enjoyed a good laugh at his pranks. At nineteen, I was preconditioned to hero worship and not an unattractive admirer myself. This gave us an automatic bond of sympathy that was reflected in our many subsequent meetings. Obviously we both evolved with the passing years, but until the last time I saw him, on his pro "circus," we were always the best of friends.

Although we had a lot of fun together, Big Bill was once a source of embarrassment to me at the Gallia tournament in Cannes early in the circuit. It happened at teatime.

A French indulgence, dating from Queen Victoria's time, was the cult of the English tea hour, "Le Five o'Clock," as they called it. At the turn of the century two kindly maiden ladies, who came to be known by the whole Riviera society as Miss Perry and Miss King, conceived the idea of an afternoon meeting place for the English colony. It was the "London Tea Shop," which started in Menton in 1900 and moved with the fashion to Nice, and then to Cannes in '27.

o

For over thirty years it was an afternoon ritual to take one's tea in the best English china, with muffins, crumpets, strawberry jam, and plum cake, in this genuine English setting.

Elizabeth Ryan's birthday was always celebrated during the Cannes tournaments, and in my time a birthday meant the inevitable cake, ceremoniously cut with equal inevitability at teatime. So every year it was only natural that we should celebrate Elizabeth's birthday with a cake at the London Tea Room.

The first year I was in a position to afford the extravagance of hosting this celebration was 1930. Considering this a social coup, I made a very careful guest list at the head of which were Toto Brugnon and Big Bill himself.

I remember Miss King being a little alarmed at having to set aside a table for ten and having it unproductive while we were likely to be waiting for Elizabeth to finish a mixed doubles, inevitably at dusk. She felt compensated, however, when Miss Perry told her I also wanted an extra special king-sized chocolate layer cake, Elizabeth's favorite, baked in the shape of a tennis court with Elizabeth in marzipan exercising one of her masterly chop volleys at the net.

Among the many well-known personalities who frequented the London Tea Room, was H. G. Wells who observed the whole scene with interest from the next table as Big Bill took charge of the proceedings. Soon after we sat down for what was to be a happy, social conversation, someone, probably Toto himself, mentioned the name of Jean Borotra. Tilden's reaction was immediate.

What began as a trickle of abusive comment by Tilden ended in a torrent of invective. I do not think any of us had previously realized the depth of bitterness Borotra seemed to have etched into Tilden's soul. In retrospect, this must have derived from two things: the similarity of showmanship and personalities, as with Tilden and Suzanne. Second, the fact that Borotra had not only dented Bill's own fierce personal pride but his equally fierce national pride by being the first foreigner to beat him in America for six years.

Nevertheless, all of us present, and we were not novices in social obligations, found ourselves reduced to absolute silence by Tilden's magnetic, insidious spell.

Toto was particularly mute and only on leaving the party Elizabeth and Desmond Morris, another friend, began to understand how deeply hurt Toto had been at Tilden's anti-Borotra diatribe.

That evening, the full embarrassment engulfed me. As the host I felt it the least of my obligations to send a note of personal apology to Toto at the Gallia Palace where he was staying. Even the following morning he lost a match in quick sets to an unknown opponent and all of us who had been at the party felt the two incidents were related.

Later, Toto, charming as always, sent me a reply, "Think no more of it. I am delighted at the opportunity to observe how well you write French."

Tilden went to the Riviera recognized, not only as a giant of the courts but a giant in stature. Apparently he was asked in two or three press interviews whether he was as tall as Ted Tinling. This may have irritated him because he said, "Let's stop all this. Let's have a picture taken together so we don't have to answer these fool questions."

It was at the Gallia courts that the picture was finally taken. This revealed that Tilden was 1 meter 84 while I was 1 meter 92. I have always found my height both inconvenient and expensive and would gladly have exchanged heights with Bill.

It was also at the Gallia that George Simond first noticed Tilden taking an unusual interest in the thirteen-year-old blond son of the teaching pro. George was even more astonished when Tilden asked him to enter them together in the handicap men's doubles event.

On the Riviera the handicap events were important to the finances of the tournament. Simond was delighted with these extra appearances of his top box-office attraction, but for a star of Tilden's stature it had become almost unheard of to play the handicaps. Even the boy himself was surprised.

Big Bill's sideshows caused a lot of comment, though the sophisticated French stars like Cochet and Brugnon took Bill's eccentricity in their stride because of their great respect for his standing. Coco Gentien, of course, aligned himself the whole way with Tilden. One of the fundamentals of French sophistication is their familiar maxim: To Understand All Is to Forgive All.

With my French/English background and the liberal attitude toward sex my progressive-thinking mother had allowed me, I was personally quite open-minded about Tilden's predilections. So the young Riviera tennis reporters usually came to me to ask if I knew who Tilden's protégé would be the next week.

My invariable answer would be, "Who can reveal the true secrets of the bedroom?"

Tilden's regular partner, Junior Coen, like nearly everyone making his first visit to the extra-slow courts and the dazzling glare of the Riviera, was well below form in the first weeks of the tour. After three weeks Coen was almost reduced to tears by the way he was playing.

On the other hand, Tilden was determined that his Riviera trip should be fun. With two friends on tour together, far from home, any

o

disparity in their relative happiness level can be a significant factor in their subsequent behavior.

Before long the new young blond protégé became Tilden's constant companion, surprisingly transformed from a hard working-man's kid to an immaculately turned-out young man who was extolled daily by Tilden as an overnight prodigy.

In addition to this, Tilden seemed concerned on many occasions to have the boy sit on his knee. He undoubtedly had very roving hands to such an extent that the boy once asked me in French, from Tilden's knee, *"Qu'est ce qu'il me fait?"* (What is he doing to me?). Needless to say, my answer had to be evasive.

Among the outstanding pleasures of Riviera life were the luxurious hotel meals. Unfortunately the price commonly paid by the guests were stomach upsets, usually attributed to Mediterranean fish.

At the Carlton tournament, Bill was complaining of "fish poisoning" and though never using this as an excuse, he lost to Eric Peters on the same court as Helen Wills lost to Suzanne four years earlier. Peters thus became the only Englishman ever to beat Tilden when Tilden was still an amateur. Walking off court Tilden said to me, "Thank goodness that's over for six months." I looked at him, not understanding. "I only have one bad loss every six months," was his explanation.

Soon afterwards it became apparent, and was noticed by several of the press boys, that the new protégé had moved into Tilden's hotel. With the exception of Monte Carlo, where the addition of the famous "Butler Trophy" precluded Tilden from playing any sideshows, he partnered the boy throughout the remainder of his visit. I was never quite sure whether his opponents in the humble handicap event were more impressed by meeting Tilden or "Mr. G," the King of Sweden. At least these two intimidating presences never met each other in our tournaments and I know George Simond had a sly hand in keeping them apart.

Bill had a facial expression that suggested he was always ready for a prank. He had very clear, appraising eyes with a searching look, a feature in common with Suzanne. His mouth seemed to tilt up at the corners at the slightest pleasure. Both Bill and Suzanne had a unique luminosity in the eyes, which, I believe, came from within, as if hoping for something to admire or interest them in the person they were talking to.

I remember vividly one conversation with Bill in which he dwelt particularly on the necessity of *enjoying* one's life. I believe he thought of his tennis as a catalyst yielding pleasure more than an end to itself. For Tilden the tennis court was a stage on which to perform. Sometimes his "performance" involved serious effort and was no fun at all, certainly no fun when he lost to Borotra.

During the week of the Monte Carlo tournament, when we were both in the Hermitage Hotel, Tilden was in very good spirits. One night Tilden was in particularly good form, and he described, with all the animation of the theatrical performer he craved to be, his two greatest ambitions at Wimbledon.

His first was to make his entrance to Wimbledon's center court, not only carrying his normal load of racquets but also a rifle! Spurred by his own momentum, Bill laughed heartily at the whole imaginary picture in which he propped the rifle against the net post and checked it at every change of ends, at the same time giving a stony look toward any linesman who had given him a doubtful call.

Those days were, of course, before the time of transsexual tennis players and chromosome tests. Tilden's second ambition was to sponsor some guy from an unknown country, dress him up as a woman and take him to Wimbledon where he would sweep through the ladies' singles. His plan was that after accepting the winner's trophy his guy would then lift up his/her skirt and pee happily on the net post.

On another evening Tilden used one of our neighbors, an elderly English dowager who resided regularly at the Hermitage for the whole winter season, as the butt of a prank. This "Lady X" invariably wore long, sweeping evening gowns for dinner. She had a bird's nest of hennaed hair swathed in a cloud of pink tulle and clasped with a vast diamond cluster, and each night she would go through a grotesque ritual of one solemn dance with the hotel gigolo.

At that time all French money was paper. A great deal of this was torn and dirty and there was a large variety of designs for every denomination. Legend had it that Lady X would deliberately tear a sizable note in half, give one half to the gigolo and invite him to pick up the twin half from her suite later.

Lady X was at the table next to us on this particular evening and Bill was so disbelieving when I told him this story I challenged him to put it to the test by inviting Lady X to dance. "Why don't you ask her yourself?" I said. "But I don't dance her way," said Bill.

However, I saw the light of a coming prank in his eye, and as we got up to leave Bill approached Lady X saying, "Excuse me, ma'am, I understand you have a very interesting collection of French notes. I make a hobby of these and would be very interested to see yours."

Looking up, Lady X examined him through her lorgnette for at least a full minute. "Are you a cowboy, young man?" she asked. "No

o

ma'am," said Bill, "but I would be very interested to see your collection."

This time two minutes' examination through the lorgnette took place while she pondered her decision. "All right," she said finally, "you have permission to ask the concierge for my suite number." Bill, of course, never took up the invitation, but was fully satisfied with his prank.

On another night Bill came to my rescue. Warned by now of the perils of Riviera fish, he had ordered his more customary steak. I had asked for breast of chicken, but when the waiter arrived with leg of chicken I remonstrated that this was not what I wanted.

All the waiters at the luxury hotels spoke reasonably good English. Mine replied, very derisively: "I regret, monsieur, breasts of chicken are reserved for the ladies."

Bill, with immediate indignation on my behalf, said to the waiter, "We are both ladies. Bring two breasts immediately!" The command was surprisingly obeyed and meant that Bill had to sacrifice his steak on my behalf!

During that week we shared many moments of hilarious laughter, but a few clouds appeared on the horizon as Bill observed his partner, Junior Coen, suddenly taking more interest in mixed doubles than men's doubles.

Distressed by his lack of form Coen also began taking more than usual interest in an extremely pretty German girl, Cilly Aussem. At the first reappearance of the Germans at Saint Cloud, Cilly made an immediate impression on the critics, not only because of her looks but because of the caliber of her tennis.

Cilly was just twenty-one. Junior was seventeen and also good looking. Together they gave the impression of an idyllic young couple. Tilden seemed to imagine a personal slight from Coen's interest being diverted to Cilly.

Cilly's mother lost no time in courting Big Bill's interest in Cilly's tennis and George Simond was soon to receive weekly entries for the Tilden-Aussem tandem in mixed doubles.

However, Junior Coen may have had the last laugh, for in the closing weeks of the Riviera season, Elizabeth Ryan invited him to be her mixed partner. Together, in an emotional match, Coen and Miss Ryan held point match to win the tournament against Bill and Cilly.

Then Coen served what everyone except Tilden thought was an ace down the center line. Tilden, however, remonstrated with the umpire and after some argument a "let" seemed the only solution.

The whole situation turned against Tilden a second time, for Coen walked back and served another ace almost on the same spot, but this time unmistakenly an inch inside the line. I think this moment gave Junior more satisfaction than any other on his Riviera visit.

At our last Riviera dinner together Bill had a quite different mood of dreamy reminiscence and I was regaled by his feelings for Alain Gerbault and admiration for his exploits. Just as Bill hypnotized others, he himself seemed hypnotized by what he described as the "mystique and charisma" of France's lone sailor.

Before Gerbault heard the call of lonely seclusion at sea, he and Tilden had been contemporaries on the international circuit. Gerbault's mysterious personality had left a lasting impression on Tilden.

I have often wondered whether the Broadway tickertape welcome that Gerbault received after his Atlantic crossing on the single-masted, eleven-meter sloop, *Firecrest*, represented a major disappointment in Tilden's mind. Despite what he achieved for America, no comparable recognition was ever given him.

The evening of our last dinner Bill was recounting a legend. To me, Bill was the legend, but I was to learn that even heroes have heroes.

During those memorable days on the Riviera, it was obvious from my many discussions with Tilden that he had a passionate desire to climb once more to the top of the Mountain. His target was Wimbledon.

It had been the French Musketeers who finally broke the six years of supremacy of Tilden and the United States. Now, at thirty-seven, Tilden was to throw himself into one last challenge to the six years of French supremacy at Wimbledon.

After leaving the Riviera, Big Bill eventually reached Paris. The record books show that of all the Musketeers, it was Cochet who could usually beat Tilden. In the Paris final Bill went down once more to Cochet. Nevertheless, it was only his second losing single in six months.

The seedings at the '30 Wimbledon were Cochet 1, Tilden 2, Borotra 3.

Tilden carved his way through the early rounds and secured a semifinal position against his longtime antagonist, the man to whom he sarcastically referred as the "Bantering Basque," Jean Borotra.

Sometime before, Big Bill made a brash forecast that he would never lose to Borotra on an outdoor surface. This was his chance for national and personal revenge.

After more than fifty Wimbledons, I am convinced that the spectators of the '30s were more understanding of the real essence of tennis than at any other time in its history.

o

So for the Borotra-Tilden semifinal of '30 the spectators came fully understanding the background of bitterness and years of personality clashes between these two master showmen. They knew in advance that high drama would be as inevitable as the sunrise—and their forecast proved correct.

The extraordinary showmanship of the two antagonists showed itself from the outset, when, instead of appearing on court together, Borotra made a lone entrance, weighed down with innumerable racquets and bath towels and a clutch of his famous berets.

Tilden was then seen at the entrance making an imperious appraisal of the center court, alone and without racquets. At least three minutes elapsed before he made a deliberately planned entrance, and this time with Ellis, the locker-room attendant, dutifully carrying his racquets. The ritual of the locker-room attendant's carrying the player's racquets has now become accepted as part of the ceremony of the men's singles final. But at that time it was unprecedented, certainly in any of the pre-final rounds.

Tilden's arrogant disdain of accepted custom caused a buzz in the crowd and fully confirmed the dramatic atmosphere they anticipated. But Tilden's initial arrogance rebounded against him. Borotra, sensing the sympathy of the crowd in his favor, began in a blaze of unbeatable tennis, allowing Tilden only a handful of points in the first set.

Two hours later the scoreboard showed Borotra leading two sets to one. It was clear that Borotra had given nearly his all to obtain this advantage. In every other championship a ten-minute interval can be taken between the third and fourth sets. Had this been the case at Wimbledon, Borotra would have had more in hand for the last two sets. It was abundantly clear to Tilden that he should not allow Borotra any possible respite.

In this long struggle, Tilden had always been the first out and ready to serve while Borotra squeezed every precious second of rest, toweling himself that one extra time at the umpire's chair.

Tilden went so far as to ask the umpire to warn Borotra for stalling. Borotra, deeply piqued, responded immediately with one of his most historic stage acts. Instead of spending the extra minute at the umpire's chair, he arranged for a ballboy to walk beside him to the baseline while still toweling himself. Almost a conjuring act took place between them as the ballboy and Borotra exchanged the towel for the balls in one single action. This comedy was frequently repeated to the great amusement of the spectators, whose bursts of laugher served only to infuriate Tilden.

Tilden's fury, and Borotra's exhaustion, combined to make the fourth set a formality, which Tilden won 6–0 in little more than fifteen minutes.

By this time the spectators were almost as spent as the players, but the stage was set for a fifth-set victory that nobody could forecast. At that time even the bookies refused any bets.

Borotra fought his way to 4–2, but Tilden, performing a near-miracle with deadly drop shots and precision lobs reached 5–4.

The crowd was reduced to silence as Borotra made one last superhuman effort to level at 5–5, finishing with an incredible smash that left Tilden stupefied.

But this was the end. This time Borotra had nothing more to give.

Tilden, who had proclaimed that he would never lose to Borotra outdoors, kept faith with his brash promise. In the last two games Borotra was punch-drunk with the punishment the old master had inflicted on his junior. Tilden won 0–6, 6–4, 4–6, 6–0, 7–5.

The public was also punch-drunk, and there was prolonged silence before they realized the match was really over. When realization came, the applause was deafening as the vast crowd rose to its feet and gave Tilden and Borotra the all-time standing ovation.

Dan Maskell and I, who invariably sat together on the actual court itself, were so limp we could hardly rise to our feet.

I remember that even in these circumstances Borotra was as gallant as ever. He had played the finest match of his life, yet he had lost. But a genuine smile of admiration for Bill never left his face. When the applause finally died down, it was I who carried Borotra's racquets, while Tilden, imperious in victory, strode off the court complete with his winning weapons.

In the final, the master's momentum was not to be stemmed.

With Cochet, Tilden's Indian sign conveniently removed in the quarter finals by the popular Texan Wilmer Allison, the final was little more than a formality, the execution taking just over an hour to perform.

It does not require much perception to imagine Tilden's feelings at this crowning moment of his comeback, probably the greatest triumph of his career.

On the last day of '30 Bill turned professional. The early pro tours, particularly in England, took some of the world's greatest tennis to cities that otherwise would never have had the opportunity of seeing the game at this level.

However, "professionalism" was still to remain a denigration for several more years. Even in the late '30s, when I was asked to escort across England a young Hungarian team that included their future international star Suzy Kormoczy, I found the train car (which had been reserved in my name) plastered with notices: Reserved for the Tilden Circus! The slur was intentional and an old confusion between our names was still going on.

Within a short time all the major players in the world, excluding Borotra, but including Cochet, Perry, and Donald Budge, became part of the Tilden "circus."

Alice Marble told me recently that when she and Mary Hardwick Hare joined with Budge and Tilden to sell War Bonds from their exhibitions, their total effort in the six years of World War II approximated $500 million. Such was the popularity of this quartet that at one resort alone they raised $2 million in two hours.

After the war Tilden left the east for California where he could play tennis outdoors all the year. But for Big Bill the next eight years were a tragic slide to poverty and public degradation.

The one light of his life at that time was Gloria Butler, whose father had been the originator of Bill's visit to the Riviera. "Angel Child," as he had always called Gloria, suddenly reappeared in his life, with affection, sympathy, and financial support.

But he was already too far gone for more than temporary salvation. All but a few single friendships, such as Gloria's and, generously, Vincent Richards's, deserted him. True to form, even the USLTA did not consider his death worthy of an acknowledgment, not to mention a tribute.

So ended sixty years of contradictions: inferiority, superiority, arrogance turned by fate to humility, victory, defeat, and victory again, insults to his national representatives but an immense pride in his nationality.

Tilden remains one of the great legends of American sport.

[13]

Elizabeth

WOMEN'S TENNIS BEFORE WORLD WAR I CONSISTED PRIMARILY OF slogging duals from the baselines. There were a few volleying pioneers, notably America's Hazel Wightman and Britain's Ethel Larcombe, but volleying, as a fundamental, aggressive technique, was first injected into the women's game by Elizabeth Ryan.

Elizabeth's unprecedented volleying talent enabled her to win her first Wimbledon championship in 1914 and establish her record nineteenth Wimbledon title twenty years later, at the age of forty-three. In so doing, her example became the generic seed that gave rise to the volleyers Sarah Palfrey and Alice Marble in the '30s. From the '40s on these were followed by Louise Brough, Margaret duPont, Doris Hart, Darlene Hard, Margaret Court, and Billie Jean King. The top woman player in 1978, Martina Navratilova, epitomizes the ultimate of the volleying concept, first foreseen by Elizabeth Ryan sixty years ago.

o

Elizabeth was born in Anaheim, California, on February 5, 1891.

In the contrasting life-styles that so characterized the early part of this century, the background of the privileged classes was not publicly discussed as it is today.

Elizabeth's upbringing was very much that of the privileged class. Although her achievements are now entwined in the folklore of our tennis community, her beginnings have never previously been recorded.

Today she is still the "Grande Dame" of tennis. Alert and lively at the age of eighty-seven, she lives alone with her memories in a comfortable London apartment. Both before and during the fifty-five years I have known Elizabeth, she has changed the history of women's tennis, but it was not until recently that I persuaded her to discuss her early Californian days.

The Irish origin of the name Ryan is unquestionable, though Elizabeth's father, Francis George Ryan, was born in London in 1855 and made his way to California with the pioneers in his youth.

Young Francis was farseeing in every way. He had the good judgment to buy Californian land that soon became a part of strategic development areas. He also had the good sense to marry a San Francisco heiress of Mayflower descent, Matilda Brooks.

As young marrieds, the couple came to possess considerable acreage in Ocean Park as well as a large ranch that extended from what is now Route 91 in Anaheim toward the sea at Costa Mesa.

To perpetuate his bride's name, Francis Ryan called his ranch "Brookshurst." Hurst, of course, implies a rise in the terrain, and the three-storied, yellowstone ranch house was built on a rise.

Elizabeth recalls a single palm tree in front of the house. La Palma Avenue owes its name to this palm tree and the original ranch house stood by the old intersection of La Palma and Brookhurst, all now submerged under the intersection of Route 91 and the Santa Ana Freeway.

The orange, lemon, and walnut trees of the ranch, and the palm tree, have long since disappeared. Even the "S" in Brookshurst has been lost in time, but Matilda Brooks's name is still perpetuated by Brookhurst Street, which connects Costa Mesa with Garden Grove, and Brookhurst Avenue, which runs north through Anaheim to the Santa Ana Freeway.

A short time after Elizabeth's birth, the Ryan family moved to Santa Monica. Elizabeth had a sister, Alice, older by fifteen months. The two girls first hit tennis balls to each other on the sidewalk of their Santa Monica home, then started their first serious tennis on the courts of the old Santa Monica Casino.

Francis Ryan died in 1898. Shortly afterwards a transportation company obtained from Mrs. Ryan a right-of-way for a streetcar service which they proposed to run from Santa Monica to Los Angeles through her property. Like the Anaheim ranch, the tramlines have long since disappeared, but for so long as the service operated, the Ryans enjoyed free streetcar transportation from Santa Monica to the "Big City."

Elizabeth, contending with a classic four-year education at the socialite Marlborough School, was always a leader, but being the school captain at basketball, she was a late starter in tennis.

Nevertheless, Alice and Elizabeth won a few tournaments together on the Pacific Coast. At fifteen and sixteen years old, they were inveterate travelers and went as far as British Columbia in search of tennis worlds to conquer. "On our first trip we won every available prize in four tournaments: Vancouver, Victoria, Tacoma, and Seattle," Elizabeth still recalls with some pleasure.

Elizabeth also remembers that she played her sister in the Vancouver singles final and that it was there she was first forced to try her hand at volleying because there was a large rough patch on the court.

"When Alice was on the good side she always seemed accurate enough to put the ball in the bad patch. After half-a-dozen untakable bounces I was furious and accused her of cheating," says Elizabeth.

Elizabeth then said to herself, "I have to stop this. I have to hit the ball before it bounces." And it was from this incident, insignificant at the time, that twenty-five years later she was still outwitting the best men in the world in quick net exchanges.

Elizabeth's angled volleys eventually became the sharpest in the game. Fred Perry told me only recently that in a mixed double in his time, she was the only woman who could kill an overhead smash against a man waiting behind the baseline.

May Sutton was the first world champion to invite Elizabeth to be her partner. Together, they beat the two older Sutton sisters, Ethel and Florence, to win the Pacific Coast championships at Del Monte in 1908. This began Elizabeth's formidable career by the end of which she had won the national singles titles of nine countries and the doubles championships of no fewer than twenty-two countries.

When Elizabeth was seven, Mrs. Ryan remarried and became Matilda Brooks Dudley. Mrs. Dudley's marriage did not endure, and in 1912 she and her two daughters set out for Europe.

The Ryan sisters were not thinking about tennis in those first days in England, but when their visit took them to Chagford village in Devonshire, "we ate so much Devonshire cream we got sick and some form of exercise became a vital necessity," says Elizabeth.

o

In search of a tennis facility, Mrs. Dudley turned to the Chagford bank teller for advice, and the two girls were recommended to the neighboring village of Mortonhampstead.

There was no store in that rural area where they could buy racquets and balls, so the bank manager suggested they make a special journey to London. At that time this involved a three-day excursion, but the girls were undaunted. They bought their racquets from a London department store and returned to Chagford with high hopes of finding some enthusiastic opponents.

Elizabeth's meticulously kept diary records that after a few mixed doubles at Mortonhampstead, "the men thought we were quite good, but the women took little notice of us."

Elizabeth's first English tournament began on May 20, 1912, at Surbiton, near London. She lost in the second round, but the following week she and Alice played at Shakespeare's birthplace, Stratford-upon-Avon.

Most tournaments in those days were played on a handicap basis. "To give everyone an equally sporting chance," was the Edwardian code, but at Stratford things did not work out as intended. "Before going to England, we had never seen a grass court," Elizabeth remembers. "We were so bad on the wet grass at Surbiton, they gave us big handicaps at Stratford and we won everything. Some of the other women were furious."

After Stratford, Elizabeth entered her first Wimbledon. Such were the sporting ethics of 1912 England that good players would refrain from practicing from fear of an unfair advantage over those who might not have an equal opportunity.

Elizabeth remembers many raised eyebrows when she first played Wimbledon. At the time she did not understand the reason. Later, she was told that some players considered her entry an impertinence as they did not think her good enough "to give the champion a good game." But she reached double match point against the six-time champion, Mrs Blanche Hillyard, so she still considers the criticisms unjustified.

From girlhood Elizabeth had always been "big." Coming to the steel-boned corsets and starch of Edwardian England, she did her best to conform. However, in a match just prior to World War I her corset split and she did not have a replacement.

"I see you do not wear stays, Miss Ryan, in spite of your size," another lady player commented with the raised eyebrows that are the ultimate in English disdain. Elizabeth says that having been temporarily relieved of the torture of steel bones, her game improved so much she never wore them again.

○

Elizabeth   115

The Ryan sisters had an uncle who resided on the Riviera, and in the winter of 1912–13, the family joined the accepted socialite migration to the South of France. Elizabeth found the palms and the blue skies there so congenial that she won the singles at her very first tournament and the mixed doubles with Count Ludi Salm.

In the first round of this tournament in Nice, her opponent was a thirteen-year-old French girl whose name happened to be Suzanne Lenglen.

This fateful day in Elizabeth's life was January 13, 1913. Those thirteens proved symbolic of both fortune and misfortune for Elizabeth. In singles, Suzanne was to be the lifelong hurdle she was never able to surmount. Elizabeth won this first meeting, but never again beat her in thirty-six subsequent encounters.

Together in doubles they lost their first-ever match by a hairsbreadth, at Monte Carlo, giving handicap points to Miss O. Ranson and Miss M. Stuart, but they were never beaten again in any championship match.

May, June, and July, 1914, were to become particularly memorable months in Elizabeth's life. First, in May, Elizabeth and the little Suzanne won the doubles in the World Hard Courts Championships in Paris. Elizabeth recalls that to celebrate their victory she was invited to visit at the Lenglen's home in Compiègne, where Suzanne was born and where she played her first tennis. Elizabeth still remembers her surprise that Papa Lenglen never once removed his hat in the house, even at mealtimes.

Then June brought a very special Wimbledon for Elizabeth for she not only reached the singles semifinals for the first time there, but won her first Wimbledon title, the women's doubles.

In July, she looked forward to what was then an unprecedented event, an invitation to compete in the Russian championships at the imperial capital of St. Petersburg (renamed Petrograd shortly afterwards and Leningrad in 1924).

She was to be partnered in mixed doubles by the German champion Dr. Heinrich (Heine) Kleinschroth. As things turned out, this was the act of destiny that enabled Elizabeth and her mother to return from Russia relatively unscathed.

In view of the political upheaval that pervaded Central Europe in the summer of 1914, it seems amazing that Elizabeth and Heine Kleinschroth accepted the Russian invitation, particularly as Elizabeth and her mother had to make the long trip from England to Russia unaccompanied.

The international danger signals were touched off as early as June

28, when a minor Austrian prince, the 51-year-old Archduke Francis Ferdinand, was assassinated at Sarajevo by Serbian nationalists. However, such was the aloof serenity of the leisured classes of that time, interested only in their own pleasures, the significance of this event failed even to raise a ripple of apprehension among the sophisticated of western Europe.

Historically, it took barely five weeks for the Sarajevo incident to engulf the whole of Europe in the calamitous escalation of hostilities which is now called World War I, and it was during this explosive period that Elizabeth and Heine Kleinschroth went to Russia.

Returning again to Elizabeth's diary, the July 20 page records that she and Mrs. Dudley were met at St. Petersburg station by a welcoming party of fifty men, all carrying bouquets.

"There was not a woman in sight," Elizabeth recalls. "Although I weighed 168 pounds in those days and was no movie star in looks, those men gave us a rousing welcome."

Heine remembers that he was the personal houseguest of the Russian Prime Minister. Even so, he recalls no sense of alarm in the household at what was to happen only a few days hence.

"Luncheons and dinners, at which there were never fewer than 100 guests, were given every day in our honor," Heine told me recently. Elizabeth adds, "The one time we saw anything strange was a column of smoke, which seemed unusual from where we were, and we were told that it emanated from the Czar's yacht because it was in a permanent state of readiness for an immediate escape."

Elizabeth and Heine Kleinschroth won all the tennis events between them. Elizabeth won four trophies. They both recall that the St. Petersburg matches were the only occasions in their lives when the ballboys were actually liveried footmen who presented the balls to them on silver salvers.

After the St. Petersburg victories, Moscow wanted to see the champions, and they, of course, wanted to see Moscow.

Moreover, the dangers of imminent war between Russia and Germany were still not discussed. Even the German ambassador advised Heine that the Moscow journey would be quite safe though they were to learn later that the Polish frontier was already closed and the alternative Archangel boat route was inaccessible.

Both Heine and Elizabeth recall that after playing in Moscow until July 30, their subsequent escape was a nightmare. They returned to St. Petersburg, and their train from there was, in fact, the last train to cross from Russia into Germany for several years.

Elizabeth recounts that they managed to get on the train only by

○

virtue of some gold rubles Mrs. Dudley had prudently concealed in a body belt. "The train stopped incessantly," says Heine. "At each stop we realized more and more the seriousness of our position." "A dozen times we thought we might be forced to leave the train so we threw piece after piece of our baggage out of the window at every stop," adds Elizabeth. The singles trophy she won in St. Petersburg is the only memento that survived the journey. She has lately bequeathed this to the Wimbledon Tennis Museum, where it is currently on display.

How close this excursion came to disaster for Mrs. Dudley, Elizabeth, and Kleinschroth is confirmed by Elizabeth. She says that it was essentially because Heine was a German national and Mrs. Dudley had the gold on hand to bribe officials that Kleinschroth managed to get the two women aboard the last train out of Berlin into Belgium.

History confirms the dangers they survived because they finally left Berlin for Liège, Belgium, on August 2. On August 3, Germany invaded Belgium and declared war on France. On August 4, four years of unending horror began when England retaliated by declaring war on the Kaiser.

Heine Kleinschroth was the German Davis Cup captain who endured three nerve-wracking hours while Donald Budge beat Gottfried von Cramm in their historic '37 Davis Cup match.

Now, at 89 years of age, he is still slim and elegant, but regretting the lost sybaritic luxuries of his youth.

At Wimbledon in '78, a young competitor overheard some of our conversation about these days, long since gone, and asked Heine how he felt about today's tennis.

"I will only quote Talleyrand to you," Heine replied after some reflection: 'He who did not know life before 1789 (the French Revolution year) never knew paradise.' "I feel exactly the same about 1914," he concluded.

In the 1914–18 years all the women of Britain's upper class did war work of one sort or another. To this day Elizabeth is still an American citizen, so she could easily have returned to the safety of the United States, but preferred to remain in England where she worked with the British Land Army to provide food for the war effort.

When the Armistice finally came in 1918, the French Riviera was still given over to convalescents from the American forces. Paris was not yet prepared for an international championship so the real "curtain up" of postwar tennis was the 1919 Wimbledon.

Although the advent of Suzanne Lenglen was described by one contemporary reporter as an "electrical disturbance," and her debut

o

there was ultimately totally successful, Elizabeth was not keen to partner her on that occasion because Suzanne had still never seen a grass court.

All this was fifty-nine years ago so it is understandable that Elizabeth no longer remembers how it came to pass that they did team together. The fact remains that they won the championship and that in doing so they lost the last set they were ever to lose together for the next seven years.

Off court, the unbeatable Ryan-Lenglen partnership was not, however, without its ups and downs and one particular "down" culminated in Suzanne's throwing all Elizabeth's clothes out of the locker-room window.

The Wimbledon women's locker room had cubicles in those days, but it was only as a result of this incident that one special dressing room was allocated to the "Lady Champion" and marked accordingly.

Suzanne said subsequently that she had wanted to share a cubicle with Elizabeth, but Elizabeth had declined on the pretext that they were partners so they would often need to be changing at the same time. Elizabeth points out that Mama Lenglen invariably helped Suzanne to dress and that there was not really space for three people at one time in a cubicle.

Elizabeth, it seems, therefore made her own choice of a cubicle and locked her street clothes in it while she went off to play a match, not knowing that Suzanne had already decided this particular cubicle "had the best light" for adjusting the famous Lenglen bandeau and applying her elaborate makeup.

Spectators outside were astonished to see a shower of Elizabeth's clothes coming out of the window. Suzanne had ordered the door opened by the attendant and with rising indignation was clearly intent on giving one of her best prima-donna performances, though she did say afterwards she had not realized she was objecting to her own partner's belongings.

On the Riviera circuit, Elizabeth and Suzanne in doubles would often win a whole string of tournaments with the loss of only a few games throughout.

On one occasion, Elizabeth suggested to Suzanne they split up as she thought it would be less boring for them to meet with different partners, and have a really close match in the final.

Suzanne took great exception to this proposal asking Elizabeth if she did not realize there were at least ten women who would sacrifice their dearest possession to be Lenglen's partner—after which comment "Suzanne did not speak to me for a week," says Elizabeth. Recalling this temporary upset, Elizabeth adds generously, "Well, Suzanne was very highly strung, so I did not raise the question a second time."

In 1920 Mrs. Mallory's return to Wimbledon seems to have caused some additional locker-room flutters.

"She would strut about stark naked!" says Elizabeth, "and this was strictly *not done* in our day."

Their mutual antagonism intensified the following year when Elizabeth beat Mrs. Mallory on her way to the Challenge Round and received the following telegram from Jack Dempsey:

> New York. June 30th, 1921. Heartiest congratulations on your winning right to challenge Suzanne Lenglen for the Wimbledon championship. I hope for America's sake you can beat this French lady just as I hope for America's sake to beat another grand French challenger for the world heavyweight boxing championship. Well wishes from a fellow citizen. Jack Dempsey.*

Although an expatriate Norwegian, Molla Mallory was a great favorite in this country. Because Elizabeth had resided in Europe for the past ten years Molla resented any expressions of patriotic affection toward Elizabeth. Some element of personal rivalry probably also played its part because that year Elizabeth won all three events in nineteen of the twenty tournaments she played and in this way was the forerunner of Billie Jean King in winning more prizes in a single year than any other player of either sex.

On her world travels, Elizabeth was invariably accompanied by a friend from either the English or the Irish aristocracy with whom she would share a personal maid.

One of Elizabeth's closest friends in the '20s was Eleanor Sears, often described as "the original Boston glamor girl." "Elio" was a competent tennis player who won the American doubles championships with both Hazel Wightman and Molla Mallory. She was also Squash-Racquets champion of America and was the first Boston socialite to dare to ride a horse cross-saddle. When she traveled to New York, her personal club car would be attached to the train and her own liveried servants would meet her on arrival.

*On July 2, 1921, Jack Dempsey knocked out Georges Carpentier (France) in the fourth round at Jersey City before 80,000 spectators, the largest attendance ever known at a prize fight at that date. However, his other hopes did not materialize for the previous day Mlle Suzanne Lenglen (France) beat Miss Ryan in the Wimbledon Challenge Round, 6—2 6—0.

o

All this luxury made Elio an exercise fanatic and in '24 she organized, for a bet, a forty-nine-mile walk from Boston to Providence, Rhode Island.

In November '26 Elizabeth was Elio's houseguest when Elio accused Elizabeth of being "sissy." "All you can do is hit tennis balls," she said.

Immediately provoked, Elizabeth challenged Elio to a replay of the walk from Providence.

Eventually, they set out from Providence station at 12:55 in the morning. Reporters were waiting to see them at every town on the route but they reached Elio's home at 122 Beacon Street, after 9 hours 53 minutes of unbroken walking. Their average speed was marginally in excess of 4¾ mph, which was consiered a remarkable achievement for socialite ladies of the '20s.

Thirteen years after leaving California, Elizabeth returned to this country to score one of her most notable victories. She beat Helen Wills at Seabright in '25, at a time when Wills was winning the American championships year after year.

But returning to Forest Hills in '26, she experienced one of the bitterest defeats of her life, losing the national final to Mrs. Mallory after leading 4-0 in the last set and holding match point in the fourteenth game.

Bad luck struck again in '31. This was the first year since World War I when neither Lenglen nor Wills entered Wimbledon and was virtually Elizabeth's last chance of winning the singles title there. Unfortunately, a severe attack of Achilles tendonitis kept her out of tennis the whole summer and the chance was lost.

Tilden, Patterson, Lenglen, and Ryan were the names I knew best when I first fell in love with tennis.

My presence was more or less forced on Elizabeth by the number of matches I called for Suzanne on the Riviera. Before long I was calling many of Elizabeth's matches as well as Suzanne's.

Elizabeth's insatiable need for exercise also had an effect on my tennis game. Tournament matches in the '20s jammed the Riviera courts from 9 a.m. till dark, seven days of every week. Because of this my job precluded me from playing any tennis at all between Christmas and Easter.

Elizabeth's need for practice came to my rescue. Although she was quite often scheduled for three matches in one day she would still ask me to hit with her at 7 a.m., and most times we played two full sets. By the late '20s we had played more than two hundred times and I had still not won one set from her.

Many of the California tennis pioneers who learned their tennis before World War I used a *chop* shot. The extreme "Western" grip used by May Sutton was the customary alternative.

Elizabeth had the world's most famous *chop* and once she accustomed herself to wet English turf the excessive spin this put on the ball made the bounce virtually untakable, except by a handful of experts. She had also a devastating drop shot, which left at least a thousand opponents flat-footed.

Having struggled against Elizabeth's *chop* for more than 400 sets, I came to know the personal idiosyncrasies of her style so well I could always detect those variations of balance or swing that upset every player's game from time to time. I was flattered, but not surprised, therefore, to receive a telegram from Paris in '32 saying, "Come at once. Can't hit a ball."

Because of Elizabeth's upbringing and modesty, she was always very reticent in her quest for doubles partners and frequently asked me to be the "go-between" on her behalf. Obviously, Elizabeth did not always agree with my suggestions, but I think I may claim "part authorship" of a dozen or so of her winning partnerships.

For instance, Jack Crawford's first Wimbledon success was his partnership with Elizabeth in '30, which I proposed.

During the championships Elizabeth sometimes found Jack's lethargic mixed doubles technique more than her patience could stand and I remember her asking me to suggest to Jack that she should serve first in each set as he was regularly losing his own serve.

Harry Hopman's book *Aces and Places* recounts that Elizabeth "saw nothing funny in the half-joking references that were being made to their partnership as "Ryan and Miss Crawford."

A century hence history may still record that Elizabeth Ryan was the best woman doubles player the world has ever seen. Hazel Wightman was the first woman volleyer of note. Elizabeth was the first to establish that aggressive volleying was to become a basic fact of women's tennis life.

It was altogether appropriate therefore that at the Wimbledon centennial in '77, Elizabeth alone was invited to represent the fifty-five other women who had also won women's or mixed doubles titles there. I think it fair to say that in spite of the number of other tennis heroes and heroines at the presentation, Elizabeth received the greatest ovation of them all.

In my boyhood, when Suzanne Lenglen was already addressing me in the second person singular, *thou*, which the French use to imply friendly familiarity, I thought the time had come when I could ask

o

Miss Ryan if I might also call her by her first name.

It was difficult to respond to her reaction. "What makes you think you should?" she asked sharply. It was at least twelve months before I reopened this question.

Having eventually been permitted to call Elizabeth Ryan by her first name, having shared in innumerable experiences with her in a number of different countries, remembering that it is fifty-five years since we first spoke to each other, it has been fascinating to discover new aspects of her that have never previously been discussed.

[14]

The Two Helens (1)

FATE, COINCIDENCE, CHANCE, CALL IT WHAT YOU WILL, THE STORY of two young girls with the same first name, who were reared on the same street, were educated at the same school and college, were coached by the same man, who lived, at different times, in the same house, and were both to become American and World champions, is one of the strangest of all tennis sagas.

Outside their tennis, however, Helen Wills and Helen Jacobs, of Berkeley, California, had nothing in common. On or off the court they exchanged only a few dozen words in fifteen years of treading parallel paths on the international circuit.

The fact that Helen Wills ruled the circuit unchallenged was accepted by all the girls except Helen Jacobs and her refusal to pay homage to Queen Wills lent credibility to a picture of antagonism.

There were also dark rumors of religious differences and differences in sexual preferences. In the '20s such things were not publicly referred to so these aspects are best countered with Tristan's reply to his king about Isolde, "What thou asks thou shalt ne'er discover."

Helen Jacobs has said, "There was no feud," but the lack of outward communication between the two Helens put an obvious question mark over their relationship. For those who wished to accent their differences some evidence of a deep rift was not difficult to discern.

Helen Wills was extremely class conscious and highly discriminating in everything from friends to fashions. She always aligned herself with all the "right" people: famous politicians, royalty, the top names in the arts world. In hotels, only the London Dorchester and the George V in Paris were good enough.

She was a talented painter herself and her works were exhibited in galleries from coast to coast. Beyond all this, Helen Wills's father was a doctor whereas Helen Jacobs's father was "in trade."

Helen Wills had a natural ability to excel and projected the impression that everyone should automatically recognize her superiority in whatever area of life she chose to favor.

With the exception of Garbo, I have seen all the best-looking women in the world face-to-face and in the beauty stakes, Helen Wills was very definitely in the top league.

I sat opposite her one eyening in the relaxed atmosphere of Noordwijk's Huis ter Duin Hotel when we were both playing the '32 Dutch championships. She had a flawless complexion. Her facial bone structure and her finely chiseled features gave an inescapable impression of serene classic sculpture. In dramatic contrast, she had the Marlene Dietrich technique of fixing her beautiful eyes with sudden intensity at the exact climax of a conversation, and I remember thinking how truly lovely she was.

Wills was certainly the Garbo of tennis, always wanting to be alone and away from her fellow competitors. This, coupled with her determinedly detached nature and unchanging countenance, both unfamiliar in tennis, gave the world's sportswriters a field day. Arthur Guiterman wrote in *Life* magazine in '29.

> The Journalists, a Ribald Race,
> Have named her Little Poker Face.

As she grew up, the "little" was dropped, but "Miss Poker Face" stuck appropriately throughout her career.

As if by intent, Helen Jacobs was one of the world's friendliest souls and I often thought that the more Helen Wills became distant and aloof, the more Helen Jacobs wanted to please.

Jacobs had a Grecian profile, which endeared her to the photographers, though she never aspired to Wills's grandeur. Wills had too much respect for tradition to innovate anything; Jacobs, on the other hand, was actually the innovator of the first shorts for women.

Wills achieved an all-time record of Wimbledon singles titles. Her personality was often considered remote and unfriendly so there were inevitably those who envied or disliked her. And these same people, spearheaded by Bill Tilden and Molla Mallory, went to great lengths to show their admiration and affection for Jacobs.

Whatever may have been the true nature of their relationship, Wills certainly used her racquet as a knife against Jacobs. Helen Wills first beat her namesake, 6–0, 6–0, in an early practice encounter in Berkeley in '23. In '38 she capped her legendary career with an unequaled eight wins at Wimbledon. She also won seven Forest Hills titles, and throughout made sure Helen Jacobs was forever the unhappy second-best.

Jacobs won the American championships four times and one Wimbledon title when Wills did not play. She beat Wills only once in all fifteen years of their rivalry and even then she was robbed of a clear-cut victory because Wills defaulted as defeat stared her in the face at 0–3 in the last set of their match.

Described as "grossly unsporting," Wills's default brought waves of criticism and indignation equaled only by those leveled at Lenglen when Suzanne "coughed and quit" against Molla Mallory in this same championship twelve years earlier.

In '33 Wills had a back injury and at the time I defended her stoutly. But this incident never lost its questionable overtones because her default made it academically possible for her to say she never lost to Jacobs, just as Suzanne was able to believe she never actually lost to Mrs. Mallory.

Helen Wills was born in 1905 and recalls in her memoirs that the fascination tennis held for her as a small child was just how high she could hit the ball into the sky. "Up, up," she said. "Where would the ball go if it didn't come down?"

This, to me, typifies Wills's mental process throughout her life. Just as her vivid childhood imagination knew no bounds, neither did her quest for unparalleled achievement nor her determination for unquestioned status.

Wills admits that at the University of California her ambition was to earn a Phi Beta Kappa key. "I had a complete lack of interest in learning for the sake of knowing something," she said. "I was, in the truest sense of the word, a 'cup-hunter' in the field of scholarship."

This same obsession pushed her career "up, up" to records never attained by anyone before or since. Twice she retired, and twice she came back to fulfill her ambition of being the greatest Wimbledon singles winner of all time.

In her junior days, Wills benefited from the inestimable advantage of having Hazel Wightman on her side at every opportunity.

Throughout the decade that spanned World War I a deep-seated rivalry existed between Hazel Hotchkiss Wightman and Molla Bjursted Mallory, who, in 1915, thwarted Hazel's hope of a fourth American singles title.

Women's tennis in every country has always abounded with bitchy theories, and it was widely said that Hazel trained "young hopefuls" with the specific purpose of revenging herself against Molla. She was certainly successful in the case of Marion Zinderstein, who put Molla out of the 1919 American championships, and then Helen Wills, who beat Molla regularly from '23 onwards.

Wills was a newcomer to Europe in '24 and was a surprise to the English. Accustomed to the glamor and panache of Lenglen, the sophisticated Wimbledon spectators were unimpressed by the expressionless, phlegmatic look of the new American champion in her school uniform of pleated skirt, middy blouse, black tie and stockings, with three large buns of hair and an eyeshade.

That year Lenglen withdrew from Wimbledon pleading "the aftermath of jaundice," and though Wills marched to the final, conceding only eleven games in five matches, she was still not experienced enough to win Wimbledon at her first try, even in Lenglen's absence.

In '24 the leading English girl Kitty McKane was Wills's final opponent. Wills won the first set and had four points to lead 5–1 in the second set. This should have given her a certain hold on the cup, but she faltered and the patriotic crowds, not having seen a British winner since Mrs Lambert Chambers before World War I, cheered Kitty to a memorable comeback victory.

It was symptomatic of Wills's mental detachment that after the most important match of her life at that time, she asked the umpire the score! Kitty McKane won the title because she never allowed herself to forget it.

Wills was bitterly disappointed at her loss and wept afterwards in the locker room. She has said it was the last match she ever cried over. She certainly had no further reason to cry at Wimbledon for she never lost there again.

Throughout her career, Wills was described as being slow and flat-footed, even "padding about the court." She was a big girl, tall, and later, very statuesque. Her concept was to achieve the best results with the least possible expenditure of energy. "Because I saved my energy conscientiously," she once explained, "I kept a reservoir of stored-up strength and was considerably slowed-up in doing so."

Hazel Wightman and Helen Wills won the Wimbledon doubles that same year, and Mrs. Wightman's spurring cry of "Run, Helen" was heard so often that it became the fashionable taunt to shout "Run, Helen," to any girl who had problems in reaching a short ball.

Like Chris Evert today, Helen Wills handled side-to-side baseline movement with the greatest of ease. Her only vulnerability was with short shots that moved her forward and, as with Chris Evert, revealed her inability to become an instinctive volleyer.

The essence of Wills's supremacy was the sheer power of her service and ground strokes. Elizabeth Ryan, who won many world titles with Helen as partner, always said that Helen could be counted on for two and a half points every time she served. If she did not serve actual aces, her service strength was sufficient to enable Elizabeth to 'poach' for outright winners.

Wills won the American championships for the third time in '25, but did not go to Europe that year.

After the Cannes match with Suzanne in '26, a new Wills blossomed on the Riviera and in Paris. She and Freddie Moody became inseparable, enjoying the golden life, the thé-dansants and the galas. Later she was swept up in the romance and sophistication of Paris, inspecting the couture collections and ordering her dresses from the top-name house of Patou. Her teenage buns of hair were soon lopped to conform with the new chic of her image.

Shortly afterwards, when she was struck down with appendicitis, some people said her tennis days were finished, but they grossly underestimated Helen's determination and ambition. She had outshone herself in her gallant defense against Lenglen. Before the appendix surgery she was already the unquestioned No. 1 in this country, and in '27 she was ready to show Europe the full extent of her continuing improvement.

Wills's first round at Wimbledon was against Gwen Sterry and is memorable for unusual reasons.

Gwen, one of the best English players of the day, was the daughter of Charlotte Cooper Sterry, who had won the Wimbledon singles five times at the turn of the century. I made a dress for this delightful past-lady-champion when she was already in her late sixties, and I made the first bridal trousseau of my new designer career for her daughter, Gwen, in '32.

o

In Helen's opening match at the '27 Wimbledon, Gwen lost the first set but won the second, and for a brief moment thought she would win the match by default. It was a cold windy day, and after losing the second set, Helen, without a word or comment, walked to the umpire's chair and put on her cardigan.

This is an unusual thing for anyone to do after two hard sets, particularly without any explanation. But Helen Wills never acknowledged the need to explain anything, least of all her own actions.

In retrospect, it seems that the moment of putting her cardigan back on in that match marked a major milestone in Wills's career. For six years she was never again to lose another set, anywhere in the whole world!

I saw a great deal of Wills in Paris when she was winning her four singles titles. The Parisians always referred to her as "La Belle Hèléne," an apt allusion to Offenbach's operetta of the same name. An etching by Childe Hassam immortalizes her in the Paris Louvre.

Paris has the known capacity to impart added bloom to a woman's beauty and I always thought Helen looked her most beautiful in Paris.

However, her greatest success in the upper reaches of society was in London in '29 and '30. In '29 she was formally presented to King George V and Queen Mary at Buckingham Palace, succumbing to the social ambitions fate had denied Lenglen. Helen's portrait was painted in oils by Augustus John and at the same time she was exhibiting her own drawings in London's most exclusive art galleries.

She had a standing invitation to most of the stately homes of England and became closely acquainted with George Bernard Shaw. One wondered at times if her social rounds would ever end. Remarkably, her tennis was never adversely affected.

Meanwhile, "Little Helen," as the press called her, emerged as a potential challenger to "Big Helen" in the late '20s. She was a tireless retriever. She was a dour and gallant fighter with an ambition to succeed undaunted by repeated setbacks.

Her backhand was particularly accurate and her ability to serve aces when most needed made her a formidable opponent. She was three years younger than Helen Wills and for fifteen years played the part of an understudy waiting for any chance to play the leading role so determinedly held by Wills.

And just as certain players are notoriously injury-prone, Jacobs seemed to attract put-downs and harsh treatment whenever any improved relationship with Wills was attempted.

A typical incident occurred in the spring of '29. Jacobs was then ranked No. 2 in this country, right behind Wills, and that year the authorities announced that they would send only a two-woman team

o

to Europe. Breaking with all tradition, the establishment asked Wills to choose her own partner. Her course of action was predictable. She deliberately passed over Jacobs and nominated the No. 3 ranking player, Edith Cross, to go with her.

For once Jacobs spoke up, and a group of San Francisco businessmen, incensed on her behalf, personally financed "Little Helen's" journey to Wimbledon.

But fate decreed she would meet Wills in the final. It was the first of four Wimbledon finals between the two Helens and Wills won all four clashes.

I still think some of the most sensitive moments of my Call-Boy* job at Wimbledon derived from the four times I escorted the two Helens to the arena court for these finals.

Because of Wills's status as Wimbledon champion, she became one of the very select gorup of women who were given membership of the Wimbledon Club and therefore had use, like Suzanne, of the members' locker room, which was upstairs.

Before winning her one Wimbledon title, Jacobs was relegated to the "lower" locker room, which was downstairs. So when they met I had first to call Jacobs, leave her near the center-court entrance, and dash upstairs to collect Wills.

At the top of the stairs there was a long passage and a door that gave access also to the Royal Box.

For security reasons the police insisted on this door being locked and the one and only key was quietly given to me in order to avoid a long detour for the players coming from upstairs to the center court. In my copy of Helen Wills's memoirs she has written a personal dedication describing me as the "key man" of Wimbledon.

The first three of the four Wills-Jacobs finals took place before Jacobs earned the privilege of using the members' locker room.

On these occasions, after I completed the routine of unlocking and relocking the pass door, Wills would sweep regally down the stairs toward "Little Helen."

---

*One of the oldest jobs in the English theater is that of the "Call Boy." His responsibility is to alert the performers when it is time to go on stage for the cues and to ensure they have ample warning of this.

At Wimbledon, before regular TV coverage (which is now seen in all the locker rooms) the players had no means of knowing when they were required to go on court for their matches as there was no contact with the play from where they were changing. In '27 the attendances were increasing daily and the new Club secretary, Dudley Larcombe, decided it was the Club's duty to the spectators to ensure against any delays between matches. This responsibility was given to me and, over the twenty-three years in which I escorted every player onto the two main arena courts, the world press gave me and my function the show biz description of Call Boy.

o

I would see her stiffen slightly as she became conscious of the presence of her victim, but she always made it seem as if there was nobody there at all. In turn, Jacobs made it appear natural that she had not seen Wills by talking earnestly to anyone nearby.

In my job I always anticipated these particular days with some apprehension though the whole ritual of our going on court together probably took less than five minutes.

The '32 final was the only time when the frigid atmosphere surrounding us was relieved by a brief moment of levity. Near the doors of the center court we passed the chairman of Wimbledon, Sir Herbert Wilberforce. Sir Herbert was a delightful, typically Victorian English gentleman. He was a high court judge who came from a long line of famous British orators renowned for their wit. He had snow-white hair, and every day wore a rose, fresh from his garden, in the buttonhole of his lapel.

Sensing and knowing the feeling between the two Helens, he greeted them with his most gallant smile and I almost detected a wink at me as he said, "Come, come. You ladies aren't going to *fight*, are you?"

He received no response whatever from either of the Helens who probably said to themselves, "What a stupid old man." Later Sir Herbert said to me, "I thought I might break the ice, but I fear I failed miserably!"

"There was no feud," said Jacobs repeatedly, but a factual interpretation of the situation must surely depend on semantics. Perhaps it is difficult to feud if those concerned never address each other.

In fact, on that same day there might not have been any women's final at all.

Helen Wills always came to Wimbledon in a chauffeur-driven limo, which she insisted was for her use alone. Any suggestion that she share the car was received with a polite but firm negative.

In those days all cars were required to display a special flag on the front if they were to be allowed through the club gates.

For some reason Helen's car arrived that day without the necessary flag and she was flatly refused admission. The chauffeur argued long and loud with the gate guards while Helen sat regally and untouched by the commotion. She disdained all suggestions that she alight, and was about to be driven back to her hotel when, fortunately, word of the problem reached us in the office.

The gate-guards' position was quickly resolved. Her limo drove up to the center court, but while Helen Wills had been sitting in state and being refused admission, Helen Jacobs walked through the gates on foot, unnoticed.

○

The Two Helens (1) 131

[15]

The Two Helens (2)

HELEN WILLS WAS NEVER ONE TO TALK ABOUT HERSELF, BUT ONE day during the Dutch championships at Noorwijk she confided to Elizabeth Ryan and me that she had strained her back, "fooling around with Freddie in the surf." This injury was to plague her for almost two years and contributed to her controversial default in the '33 Forest Hills final.

Wills says in her memoirs she aggravated her back injury lifting rocks at a California beach in the spring of '33. She then went to England where increasing twinges forced her to consult a top London specialist.

Helen had not lost a set at Wimbledon since '27, and it was significant that in winning her sixth title a few weeks later, she lost a set to England's Dorothy Round in the final.

Since the beginnings of the game considerable prestige was attached to the Eastern grass-court circuit in this country, which followed immediately after Wimbledon and the European circuit. Even after the Depression of '29, many of America's top socialites retained their summer homes in well-known resorts down the coastline from New Hampshire to New Jersey.

Most of these resorts held invitational tournaments, and it was accepted that in some, such as the Easthampton tournament for women or the Southampton tournament for men, the top-ranking players would compete.

In '33 the Easthampton event took place a few weeks after Wimbledon. It was to be Wills's first tournament on returning to this country. She was to play singles and partner the new rising star Alice Marble in doubles.

However, her back injury, which had obviously contributed to her losing a set at Wimbledon, was still bothering her and she withdrew from the singles.

Two weeks later she also withdrew, at the last minute, from the American Wightman Cup team. I had been asked to report on the Cup matches for a London newspaper. With uncertainty surrounding the fitness of the world's leading star, we were back in a "Will she, won't she," situation, reminiscent of Lenglen in Cannes.

At the end of August, while the women's championships were being played at Forest Hills, the premier men's tournament of the Eastern circuit was being played in Newport, Rhode Island.

In those days, invitations to compete in Newport were almost gold plated. The entry was restricted to thirty-two men, and the unbelievably lavish scale of entertainment offered each night at the great Newport residences made the tournament a major attraction for all the players.

One of the queens of Newport society was Mrs. Maude Barger Wallach. Mrs. Wallach had been the U.S. national champion in 1908. She was a frail aristocrat who would sometimes have a trained nurse in attendance when she played her matches.

Mrs. Wallach went to Wimbledon in '33 and I was introduced to her by Frank Shields. Frank is credited with being the most handsome athlete of all time in any sport. He was a great favorite of Mrs. Wallach's, and it was Frank who suggested that she allow me one of the treasured spots in the Newport tournament.

I particularly remember an evening at the Curtis Jameses' palatial home. The beautiful gardens were extensive enough to accommodate three separate dance bands. For those who became bored with moonlight revels on the grounds, or stuffed themselves at the

o

The Two Helens (2)   133

hundred-foot-long buffet, there were launches to shuttle them out to the James yacht *Aloha*, where guests enjoyed, anchored offshore, the bootleg liquor they all brought with them.

The parties always went on until well after sunrise, and I remember remarking to another guest how lavish it all was. "This is nothing," he replied. "You should have been here before prohibition!"

In the tournament I played one of the best matches, and experienced one of the biggest disappointments of my tennis life. I reached match point on the Newport Casino courts against Manoel Alonso. Alonso was then thirty-eight, but had been one of the world's leading players. To beat him would have added considerably to my prestige.

That weekend everyone in Mrs. Wallach's entourage was on cloud nine because Frank Shields won the tournament, beating Ellsworth Vines and Wilmer Allison, America's No. 1 and 2 respectively, on his way to the title.

Meanwhile the women's nationals in New York had been delayed by rain, and on my return to the old Vanderbilt Hotel there, I found Elizabeth Ryan waiting to tell me that Helen Wills had again lost a set, this time to the British girl Betty Nuthall.

The gallery was astonished, and the umpire was so enthralled at Nuthall's achievement he allowed Wills to serve twice in succession. Neither girl noticed the irregularity, and as Nuthall won both service games she did not complain.

After defaulting at Easthampton and in the Wightman Cup, Wills played Forest Hills against doctor's orders, partly to avoid disappointing her doubles partner, Elizabeth Ryan.

Wills's win over Betty Nuthall put her in the final. In the other half Jacobs was to meet Dorothy Round, but the rains came. The rain cleared on Sunday, but because of her religious beliefs, Dorothy would never play tennis on the Sabbath. Ironically, the rain started again the next day.

Because of Dorothy's religious scruples and the rain, the tournament dragged on for twelve days. On the eleventh day Jacobs and Round eventually played their semifinal on soaking-wet turf, and while their match was in progress, Helen Wills asked if I would give her a gentle hit.

This in itself was significant. For the past three days she ha⁴ only occasionally been tapping volleys on the clay courts during short breaks in the clouds. In normal circumstances Helen would have needed a testing workout in preparation for her final.

I knew Helen's game well from long years of observation and I had played a couple of sets against her a few weeks before at Easthampton.

o

As soon as we got on the wet practice court it was obvious to me that something was wrong. She was not bending properly and was nervous to move. Putting all the circumstances together, I realized she was still having trouble with her back and wondered how she would play the next day.

Jacobs and Round were playing their match inside the stadium. Helen and I were hitting on the court immediately outside and I noticed that Helen was paying attention to the stadium score.

Jacobs won the first set and had a commanding lead in the second when Round fought back and they eventually split sets. At this point I thought I detected some distinct displeasure in Helen Wills. Later, I concluded that Wills had not the slightest apprehension about meeting Jacobs in the final. However, because of the bad time Round had given her at Wiimbledon, there was no doubt where her preference lay in opponents.

Jacobs came back to win the third set decisively, and I detected a sense of relief in Helen Wills.

All this is to emphasize that what happened the following day came as a great shock to Wills. The two Helens had met seven times in the States and Europe, and until this eighth clash Wills had never yielded a set to her rival.

The next day Wills made history by defaulting to Jacobs at 0–3 down in the third set.

It is a controversial event when any player retires from a match in a losing position. Everyone present on this occasion was stunned into silence when it became clear that Wills was quitting.

My memory of the incident compares exactly with the description recounted by Helen Jacobs. So I quote the words from her book *Gallery of Champions*.

> Leading 3–0 in the third set I had changed ends. I turned to the ball-boy for the balls, speaking to him once, and then again, before I realized his eyes were fixed on the opposite court. I repeated my request before I turned to see that Helen (Wills) had walked to the umpire's chair and was reaching for her sweater.
>
> It was a confusing moment. I hurried to the stand as Ben Dwight, the venerable umpire, announced that I had won by default. As Helen put on her sweater I went to her. "My leg is bothering me, I can't go on," she said. "Would you like to rest for a while?" "No, I can't go on," she answered.
>
> I went back to the dressing room where Molla Mallory was waiting for me. A radio commentator had immediately asked Molla to broadcast a statement on the default in view of her similar experience with Suzanne Lenglen. She did, in biting terms, and was still full of it when we met.

○

I also recall seeing from my court-side box seat that Jacobs in trying to show sympathy with Wills's distress, put her arm on Wills's shoulder. This gesture, for all its kind intentions, seemed repugnant to Wills, and before replying to Jacobs, she pulled sharply away.

In Helen Wills's account of the incident several years later, she wrote:

> If I had fainted on the court, it would have been thought a more conclusive finish to the match in the eyes of many on-lookers, for they would have been convinced I could not continue. Had I been able to think clearly I might have chosen to remain. Animals and often humans, however, prefer to suffer in a quiet, dark place.

No matter how one sees this odd occurrence, Wills's withdrawal when facing defeat brought eerie echoes of Lenglen's "cough-and-quit" episode in '21, and Molla Mallory was quick to elaborate on these in her broadcast twelve years later.

It is a strange coincidence that the two greatest women players of tennis history were to lose only one major match after reaching their peak of world supremacy, and both times—by defaulting—they could claim they were never truly beaten.

A further coincidence is that both supreme stars quit at the very same Forest Hills Club and neither star ever played there again.

Helen Wills did not go to Wimbledon in '34. Except on two occasions it was the first time in fifteen years when neither Wills nor Lenglen took part in the women's singles final there, and it seemed their long reigns were at last finished.

But Wills reappeared in '35.

It was then Dudley Larcombe began receiving letters from a patient in a mental home. The writer claimed he had been driven insane by Helen's beauty and was incarcerated only because she refused his advances.

Fortunately, his hospital was aware of his particular obsession because, one morning during the championships, Larcombe received a warning phone call from the clinic saying the patient had escaped and they figured he was on his way to Wimbledon.

The police, of course, were alerted and were on hand, when, by arrangement with them, he was allowed to penetrate Larcombe's inner sanctum. An alarm bell had been fixed under the carpet by Larcombe's desk, and I have often thought how courageous Larcombe was not to have given the alert until the man was backing his demands to see Helen Wills by actually pointing a revolver at Larcombe's head.

o

Wills's meeting with Jacobs in the final that year assumed even greater-than-ever dramatic proportions. Once again Wills was to lose a set, and this time faced unquestionable defeat, when, after a ninety-minute tug of war, Wills found herself at 3–5 and match point down on her service.

At this point Wills put up a defensive half-lob. It is said that Jacobs missed an easy overhead, but in fact Wills's lob was never high enough for a classic smash. Jacobs let the ball bounce and then found it too low for the easy smash off the ground she had anticipated.

I was in my customary place on the court with Dan Maskell. Dan and I knew just how much was at stake for both girls. Jacobs was extremely popular with the Wimbledon crowds, and there was an audible groan as she misjudged the match point and hit her shot well down into the net.

Fate was again kind to Wills in the next game as Jacobs was 30–15 on her own service, but put a certain winner a fraction of an inch outside the line.

I see from the umpire's blank, which I still have, that the match lasted exactly one hundred and seven minutes. Strangely, though the score was 6–3, 3–6, 7–5, to Wills, each girl won exactly one hundred and seven points. As usual, Papa Lenglen was right. He always said that traditional tennis-scoring could be unfair to the loser.

Escorting Helen Wills back upstairs to the members' locker room, and still tense with excitement, I was fumbling for the key of the pass door when, to my amazement, Helen flung her arm round me and embraced me. "Isn't it wonderful," she said. This occasion and during the match with Suzanne in Cannes were the only times I ever saw Helen allow her "poker face" any outward emotion.

Wills had already won the American championships seven times. With this latest victory over Jacobs she reached the same count at Wimbledon and also equaled Mrs. Lambert Chambers's record total of Wimbledon singles titles.

Afterwards Wills disappeared from England, this time for two years. In her absence Jacobs finally achieved her lifelong ambition by becoming the '36 Wimbledon winner.

To everyone's amazement Wills reemerged in '38. The natural assumption was that her boundless ambition would give her no rest without becoming the unquestioned singles record-holder of all time at Wimbledon.

In her quest it seemed unbelievable that Jacobs would again be her final opponent; and again their match would be highlighted with drama.

Big finals such as the Wills-Jacobs encounters always produced a

o

flood of telegrams from fans. I remember on this occasion there were ninety-six addressed to one or other Helen, with one in particular addressed "The Two Helens."

I took advice from Norah Cleather as to what we should do about this. Before deciding, Norah felt she should read the contents. It was just as well for the telegram read: "Good luck. Wish you could both win."

I think Norah was right in decreeing this particular message should not be delivered to either girl.

In '38 Wills spared me the ordeal of walking down the long passage and the stairs from the members' locker room between the two antagonists.

I have often wondered if Wills also wanted to spare herself this tense moment, because, an hour before the final, she told me that when the time came for the match she would be outside on a practice court hitting with Dan Maskell. After the tensions I had experienced in my Call-Boy duties at their three previous Wimbledon meetings, I was really glad to hear this.

At the start of '38 Wimbledon's second week, Jacobs injured the Achilles tendon in her right foot. All week she had been receiving treatment from a London chiropractor, Hugh Demptster, who was very popular with the players.

As I took the girls onto court, I noticed her ankle seemed very tightly bandaged and a slight swelling was already showing above the Elastoplast.

In the first set, Jacobs was within a point of leading 5–4, but in an attempt to reach a wide passing-shot she turned awkwardly and gave a cry of pain.

Helen Wills, with her usual detached air, put her lace handkerchief to her nose and appeared not to notice.

As the match progressed, Jacobs became more and more lame till Hazel Wightman, intervening as always, surprisingly appeared at the umpire's chair and told her she should default.

But Jacobs, obviously remembering the reverse situation of their '33 Forest Hills meeting, was determined to finish the match and allow Wills a clean-cut record for the history books.

This was an unhappy finish to Helen Wills's illustrious record. Many spectators were shocked by her relentless detachment from Jacobs's obvious injury.

Her incomparable feat of losing only one singles match at Wimbledon in a fifteen-year span would normally have received a tumultuous reception. But she climaxed her career before an apathetic crowd,

o

hushed in sympathy for her victim.

Helen Jacobs records that after shaking hands on that day, the two Helens never saw each other again.

I did not see Helen Wills for the next fifteen years in which time she had divorced Freddie Moody. She had also remarried and divorced her second husband, Aidan Roark.

In '53 I was hitting with Elizabeth Ryan in California, when Helen Wills appeared. She was very gracious and seemed even more beautiful than I remembered.

She played a social game on a nearby court. She wore exactly the same clothes as in her golden years of the '30s, with one small difference in detail: she now wore a pastel blue eyeshade that made her beautiful eyes seem even bluer than before.

I recalled a line by the poet Keats: "'Tis the eternal law that first in beauty should be first in might." Keats could have written this line for Helen Wills.

Helen caused a small flutter when she announced she was considering returning to Wimbledon to play mixed doubles in '53. But she never came and instead retired to the life of a recluse, immersing herself in her beloved painting and refusing all but one or two interviews by today's sportswriters.

Had her incomparable tennis talent reached its flowering in the late '70s instead of the late '20s, she could easily have become a millionaire in a few years.

My long-time friend Will Grimsley of the Associated Press wire service met with Helen Wills in '77, and his impressions only served to confirm my earlier memories of her. Will Grimsley described her as "an elegant and lovely woman who looks twenty years younger than her seventy-three years."

Helen Wills told Grimsley, "I read about fierce feuds I am supposed to have had with Suzanne Lenglen and Helen Jacobs. It was never so. We were so different eras—Suzanne older than I, Helen younger. I never had an argument with either of them."

Grimsley comments, "Helen Wills is still an aloof and very private person."

The last time I had any contact with Helen Jacobs was through my tennis-dress business.

In World War II she had been a commander in the U.S. Navy and had since been appointed sports-fashion adviser to Saks Fifth Avenue in New York. She was as delightful as ever and gave my partner, Henry Turner, every assistance in his negotiations with Saks. Today she lives quietly in Easthampton, Long Island.

More than half a century has elapsed since Helen Wills won her first American and Wimbledon titles and Helen Jacobs began her frustrating challenge to the "Queen of Ice and Snow."

But the strange coincidences of their likenesses, their differences, and the curiously parallel paths of their lives will rank among sport's most fascinating histories.

[16]

Big Guns

IN '53 A GROUP CONSISTING OF MYSELF AND TEN WIMBLEDON champions were discussing tennis in Lennons Hotel in Brisbane, Australia, during a Davis Cup match between the United States and Belgium.

Inevitably our debate turned to the greatest players in the game, more precisely the best players since World War I.

It was agreed that Wimbledon be the basis for assessment as it was the goal of every player in that period. However, it was also agreed that the different eras, bringing changes in playing style, advances in tennis equipment and training methods, would preclude us from naming one man as the outright greatest.

The consensus was that four players, William Tilden, Henri Cochet, Fred Perry, and Donald Budge, were unquestionably the elite of the game *to that time*.

Only Budge had won the Grand Slam of tennis. I should add here that the Grand Slam was never an official title, rather a convenience invented by sportswriters to describe the elusive achievement of winning, in one calendar year, the four major championships of America, Australia, France, and Wimbledon.

Later Rod Laver achieved this feat not only once but twice, and thereupon inevitably joined the four tennis deities we had enshrined. My own opinion is still that though Tilden was the top technician, Perry was the most capable match winner I have ever seen. I always firmly believed Perry was the greatest all-round player until Laver forced me to update my assessment.

From '33 to '38 Perry, then Budge, dominated the American and Wimbledon championships and the Davis Cup, the supreme event in tennis. In fact, from the fall of '33 to the fall of '36 Perry lost only two matches of significance.

Budge was already the world's most promising prospect and Perry the world champion. After beating Budge in the '36 Forest Hills final, Perry turned professional, leaving the way clear for the redheaded Scottish-American to steamroll all the world's best players for the next two years.

During the glory days of the mid '30s, Perry and Budge had an ideal foil in the immaculate German Baron Gottfried von Cramm. But he was an unlucky player. Only three men in Wimbledon's history have lost in three successive finals, Herbert Lawford in the 1880s, von Cramm the '30s, and Fred Stolle in the '60s. Von Cramm lost two of his finals to Perry and one to Budge.

In '29 Perry was required to play through the qualifying event for his admission to the main championships of Wimbledon. Within seven years he had won the title three times in succession, the only player to scale this ladder from bottom to top with such startling success.

Perry had already made his mark at another game, table tennis. In fact, in '29 he won the World Table Tennis championships in Budapest. Fred had no aspirations to be a Bruce Jenner, but in '31 he performed the remarkable feat of reaching the semifinals of both the American and Wimbledon tennis championships, also carrying Great Britain through six matches to the Davis Cup final and winning the International Table Tennis championships in Paris.

Fred had the lithe grace of a panther. His lateral movements across the court had the easy rhythm of a pendulum. His dash, daring and aggressive approach to lawn tennis, seemed an obvious carry-over from the rapid-fire sport played on the small surface of a table.

He had a mercurial mind that perfectly matched his speed of foot. He seemed always faster than his opponent; after the change of ends,

o

he was always ready before his opponent. In his matches one felt the key was pressure, pressure, pressure.

Fred also had enormous appeal to the female section of the audience. Women were much more attracted by his obvious virility than touched by his lack of traditional sportsmanlike demeanor.

Perry was born on May 18, 1909. He was twenty-four when he first won the American championships. He was twenty-five when he first won at Wimbledon. By a strange coincidence the last Englishman to win Wimbledon did so the year Fred was born. No Englishman has won there since.

Perry's father was in the construction industry; later he served as a Labour Member of the British Parliament at Westminster. It was soon pointed out that Fred did not have the classic private school upbringing of most British tennis players. Inevitably, there were to be questioning comparisons with his contemporary Bunny Austin, a product of one of England's top private schools and Cambridge University.

Fred never missed a trick when it came to the psychology of winning. He was the master of one-upmanship. In the locker rooms he had a sharp tongue and took every opportunity to make cutting comments, sometimes to the point of being extremely personal, with the aim of gaining a psychological advantage over an opponent. On court, he was never averse to using a caustic one-liner to distract an opponent.

Perry's flash smiles and easy language were really the outward glow of his inner steel. F. R. Burrow, Wimbledon's traditional tournament director, who was always sparing in his praise of tennis players, nevertheless said, "I always made a point of watching Perry's matches. I liked to see a man play as if he was certain he was going to win."

I remember Perry always made a point of spinning his racquet quickly, forcing his opponent to call for the choice of serve or end. Fred maintained that by placing the pressure of the first decision of the match on his opponent, he gained an advantage, however small.

Possibly some of the strength of Fred's determination derived from being one of the first players of note not to have the traditional accent and demeanor of the leisurely upper classes.

Since the last century the sophisticated "Blues" of Cambridge invited tennis clubs to play friendly weekend matches at the university. I took teams there for several years, and the atmosphere at Fenners, the Cambridge University tennis club, resembled a peaceful afternoon on the lawns of a stately home.

When Fred went to Fenners with his Chiswick Park team in the early '30s, his undisguised drive to win-at-all-costs so ruffled university feathers it was suggested it might be best not to include him in future matches.

The American Jimmy Connors, brash, arrogant, cocky, and belligerent, could be regarded as a contemporary version of Perry.

Connors has to contend with Borg, Vilas, Dibbs, Gottfried, Gerulaitis, Orantes, Ramirez and Panatta. Perry had to contend with Vines, Budge, von Cramm, Crawford, Austin, Cochet, Borotra, and Quist, not to mention Allison, Shields, Stoefen, and Sidney Wood. For me it is not difficult to judge which era had the greatest depth.

Perry had the advantage not only of being a great individualist but a great patriot. Borotra has spoken of the remarkable team spirit that was a major factor in the French campaign for the Davis Cup. Something akin to this national pride was shared by the British team of Perry, Austin, Hughes, Lee, and Tuckey when they in turn wrested the Davis Cup from the French in '33.

The English have always liked good losers rather than winners. Perry was a winner and the very qualities that gave him the capacity to win were those that made him unpopular with the British public.

Many Americans today have an antipathy toward Jimmy Connors and the image he projects. One can imagine the impact Perry had on Britain of the '30s, for he was the first Englishman to see tennis as a battle rather than a game.

During the early '30s two young men, one the son of a German baron and the other the son of a former Scottish first-division soccer player, were treading entirely different tennis paths. Both were to lead to Perry's door, and at the same time, converge to produce some of the best tennis ever seen.

Gottfried von Cramm was one of seven sons of Baron von Cramm. He was born on July 7, 1909, on the family estate at Nettlingen, situated in the ancient German kingdom of Hanover, which sired the Georgian kings of England. By heredity Gottfried was a baron in his own right, but throughout his tennis career he preferred the modest "Mr. Cramm."

Educated in the traditional manner of an aristocrat, von Cramm was an impeccable gentleman both on and off the court. Handsome, with heroic Germanic features, he was an outstandingly popular figure.

His father had been a tennis enthusiast since the turn of the century and encouraged Gottfried on the courts of the von Cramm estate. Ironically, like his close friend of later years, Bill Tilden, von Cramm lost the top of a finger of his right hand. As a youth he was bitten while feeding sugar to a horse and lost a part of his index finger. Fortunately, as with Big Bill the injury had no adverse effect on his playing career.

Meanwhile a skinny redhead in San Francisco, John Donald Budge, had been launched into tennis from a vastly different background. Budge has always maintained that fate played the complete hand in his being a tennis player. His father's emigration from Scotland to California was the key.

Donald's father, John Budge, was born in Wick, the northernmost township of significance in Scotland. He was injured while playing soccer for the renowned Glasgow Rangers team. Pneumonia followed, and the doctors advised that only a climate such as California's could ease his chest problem.

Don once told me that his mother was the redhead of the family. But during the great San Francisco earthquake of 1906, she was tossed violently around a room, and within ten days the flaming red hair had turned completely white.

Don Budge was born in Oakland on June 13, 1915, and had not played his first tournament when Perry made his Wimbledon debut.

As a kid, Don preferred baseball and basketball to tennis. It was not until May of 1930 that his brother goaded him into entering the California fifteen-and-under championships. His father promised that if he won his first-round match he would buy him some proper tennis gear.

Budge went to the tournament dressed in a white T-shirt, fawn cords, and colored sneakers. His first opponent was the No. 1 seed. But the young Budge, who had had little more than a few crude practice sessions on park courts, beat his opponent and went on to win the tournament. Within hours he had a new tennis wardrobe.

Don Budge won the junior championships of America in '33, beating Gene Mako in the final. I had my first sight of him a week later. In the Los Angeles Club, Perry Jones beckoned me. "The two best young players in America, Budge and Mako, are having a hit on Court Two," he told me. "They are very exciting. Go take a look."

Like Helen Wills's, Budge's philosophy was to hit the ball as hard as possible but with the least amount of errors. I clearly remember the sheer, raw power of the slightly built youngster who stood over six feet tall yet never, in all his playing days, weighed more than one hundred and fifty-five pounds.

A year later it was in a match on Perry Jones's star-studded center court that Budge came within a few points of beating Perry. From that day he was marked out as the natural successor to the world champion.

Meanwhile, during a private education in Hanover, Gottfried von

o

Cramm was being taught his tennis by the German coach Ramon Najuch, who was later to have some memorable struggles with Tilden on the professional circuit.

Von Cramm was first noticed internationally while studying law in Berlin. There he beat Tilden's protégé, Junior Coen.

Just as Fred Perry was about to win the American championships in '33, von Cramm also won his first big title, the Wimbledon mixed doubles with his countrywoman Hilda Sperling, as well as his second German championship. The following year he moved up in the world's first ten from No. 9 to the No. 3 spot.

In '34 von Cramm was to win his first international singles title, the French championship. But this was to be Perry's year.

The summer of '34 was unusually hot, dry, and dusty in England, and Wimbledon was hit by an extraordinary epidemic, called "Wimbledon throat." The infection, which doctors likened to diphtheria, caused sixty-three players to withdraw from competition. Both Fred and I had lucky escapes, but Dudley Larcombe and Norah Cleather had the heavy handicap of being voiceless throughout the championships. Von Cramm had a severe attack. But with his usual code of sportsmanship he played and lost badly to South Africa's Vernon Kirby rather than default.

As the number of infected players grew and grew, only those in the privacy of our offices knew how frightened and worried we really were. Eventually the drains were examined, the water tested, and late at night in the closest secrecy, sprays and syringes of potent disinfectant went into action against the insidious enemy.

The two top throat specialists in London, Sir Milsom Rees and Ivor Griffith, were brought to Wimbledon every afternoon to examine and spray the players' throats.

Eventually Buckingham Palace was told it was safe for the Royals to come to Wimbledon.

It was in this strange and anxious atmosphere that Perry's Wimbledon victory came to pass.

In a post-match account Perry wrote, "Everything I did against Jack Crawford in the final went right for me. Everything went wrong for him, including a foot-fault call against him at match-point. Luck was on my side in the draw and in my matches, too. Luck, indeed, plays a very considerable part in any Wimbledon."

National ascendency in tennis always seems to come in waves. Just as America dominated tennis in the early '20s and the French in the early '30s, England produced a girl prodigy, Dorothy Round, at the same time as Perry. Dorothy won the women's singles at Wimbledon the day after Fred won the men's title.

o

Dorothy was a charmingly modest champion. In England she was a heroine even before succeeding Kitty Godfree as the first English girl to win for the past eight years. Dorothy's victory roused spectators to fever pitch. The previous day Fred's achievement had been greeted only with cool acknowledgment.

Fred had a strong personal affinity with Roper Barrett, the British Davis Cup captain and former world doubles champion. Each time I took Fred onto the arena court he always asked me to tell him where Roper Barrett was sitting, which often led to a curious succession of signs and signals between the two of them.

In the women's final, Roper Barrett had volunteered to be a line judge. As I went to escort Dorothy Round back to the locker room, tears of joy mingled with deafening cheers around the court. Even King George and Queen Mary seemed quite overwhelmed in the Royal Box. Roper Barrett gazed wistfully at the frenetic scene and said to me, "Fred could have had all this yesterday, if only he'd let them understand him."

I still have fond recollections of the private celebrations Fred, Dorothy, Norah Cleather and I had in the flowered bower of Norah's office.

Fred ordered champagne. He and Dorothy were sitting on Norah's table, swinging their legs merrily, when Fred suddenly let forth a loud "whoopee." He could not contain his emotions. "My God. We've really done it!" he shouted as he embraced Dorothy and twirled her around in a moment of irrepressible joy.

In '35 and '36 Budge, Perry, and von Cramm crossed swords on every center court in the world.

At Wimbledon there was a day's interval between the semifinal and the final. I always thought the waiting time played havoc with Gottfried's nerves. When he beame overtense his pale Germanic complexion would develop two flushed Dutch doll circles on his cheeks.

Taking him on court for his finals against Fred, the two flushed patches were conspicuously present on both occasions. I felt instinctively he would not do himself justice. The red patches were particularly noticeable when they met in the '36 final.

Coming off court, Fred, with the incisiveness that made him unpopular in so many English places, said, "It didn't take me long to fix him, did it, Ted?" In fact, in the second game of the match von Cramm injured himself and won only one more game.

Actually, Fred as well as Gottfried, was nervous on that occasion, but Fred for a more outstanding reason.

Fred had made up his mind to turn professional at the end of the

o

year. He was frightened he might aggravate an earlier injury. Fred told me he wanted to insure himself heavily against this, but could not do so because as an "amateur" he could not disclose that he would lose financially if he could not play.

Perry was the cornerstone of English tennis supremacy in that era. At the Wimbledon Ball after his 1936 victory, various speeches from the establishment pointedly "regretted" his known intention of deserting the Davis Cup team.

Fred's speech in reply was typical. "If anyone would like to make it worth my while to play another year, I would be glad to do so."

However, Norah Cleather and I, and certainly Fred's trainer and confidant, Dan Maskell, knew this outer brashness really concealed an inner sadness.

A month later, after leading Britain to its last Davis Cup victory at Wimbledon, the groundsmen were tidying up and we all went out to have a last look at the scene of the earlier celebration.

As we stood there with all the crowds gone home, Fred said wistfully, "Let me stay here a moment by myself." He remained on the court alone, the court where he had made himself a world-famous figure; where he changed British tennis history, winning not just in a leisurely pastime but in international confrontations. He knew then he would never again play at Wimbledon.

Afterwards, in a monumental struggle against Don Budge, he went on to win his third American championship and turned professional.

With Perry gone and Budge just reaching his peak, it was the Californian's turn to run riot in the amateur ranks. In '37 and '38 he won eleven of the twelve possible titles at Forest Hills and Wimbledon, losing only the doubles to von Cramm and Henkel at Forest Hills in '37. Winning also the Australian and French singles titles in '38, Budge became the first player ever to achieve the Grand Slam. In the previous five years both Perry and Crawford had missed it by one match.

But probably the most historic moment in both Budge's and von Cramm's careers came in the last match of the Davis Cup semifinal at Wimbledon in July of '37. Perry was gone, and in the circumstances the whole outcome of the cup rested on the match between America and Germany.

At that time Adolf Hitler was building a massive military force and the clouds of war were already appearing on the horizon.

Hitler's Nazi propaganda was far reaching. He was determined to build an Aryan race of super athletes. Max Schmeling's stunning twelfth-round knockout of Joe Louis in Madison Square Garden in '36 had delighted Hitler.

o

Also in '36 Hitler had planned a show of strength to the world at his Berlin Olympic Games. However, the Germans were humiliated by the might of America, led by Jesse Owens who won four gold medals. In one of sport's historic incidents, Hitler snubbed Owens and America by refusing to preside over the medal presentation.

Now Germany had the chance to show the world again, this time on the Wimbledon tennis courts. For three single days in history the swastika fluttered over the lawns of the All England Club.

Ironically, Bill Tilden was coaching the German team. Some called him a traitor. The atmosphere was all very tense.

With the teams locked at two matches apiece, a crowd of 17,000 waited anxiously for the world's two best players to appear for the decider.

The drama began in the locker room.

I was anxious there should not be a moment's delay and was hurrying Budge and von Cramm out of the locker room when the telephone rang.

Donald Budge himself picks up the story that he repeated to me at the Wimbledon centennial. "You had me by one arm, Ted, and Gottfried by the other. You were bustling us along and we hardly had time to acknowledge each other. We were just about to go out into the stadium when the phone rang. None of us paid any attention, but Ellis, the locker-room attendant, picked it up and called to Gottfried, 'Long distance for you, sir.' "

Don said that I intervened at this point, "Come on, you can't keep Queen Mary waiting." But handing me his racquets, von Cramm pulled himself free from my arm to pick up the receiver. "Yes, hello," he said. "This is Gottfried von Cramm."

As the switchboard operator connected his call von Cramm, with his inherent Germanic instinct, stiffened and stood to attention. For the next minute or more he listened intently. The only words he uttered were "*Ja, mein Führer,*" which he said about eleven times.

When he finished he turned to Budge and me and said, "Excuse me gentlemen, it was Hitler. He wanted to wish me luck."

With that I swept them both onto the center court for what has been described by many of the world's most experienced tennis critics as "the greatest match ever played."

The score is history. Budge won for the United States 6–8, 5–7, 6–4, 6–2, 8–6.

I have the original umpire's blank in my hand as I write. For posterity it is interesting to record that after the first two sets, won by von Cramm, both players had each won exactly eighty points. In the three remaining sets, all won by Budge, the American each time won

o

seven more points than his opponent.

I see also from the umpire's blank that von Cramm led 4–1 in the fifth set. The two team captains were in their traditional places below the umpire's chair, Heinrich Kleinschroth for Germany and Walter Pate for the American team. Norah Cleather recalls that at that stage Walter Pate seemed resigned to prayer, "for his hands were clasped and his eyes turned heavenwards."

Again Budge takes up the account of what he actually said as he changed ends, when all seemed lost from the American point of view. *"Don't worry Cap, we are not licked yet. I'm not tired so don't give up the ship. I'm only one service break down, so stick with me."*

Tilden, who had brought a lot of criticism on himself by accepting the appointment as coach to the German team, was sitting in the stands. The other members of the team were two rows behind Tilden. Between them were three American celebrities, Ed Sullivan, Jack Benny, and Paul Lukas.

At the vital changeover, a grinning Tilden turned and gave a conspicuous victory sign to the Germans behind him. Sullivan was so incensed at Tilden's arrogance he jumped from his seat and had to be restrained by Jack Benny and Paul Lukas.

A week later the American team inevitably beat Britain. Less than a year later Gottfried von Cramm was imprisoned by the Nazis.

Don Budge's voice was the most indignant of all in the defense of von Cramm. In an appeal to the Nazis to withdraw the charges, he gathered scores of famous signatures, including those of Joe DiMaggio and Alice Marble.

But at the time it was still "Deutschland Über Alles," and the Third Reich was impervious to all outside opinions.

Von Cramm served a year in prison and during that time the American players refused to participate in any German tournament.

The charges against von Cramm were never made public, but were assumed to have related to homosexuality, although homosexuality was widely condoned in the cases of other well-known German figures.

Soon after World War II, John Olliff, the ex-Davis Cup player and well-known London tennis writer, researched the case and obtained the following information from an official in Germany whose position, said Olliff, "guaranteed its authority." The evidence he received read as follows:

"Baron Gottfried von Cramm was charged and found guilty under German Statute No. 165, which deals with homosexual offenses. I briefly examined the case records. It appears that some substance had been provided for the case. The file had also been marked as a prosecution brought by the Reichführer der S.S. At that time this was Himmler. The case was further annotated with instructions to both prosecuting and defending counsels: *"The defendant WILL BE FOUND GUILTY."*

The Germans were banned from Wimbledon for six years. After World War I it was nine years before they were readmitted.

Von Cramm played once more at Wimbledon in '51 and three times in the Davis Cup for West Germany, in '51, '52, and '53.

As popular as ever, Gottfried reestablished himself completely in the international jet set by his marriage to Barbara Hutton. His life was to end tragically in a car wreck on a desert road in Egypt in '76.

On turning professional in '38, Budge received the largest guarantee ever made to a tennis player at that time. Later, his charm and skill raised millions for the war effort.

Budge seems to possess the secret of eternal youth. In Los Angeles in '53 I was glad to see him still playing marvelous tennis in a pro tournament against Pancho Gonzales.

With our conversation about Hitler at the Wimbledon centennial we celebrated forty-four years of friendship and our survival of the world's greatest crisis.

Fred Perry launched himself into the manufacture of tennis wear in the early '50s. At that time it was already estimated that he had made close to a million dollars since turning professional in '36.

In my youth Fred was a warm and generous friend. Later we had almost a commercial dual to the death over our relative dominance of tennis wear around the world. In older age the smoke of battle is behind us and we are able to reminisce happily over the countless dramatic encounters we fought and shared.

Until Wimbledon '78 I was convinced Fred Perry was one of the five best tennis players I ever saw. But since the Wimbledon '78 men's final I have to think that Sweden's Björn Borg has now made that exclusive club into a round half dozen.

[17]

Alice Marble (1)

I HAVE KNOWN ALICE MARBLE THROUGH THREE DISTINCT PHASES of her life. The first was in the early '30s. She was then a friendly, smiling, nineteen-year-old, full of aspiring hopes, enormous talent and ambition, but soon to be struck down by illnesses that left her incarcerated in a sanatorium.

The second phase was the golden summer of her career. This was in the late '30s, when she had risen from despair to emerge as the unquestioned champion of America and the world.

The third phase is the Alice of today: effervescent, feminine, gracious, and still youthful in her mid-sixties, a woman who has sailed the roughest seas, survived the storms, and now finds, in the sunshine of her personal haven in Palm Desert, the serenity and fulfillment of a legendary life.

The story of Alice Marble, the "Girl from the Golden Gate," is an

o

amalgam of many factors, the most significant of which was her soulmate association with one of tennis' most outstanding women characters, Eleanor "Teach" Tennant.

Her victory over her health problems was a physical triumph. The emotional crises involved in her eventual parting from Teach would have destroyed many less courageous souls. On the courts, Alice's success came from a new interpretation of how women's tennis should be played.

The heroines of women's tennis in the '30s were the Americans, Helen Wills, Helen Jacobs, and Sarah Palfrey. Following close behind were Betty Nuthall, Dorothy Round, and Kay Stammers of Great Britain, Cilly Aussem and Hilda Sperling of Germany, Jadwige Jedrezjowska of Poland, the little Chilean, Anita Lizana, Nancye Bolton and Joan Hartigan of Australia, and Simonne Mathieu from France.

Sarah Palfrey was a natural volleyer, but except for Elizabeth Ryan, all the other girls were the epitome of traditional female tennis, inherited from the beginnings of the game—"steady-as-a-rock" baseline players, some of whom could volley and most of whom could not. All generally followed the accepted code of behavior, no tempers, no antics; they played tennis and behaved as we had all been conditioned to expect ladies to behave.

Then came Alice.

She was the first woman to follow her serve consistently to the net like a man. She had the manner, demeanor, the clothes, and all the wisecracking jargon that made her the first tomboy type to attain the upper reaches of world rankings. With her jaunty jockey cap, the short shorts of her champion era, her American-twist serve, and her incisive volleying, she was not averse to kicking a loose ball into stands and generally revealing her feelings. She wanted to win and she saw no reason for any class-conscious façade to hide this fact.

With this approach she broke down many of the traditional codes of ethics and disgusted the Old Guard. Hazel Wightman, sitting next to me during one of Alice's Wimbledon matches, was so outraged she left the stands altogether.

These characteristics made Alice the first woman since Lenglen the men wanted to watch. Suzanne communicated with men through her sexual message. Alice was the clean-cut, all-American girl who gave the women's game a new dimension, the girl who played the same game as the fellas.

Alice won the American championships four times in five years, and at Wimbledon she is one of only five women in a century of

○

Alice Marble (1) 153

history who has won all three events in one year. Except for the interruption of World War II and the lure of professional gold, which came at the same time, who knows what records she might have achieved?

Alice's nature was a fascinating paradox. She was a leader in her chosen craft, but a follower of other people. In many ways she was the embodiment of "People Who Need People."

Among the people Alice needed most was the well-known tennis pro Teach Tennant. More possessive than a coach, more demanding than a mother, Teach became the female Professor Higgins to Alice's Eliza Doolittle.

Alice was the fourth of five children, born in Beckwourth, California, in 1913, to what she describes as "backwoods farm people." Her father was a logger, and she remembers her mother as a strong-willed woman with the unusual status of being the last of twenty-two children.

Their home was in California's Feather River country, where the natural pastimes were hunting and trapping. Woodland escapades with her brothers are her earliest memories. The tomboy projection seems to have been born there and then.

When she was six, the Marble family moved to San Francisco. Alice told me the transition from small-town-country to big-city life was her first milestone. Once in the city, her tomboy inclinations ran riot and she wanted to play all the boys' games. She ran track, kicked a football, played baseball, and even at home was called Miss Perpetual Motion because she practiced her basketball shots with scraps of paper or rubbish thrown across the room to a trash can perched high on two chairs.

By the time Alice was eight, she was picking up baseballs for the local pro team, the San Francisco Seals. Soon afterwards they made her their official mascot and nicknamed her the "Little Queen of Swat." The great Joe DiMaggio was playing for the Seals. Years later he told Donald Budge, Alice's mixed doubles partner, that she "had a pretty good arm."

Then Alice's father died, and her older brother Dan became the father figure of the family.

Dan did not consider her actions "ladylike" enough for San Francisco and thought his kid sister should develop her obvious athletic talents in a more genteel "girls' game," like tennis. So he bought her a racquet, and her tennis life began on the municipal courts of Golden Gate Park.

Dan did all he could to encourage Alice's tennis; he took her at

o

thirteen to see Suzanne Lenglen play Mary K. Browne when Lenglen's exhibition tour reached the West Coast in '26. "But with all the smoke in the hall and everything," Alice recalls with disappointment, "I fell asleep and never did get to see Suzanne play."

Alice was not to know that Suzanne's opponent, twenty-one years older than Alice, would play a significant part in her career. In later years "Brownie" became such a close friend that she ended her days as Alice's living campanion.

On the tennis courts, young Alice had outstanding natural coordination, and in her years as a champion this was to contribute immeasurably to her easy-swing, masculine, serve.

Yet she started out with only a very vague concept of what tennis was all about. Having virtually no ground strokes it was her quickness of eye that made volleying came naturally to her, and she remembers that for years she was always anxious to rush to the net to avoid having to take the ball on the bounce.

In this respect Alice was the exact opposite of most beginners and the first woman to adopt the complete masculine serve-volley game. She was just doing what came easiest to her and gave her the most fun.

Alice's assertive technique compensated for her lack of ground strokes sufficiently for her to reach the top spot in the California junior rankings. The second milestone of her career was being runner-up in the Philadelphia Under-18 Girls' Nationals in '31. She lost the final to Ruby Bishop, a pupil of Teach Tennant.

In the years of prohibition I played escort to Ruby Bishop at quite a few evening parties in Hollywood. In that era evening parties meant tuxedos and long dresses, but in spite of this we would arrive conspicuously waving tennis racquets and boxes of balls. Perhaps it was just luck the inspecting traffic cops never discovered the "tennis-ball" boxes really contained two half-bottles of Scotch or gin!

After Ruby returned to California, she obviously discussed her Philadelphia victim, Alice, with Teach. All coaches have their eyes peeled for promising juniors. Teach, realizing Alice's potential as the National Under-18 finalist, approached Alice's family with offers of coaching. The family had their own ideas, however, and were not impressed at the time with Teach's proposal.

Then Alice and Teach decided themselves to work together. At the time Alice was eighteen and Teach thirty-four. What took place later derived from a decade of interplay between these two women of different ages and characters.

Teach Tennant is not a name one is likely to find in the world's tennis records. Nor is her name engraved on the honor rolls of any major championships. But from the home, and the sidelines, she could influence a "protégée" in a way to be compared only with Papa Lenglen.

Teach was born in San Francisco in 1895, and admits to starting her tennis by stealing her first racquet at the age of eleven.

She had no idea what tennis was. She was just fascinated when a houseguest arrived with a racquet, so she stole the racquet and hid it behind a woodpile in the yard until the mystified guest had departed.

Then she looked around avidly for somewhere to try out her new toy. Quite fortuitously she noticed a woman with a tennis racquet boarding one of the horse-drawn buses of the day. She had no idea what the woman was going to do with the racquet, neither could she know the woman was Mrs. Golda Meyer Gross, one of the top players of the Pacific Coast at the time.

It seems almost incredible today, but Teach then ran alongside the bus until Mrs. Gross alighted at Golden Gate Park.

Having eventually caught up with Mrs. Gross, Teach hid in the trees to see how she used her racquet. In a few short days Teach became obsessed with the idea that she, too, could play like Mrs. Gross. Through this strange fascination she was unwittingly committed to a lifetime of tennis. I wish I had known this in the '20s as I well recall playing against Mrs. Gross in a Riviera tournament of those days and we could have laughed together at this incident.

But with limited family fortunes, Teach soon found that if she was going to play tennis she also needed a job. For several years she tried everything, even selling newspaper subscriptions from door to door.

At the time of World War I not every woman could drive an automobile. Teach, being Teach, had contrived to learn, and with this as a sales pitch, she talked her way to becoming the first and only woman traveling rep for Standard Oil. "But I found myself talking tennis strokes to the customers," she said. Having earned enough money for a vacation, she decided that Southern California was likely to give her the most opportunities for her tennis compulsion, and the Standard Oil people never saw her again.

Through a chance meeting in Los Angeles with ex-American champion Maurice McLoughlin, Teach then began a very successful two-year association as hostess and tennis coach at the newly smart Beverly Hills Hotel.

I did not meet Teach until twelve years after all this, but it was easy to see her stint with the fashionable Beverly Hills Hotel set had been the launching pad for both her career and her personality. Teach had an outstanding capacity to communicate and to amuse people. In later years she became snobbish enough to indulge in a great deal of name-dropping, but she remained a breath of fresh air at any staid party, with a large repertoire of fun stories.

These characteristics made her an automatic favorite with the Hollywood movie colony. The stars of that era, Tony Moreno, Douglas Fairbanks Sr., Enid Storey, Norma Talmadge, and young Marion Davies, were soon asking her for lessons on the courts of their homes. Several of her rich pupils have told me that Teach's incisive idiom and her great sense of humor made their court sessions more of an entertainment than a lesson.

Throughout her life, however, Teach's associations seemed destined to dramatic terminal breaks. After two happy years at the Beverly Hills Hotel a devastating scene with the management put her future in jeopardy once again.

Nowadays, almost every tennis magazine includes the questions of when, or at what age, some player will turn pro. Leaving the Beverly Hills Hotel with only dark clouds on her horizon, Teach put the question to herself in reverse. How and when could she turn amateur?

Somehow, in a way that seems typical of both Teach and the establishment, Teach convinced the authorities that her coaching had been done "as an amateur." Teach had a great knack of convincing herself—and the others—that what she wanted was right. Amazingly, she was allowed to embark on the amateur tournament round.

By '20 she was ranked third in this country with only Molla Mallory and Marion Zinderstein ahead of her. She was good enough, in the last women's national championship held in Philadelphia, to take Molla to a three-set match that was described as the best in the tournament.

Then love stepped into her life. Like everything she did, Teach indulged her new status to the full and "gave away tennis for ever." But again the apparently inevitable break came, this time in three years.

On the rebound, Teach became involved in what she describes as "intimate terms" with a notorious lesbian called "Madame Hélène." Unfortunately, Madame Hélène was not a tennis enthusiast, so the inevitable emotional scenes recurred, and once more Teach took refuge in what she really knew best, teaching interesting people to take an interest in tennis. Eventually she more or less bulldozed her way to the coaching spot at the elegant Bishop School in La Jolla.

Meanwhile Hollywood had gone All-Talking, All-Singing, and All-Dancing. The old silent stars had to reorient their whole lives.

○

Alice Marble (1)   157

Many of them disappeared from the screen, and Teach realized the need to work on a list of new famous faces.

Her new list soon included Carole Lombard, Joan Crawford, Clifton Webb, Jean Harlow, and the great Charlie Chaplin himself. With this star-studded clientele and the Bishop School job, she managed to survive the '29 Depression almost unscathed. And her first real appointment with fame was still round the corner.

In '31 the Marble family finally succumbed to Teach's advances and Alice became her permanent "protégée." In Teach's memoirs she recalls her first sight of Alice. "Alice was fat and heavy. Her stroke production was eccentric, worst of all she had no control over her temper. When she didn't get the play she thought she should have, she would sock the ball, and I'm not kidding you, honey, right over the chicken coop, a block from where we were playing." She also adds: "Something happened to my solar plexus. This thing came to me which said: 'Alice can be a world champion.' "

How easily gold can turn to dust in one's hands! Having achieved her ambition of having Alice completely under her domination, Teach found herself not knowledgeable enough to improve Alice's wayward ground strokes and had to seek outside assistance. Alice recounts that Teach took her to a Santa Barbara tennis teacher, Harvard White, whose comment on first sight of Alice was hardly helpful: "That's the worst tennis game I have ever seen." Teach then turned to Mary K. Browne to help with the problems.

Undeterred, Alice moved to La Jolla to live with Teach. She pursued her lessons with Harvard White, and she thinks his provocation, Brownie's belief in her, and the discipline Teach imposed, were the factors which took her at the age of nineteen, to seventh place in the national rankings at the end of '32.

In the previous decade, Bill Tilden's running battle with the tennis hierarchy had been virtually a head-on personality clash with Julian S. Myrick. Myrick was the vice-president on the USLTA immediately after World War I and president from '20 through '22. In one top-establishment appointment or another he ruled American tennis for twenty years. In '33 he was still chairman of the Wightman Cup committee and of the Easthampton tournament, one of the women's circuit events that was mandatory for those aspiring to national ranking.

Myrick held great sway over all his committee colleagues and made it abundantly clear that he could use this at will. When I first met him, at Piping Rock in '33, he made it determinedly clear that I was meeting with an emperor, or at least a dictator, of tennis. He did not mellow as he grew older.

o

In those days the term "Lawn" Tennis (deleted only in '76 from the official terminology) was still endowed with its true meaning.

The establishment, being led mostly by Easterners, gave absolute priority to its own Eastern tournaments, which were all played on grass.

Ironically, California, with its cement and asphalt courts and regardless of the high percentage of world champions who had been bred there, had a fifty-year fight for appropriate recognition in establishment eyes. The rain-soaked turf courts of the Eastern circuit stretched the length and breadth of the "in" resorts from Boston to Philadelphia, and before being "acceptable" to the various national selection committees, all California players had to prove themselves in these areas.

So with her seventh-ranking position achieved at last, Alice prepared through the early spring '33 for the unavoidable Eastern tour. Teach could not afford to travel with her. Had she done so, this could have changed the whole course of events, because, with Teach around, Alice would never have been subjected to the traumas that followed.

Even traveling alone, Alice notched up a few brilliant wins in the early part of the tour and reckoned she was in direct line for a coveted spot in the Wightman Cup matches in August.

Her seventh-ranking position gave her no automatic place in a national team of five girls, but between March and August of that year she beat most of the players above her, and everyone considered her a natural to make the team against Britain.

Myrick, however, had the interest of his pre-Cup, Easthampton tournament at heart and used this relentlessly, making it a condition that if Alice did not play both singles and doubles at his Easthampton tournament, she would not be considered for international selection.

Elizabeth Ryan was also at Easthampton. We had traveled from England together, and she suggested I go with her, even though the men were playing separately at Southampton.

But to go to Easthampton one had to have Myrick's blessing since he controlled all the tennis accommodations. Elizabeth insisted on my behalf, and eventually Myrick rather reluctantly agreed that I might stay at the small local inn at my own expense.

This was not exactly a warm welcome, but I did not let it bother me. I had been watching Helen Wills, Helen Jacobs, and Sarah Palfrey for years. I particularly wanted to have my first sight of America's new "Golden Girl," Alice Marble. So Elizabeth and I set off together.

There was a strong entry, including all the leading players from Britain. Helen Wills was still nursing a back injury from the previous year, so would not play the singles. Myrick, therefore, counted on the Wills-Marble doubles team as a major attraction and also counted heavily on a singles final that would include the new rising star, Alice, from California.

Easthampton was a three-day tournament, which meant that any player reaching the singles and doubles finals would have to play nine matches within that short time. Alice had been playing the Eastern tour almost daily for weeks and came to Easthampton saying she could play only one event. This started immediate trouble. On the first morning, she found Myrick would not entertain the idea, and he again threatened her with being excluded from Wightman Cup considerations.

How well I remember the heat! There was no air-conditioning in my inn, nor in most of the private homes of those days. Elizabeth and I, recently arrived from Europe, went around like sleepwalkers in slow motion. Every quick movement meant that one's clothes were a soaking mess in less than a minute. Every day we were there the temperature passed a hundred degrees with humidity in the high nineties.

In these conditions and with so little time available, Alice restated her case: there was no way she could play nine matches in three days. Worse still, she had a long first-round single and was already too exhausted to partner Helen Wills in a doubles that was scheduled to follow. I shall never forget this because I was called in to fill the gap in the schedule and played two exhibition sets with Helen Wills in the blazing heat.

For Alice, the last two days at Easthampton were the beginning of a two-year nightmare that could have ended her career before it began. On the final day she was forced to play the semis and finals of both singles and doubles. Within hours she collapsed with sunstroke and serious dehydration.

The Wightman Cup followed two weeks later. In the interim Alice's doctor said she was developing anemia, and she was warned not to exert herself for the rest of the summer.

As a "consolation prize" for gutsing it out at Easthampton, Alice was picked for the Wightman Cup team, but played only one losing doubles match. Sick, tired, and worried by the anemia diagnosis, she returned to Teach in California with a large question mark over her future.

Meanwhile Elizabeth and I traveled by overnight train to Boston where Elizabeth was to play the national mixed-doubles with Ellsworth Vines.

o

It was an eight-hour journey in '33. In pajamas and with my own down-filled pillow (which I still take on my travels), I settled down for the night in my sleeping compartment. Unfortunately the attendant did not wake me before we arrived in Boston station, and I was forced to leave the train still wearing pajamas and carrying my pillow.

Elizabeth, always punctual and punctilious, was disgusted when she saw me on the track looking like an adult version of Wee Willie Winkie about "to run through the town, in his night-gown!"

And Boston is Boston. Elizabeth had always been a part of the "upper-crust" social set there. I remember her valid embarrassment at having to check into the top hotel with a sheepish, pajama-clad companion, still carrying his pillow!

After Elizabeth and Vines beat Perry and Dorothy Round to win the championship, we went across the continent for the Pacific Southwest tournament in Los Angeles and to my first meeting with Teach Tennant.

The train journey from Boston took three days and nights. California to a European was not just the other side of the world, it was another world.

Some years before, Elizabeth, on returning to her West Coast home from her early triumphs in Europe, was the first to suggest that Los Angeles should be as important a tennis center as the capital cities she had visited in Europe. The eventual result was that a committee of leading businessmen was formed, and the Southern California Tennis Patrons Association was born, due primarily to Elizabeth Ryan's enthusiasm and foresight.

Perry T. Jones, whose official title was that of director of the association, became the lifelong driving force of the scheme. Maybe it would have been more appropriate to call him the czar! He had a marvelous organizational brain, and he became, to Southern Californian tennis, what a hairspring is to a watch.

The Patrons Association was then unique in international sport, in that it helped discover, groom, train, and give financial support to young players of promise and send them to major tournaments around the world. Within a few years Jones also made his Pacific Southwest tournament one of the top prestige-events in the calendar.

When a poll was taken in the '50s that quizzed all the leading players on which tournament they enjoyed most, Wimbledon and the Pacific Southwest were listed in either first or second place in every player's reply.

Jones did me the honor of meeting me at Los Angeles station. His manner was similar to Larcombe's at Wimbledon. They were both men of quick decisions and no unnecessary words. "You look hot and dusty," was his typical greeting. "Better wash up before anyone sees you." In those star-image days, this was the very essence of Hollywood, where you had about thirty seconds flat to make your mark before the person speaking with you passed on to someone more interesting.

Jones took me to the Ambassador Hotel, and I was easing into a welcome bath when I was called, dripping, to the phone by a salesman wanting to sell me a hat. He had seen in the lobby that I had checked in without one. All movie heroes were portrayed wearing hats. "No one should ever be seen without one," he told me.

Back in the bathtub I was confronted by another man who had three elegant, but huge, white Borzoi dogs on a triple leash. The maid had opened the door for him without knocking. While I was in the bath, with the dogs lapping the water and licking me, the man said he knew I was English and therefore interested in royalty. I should buy the dogs, he said, because they were "royal," having recently been used on the movie set of *Catherine the Great*. These were small but typical happenings of the old Hollywood days.

The movie stars, Loretta Young, Marlene Dietrich, Bette Davis, Myrna Loy, Norma Shearer, Kay Francis, Claudette Colbert, and a host of equally famous men, came regularly to the tennis matches. Fred Perry won the tournament, and at the Los Angeles Club he behaved like an old-time jousting knight, flashing challenging glances at each court-side star in turn, as he reeled off his winners.

Fred was always grateful to me for taking special care of his Wimbledon matches, and he made a point of introducing me to many of the famous movie characters I might not otherwise have met.

Everyone was surprised that Louella Parsons also took me in her care. Movie people were not accustomed to kindness from Louella, but she arranged for me to be invited to several parties where every star in the system was on show.

Bing Crosby's first record hit, "Learn to Croon," was just released, and I remember the current heart-throb, Robert Montgomery, drove me to Bing's celebration party. Harold Lloyd had his own projection theater and delighted us with replays of his hilarious escapades, usually set at the top of church steeples or on the crumbling faces of aging clock towers.

Garbo was filming *Queen Christina* at the time and disappointed us all by driving to the MGM lot every day in a limo with all the shades drawn. Mae West's *She Done Him Wrong*, was the talk of the city, and I remember spending four anxious hours in the lobby of her apart-

o

ment block, to be rewarded with a purring smile and an autograph.

My room at the Ambassador Hotel was a few floors above the old Coconut Grove nightclub, and I still hear the sweet sounds of the tenor saxes as they lulled me to sleep after long, exciting days.

Jones had a tremendous caste sense. The movie colony was not well thought of by the older Los Angeles residents. Jones wanted the money and the status the socialites represented, but he also wanted the famous faces arrayed around his stadium court, so he arranged for both cliques to have their own groups of court-side boxes, clearly segregated on opposite sides of the arena.

Jones allowed me the privilege of being one of his socialites, but once I was seated in direct line across the court from Norma Shearer and the Adonis-like Robert Taylor, another time from Janet Gaynor and Charlie Farrell, and I readily confess to wishing I was sitting among the stars on the opposite side.

Alice introduced me to Teach Tennant at this tournament. Teach, of course, sat with her movie friends. Elegant and graceful, she already had snow-white hair in contrast to an olive, almost waxed complexion that resembled that of a Tibetan monk.

I found her famous idiom fundamentally tough and with an unabashed incisiveness that reached the heart of any subject in two sentences flat. She made frequent wisecracks, reminiscent of an early Mae West script, expressed in dry, movie-gangster style.

Among Teach's star-spangled coterie she spread the impression she was Alice's second mother. This infuriated Perry Jones who wanted to claim Alice's discovery for himself. With two characters as potentially abrasive as Teach's and Jones's, head-on collisions were inevitable. And they occurred with unfailing frequency.

Elizabeth Ryan asked Alice to partner her in Perry Jones's tournament and again the following week in San Francisco. They beat England's leading pair, Round and Heeley, in the Los Angeles final, but lost to them in the San Francisco final the next week. In reverse order, Alice lost the Los Angeles singles final to Round, then beat her in San Francisco.

Having survived so much strenuous tennis in California, in spite of the Easthampton debacle and incipient anemia, Alice seemed, on the face of it, to have recovered from her collapse and her skirmishes with Myrick.

But the Easthampton experience became a fateful foreboding, and the happy California weeks just a happy interlude. The following year, Alice was to make her first trip to Europe and be taken back to California by Teach in a wheelchair.

o

Alice Marble (1) 163

[18]

Alice Marble (2)

DESPITE HER SUCCESSES IN CALIFORNIA, ALICE MARBLE DID NOT recover for several years from her collapse at Easthampton in '33. Alice told me later that while she was beating Dorothy Round and playing doubles with Elizabeth Ryan, she felt constantly below par, prompting Teach to arrange a series of medical tests in an attempt to get to the root of the problem.

Ever since '26, when Suzanne refused to cooperate, the French authorities had been negotiating for an American/French women's team match. It was at last decided in '34 the U.S. team would play a French team in Paris on their way to England.

Teach was skeptical about Alice's health when she was chosen for the team, but after all the arguments and the fights, national acceptance of Alice meant a lot to them both. With Helen Wills out, Alice was now the country's No. 2 behind Helen Jacobs. The Wightman

Cup in London was the team's prime objective, and whatever the risk, the trip would also allow Alice her first crack at the French championships and Wimbledon. Alice gambled and lost.

Helen Jacobs was appointed team captain, and by the time the team arrived in France she was already apprehensive about Alice's condition. Her fears were confirmed when Alice became sick after a practice hit, and Helen immediately summoned a doctor. He agreed with the original anemia diagnosis, but between them they decided it was not serious enough to prevent Alice from playing the French match.

Alice was drawn to meet the No. 2 French player, Sylvia Henrotin. Sylvia was an extremely talented player. She enjoyed cunning little dinks, short angles, precision lobs, and always had the capacity to come to net and finish the point with some incredible volley. She ran Alice to every conceivable spot on the court and soon built up a 4–1 lead.

At the start of the sixth game, Alice, blown and taken by surprise by Sylvia's cunning, served a double fault, then collapsed, crumpling into a heap on the court.

She was rushed to the American Hospital in Paris where her temperature rose and her general condition became worse. At first the hospital agreed it was anemia, or possibly gall-bladder problems. Eventually they said it was tuberculosis, a traumatic experience for any patient. Later she was told she would never play tennis again.

Alice recounts that Helen Jacobs was like a sister to her in those frightening days in the hospital. But finally Helen had to move with the rest of her team to London, leaving Alice to recover sufficiently for the lone journey home. Helen asked the American Embassy to arrange Alice's return passage, and at the same time she cabled Teach, asking if she could travel to Paris, or at least, meet up with Alice at the dock in New York.

Teach could not afford the journey to Paris, but with the aid of a friend, made the long automobile trip across the continent from California to meet the liner *Aquitania* when it docked in Manhattan.

Waiting for Alice to arrive, Teach had a blazing confrontation with Julian Myrick. Teach laid the whole Easthampton disaster at Myrick's door and told him she thought the USLTA should pay all Alice's traveling and medical costs. She said—rightly at that time—Alice's whole future could be in jeopardy. Myrick was incensed and told Teach they had already paid up enough for Alice, that she was a bad investment, and they would not spend another dime on her.

"Just whose money was he protecting?" argued Teach at the height of her indignation. She had a strong point, because before sponsor-

o

Alice Marble (2) 165

ships, national associations' funds derived almost entirely from tournament receipts, which in turn derived essentially from the box-office appeal of the players. Tilden had had the same argument with Myrick year after year in the previous decade.

During this stalemate Teach took Alice to her own home in San Francisco, but once again the situation was impossible because Alice's mother was sick and unable to help Alice in any way. Distraught, Alice had to appeal once again to Teach for assistance.

Teach already had all-consuming family problems of her own, but she did not fail in the crisis. At her own expense, Teach had Alice taken to the Monrovia Sanatorium, thirty miles from Teach's home in Beverly Hills. To fund the medical costs, Teach spent countless hours in the sun coaching from dawn till dusk. And she also managed to make the return trip to Monrovia twice every day to see Alice and keep up her spirits.

But Alice's condition continued to deteriorate. Confined to her room, she became fatter and weaker by the day, her weight ballooning from 140 to 185 pounds. A fine athlete was being reduced to a vegetable.

Alice became convinced she would spend at least three years in the sanatorium, probably longer, and even then she might get out only with an arrested case of TB. "One day, after I spent eight miserable months in the place," she related to me, "I was so depressed I told Teach: 'I shall never get out of here alive.' "

Teach acted fast. She was not personally convinced by the doctor's diagnosis of tuberculosis. So she arranged an abduction.

Without a word to the sanatorium staff, Teach packed Alice's clothes and sneaked them in her tennis bag to her car. Then she went back for Alice, but found she was too weak to dress herself. Teach bundled some sweaters around Alice and carried her down the fire stairs, terrified all the time they might be observed.

Once well away from the sanatorium, Teach called the head of the institution and admitted what she had done. He described her action as "dastardly," but Teach gave him her customary bulldozing treatment and he eventually capitulated, promising he would "forget" the matter.

Few athletes, or coaches, would have survived this trauma. Even fewer would have bothered to try. But with Teach's constant love and care, Alice showed the first real signs of progress. Teach imposed her own diet to reduce Alice's weight, then encouraged her, bit by bit, to start taking short walks. Alice had always been musically inclined, so Teach also arranged singing lessons to improve Alice's breathing problems.

o

All this time Teach was paying the bills. She slaved, literally, day after day, on the courts to earn enough to meet the ever-present problems of finance for two.

The final inspiration for Alice was the movie star Carole Lombard, whom Teach was lucky enough to have among her pupils. One has only to visit Alice's home today to know what Carole meant to her in those troubled times. Amid all the trophies and awards, one beautiful photograph dominates her bedroom . . . Carole Lombard, glamor personified, at the height of her movie fame.

Carole had had her own traumatic experience, an automobile crash after which she required well over a thousand stitches. She knew from this what it was like to face the overnight termination of a brilliant career.

Though extremely beautiful, Carole Lombard was also contemporarily described as being "earthy" enough to communicate with movie audiences more warmly than Garbo or Dietrich. Although one detects Teach's hand in the actions, it was Carole's determined phone calls and letters of encouragement that eventually spurred Alice back to the tennis courts.

"Carole told me the doctors said she would never work again," Alice remembers. And she sent Alice a telling challenge, "If I could make it back, so can you," she declared.

Alice made it back, but the way was long and nerve-wracking. The doctor Teach consulted emphasized the need for extreme caution and at first would only allow Alice to play for five-minute stints. Slowly Teach weaned her, mentally and physically, back to health until she began to look more like the Alice we had known and loved.

It took two full years after the collapse in Paris, three years since Easthampton, before Alice was ready to resume competitive tennis. She was still only twenty-two, but had already experienced enough emotional stress to last most people a lifetime.

After her return to some minor tournaments in California, Perry Jones sent Alice's entry for the national championships to New York. Even Jones, with all his knowledge of the establishment, did not anticipate the mixture of alarm and antagonism this would arouse in Myrick. Teach had already blamed the whole of Alice's troubles on Myrick, and he was afraid that if Alice had a third breakdown Teach would be instantly at his throat. In the circumstances, Myrick and his committee must have wished Teach and Alice at the bottom of the sea!

Alice's entry was refused.

Teach's fury knew no bounds. Alice's recovery had cost her two whole years of hard labor in California and all her savings. Now the authorities in the East proposed to ruin both her and Alice on the pretext of Alice being "unreliable."

The name of Mary K. Browne weaves through the pattern of women's tennis like some clear, bright thread in an otherwise complex design.

Throughout her life of tennis, and golf, Brownie was liked by everyone. In this latest impasse she was the obvious go-between, and she herself suggested to Teach that she should intercede with Myrick. She managed to convince Teach that another slanging-match with Myrick would get Alice nowhere.

At least Brownie kept the doors open. But Myrick's incredible condition was that to prove her fitness, Alice would have to play singles against three men in one day. Afterwards his committee would vote on her acceptability.

Alice recalls vividly that only Teach's fury, Brownie's belief in her, and her own blind obstinacy enabled her to come through and beat all three men on a red-hot day at Forest Hills.

Even so, the committee's vote was only 3–2 in Alice's favor. She still shivers as she remembers that on that afternoon her whole future hung by a thread. Personally, I suspect the committee's fear of the earthquake-repercussions Teach would have caused had they rejected Alice a second time, also had a part in their capitulation.

How sweet a victory it must have been for Alice to come off the Forest Hills stadium court with the winner's trophy, having beaten Helen Jacobs in the '36 final.

Afterwards Teach had just four words to say: "Was Myrick's face red!"

The English grass-court season includes an early tournament at the Chiswick Park Club. Chiswick Park was one of the historic clubs built in London's suburbs in the Victorian era, and Teach thought it appropriate to introduce Alice and England to each other at this traditional event in '37.

Chiswick Park had one of the strongest playing memberships in England led by Fred Perry, no less, and Betty Nuthall. Always preferring to be the worst player at a strong club rather than the opposite, I had become a member of the club in the days just prior to Teach's and Alice's arrival.

So I was particularly delighted to discover Teach and Alice, sitting in the tea marquee of my new club, wreathed in smiles at the sight of me.

I had not seen Teach or Alice since '33. Now Alice looked fit, slim, tanned, and radiant. Teach was her starry-eyed, exuberant self. They were both obviously set for the victory trail.

o

But everyone, including Teach, always underestimated the obstacle course that is Wimbledon. In '37 only four women in fifty-three years had won the Wimbledon singles at their first attempt.

Teach made few psychological errors. Most often she was right. But in forecasting Alice's victory to all and sundry, she unwittingly put enormous pressure on her protégée, and it was inevitable that an overdegree of disillusionment set in when Alice lost in the semifinals.

Back at the U.S. nationals, Alice lost even sooner—in the quarters—and became so discouraged that the self-analysis and the soul-searching began all over again. Alice well remembers that by the time she got back to California in '37, she was on the point of giving up tennis altogether.

Once again, but in a completely different way, Carole Lombard was to be her savior. I have described how Perry Jones, at his Pacific Southwest tournament in Los Angeles, always arranged for the movie colony to have its own court-side boxes well away from his socialites.

Among the movie stars, Carole was occupying a box with her friend Clark Gable. Alice, going on to the LA stadium court for a match at one of the lowest moments of her morale, had to pass the box where Lombard and Gable were sitting.

Obviously, Carole had just expressed some comment of concern to Gable about Alice, because, as she passed, Alice heard Gable say to Lombard, "Honey, we all love Alice, but I don't want you worrying about her! Let's face it, Alice just hasn't got what it takes."

To have one of the best-looking and best-known men in the world administer such a public putdown would provide the necessary motivation for lesser souls than Alice to prove him wrong. Alice recalls that she barely managed to refrain from punching him because of Lombard. With her tomboy beginnings, she could well have done some damage to his million-dollar smile!

This incident was the turning point of her turbulent life. Gable's cruel comment was exactly what she needed to rekindle her spirit. All the magic came back in her game, and she was only to lose one more singles match ever throughout her amateur career.

Alice had won her first American singles title in '36. She won her first Wimbledon title in '37, two Wimbledon titles in '38, and in '39 she achieved the Wimbledon ultimate, winning all three events. After the Gable incident she was never again beaten in the American championships, and the one match she lost was the '38 Wimbledon semifinal to Helen Jacobs.

Mention here of Bobby Riggs may seem a distraction, but Riggs is, in fact, related to Alice's history in two ways that cannot be disregarded.

First, Bobby had been one of Teach's pupils. Bobby had the type of personality and the game that flourished when infused with the spark of Teach's confidence and vitality. Teach once told me, "When I met Bobby first he was 'wet and negative.' When I finished with him he was '*positive-plus*' and volleyed almost as well as Alice." Again, this was typical Teach idiom, and typical Teach confidence.

The second factor is that in '39, the year of Alice's "triple," Bobby Riggs achieved a similar success. Theoretically he did better as Riggs remains the one and only player in Wimbledon's one hundred years ever to achieve the triple on his first visit.

Over fifteen hundred people assembled to congratulate Alice and Bobby at the Wimbledon Ball after their joint triumphs in July '39. The picture of them together, dancing the lap of honor, must be one of the happiest ever taken.

I wonder if it crossed anyone's mind then that in less than eight weeks Wimbledon would close for six years and that World War II would end forever a whole life-style.

History records that on the eve of the Battle of Waterloo, at the Duchess of Richmond's famous ball, which she arranged less than three miles from Napoleon's massed armies, the Duchess herself sang "a patriotic song to inspire the gentlemen."

At the '39 Wimbledon Ball, Alice crooned "Stardust." She was wildly encored, returned to the rostrum to sing "This Can't Be Love," and inspired everyone.

For her crowning night Alice chose a cherry-red chiffon dress with a sequined bodice. With good reason she looked radiant, and her golden hair was effectively enhanced by a corsage of cypripindium orchids at her shoulder.

Amid the applause for her singing and her achievements, she passed my table, unpinned her orchid corsage, and tossed it to me. Pressed and flat, but with the memories it recalls still unfaded, I have it to this day.

Within weeks World War II put a stop to all European tennis, but Alice went on to win two more national championships at Forest Hills.

It was then sixteen years since Alice had fallen asleep in the San Francisco Auditorium while her close friend of later years Mary K. Browne was performing against Suzanne Lenglen in the first professional appearances made by women.

Meanwhile the pro "circus," after its uncertain beginnings in Suzanne's days, began to assume valid status when Tilden formed his own professional company in '30. By the middle '30s Tilden's glamor and personality enabled the tour to enlist, one by one, all the best

o

men players in the world. By the late '30s it was a viable concern. Class consciousness was easing, and it was no longer demeaning to be a performing tennis pro.

As soon as Alice won her first Wimbledon doubles title in '37, Teach started receiving offers for Alice to join the men pros. Teach immediately appointed herself Alice's business manager, and the domination she assumed over Alice's life in the following three years seems to have sown the seeds of their eventual breakup.

In '38 and '39 Alice and Teach had been faced with the same poker game as Suzanne in '26. Which professional offer to accept and when best to accept it? Just as Suzanne anticipated a much higher reward for facing up to and beating Helen Wills in Cannes, Alice and Teach had the nerve-wracking problem of knowing Alice could at least double her price if she could win the Wimbledon singles.

They waited, and this time the gamble paid off.

In '41 Tilden induced Alice to join a pro foursome with himself, Don Budge, and Mary Hardwick Hare. Throughout the war years they conducted an enormously successful campaign, both in entertaining the troops and in raising many millions for War Bonds. Mary Hare, being English, also made a considerable contribution to the British Red Cross by the same effort.

Meanwhile Alice and Teach were receiving financial guidance from Willie duPont, who was later to marry Margaret Osborne. Teach and Alice had a joint account in a duPont bank. Alice eventually received the rewards of their combined efforts, and some deep difference arose between them about the division of the money Alice had earned.

Also, being Champion of the World quickly widened Alice's horizons. A natural desire to emerge independently from Teach's hour-to-hour domination caused them first just to drift apart, but soon to split up irrevocably.

I have always held that after winning the Wimbledon crown no one is ever the same again. The success and publicity this brings changes, quite fundamentally, all those who achieve it.

The change in Alice was too big a shock for Teach to comprehend. Her reaction was one of jealous possessiveness to the extent of intercepting Alice's phone calls and deeply resenting a love affair she had with a young Air Force officer. The man Alice refers to only as "Captain Joe," was shot down and killed during the war. This love affair would have seemed the most natural thing in the world to anyone but Teach. Teach thought the years of personal sacrifice she had made on Alice's behalf were being conveniently overlooked.

Teach was quite unequipped to accept this situation. She was an

o

"all-or-nothing" person in every respect. Once she could no longer have all of Alice, the only alternative in her mind was nothing. Her bitterness was total. When Alice appeared on the nationwide "This Is Your Life" program, Teach said the few words given her in the script, but declined all other contact with Alice.

Teach was lucky that within a few years of her parting from Alice, Maureen Connolly came into her life and succeeded Alice in a very comparable relationship. Alice went on to find companionship in later life with Mary K. Browne.

Brownie was a sporting, gay person who married at sixty-nine and divorced at seventy-one. Having won the national tennis singles title three successive times before World War I, Brownie again reached the national final in '21, and three years later, appeared in the final of the national golf championships. She promised herself that on her seventy-fifth birthday she would go round in 75 and was shattered to manage only a 76. "One over par" in a new way!

Brownie died in '72 at the age of eighty, sixty-three years after being first noticed in the press as "a wee whippet of a girl," at the old Hollywood Hotel tennis tournament in 1909.

Alice's character, including her indecisions, has always been compatible with her Libra zodiac sign. The scales, symbolizing this sign, imply, of course, balance and fair play. In spite of all that had gone before, Alice forced Teach to "bury the hatchet" with Julian Myrick before his death. She recalls that with the help of a few martinis, Teach even managed to tell Myrick he was "a good guy, after all!"

But unhappily, the echoes of Easthampton lingered on. In '49 Alice's chest problems recurred, and she was forced to have a lobectomy.

Talking with Alice, three years after Teach's death, Alice said, with the deepest sincerity, "I owe my life and my career to Teach."

In youth, and in the first days of her association with Teach, Alice may have been a tomboy with an ungovernable temper. In gracious middle age she bears no trace of bitterness, either toward her dramatic parting from her onetime soulmate, or toward the rough hand life dealt her on so many occasions.

Near Christmas in '77 Rod Humphries and I visited Alice at her Palm Desert home, and I had the impression that complete fulfillment and serenity were the keys to her present happiness.

Alice's Libra scales crashed down at both ends with horrifying alternations throughout the life.

Today they are as level as those seen on any Statue of Justice.

○

[19]

Thirties Diary

IN THIS CHAPTER OF MY STORY I HAVE TO GO BACK SOME YEARS because my twenty-first birthday coincided with the second day of '31 Wimbledon. My father contributed a case of Dom Perignon, and Daisy, his wife, arranged a vast, white-frosted birthday cake, decorated with twenty rosebuds and one full-blown rose.

The symbolism of the full-blown rose depressed me beyond words. The golden interlude of adolescence was over, and I remember thinking, "My God, today I am supposed to be a fully fledged adult and I haven't even made a start on a life career." That day, I felt I identified with the growing pains of the whole world.

Mentally, I had already resigned myself to the bottom rung of the dress-designer ladder in London starting that fall, but I was still in love with tennis and looking for any excuse to postpone the unavoidable ending of my Riviera boyhood.

○
173

An opportunity came when a friend unexpectedly offered me a ticket for the Wagner festival at Bayreuth. I had been a dedicated Wagner fan since my early teens. In Nice there was a library where one could obtain the musical score of any opera for a minimal subscription.

By the time I was sixteen I knew most of Wagner's operas line by line. In '76 I made the thirty-hour journey from Australia just to catch some of the "Ring" at the Academy, which adjoins my Philadelphia home. Only later, when storing away the program, I realized this was my seventy-fifth *Walküre*.

Bayreuth was an unforgettable experience. I had a particularly lucky year because Furtwängler conducted the "Ring," and Toscanini followed with *Parsifal*.

I had heard my first *Götterdammerung* the previous year in Zurich, Switzerland, with Toscanini in charge. Wagner spent several periods of his life in Switzerland, and like all Wagnerian addicts, I had visited the Wesendonck Villa in Zurich and also had been dutifully to Triebschen, near Lucerne, where Wagner's son was born and the wonderful Siegfried Idyll has deep associations.

I have never enjoyed Salzburg as much as Covent Garden, the Scala, or the Met, but opera everywhere has given me some of my happiest moments.

In '44 at the height of the Allied campaign in Italy, we were quartered in the rococo palace of Caserta. There was no plumbing as we understand the word, but there were individual crucifixes hanging in each of the eighteenth-century paneled mahogany horse stalls and a beautiful private theater in which past kings of the Two Sicilies entertained their guests. Presumably, our commanding officer, General Mark Clark, was also an opera fan, for the neighboring San Carlo Opera Company was often summoned from Naples to perform for us.

It was during my pilgrimage to Bayreuth that the first devaluation of British sterling was announced. The French, who had welcomed British visitors and workers for at least half a century, took the opportunity to close ranks by making work permits mandatory overnight for all foreigners.

So inevitably my fourth summer as George Simond's assistant in the glamor life of Le Touquet had to be the last. This time there could be no looking back.

After a year in my London walkup I had to rent additional space, because by then I had enough work for a staff of five. I reckon I worked fifty weeks that year. In fact I only took two weeks away from work to maintain my Call-Boy job at Wimbledon and a few days to participate in the Dutch championships.

o

In spite of this, '32 was a particularly happy Wimbledon made memorable for me by the first return of Suzanne Lenglen to the scene of her former glories.

Since her exhibition tour in this country in '26, Suzanne had lived in great happiness with a rich young American charmer, "Lucky" Baldwin. But once again she decided against marriage and the affair finished at the beginning of the '30s.

Her reappearance in London was sudden and dramatic. During Suzanne's romance with Baldwin she seemed to cut herself off deliberately from her previous friends. Only the night before her return to Wimbledon, Sophie Wavertree received, out of the blue, a telegram that said simply: "Arriving tomorrow. Suzanne."

I happened to be standing by the door of Wimbledon's center court when Suzanne arrived and gave me a very affectionate greeting. It would not have made any difference, but she did not know at the time that I had been brought to Wimbledon by Dudley Larcombe specifically because of the administrative foul-up that caused her sad and stormy walkout six years earlier.

Almost as we were embracing, Ellsworth Vines appeared in the doorway and obviously wanted to ask me something about his matches.

I thought Vines would be interested to meet with Suzanne. She was in her most gracious mood. Although Ellsworth was seeded only second that year behind Henri Cochet, she told him, "I hear you're going to win Wimbledon." In fact, he did so, beating England's Bunny Austin in one of the quickest men's singles final on the record.

Suzanne's shock return caught Wimbledon completely by surprise. They had no seat for her. Moreover, like Mrs. Lambert Chambers, she was a professional. She had openly made money from the game, was therefore a pariah, and must not sit with the simon-pure "amateurs."

As outcasts, these two immortals of tennis were eventually found seats together in the boondocks. But everybody noticed. "Look, Suzanne. There's Suzanne!" The whisper went right around the center court. Ex-king Manoel of Portugal,* Suzanne's partner in so many fun matches at the Beau Site in Cannes, was in the front row of the Royal Box. He saw her, and blew her a kiss.

In business I was fortunate that the many socialites I had met on the Riviera came to me with their orders. This was probably partly out of curiosity, but these women also brought their debutante daughters, and within a year I was able to arrange a first showing of a collection.

---

*It was the last match he ever saw. That night he died of a heart attack.

o

At the time my biggest upward step was to receive, in *Harper's Bazaar* in '32, the first-ever mention of my designs.

Suzanne Lenglen stayed on in London and soon interested herself in my new life. Having recently terminated her five-year romance she was herself finding a new life.

We shared in this experience, and I found myself even more fascinated than before by her lively interest in everything. Since she was no longer performing day-by-day, she had become a delightfully relaxed companion. Perhaps also, because I was no longer her "stableboy," I was able to have a more balanced conversation with an Empress.

I recall that when the time came for my second dress show, Suzanne said she would like to be there and would also like to wear one of the models from the collection.

She chose a pale gray, wool-knit suit with a scarlet shirt, which showed her dark hair and coloring to great advantage. Suzanne always preferred strong colors for her tennis accessories and only wore the pale salmon-pink bandeau on the big days because she believed it brought her luck.

Suzanne was the salvation of my second show. It was one of those days when everything went wrong. There were interminable stage waits, and during one of the nail-biting delays Suzanne, sensing the situation, said, "Leave this to me."

On that note she left me and walked conspicuously the full length of the catwalk to greet some imaginary friend.

There were some two hundred restless people in the Garden Room of London's Mayfair Hotel. Even after a five years' absence almost everyone recognized her. For the few who did not, her professionally poised walk made it clear she was a world-famous star. The delays in the show were quickly forgotten as she put on this impromptu performance to help out my embarrassment.

On another occasion she came late one evening to my design studio. All the staff had gone, and we sat on one of the workroom tables, her wonderful legs dangling. We reminisced and chatted about the memories we shared as twilight faded into darkness.

I asked her opinions of the current stars, Helen Wills and Helen Jacobs.

"They don't use the court as I did," she said, the vanity of her tennis supremacy echoing clearly in the darkening room. "For men the court is not that big," she said. "But for women it is enormous. I used every centimeter of the court. Today's girls do not seem to understand this. I had no need to serve aces."

○

The next night we saw a movie together, and were both fascinated by Adrian's fabulous Hollywood designs for Joan Crawford. In the story the hero died as he was singing "All Night Through I Dream of You." I remember Suzanne saying how wonderful it would be to die dreaming of one's lover. All the sadness of her life of stardom and privation seemed reflected in those few words.

By the summer of '33 my business was growing fast, and I felt if I did not make the "Grand Tour" soon, I might never again have the opportunity.

So I made my first trip to America, traveling with Elizabeth Ryan. After my visit to Hollywood and meeting with Perry Jones, I went with the young guys of the '33 Japanese Davis Cup team and spent some unforgettable weeks in the Far East.

In my teens I would make special visits to the Gare du Nord in Paris just for the fascination of seeing the Tran-Siberian Express glide off silently on its 5,000-mile trek to Vladivostok.

From the Orient I was sorely tempted to make the return journey to England via Siberia, but decided instead to take the boat because I wanted to see Shanghai, Malay (now Malaysia), the paddy fields of Ceylon (now Sri Lanka), and the Pyramids. In '34 I was back at work. The years '35 and '36 were boom years for those of us involved in fashion. They were the years of the King of England's passionate romance with Wallis Simpson. Every hostess, every guest at every party seemed to want to outdo the other with new dresses and more sparkling jewels.

Then, with the king's abdication, everything went into reverse. None of the socialites bought anything for months. The fledgling British fashion trade that Norman Hartnell, Hardy Amies, Digby Morton, and I had pioneered and that was just establishing its first identity, almost owed its survival to the big theater productions of the day.

Happily, in '37, the Coronation of George VI and Queen Elizabeth, the present "Queen Mum," put everything back in place.

I was lucky to have among my clients the Marchionesses of Bute and Exeter, the matriarchs of two families in England, who by centuries-old privilege, had the right to drive to the Westminster Abbey coronation in their heirloom horse-drawn coaches. Their coronation dresses, under all the red velvet and ermine of their official robes, had not only to be a suitable backdrop for their fabulous family jewels but blend also with their painted coaches.

The year 1937 also brought London's first sight of tennis on television. I have a clear memory of the baseline on the primitive screens being arched like a rainbow so it seemed impossible for anyone to hit over the lines.

That same year Suzanne had her first look at Alice Marble, who was wearing short shorts and a jockey cap. Suzanne was then planning a comeback exhibition tour of England and asked if I could make her a tennis outfit that would not only express her own femininity but would project Alice's more contemporary masculine image as well.

After long discussions we achieved this by making an abbreviated version of Suzanne's legendary pleated dresses, but with the skirts split to the waist to show the "Marble" shorts underneath. In retrospect, this outfit was a forerunner of the first hot-pants tennis outfits I made in '50 and repeated for Virginia Wade and Evonne Goolagong in '70.

In '37 I had the excitement of making one of the first radio broadcasts on fashion from Europe to America (on station WCAU in my present hometown of Philadelphia). That year I also showed six dresses in the first-ever televised fashion show in Europe.

The historic Budge–von Cramm Davis Cup match took place at Wimbledon that summer. At the notorious Berlin Olympics of '36 Hitler had already made the world conscious of his intrusion into sport. In '37 his voice actually reached the Wimbledon locker room while his sports minister, a guest in the Royal Box, brought a dark foreboding of what lay ahead.

King Edward VIII, always a trend-setter, set a new fashion by cruising in the Mediterranean on the yacht *Nahlin* with Mrs. Simpson in midsummer.

For fifty years the sun had been taboo for milk-and-roses-complexioned Edwardian socialites, but the sun-tan cult spread to all levels of society in the mid-'30s. During my boyhood Monte Carlo and Cannes had been as empty as cemeteries from May to September. Suddenly, they became the in places to be during July and August, and like migratory birds we all found ourselves back there, gambling and dancing, but this time in summer instead of winter.

The year '38 was probably my best year as a society "couturier." In London the Church of St Margaret's, Westminster, rates second only to Westminster Abbey in social distinction for weddings. In the '38 London season I made no fewer than fourteen bridals for some of the year's most elite weddings held there.

On July 2, 1938, Helen Wills achieved her all-time record at Wimbledon. On July 4, Suzanne died in Paris of pernicious anemia.

All the official tennis bodies in England, remembering my Paris contacts, asked me to help out with the wreaths and tributes. Jean

Borotra's faithful Suzanne Duboy was our salvation, and I remember calling her at least half-a-dozen times on that sad Monday morning.

Suzanne's friend and partner Pierre Albarran, who came closest of all to marrying her, records that on his last visit to her she confided in him. "The happiest years of my life were '19 and '20, the years I spent mostly with you and Alain (Gerbault)," she told him within weeks of her death. The period she referred to was, of course, at the beginning of her career, when her supremacy, and all it cost her, was still unrealized.

So Suzanne died, dreaming nostalgically of her youthful companions rather than of the many famous men who would happily have married her.

On August 23, 1939, I left my precious Riviera knowing that war with Germany was inevitable. I was not quite on the last Blue Train from Cannes, but almost.

How well I remember that sad journey along the coastline, once the Land of Lenglen. The train passed a succession of red rocks protruding from royal blue bays. Every inch of the way seemed more beautiful than ever, and I traveled with my back toward the engine so as to savor every last moment of its romance.

In London, I found countless busloads of children being evacuated to the country, away from the anticipated bombing, and blocking every exit from the city.

The last of the circuit tournaments was still being played. I remember thinking, "I may never play tennis again, so I might as well play this week." My partner and I won the doubles. I went home and buried the cup in the garden. I was not about to have Hitler bomb my trophy after the toil and emotion we had spent winning it.

On Saturday, September 2, I paid off my staff of one hundred girls and told them that if war was declared there was no point in coming back. The previous night all the lights of London had been blacked out and were not to be relit for the next six years.

Neville Chamberlain announced the declaration of war at 11 a.m. the following morning, Sunday, September 3. The air-raid sirens sounded immediately, but it was nearly a year before the bombing began in London.

While I was trying to sort out the ruins of my curtailed professional career, I passed the time making nearly a hundred pounds of jam and a dozen Christmas plum puddings.

In World War I food-rationing was not introduced for the first two years and by that time shortages were very serious.

In 1916 jam was virtually unobtainable in English shops. I remembered my older brothers standing in line at dawn for the prize of a single pound of margarine or sugar and decided to learn from this experience. It was a wise decision, for my store of jam was a wartime luxury for me almost until V-J Day.

When, eventually, my apartment was bombed, the last of the Christmas puddings remained intact, but its basin was shattered and the tiny fragments of broken china made a clean white halo on the shelf around it.

I felt a sense of personal grievance against the entire Luftwaffe for bombing my plum pudding and immediately re-boiled it in a new basin.

The Wimbledon Club was also bombed when Norah Cleather was in charge and living on the premises.

Some years later, on V-E Day, Norah and I sat down to lunch together. As a token revenge for what we had endured, we solemnly ate the bombed pudding and saluted it for its private victory over Hitler.

In '39–'40 auxiliary services of all kinds were organized in England while the enlistment processes for the three main forces were being arranged. Everyone had to sign dozens of forms and declarations of his ability. One sent me asked whether my education had been "primary," "rudimentary," or "elementary." I settled for "primary" and often wondered if this was why I was kept in the army for seven years.

In May '40, ironically one of the loveliest Mays in the long story of wet English weather, we lived the true-life version of the movie *Mrs. Miniver*. In the nine days of May 27 to June 4, 338,000 men of the Allied fighting forces were repatriated from Dunkirk in the historic armada of thousands of little boats. Hundreds of these were piloted across the English Channel and back by volunteer private owners.

For a short time the London parties and celebrations were such one could have thought the war had ended instead of just starting.

At the same time some 30,000 Frenchmen opted to join General de Gaulle in London rather than General Pétain in Vichy.

On a glorious June day, when the flowering English gardens seemed to refute the very existence of the word war, Bertie Gillou, a boyhood buddy from my Riviera days, arrived on my doorstep, penniless and wearing only some tattered clothing given him by the Red Cross. His ship had been sunk in an estuary off Scotland; he had swum ashore and hitchhiked to London.

Bertie's father, Pierre Gillou, was the captain of the "French Musketeers" and the architect of their Philadelphia Davis Cup victory in

o

'27. The Gillous were one of the first tennis families in France. Pierre's sister, Katie Fenwick, was four-time champion of France before Marguerite Broquedis. Suzanne Lenglen's closest confidant, Coco Gentien, was Pierre Gillou's nephew. I had been part of their tennis milieu since the beginning of my own tennis days.

In '40 Bertie made the heartrending decision to break with his Paris family in order to serve with the Free French in England. A decade earlier we had shared in many youthful pranks in Monte Carlo. He had become outstandingly sophisticated and cultured and I was gratified he should seek shelter with me at this soul-searching time when both our futures were unforeseeable.

Meanwhile all the circuit tennis players, awaiting their call to duty, played exhibition matches to raise funds for the Red Cross.

On Sunday, August 24, 1940, we played an exhibition at a club just north of London. The sirens wailed all afternoon, but we still believed in false alarms.

As we left the club and looked across London's twilight, most of the skyline was lost in a flaming blaze. It was the first night of the London blitz, and we learned later the London docks had been totally destroyed. The American press described it as "indiscriminate arson."

In the previous weeks Bertie and I laughed and swam and sunbathed each morning, read Proust and Verlaine and explored Shostakovich together in the afternoons. At night we indulged in a splurge of carousing around blacked-out and search-lit London.

Since Dunkirk anyone in an official capacity was required to carry a combat helmet and an anti-gas respirator at all times.

When we went swimming on those glorious fall mornings, thinking every one could be the last, it was odd to see bodies on sun decks with combat helmets and respirators constantly beside them. On one occasion, when the sirens sounded, I remember a friend reaching dutifully for his helmet, only to place it carefully over his private quarters before dozing off again. We laughed hilariously at the time. In a week he was dead, hit by a bomb. In the circumstances, even the helmet on his head would probably not have saved him.

At that time there were many restrictions on news items being put out by English reporters and we often heard more about what was actually happening from the overseas war correspondents in London.

On the first night of the blitz, a quartet of well-known observers was doing a CBS radio commentary to America from various strategic spots in the beleaguered city. The four involved are now all famous names: Ed Murrow, Eric Sevareid, J. B. Priestley, and Jimmy (Vincent) Sheean. Sheean was in London's Piccadilly Hotel.

o

That night a regular-Army friend of mine was spending, as it turned out, the last furlough of his life at the Piccadilly Hotel. From listening to Jimmy Sheean's broadcast in the next room, he told us more about the beginning of the blitz than we would ever have known from our own people.

Shortly afterwards, I received my call to the Army and I never saw Bertie again.

The life-styles our fathers had known died that fall, never to return, even as ghosts. Churchill had warned: "The lights are going out all over Europe."

In August '40 Bertie and I participated in the final wake for the old world.

"The Way We Were"*

Memories
Light the corners of my mind
Misty waters cull a memory
Of the Way We Were.

Scattered pictures
Of the smiles we left behind
Smiles we gave to one another
For the Way We Were.

Can it be that it was all so simple then?
Or has time rewritten every line?
If we had the chance to do it all again
Tell me: Would we? *Could we?*

Memories
May be beautiful and yet
What's too painful to remember
We simply choose to forget

So it's the laughter
We will remember
Whenever we remember
The Way We Were.

*By agreement with Screen Gems-EMI Music Inc.

o

[20]

Fancy Pants

ON A SCORCHING DAY IN '51 I WAS SWELTERING IN THE PRIMITIVE customs shed of an airstrip on the Canadian border, when the customs inspector pulled out of my luggage some rather transparent nylon tennis panties I had promised to bring from England for a friend in Toronto.

In those days one could have unforeseen entry-permit problems. There had already been some difficulty over mine, and for a time it seemed doubtful I would be allowed to continue my journey. I felt cut off and miles and from a friendly face. To add considerably to my bad humor, the inspector waved the flimsy garments around for all his colleagues to inspect.

"What, Mr. Tinling, no lace this time?" he said suddenly with a grin. The tension was immediately relaxed, and I was surprised he recognized my name. Such was the power of Gussy's panties. After that I knew my entry permit was going to work out okay.

o

The story of Gussy Moran and the lace panties I made for her in '49 still remains one of the most unlikely happenings in the many legends of tennis.

Gussy's panties caused shock waves that reverberated from Alaska to Antarctica. On the way they even led the English minister of St. Andrew's Church, Buenos Aires, the Reverend John Cummings, to preach a sermon, the theme of which was the sinful implications of wearing this unsuspecting garment.

Thirty years later it is still almost impossible to comprehend how a yard of lace, added to a player's normal undergarment and barely seen at five-minute intervals, could cause such a furor.

Yet the "Gussy sensation" was tantamount to a star of today suddenly appearing topless on Wimbledon's center court. Even this might not cause quite the same buzzing of intercontinental cables.

In '77 the extraordinary Gussy story was still prominently quoted in almost every review of Wimbledon's one-hundred-year history. To understand it one must also understand the unique news exposure of the Wimbledon championships and the out-of-proportion importance that can be attached to quite small happenings there. Major Wimbledon controversies have been related many times to items of women's tennis wear. Mostly, these have been brought on by the blind chauvinism of a club that has never yet appointed a woman to its committee.

Whether it was showing one's wrists for the first time, as May Sutton did in 1905, or Suzanne's frocks "indecently" revealing a woman's natural silhouette in 1919, the resulting indignation stemmed each time from Wimbledon's all-male philosophy at its worst.

Besides, before TV coverage, tennis was reported to the world exclusively by men. Today there are more and more women reporting the game. Had this been the case in '49, Gussy's panties could not have caused the same shock reaction. Women journalists would never have accented the panties' sexual implications to the same degree as the men writers.

But very few things in life derive from a single cause, and like the roots of some aging tree, the Gussy episode had its origins in a complex tangle of happenings that had gone before.

The era of masculinity in both the style and dress of women's tennis was spearheaded by Alice Marble in the late '30s. It was carried over to the postwar years when Louise Brough, Margaret Osborne, Pauline Betz, and Pat Todd arrived in the first plane to touch down in '46 at London's new Heathrow airport.

○

The masculine look of the women players who came to prominence during the war years related to the regimentations of war, when it was unavoidable that unisex duties should lead to unisex clothes. One of the major factors in the explosive reaction to Gussy's panties was the conscious, and subconscious, revulsion against this masculinity that was still obvious in tennis even four years after the war had ended.

Christian Dior's Paris "New Look" created an international hunger for a return to femininity and sexual attraction in clothing. This was just beginning to find expression in the designer collections but not yet in the sportswear of the late '40s. In fact, Pauline Betz recalls that in '46 sportswear hardly existed, and it was almost impossible to buy a tennis dress at all in this country. I remember that this was also true in London.

Having been a prewar designer of evening clothes and bridals, and also preconditioned to femininity by the glamor cult of Lenglen, I was the first to rebel against the uniform appearance of the postwar tennis players. I felt that in looking like modern-day Amazons, the sports girls were reneging on their birthright. There was no "Peacock Age" at that time. All the men looked alike, and it scandalized me when women also looked identical to one another.

For this reason, in the beginning of '47, I conducted a strong campaign for femininity in tennis, demanding, for starters, that the girls wear dresses as opposed to the severity of the shorts and culottes they all had at that time.

Joan Curry, one of the few British internationals who could demonstrate on an arena court that tennis wear could be pretty as well as functional, came to me. When I was released from the Army after seven years in uniform and picking up the threads of my dress-designing career, one of my first thoughts was to make her an attractive tennis dress.

Soon afterwards, a Mrs. Hilda Gannon also came to see me. "I would like you to design something very special for my daughter's first appearance at Wimbledon. As you know, Joy can look very pretty," she said. This was a welcome commission in '47.

By tradition, Wimbledon dresses had always been white. Although there were no rules, I had no thought, then, of offending anyone. But I did suggest that a diminutive sky-blue or rose-pink hem could be added to an otherwise conventional white dress.

Joy Gannon, who was later to become the mother of current-day professional Buster Mottram, made her Wimbledon debut in my "new look" in '47. She looked adorable, and apart from one flattering paragraph in a London evening newspaper, nobody regarded the colored hem as the least bit unusual.

The news of Joy's color-trim dresses soon reached this country, and within a few weeks I received a letter from a pretty American ranked player: Bobbie Schofield. "I'm making myself some new tennis clothes," she wrote, "Would you allow me to put blue hems on my dresses?"

"Of course, of course," I replied. In a world where it is only regarded as smart to copy someone else's worthwhile ideas, it was refreshing to be asked permission when there was no need in fact.

When Joy came on a visit to the United States shortly afterwards, she and Bobbie became identified as the pretty tennis twins of two continents, linked by their natural prettiness and by the sky-blue hems on their tennis dresses.

In '48, the following year, Britain's No. 1 player, Betty Hilton, approached me before the Wightman Cup matches. She said she thought Joy Gannon's dresses were charming and asked me to design her a tennis dress that also featured a colored hem. The dress I made for her had a colored hemline, but the hemline was a half inch wider than Joy's and with a zig-zag top edge to the color.

Betty duly appeared in my design in the opening Cup match.

Hazel Wightman, who had donated the Cup and was still captain of the U.S. team, considered herself the First Lady of women's tennis. She had decided some years before that she was the ultimate arbiter of tennis etiquette across the world, and it so happened that she took great exception to Betty's dress.

Another factor was that Betty lost to Louise Brough (I thought predictably), 6–1, 6–1. At the time this was the quickest Cup defeat on record, but I was still amazed when Hazel said to me, "Betty lost because she was self-conscious about the color on her dress!"

The next day I was shocked to hear that Hazel had asked the Wimbledon Committee to ban both Betty Hilton and Joy Gannon from wearing the dresses I had designed for them.

When I arrived at Wimbledon to carry out my Call-Boy duties, Hazel embraced me superficially and kissed me on both cheeks with the smug smile she used on people she had just beaten in a match. "No hard feelings, of course," she said. "But we DO play tennis in white, DON'T we?"

My mind immediately went back to an incident in '33 when Hazel Wightman saw Helen Jacobs about to go on court for a similar Cup match at Forest Hills. At Wimbledon in '33 Helen Jacobs had actually launched what was then the novelty of tennis shorts for women and looked particularly good in them. "Take them off and put on a dress," Hazel had ordered her, two months after this. Helen had to dig out a soiled dress from her luggage.

This renewed example in '48 of Hazel's tennis power complex reminds me of a history-class legend that is singularly appropriate. Every English schoolboy knows it.

When the centuries were numbered in three figures, there was a King of England called Canute, whose ego trip was such that he declared his power greater than the oncoming waves. His courtiers respectfully questioned this, so in order to prove his point, Canute had himself carried, on his throne, into the surf. There he commanded the rising tide to stop, and it was not until he was within a gurgle of being drowned that Canute was forced to admit his ideas of grandeur had been overstated.

In '48 I told Hazel Wightman that henceforth I would call her "Queen Canute." World frontiers had been changed, civilization had barely survived its greatest threat, but Hazel Wightman thought she could hold back the tide.

A short time after this the suntanned, shapely form of Gertrude Augusta Moran arrived in Europe from California.

The press soon discovered the name "Gussy" had been substituted for Gertrude as a more polite version of "Goosy," the nickname one of her teenage boyfriends thought appropriate. "Gorgeous" was added later.

Even at first sight, Gussy looked to me like a person who loved life, enjoyed being attractive, and enjoyed the excitement she gave to men. According to her mother, she always went barefoot at home, never wore makeup, and slept in a T-shirt. This was innovative, to say the least, in those days.

The late '40s were the "Lana Turner era" when curvaceous figures were emphasized. Gussy epitomized this with her provocative, sexy bodyline and a walk that had so much bounce she appeared to be treading on a succession of rubber balls. The length of her stride seemed unreal, but it was instinctive and not at all artificial. She had a beautifully modulated, laughing voice, and her skin had a lustrous California gleam. I thought of her as a person who actually shimmered.

Gussy's father was a sound technician in a Hollywood movie studio. Her childhood playmates were Tom, Bob, and Jinx Falkenburg. In the late '40s Jinx became one of the most famous cover girls in fashion history, and it was all but impossible to buy any glossy magazine that did not feature her.

o

Fancy Pants 187

One day Jinx received a phone call from Hollywood movie magnate David Selznick, who said he would like to give Jinx's kid sister a screen test. "I'm fresh out of kid sisters at the moment," replied Jinx. "But perhaps you mean Gussy Moran."

Gussy secured several bit parts, and it is surprising her 37–25–36 measurements did not take her further. This was possibly due to Hollywood Central Casting's world-renowned reputation for curious associations of ideas. Gussy was cast as a Soviet nurse in a movie called *The Three Russians*.

In the war her only brother, Harold, was killed in the Pacific, and Gussy herself worked the "death-shift" in an aircraft factory for $40 a week.

Bill Tilden had picked her out for special coaching at the Los Angeles Club in '38. After a short while he told her, "If I could put my brain inside yours, you'd be the top player inside a year." Touring the service camps, Tilden recruited Gussy; she quickly became the No. 1 pinup girl. Soon after, Tilden wrote: "I think of Gussy as the No. 1 glamor girl in the United States. She also hits harder than any girl since Alice Marble and has as beautifully rounded a game as she has a figure."

Another writer declared, "Gussy is a girl who could shovel snow at Forest Hills and still draw the crowds."

The late '40s were a time when American women's tennis probably had its greatest depth. When Gussy came into my life, she was, in fact, ranked fourth among the top-ten women and was also the covered-courts national champion, which proves beyond argument she was a first-class player.

For two years I wrote the first postwar tennis fashion column in a magazine called *British Lawn Tennis* while Gussy did the same job in the counterpart magazine *American Lawn Tennis*. She was excited by the Gannon and Schofield dresses and mentioned them several times in her column.

Until '49 we had never met, but Gussy wrote me in the spring of that year telling me she was about to make her first trip to Wimbledon. She said she had red Indian blood in her and was extremely fond of color. She said she always wore bright ribbons in her hair, even around her wrists, and wanted as much color as she could have in the clothes she hoped I would design for her.

The day Gussy arrived in England I was playing in the doubles final of an English circuit tournament, Beckenham.

All my biorhythms must have been on a high that week, because, in addition to my fateful meeting with Gussy, I remember the semifinal the previous day was the one match in thirty years of tennis in which I did not make a single error. In a sense this was the best performance of my tennis-playing life.

Gussy came straight from the airport to Beckenham to see the finals, and we were introduced by Mrs. George Pierce Butler, the mother of Monte Carlo's tennis angel Gloria Butler. Laurie Pignon, of London's *Daily Mail* was standing beside me.

Gussy and Mrs. Butler sat in the courtside seats, and I was delighted Gussy was able to see me at my best in tennis. But a lot of the time my concentration wandered from the game because of Gussy's sexy, suntanned legs that I could not help looking at each time I went back to serve.

"I hope you're going to take care of my tennis clothes?" she said to me later. Naturally, I agreed immediately, but when I went to show her some sketches the next day I had to explain that though there was no reference to "all-white" in the Wimbledon entry blank, I was convinced, from Hazel Wightman's actions the previous year, some last-minute restrictions would be imposed.

Gussy stared at me in disbelief, and I realized the full degree of her disappointment. Such a situation was unimaginable to her. As well it might be!

Designing for a player as stimulating as Gussy, I first had to find a fabric that suited her ultrafeminine image. But '49 Britain still had what were called "Utility" restrictions on all fabrics and clothing. The government would not allow us more than five buttons on any dress. We were restricted to a limited yardage around the hem. The seams of every dress could not exceed a certain number. All this naturally made a lot of difficulties for designers.

Looking for an appropriate fabric, I approached a number of my influential textile friends, until Nance Ellis, then head of public relations at the Celanese Corporation, produced out of a secret drawer, a highly prized, experimental sample of soft rayon knit. More than a quarter-of-a-century later this probably sounds very prosaic, but at the time it was an absolute curiosity and a pioneering miracle.

I thought of Gussy as a shimmering personality and to capture this image I decided to trim her dress with white satin. She had never seen satin on a tennis dress and was startled, but greatly intrigued, at the first fitting.

Finally, I took the finished garment myself to the Dorchester Hotel in London. Adding a spray of orchids from the lobby flowershop, I waited impatiently for her verdict.

Gussy eventually called me from her suite that she was absolutely

○

delighted with the dress, but three hours later, back in my office, I received another call. Gussy was agitated and was asking what she was going to wear underneath.

I had been completely unaware that Gussy had always worn shorts, that she had truly had nothing to wear under a tennis dress because she had never owned one. "What you wear underneath is up to you," I told her with some skepticism. "I do not think your underclothes are my responsibility."

Gussy explained that she was playing Margaret duPont in the semis of the Queen's Club tournament the next day and would not have time to go shopping for anything at all. We both became rather irritable and finally she said, "You'll have to make me something. You promised to take care of my tennis clothes."

I had a French fitter at the time and told her, "We have got to make Miss Moran some panties." She frowned, but eventually produced some panties made from the leftovers of the dress fabric. "They look awfully dull," I said, when she showed them to me. "We cannot have any color, so let's try some lace on the bottom!"

My fitter returned with what we called "handkerchief" lace, and again I thought we had missed out completely, remembering Gussy's startling mahogany legs. Spectators never see championship tennis from close quarters, and I felt what we wanted was some lace with a bold design that would be visible from the stands when Gussy served. We finished up with coarse cotton lace my mother would have called "kitchen" lace, because it was often used on household linen.

So the notorious lace panties were born—not out of some erotic urge, but through niggling attention to detail and a special insight into the ingredients required to project the inner character of the players I take care of.

My philosophy is that the ideal designer makes frames for pictures, and when the frame is more eye-catching than the picture the designer has done a bad job. I certainly did not devise the "picture" of Gussy, but history seems to think I created the perfect "frame."

One has to remember that tennis dresses of that era were close to "kilt-length." In Scotland, kilt hems are measured one inch from the floor when the wearer is kneeling down.

A sexy projection made Clara Bow the original "IT" girl. I am always telling my tennis girls that men are hunters . . . they want to be titillated. Men want to look for "IT" when they feel inclined and do not want it thrown at them. The French describe intermittent sights as *"entrevu"* (seen between). "IT," *entrevu*, is a hundred times more provocative than seeing everything at first sight.

o

The length of Gussy's dress provided exactly this situation. One only saw the lace-trimmed panties once or twice every five minutes. It was said the lace drew the eye to the sexual area and this deeply shocked the establishment. But it delighted ninety-nine percent of the world, and Gussy gave press photographers their new position for '49, lying flat on the courts.

Wimbledon's "Ladies' Day" duly arrived with my prediction coming true. Notices were put up in all the women's locker rooms, which read: "Competitors are required to wear *all-white* clothing."

The fireworks really began the day before Wimbledon at the annual Hurlingham Garden Party arranged to give the players some carefree practice on grass when all the other clubs were closed under the no-Sunday-play rule.

Gussy appeared in her new outfit, and before I knew what was happening, the wife of the Queen's Club Secretary, Daphne Ritchie, came to me and said, laughingly, "I think you've cost me my husband." I was taken aback. "What do you mean?" I asked. "All the men are lying on their stomachs watching Gussy," was her reply.

I went to the court to find some twenty photographers in this position. Out of the blue the *Life* magazine photographer appeared and asked for a court where he could take some exclusive pictures of Gussy smashing, guaranteeing a tantalizing peep of the panties. One has to be very naive not to appreciate the significance of *Life* magazine's interest.

Overnight, Gussy was not just a tennis player but a sex symbol.

The press reports were worldwide and incredible. The next day, Gussy, locked in her hotel suite, was besieged by reporters wanting to know whether she was really going to wear the panties at her Wimbledon debut.

"Will she?" "Won't she?" was the press-room question of every hour. The phone lines were jammed as frantic editors demanded an answer for their deadlines. The press boys even organized a bulletin board that reported Gussy's latest available answer from her hotel room. Every fifteen minutes a different forecast was posted.

This was the climax of the Wimbledon Committee's antagonism. The focus of interest had been taken away from actual tennis to something they considered vulgar and out of place, particularly since the press represented the whole subject with sexual connotations.

Eventually Gussy felt, and I think quite rightly, the publicity was too much for her. She had a singles to play against a competent competitor, Bea Seal. Her first match at Wimbledon was going to be a difficult one, so she wore some old shorts and a shirt.

As soon as she appeared the crowd started a questioning chorus right around the stands whispering, "Where's the lace?" The "S" sound reverberated across the courts, and Gussy at first thought she was being hissed.

Then the world asked the same question, "Where's the lace?" and Gussy's indecision was interpreted as a masterstroke of showmanship and public relations.

Her next match was scheduled for the grandstand court. By now even I was on tenterhooks wondering if, and when, Gussy would appear in the panties outfit. To this day I make a point of never asking a player what she is going to wear before a match. Their tennis must come first, and I purposely avoid embarrassing the players or myself by raising a question that could lead to a disagreement.

But I was still Call-Boy for the arena courts, and my heart was in my mouth when I went to fetch Gussy. With the immense publicity surrounding her, I now had a vested interest in what she was going to wear. It was one of those moments in life when one feels one's whole future depends on the outcome. I had the same gut feeling as on the day Suzanne was asked if she minded a thirteen-year-old boy calling a match for her.

However, for her second match, Gussy glided out of the locker room, giving me a conspiratorial wink and wearing my dress with the much-discussed panties underneath! The huge crowd, feeling its curiosity at last rewarded, approved loudly and welcomed Gussy with its fullest roar of applause.

At the time so much emphasis had been placed on the undergarment, everyone forgot to consider the dress itself. The dress has certainly been forgotten in the years since '49. I always thought it a very pretty dress on its own merits, so I was particularly pleased with the crowd's applause. In fact, walking behind the two girls, I felt rather sorry for Gussy's opponent, Betty Wilford.

Then we saw a rush of reporters scrambling to their telephones. The official count said there were nearly two hundred present. The match was unimportant. Gussy was wearing the lace panties! On court, the photographers machine-gunned Gussy merrily, led by Bob Ryder of Associated Press whose afternoon's work earned him the "Photographer of the Year" award. The *Life* magazine picture was also the "Picture of the Week" feature.

Then the situation began to snowball out of all proportion. Gussy was inundated with requests for personal appearances—everything from hospitals and garden fetes to judging beauty contests. The Marx brothers, in London at the time, invited her to join their act. A racehorse, an aircraft, and a restaurant's special sauce were named

o

after her. The following week she was voted "Best-Dressed Sports Woman" by the U.S. Fashion Academy. The whole thing was staggering.

Meanwhile the Wimbledon Committee resorted to the essentially English defense: "If you don't like something, just disregard it." Nothing was said to me at all. There was even a cold war from my colleagues in the inner sanctum of Wimbledon. Very determinedly they made no mention whatever of Gussy in my presence. I could only go about my job as if nothing unusual had occurred.

The tangled story of my break with Wimbledon after "the Gussy affair" actually originated before the war.

In '37 I was offered what was really an apprenticeship as the future secretary of Wimbledon. Dudley Larcombe was due to retire in a few years, and the committee made the proposal that I have a trial period under his guidance, no longer as temporary Call-Boy but as his bona-fide successor on his retirement.

I had been climbing the ladder of dress-designer prestige in London's Mayfair, slowly but steadily since '31. The Wimbledon Call-Boy job was my vacation hobby. I loved every moment of it, but I was equally determined to be as successful as possible in the remaining fifty weeks of the year.

Considering the Wimbledon offer of permanent employment was a real dilemma. To accept would put me back again at the heart of my beloved tennis. The job also offered unlimited social advantages, including contact with the Palace and the Royal Family as well as other privileges well beyond my normal horizons.

But the money was negligible, and after a great deal of soul-searching, I decided to stay with my dress designing. So I wrote a polite letter of refusal, formally and correctly addressed to the secretary. The correspondence is still in my files, and I am still surprised when I read it.

Apparently its substance was never conveyed to the chairman, Sir Louis Greig, because he stopped me in the men's locker room one day soon after and said, "My dear fellow, I am so glad you are going to join us. I'm sure you are going to do a good job."

Although I realized he was caught unawares, I had to say, "I'm sorry, Sir Louis, but I have declined." From that moment on our previously cordial relationship began an irrevocable slide toward mutual antagonism.

Evidently Louis Greig's change of attitude toward me began to crystallize ever more with various happenings that involved me in '47 and '48.

One factor was that Jack Kramer, after winning Wimbledon in '47,

o

Fancy Pants 193

made me a gift of six very loud, contemporary American neckties. They were extra-wide in the latest American style, and I was very proud of Jack's gift because there were no ties at all like them in England.

The second factor was a stupid incident in '47 involving bouquets of flowers that have since become a traditional part of every women's singles final. For years these were always sent by the secretary and the tournament director as congratulatory gifts to the two women finalists in the locker room. In '46 Pauline Betz and Louise Brough had been so delighted when they received the flowers they automatically took them onto the court with their racquets.

The next year, when Louise and Margaret Osborne were due to play the final, Louis Greig and the new secretary, Duncan Macaulay, took me aside and said the committee had decided they did not want the women to take their flowers on to court. It was Wimbledon's way of attempting to stifle any semblance of color or intrusion into what they considered the "proper" way of playing tennis.

"I think it's a great pity," I replied. "Last year everyone loved the new picture." Greig murmured that there had been complaints, but the new club secretary, Duncan Macaulay, suggested, "Why not leave it to the players' discretion?"

Greig's eventual decision was a typical example of his ambiguity. Nodding to Macaulay he instructed me, "Leave it to the players. Don't tell them to leave the flowers behind if they bring them, but if they don't, don't raise the matter."

When I went to fetch the players, Margaret asked me the leading question, "Shall we bring the flowers, Ted?" My inclination was to say, "Of course." But after thirty years I am still glad I was scrupulously loyal to my job and replied, "It's entirely up to you."

"Right," said Margaret and Louise with one voice. "We'll take them."

We passed Greig and Macaulay on the way to the center court and I knew from their sickly expressions they thought it was because of me that Louise and Margaret were carrying their flowers. As far as Greig was concerned, it was just another tick against my name in his black book.

A third factor was the '48 episode when Hazel Wightman delighted the Wimbledon Committee with her disgust over the color-trim dresses I made for Betty Hilton and Joy Gannon.

With all this happening, the '48 Wimbledon was the first of my life that was not to be a total enchantment. My clash with Hazel and the banning of my dresses in her Cup matches two weeks previously cast the first and unexpected clouds over our idyllic relationship.

Conversely, there was a new note of anticipation because I had decided this would be the first time I would actually compete in the Wimbledon championships. I could have played there several times before the war, but because I was being paid in cash for my Call-Boy job, the so-called "amateur" rule precluded my doing both.

After the war I was persuaded to resume the Call-Boy job on an honorary basis. I had played twenty-six tournaments on the '47 circuit. I was also captain of one of the top English county teams, but I had never played Wimbledon, and my friends rightly pointed out that if I did not enter soon I could end my playing days without ever doing so.

Fate scheduled my Wimbledon debut for my thirty-eighth birthday (once again a Thursday!). I need hardly say I went to Wimbledon, proud as Punch, wearing one of my Jack Kramer ties, and without the thought that it would strike horror in the chairman's soul.

After my match I was changing quickly to resume my job and was adjusting my tie when Louis Greig appeared in the locker room. He made some caustic remark I have forgotten and looked in revulsion at the loud tie. It might have been something unclean.

"Your ties are your worst enemy," he announced scathingly. Astounded, I realized he was not joking.

"I'm not so sure about that," I countered, very tactlessly, because of the unexpectedness of his attack.

This exchange was merely a storm warning. From then on I sensed that I was unwittingly caught up in a gathering squall. Gussy's panties were at the eye of the hurricane.

[21]

Where Fashion Lags Behind

In late '48 Gussy and I, although not having met, had written some mutually admiring comments in our respective fashion columns three thousand miles apart.

In one of my columns I had said: "Men go mad, we are told, when La Moran smiles at them and swoon when she takes off her sweater. The sooner all the lads are sun-tanned from the blaze of her tropic eyes the happier we shall be." Later, I was told these lighthearted remarks had been found particularly obnoxious by Louis Greig.

Ever since '28 I received, around Christmastime, Larcombe's curt invitation: "I hope you will join us again for the championships. They begin on June—Yours sincerely." This was his usual peremptory style.

In '49 I thought the new secretary's letter had gone astray because by the end of March it had not arrived. In April I received a personal call from Louis Greig. I immediately sensed the tension and irritation in his voice, in spite of the ritual hypocritical English opening, "My dear Fellow."

Greig explained why the customary invitation had been delayed. "My committee feel I should stress a few points. Some of us consider your ties are not quite . . . er . . . that you . . . er . . . if you could just . . . er."

I cut him short. "Let's not worry, Sir Louis. The time has probably come when we should all have a change."

Wimbledon had been my personal wonderland for twenty-three years, and I still marvel that I could even suggest severing a bond that meant so much to me. But I was not about to burn all my bridges in one phone call, and the conversation ended with my saying I would think about his invitation, and his words.

In early June I was still uncertain about what to do. I had made no further comment about going to Wimbledon since Greig's call two months previously. Then I had a call from the secretary, Duncan Macaulay. Macaulay and I had known each other for more than twenty years and had built up some degree of mutual respect while we were both on the Wimbledon organizing team with Norah Cleather in the '30s.

On the phone Duncan told me he was leaving London the following morning for the Paris finals and thought it only fair to his own responsibilities to have a firm decision from me before he left. I had "played a leading part in the organization of the championships for more than twenty years," was the reason he gave.

That evening we had dinner at his apartment and discussed every aspect of Greig's and my own feelings until 3 a.m. Trying to be tactful, Duncan opened the discussion by saying, "I think the press are your worst enemies." All my life the press has been extraordinarily generous to me everywhere, and I was certainly not having my "problem," which appeared to be what we were discussing, blamed on my newspaper buddies.

"Funny you should say that," I countered with this in mind. "Sir Louis thinks it's my ties." Duncan then told me the comments in my fashion column about Gussy had incensed Louis Greig with their "vulgarity."

After six hours of discussion I was close to deciding my long stint with Wimbledon should finish. Conversely, as a friend, I did not want to renege on Macaulay only three weeks before the biggest job of his life was due to start. So I promised to "sleep on it" and write him the next day.

I have the copy of the correspondence in my hand as I recount this story and see that I said, "In light of our long association I shall not let you down at the last minute. However, I trust there will not be too many regrets, either on my side or in the Committee Box."

The Hurlingham garden party had taken place on Sunday, and Gussy's panties made headlines the following day before Wimbledon even started. Gussy did not wear the panties at Wimbledon until Wednesday, but the London *Daily Express*, in spite of carry-over wartime limitations to six pages, made Gussy a front-page leader story for five days in succession in the first six days of Wimbledon.

On Thursday Gussy, still shocked by the enormous amount of press exposure she had experienced, was scheduled to make her first center-court appearance. This was a third-round single against the diminutive Chinese prodigy Gem Hoahing, whose total height was less than twice the circumference of Gussy's most expressive dimensions. The combined emotions of the whole situation proved too much for Gussy, and she was beaten.

At Beckenham, when Gussy arrived, I had had difficulty concentrating because she sat in the courtside seats. At Wimbledon I was again involved in a men's double, but this time in full sight of the electric scoreboard of the center court during Gussy's defeat. It seemed that each time I received service, the board flashed the message that Gussy had lost another game. My poor partner George Godsell was distracted, and we also lost. I think it was to the Irish Davis Cup team, Kemp and Jackson.

The day after her singles loss, Gussy was surprised to be summoned personally by Louis Greig. She told me afterwards she expected to be reprimanded about her panties. But he only told her her mixed-doubles partner, Bob Falkenburg, had pulled out of the event.

The imparting of this type of information is strictly the job of the tournament director and in no way the normal function of the chairman of the world's most famous tennis club. I have often thought, and so has Gussy, that in sending for her Greig intended, in fact, to raise the panties question, but confronted with her personal charm, and hearing her lilting voice in his office, he chickened out.

The cold war against me went on until my birthday on June 23. I had played, and lost, my first match at Wimbledon, and with other members of the staff I was having our customary late dinner in the Royal Tea-Room after the rush and pressures of the day.

The caterers produced an imposing birthday cake for me, when, because of a late mixed doubles, Jean Borotra appeared and asked if he might join us. Seeing the birthday cake on the table, he immediately ordered champagne for everyone. Then, with his usual infectious chuckle, he exploded the whole situation by saying, "I don't know if we should drink to your birthday or your panties."

There was deathly silence. Jean looked startled, and I felt I was being engulfed in a wave of open hostility. The romantic clubroom that held so many happy memories for me in those twenty-three years of Wimbledon suddenly became a courtroom. And I was clearly being declared guilty.

But I kept all my thoughts on the matter to myself until an incident at Queen's Club. Notwithstanding the championships, Wimbledon always closes for the middle Sunday because of the no-Sunday-play rule there.

During Sunday lunch at Queen's Club, which does not close, one of the Wimbledon Committee attacked me bitterly before all the members. "How could you do something so tasteless having been with us for so long?" he asked. "What do you mean?' " I inquired. His reply was quick and caustic. "You have put sin and vulgarity into tennis."

This accusation really released my bottled-up feelings. In the previous week I had been asked innumerable times for interviews about Gussy's panties. I still hoped the ridiculous storm would blow over and refused all comment, although I never denied having made them. One of my feature-writer friends had already called me that morning and was annoyed by my silence. Now I was ready.

So on Wimbledon's second Monday morning a column appeared in London's biggest circulation daily that quoted me as saying I did not communicate with the Wimbledon Committee's attitude because I had added at least an extra thousand spectators each day to their attendance.

This set the stage for the eventual jealous showdown with Greig.

Gussy had refrained from wearing her panties outfit after her second-round singles. But she and Pat Todd reached the doubles final against the titleholders Margaret duPont and Louise Brough. In spite of all that had already been written, the question of whether or not Gussy would wear the panties in the presence of Queen Mary once again hit the headlines.

Throughout the history of Wimbledon controversies, pressure was frequently put on center-court players by telling them, "Queen Mary might not approve." In fact, she was a sporting old lady who smoked in public when this was still considered a questionable habit for ladies, and she always enjoyed a good joke.

On the final afternoon Gussy called every thirty minutes from her

Dorchester suite to ask, in a frenzy of indecision, whether Queen Mary would be there to see her match.

Queen Mary was then eighty-four, and the intense heat of the day had already raised questions in the midday newspapers about her presence. Louise Brough was involved in all three finals, and her doubles match against Gussy and Pat Todd could only be a late starter. Queen Mary often arrived at Wimbledon about 3 p.m., but that day it was not until 4 o'clock that her equerry called to say she had decided not to venture out in the heat.

When Gussy was told Queen Mary was not coming she hurried straight to Wimbledon. Her emotional conflict was at least partly resolved, and if she could only pluck up the courage she was free to show off, on the center court, her panties and the pretty dress that went over them. Nevertheless Norah Cleather, who was in the locker room at the time, told me Gussy put on, and took off, the whole outfit at least three times before deciding.

With the enormous publicity, Gussy developed an oversensitive self-consciousness. She began holding her racquet in front of her face when going onto court until the press photographers protested she was preventing them from earning their living. Another time she protested that all the passersby stared at her on the sidewalk. "They looked at me and their faces fell," she said. "What did they expect. A goddess or something?"

Originating in their younger California days, there was a natural antagonism between Gussy and her final Wimbledon opponents Louise and Margaret. They represented the ultimate difference in concept as to how tennis should be projected. Their feelings were as polarized as those of Mrs. Lambert Chambers and Suzanne in 1919.

Both times a new world was emerging from the old, and both times the evolution was a painful shock for the purists. Margaret's and Louise's philosophies were exactly aligned to Louis Greig's, which did nothing to ease my situation.

The older girls' antagonism toward Gussy, and what she stood for, was very apparent the night before the match. I was helping sort out the complimentary tickets for all the finalists when Gussy's allocation was inadvertently handed to Margaret duPont. Margaret stiffened visibly and handed the envelope straight back. "I doubt Louise or I will be seeing Miss Moran," she said, coldly. "And anyway she would not like to receive her tickets from us."

The players' entrance to the center court for the final verged on comedy. As Louise and Margaret walked on, Louise, unable to conceal her curiosity any longer, bent nearly double to look at the famous panties she was seeing for the first time.

o

In spite of a really sincere ovation from the huge crowd, Gussy, with her self-consciousness aroused to the full, hardly dared bend down during the preliminary hit. One ballboy tossed her a low ball, and she watched it, frozen, as it rolled by her feet. Other competitors in the stands roared with laughter, and Gussy signaled them to be quiet. It was only after she let two or three balls go by untouched that she plucked up enough courage to hit some.

An astonished Louise and Margaret lost the first four games, but then asserted their superiority to win in straight sets.

This was the end of two unbelievable, certainly unforgettable weeks for Gussy.

As she left England the following morning, Gussy did a strange thing, which proved symptomatic. In the lounge of the London airport, Gussy met Jackie Smythe, a Wimbledon diehard who had been one of Gussy's sternest critics in his role of tennis writer for the London *Sunday Times*. Gussy took a pair of scissors and, before the bewildered eyes of the onlookers, snipped off her pigtails. "If you still want masculinity," she seemed to be saying, "you can have it."

Jackie Smythe always had an infallible instinct for faux pas. After I had already been dressing Doris Hart for two years, he said to me, "What a pity all that Gussy business was for you. Why don't you dress one of the *serious* players, like Doris Hart? She's *always* impeccable."

Gussy had left, but for me the real drama was yet to come.

After the finals the chairman held a private cocktail party in the committee room to which guests from the Royal Box were invited on their way home. Greig asked if I would recruit some of the stars for the party. Already among his guests was the current Prime Minister, Lord Attlee, who told me with a sly smile, "You've done a great job for tennis this year." Next, Macaulay stopped me on the stairs to say, "Princess Marina (then president of the Wimbledon Club) thought the panties great fun." During the party Louis Greig shook me (as I thought) spontaneously by the hand and said, "My dear fellow, thank you so much for coming to Wimbledon this year. We could never do without you!"

This was reassuring. Stupidly I believed it and went to the Wimbledon Ball relieved.

But somewhere, deep down, I had an instinctive feeling I was again at a crossroads in my life. Something had happened in the previous three weeks that was too big for me to analyze. It was the hottest summer night in ten years and I walked back to my apartment confused and alone.

Thirty-six hours later there was a ritual farewell cocktail party for the players, which I had attended for years past with Norah Cleather.

o

Greig, as chairman of Wimbledon, was asked to say a few words. This time, the expectable pleasantries completed, his whole appearance suddenly changed, even the muscles of his face seemed to go into spasm. "Never," he thundered, "never shall we allow our center court to become a stage for designers' stunts."

You could have heard the traditional pin drop with ease. Norah was so shocked she dramatically dropped her champagne glass. A hundred heads swiveled to see my reaction. Even knowing Greig's uncertainties I could not forget the unnecessary congratulations so recently offered. I felt betrayed and offended in a situation in which I had no means of defense.

This was the crossroads I had sensed. Now the direction was quite clear. I went back to my office, wrote Macaulay, and reminded him of my warning: "I trust there will not be too many regrets——." Indeed, I told him, I now had a great many.

The whole "Gussy episode" carried over to '50 when she returned to Wimbledon. In the interim she toured the world loaded with unfamiliar trappings of stardom. Her reputation was somewhere between famous and notorious.

In India she had a romance with a handsome young British army officer, Tony Davenport, which was widely publicized. Even though Gussy had read Sigmund Freud and Karl Menninger and had been seen carrying such books as *Man Against Himself* or *Love Against Hate*, this had not impressed her fiancé's father and he made a dramatic denouncement from his English country home forbidding the wedding. This caused another rash of world headlines.

After visiting the Taj Mahal and inspecting all the other marvels of India, Gussy went on safari in the jungle. After this she told the world she would be wearing leopardskin panties and dyeing her hair blonde because "rajahs do not seem attracted to brunettes."

It was in India they washed her limited wardrobe on stones in the river, and her tennis wear became so tattered she played in her beach shorts. In most countries on her travels nobody minded, but when she arrived in Egypt and appeared in black shorts the ultra-tradition-conscious clubs in Alexandria and Cairo were outraged.

Still another affront, this time to Egyptian dignity, occurred when Gussy was to receive the winner's trophy from King Farouk himself, and through a misunderstanding she did not show up. She used illness as an alibi though this was presumably a "diplomatic indisposition" because of the criticism expressed in the newspapers about her black shorts. Overnight the Egyptian troubles blew up into an international incident. There were phone calls of explanation, and even an apology to the palace from the American ambassador.

o

As Gussy began to think of Wimbledon, she realized she would need some more tennis clothes, and I received a letter saying, "Make me something even more feminine than last year. *Let's Dig Deep!*"

Back in England the British writers anticipated yet another dress controversy. Headlines appeared asking if Gussy would be banned from this Wimbledon. Others asked pointedly what would happen if she were banned.

Louis Greig, still peeved over the '49 "indignities" announced, "Wimbledon needs no panties for its popularity." In another interview he said, "Tinling's clothes are designed to keep everybody's eyes off the ball."

I was approached by the whole British press asking if I was going to dress Gussy again, but I released only the letter she sent me. Then, following demands that I give a reply, I issued a statement through the Associated Press to the effect that if Gussy wanted "practical and attractive garments" from me, I would be happy to take care of her.

This was my first experience of the new era of communications, the first time I was able to have a dialogue with a client across the world through the news media.

Our dialogue soon raised another question, "Surely if you design another Gussy sensation Wimbledon will throw *you* out?"

It suddenly hit me that I had made no public mention of my break with Wimbledon six months previously. Now I decided to speak out because my own friends needed to know that I would not be in my customary Call-Boy position at the '50 Wimbledon and would be asking the reasons why.

John Olliff, who was the tennis writer for London's *Daily Telegraph*, asked me about this, and he reported my differences with Louis Greig for the first time. Unbelievably, they made lead position on the front page.

As soon as the first editions hit the streets I was besieged by all the other London newspapers. The first call came from the *Daily Mail* just before midnight. The phone rang all night without stopping, and by dawn reporters from the next day's evening newspapers were already on my doorstep.

Features and readers' letters went on for weeks. Hundreds complained about the "dictatorial" attitude of Wimbledon attempting to impose its wishes on the players. Photographers from all over the world lurked round my design studio hoping to catch me snipping a piece of fabric that would give them a clue to my plans for the next "Gussy sensation."

And it was not long before other designers started to get in on the act. Emilio Schuberth, one of Italy's top names, made Gussy an outfit that she actually wore at Beckenham, on the same court where we met less than a year before.

The week before Wimbledon Pierre Balmain, of Paris, staged a press show in London at which Gussy modeled his creation. Fortunately for me this was composed of yard upon yard of flimsy silk chiffon and was totally unwearable for tennis.

Finally Wimbledon was three days away. After almost hour-to-hour contact with Gussy from Egypt, I had not heard one word from her in four months so I called the Dorchester and said, "What in the hell goes on? Is Schuberth dressing you, is Balmain dressing you, or am I? What's the score?"

Gussy was distinctly embarrassed and said she would "explain everything" if I would see her immediately. She received me in an apricot-colored negligée, looking absolutely divine. She said she became "caught up with those guys" and really did not know what she was doing. She excused herself, saying, "I guess I just got carried away. You know how it goes."

I went back to my workrooms and slaved until 5 a.m. on the morning of "Ladies' Day," finally coming up with a shirt-and-shorts outfit in white Swiss embroidery. I had never before made any shorts, but I decided this was my best insurance against Gussy's self-consciousness. Although I was assailed by doubts all through the night, my instinct kept me working. Around 5 a.m. I cursed myself for a fool, but I have never regretted the effort.

Later that day the outfit was delivered to Wimbledon with a note: "I thought you might not feel like a dress today, so how about this?"

All I could do then was to sit back and wait. Once again she was scheduled on the grandstand court where the panties made their first Wimbledon appearance. Once again the crowd was seething with anticipation. The United Press International wire service put out a story that read: "The lips of every woman and the eyes of every man are asking the same question: 'What will she wear this time?' "

The wait was agonizing. This was the first time in my life I was at Wimbledon without any duties, which also meant without any privileges, so I had difficulty in even making the bleachers, the crowd was so dense.

Suddenly Gussy appeared for my moment of truth. My knees went quite limp as I saw her looking dazzling and as sexy as ever. The tight-fitting embroidered shorts seemed to enhance her already provocative, long stride. The press quickly dubbed it the "Peek-a-Boo suit" because the embroidery had holes in it and the deep suntan of her shoulders was visible through the shirt. Her appearance was a smash hit. Phone calls came from six thousand miles away in California. "We must have it," they said. "Reproduce this outfit immediately and send it over."

After the '50 Wimbledon everything went awry for Gussy.

Bobby Riggs induced her to set out on an exhibition tour with Pauline Betz. Riggs presented Gussy and Betz in Madison Square Garden on October 26, in '50 but he totally misread the situation, which was unusual for him.

Gussy, very much wanting to be respected for her tennis, had to accept the bitter pill that her real attraction was in her clothes and her sexual projection.

She was the houseguest of Jinx Falkenburg's mother, Mickey Wagstaff, for her New York debut. On the morning of the opening, Mickey happened to ask Gussy what she was going to wear for the match. "What new sensations has Riggs dreamed up for you?" she asked. "Nothing at all," replied Gussy, amazingly.

So Mickey hunted around New York. With a few hours to spare they finally decided on some little white satin cabana dress on which they sewed some gold trim. Meanwhile Pauline Betz, who was normally not the slightest bit clothes-conscious, appeared in a gold lamé tunic over apricot-colored fur panties! It was an unbelievable turnaround. Pauline not only swept the boards by obliterating Gussy with a 6-0, 6-3 beating in thirty-three minutes. But she swept the sensation stage as well. The tour was the ultimate bomb from the start.

Gussy's marriage rounds had started with two broken engagements; now she had two broken marriages. At one stage she was involved in problems with *Confidential* magazine over accusations of nymphomania.

However, she went on to become a successful public relations expert, radio commentator, and newspaper columnist. She always had a ready wit, and when all color was banned from Wimbledon for the second time in '62, her incisive comment was, "If they want only one color why don't they choose black? This would be appropriate mourning for the game they are trying to kill."

During my travels in the States Gussy and I have since met many times. On one occasion she gave a glamorous reception for me at the Beverly Hills Town House.

In '70 she wrote me from Vietnam where she was ostensibly making a USO tour with Nancy Chaffee, playing tennis, but really entertaining the troups. In her letter she told me the armed forces television program recounted the old story of the panties once again. "My God,

Ted, how long can this go on?" she said. "The panties went yellow twenty years ago!"

Gussy's pro fling earned her a bit short of the $75,000 that was publicized at the time. She does not resent the large sums being earned by professional tennis players today. "As long as they can get that kind of money I'm all for them," she says philosophically.

At fifty-five, Gussy is still on the courts, coaching kids six days a week. She works primarily with youngsters from three to eight years old, and she works one day each week with deaf children at the John Tracy Clinic.

"I had the most exciting experience the other day," she said recently. "Working with two kids, both five and a half years old and deaf, they actually got a rally going. They hit the ball back and forth. It was gorgeous," says the erstwhile glamor queen of tennis.

Thirty years ago destiny linked me with Gussy through the common cause of believing the word "feminine" could be a reality in women's tennis.

Our association had to survive many storms and stresses before we emerged amazed by the whole thing, perhaps a little scarred in the process.

But meanwhile we initiated a tide of fashion progress, the irresistible tide Hazel Wightman—like the legendary King Canute—was unable to comprehend. A yard of lace under a tennis dress proved, for the first time since Lenglen, that functionability could have an affinity with adornment.

Within a few weeks of the lace panties' first appearance, lace was to be seen on swimwear, ski wear, leisure wear, and every other conceivable type of garment.

Together, in less than three weeks Gussy and I changed the entire concept of how sports girls could look.

Across the world, and forever more.

by Sagittarius

FRILLS *

It fell upon the Doomsday eve
When the Atom race was on,
That from the U.S. came a bonny lass
To play at Wimbledon.

*By courtesy of the New Statesman, London, March, 1950.

○

A Colonel there in the tennis set
　Who long the stars had dressed,
Showed her new designs on sporting lines
　And one she liked the best.

O, tennis frocks are plain and straight,
　And tennis shorts are bare,
But a style she wore not seen before,
　With frilly underwear.

Next morning all the daily press
　For A-bombs had small space,
For each front page showed the tennis rage,
　The undies flounced with lace.

Then up the Tennis Chairman spake,
　And did the Colonel chide,
"Publicity for frills," quoth he,
　"Is most undignified!"

"No seemly clothes—no simple smock,
　The Tennis Club condemns,
But we owe our fame to the well-played game,
　Lay off those lacey hems!"

Strong words are spoken anigh the courts,
　The Colonel has resigned;
"I will be gone from Wimbledon
　Where fashion lags behind."

"Ye have banned the lassies in ankle socks,
　And lassies in short-sleeved shirts,
Ye have frowned on shorts on Wimbledon courts
　Ye have thundered at knee-length skirts."

"Queens of Wimbledon I have gowned
　Since skirts round the ankles swirled!
Say what you will of my fancy frill,
　My frill's gone around the world!"

⎡22⎤

Tug of War

ALTHOUGH IN '49 AND '50 GUSSY AND I HAD BLOWN UP THE TRA-
ditional edifice of sports fashion, I could still not see the way out of the
bomb crater to my future. Perhaps I was naive.

Gussy's outfits attracted more worldwide exposure than anyone's
since Lenglen. Both women were immediate products of a postwar
era. In both cases the public was longing, consciously and subconsciously, for something artistic and titillating to replace the years of
regimentation and restriction.

In 1919 Wimbledon called Suzanne "indecent," "brazen," a
"French hussy." On one occasion two spectators even spat on her car
as she was leaving Wimbledon. Perhaps, with Gussy, I should have
anticipated some comparable antagonism from the diehard minority
that always resists change.

I realized that in the years '49–51 I had created a sportswear

○

revolution. I expected some resistance, but what hurt me most was that the strongest criticism emanated from my own countrymen who had the most to gain from my work. In fact, the English could not have cared less what I had to offer them.

It seemed that every morning I would read in the newspapers another derogatory quote or comment. The most pungent usually originated from Wimbledon's Louis Greig.

One morning, for instance, I read: "Tinling's dresses seem designed to keep everyone's eye off the ball."

Two days later Louis Greig told the Associated Press, "We want to tell young players not to spend their money on a designer's ideas which might make a bad impression on the British public."

At the end of the same week Louis Greig asked Margaret duPont, the captain of the American women's team, to have a "private word" with her players. "Frills are unsuitable for Wimbledon," she was instructed to tell them.

This statement was followed up by threats. "Wimbledon retains the right to refuse players' entries without giving a reason," Louis Greig reminded many of the questioning journalists.

Yet through all this the rest of the world seemed to be on my side. The French decided that something other than moral susceptibilities were being violated. *"British puritanism goes too far at Wimbledon,"* Paris readers were told. The Italians were equally quick to comment on what they termed *"the subversive force of English tradition."* *Women's Wear Daily* reported with amusement: *"Wimbledon Outlaws Galloping Godivas."*

Fortunately the British fashion press ranged itself on my side against Wimbledon.

"Enchantingly feminine," said one national daily about my new collection. *"Everyone should record their thanks to Ted Tinling for changing the dreary scene,"* said another.

All this prompted me to make my first postwar trip to New York. I felt I had to get away from the Old World and make contact with the receptiveness and initiative of the new.

In the spring of '51 my business associate, Henry Turner, brought one of my most avant-garde tennis collections to show to American buyers. In it I included flimsy lace tunics, nylon sheers, the first flower-print hot pants with matching bras, hand-printed organdies, the whole bit.

Henry did a first-class job on prepublicity and selling the best American stores.

On arrival at Idlewild Airport (now JFK) I was rushed with the dresses to the NBC studios. Five scriptwriters pounced on me immediately and analyzed my philosophies. Within hours of landing I was to appear with Jinx and Tex McCrary on their prime-time personality program, and Jinx herself wanted to model one of the new styles.

The scriptwriters did a great job. Tex's opening words to me on camera were "Say! You're the guy who makes girls look the way guys want 'em to look!" As always, the American idiom packed a punch that made English English seem colorless. After endless negatives in London, I felt the throb of American stimulus right there in that opening sentence.

Jinx then appeared on the set in a soft rayon-knit dress that had gold-bead embroidery on the shoulders. It was a proud moment to see the most photographed cover girl in the world, a legendary American beauty, modeling my English dress.

At that time British currency restrictions allowed us only a daily total of eight dollars. Some kind New York friends who themselves lived on a very limited budget, accommodated me in their apartment.

The day after my TV appearance with Tex and Jinx, the janitor of the apartment block recognized me.

"Was dem beads or sequins?" he demanded.

"Uh?" I queried.

"Last night," he mumbled. "That dress Jinx wore. My wife has gotta know."

It was a telling instance of the new power of TV. In that moment I knew my future designs would have to be thought of in terms of TV projection.

For nearly thirty years now I have been indebted to Tex McCrary for the image of me he created in a single sentence. Whenever I have doubts about my work I recall his words and remember the importance of living up to the terms of reference he invented so opportunely for me in '51.

After the first hectic days in New York we got down to the business that seemed so elusive in the old world of England.

Vogue summoned me to their offices. Other exciting phone calls came from New York's top fashion personalities Eugenia Sheppard and Eleanor Lambert. I was feted by some of the most powerful personalities in American fashion, and later became the first British designer to work with the volume trade on Seventh Avenue.

That week was also exciting for another reason. The U.S. Covered Court Nationals were being held at New York's Seventh Regiment Armory, and it was there I had my first sight of the shapely 36–23–36 silhouette of Santa Monica's Beverly Baker.

o

At the time she was playing barefoot on the armory's polished parquet courts. She was ambidextrous, playing an equally aggressive brand of tennis with either hand. "Sugar Candy Kid" and "Good Enough to Eat," the descriptions given her by the New York press, were exactly right.

I thought I had never seen a sexier tennis girl. She was certainly going to be Gussy's successor as the new No. 1 pinup at Wimbledon. She was already planning her first trip to the British circuit, and I was overjoyed when she asked me if I would take care of her tennis clothes.

Two days later I went back to London, and it was time to reflect on the excitements of my American visit.

In England the new, even the unfamiliar, was a target of constant criticism. I found New York hungry for novelty and generous with its praise.

The diamond glitter of the Empire State disappeared in the distance as I left Idlewild.

But I had been caught up in the vibrant upbeat of America, and I knew I must come back soon. The way ahead had become clear at last.

Beverly Baker made her British debut at Bournemouth on May 1, 1951. London's leading national daily described it as follows:

> The latest beauty from California, Beverly Baker, twenty-one years old and brown as a berry, walked onto court today wearing a sharkskin and satin ensemble specially designed for her by Ted Tinling.
>
> The spectators left all the other courts to look at her. At the sidelines they were saying things from "Isn't it simply lovely?" to "A little like a swimming costume, don't you think, dear?"

There was no doubt I had a successor to Gussy on my hands. By coincidence, like Gussy, she was the No. 4 ranking American player. But it was probably not a coincidence that she suceeded Gussy in drawing howls of dismay from the Wimbledon hierarchy.

For the past two years Gussy Moran had already excited the men sportswriters to fever pitch. When they saw Beverly Baker they could hardly believe they had another sex symbol to write about. The resulting press exposure was extraordinary. It was so extraordinary, BBC-TV took the then unique step of flying Beverly to London and back between matches to take part in a specially arranged program.

The TV interview proceeded normally until Beverly was asked about her new tennis wardrobe. "Ted Tinling's making me. . . ." she began. The rest was silence. She was faded right off the screen. Ten

o

months after Gussy the name Tinling was still considered too sensitive a subject for British viewers.

At Wimbledon Beverly reached the semifinals, with a shock victory over Margaret duPont in the quarters.

Beverly was the first-ever player to wear a different outfit in each match at Wimbledon. Press exposure about her statistics and her tennis gear had heightened the growing hostility of the self-appointed guardians of morality. Unable to accuse her of anything else, they decided her outfits were "transparent."

As Beverly and Margaret came out to battle, the atmosphere was electric. Thousands of men spectators hoped this would be a breakthrough for Beverly's glamorous and sexy image. The diehards hoped that safe, reliable Margaret would put this disturbing influence where it belonged.

Perhaps the pioneer ghosts of May Sutton and Suzanne Lenglen smiled that day on Beverly. In a more partisan atmosphere than I had ever known at Wimbledon, Margaret duPont was beaten.

The purists greeted Beverly's victory in stunned silence. Naturally, I shared in the delight of the thousands who were her genuine admirers.

But the diehards had to say something and on leaving my seat I became aware of two heavily tweeded ladies beside me.

Looking at me more than at each other, they staged what seemed a prearranged dialogue.

"It must be like playing a freak to play that Baker woman with her two hands," declared the first.

Her friend went even better for my benefit. "Well, she certainly dresses like one," she pronounced.

Louis Greig, playing the same game as with Gussy, summoned Beverly from the players' lunchroom before her next match.

Beverly said later that he never accused her of wearing transparent outfits, and said only that there had been comments on this aspect of her clothing.

Beverly's comment was appropriate. "I did not think I would be summoned to his office," she said. "I would have thought an English gentleman would have come to me, especially as I was in the middle of lunch."

In her next match, her first appearance on Wimbledon's center court, Beverly was annihilated by Doris Hart. One of the guests in the committee box was Russell B. Kingman, then president of the United States Lawn Tennis Association.

Obviously Kingman identified totally with Louis Greig's outdated thinking, and on his return to New York attacked Beverly bitterly.

I had made it back to this country when Russell Kingman returned. But, reading the headlines in some New York and Boston newspapers, I could have thought myself back at Wimbledon.

"Fancy Dress Ended By Kingman."

"Girls Must Show Only Tennis Form From Now On."

"Henceforth Kingman Will Insist On Good Taste Instead Of Questionable Fashion Displays."

These were just three among many.

That same week, at the Eastern Championships at Orange, New Jersey, a pretty umpire, Aili Tesloff, was refused permission to take the chair because she was wearing a strapless sundress.

This gave Kingman the confidence to become even more personal. *"Poor Beverly couldn't have known how bad she looked at Wimbledon,"* he said in an interview. *"Innocent kids are being conned into wearing daring tennis costumes for purely commercial reasons. It's time this was stopped."*

Both Gussy and Beverly were delightful, sophisticated women in their twenties. They well knew what they were about and must have been amused, at best, to be described as "innocent kids."

But strangely the British National Association, in direct contrast to Wimbledon's Louis Greig, invited me to design the official uniforms for the upcoming British Wightman Cup team in Boston.

Coincidentally we were told that the Australian authorities in Sydney had banned all press photographers from taking rear-view pictures of women tennis players.

At the time the whole situation was confusing. In retrospect, the record shows it for what it really was: a stupid, ridiculous farce.

Yet the double-talk still endures in some areas. Even twenty years later, when almost every tennis girl in the world wears frilly panties, Peter Schweb, in his *Fireside Book of Tennis*, thought fit to reproduce an article titled "The End of the Fancy Pants Era," already an idiotic piece when it was current.

Beverly went back to Wimbledon twice more. In '55 she was unlucky to lose the singles final by a hairsbreadth to Louise Brough.

Today, after twenty-five years of happy marriage to John Fleitz, she looks as glamorous as ever and unbelievably unchanged from the day I first saw her in the Seventh Regiment Armory.

Beverly and John now manage their own sports complex, the Los Caballeros Club, with close to seventy tennis courts near Newport Beach, California.

The years '49 through '52, when Gussy and Beverly came into my

o

life, had all the excitement of an adventure into the unknown.

All three of us were deeply sincere in our beliefs. Perhaps the insults and the resistance we received from the establishment even strengthened our motivation. And the tide was with us, the timing was right.

I have never really enjoyed being right after the event, but I know Gussy and Beverly would be the first to agree with Sagittarius's satirical lines:

> Say what you will of my fancy frill,
> My frill's gone around the world.

[23]

Little Mo

MAUREEN CONNOLLY, ALL TINY SIXTEEN YEARS OF HER, APPEARED suddenly from the locker room and confronted me. "Hi! I like your work and I'm going to wear your dresses!"

I had never before seen "Little Mo," as she was called, and in that first meeting, during the Longwood Wightman Cup matches, in Boston '51, I got the impression I was being addressed by an animated toy in which a rapid-fire voice tape had somehow been implanted. The spring was overwound. Her eleven words took less than eleven seconds. Then she was gone.

Already in '51 this kid prodigy knew exactly where she was at, but even she could not have imagined what her meteoric rise to stardom would involve.

Within weeks she was to become the youngest player ever to win the American championships; within nine months she had captured

○

the first of her three successive Wimbledons, and in two years she achieved what no woman had ever done before, the Grand Slam of the Australian, French, Wimbledon, and the United States titles. For good measure she added the Irish championships, which were particularly dear to her heart because of her shamrock ancestry.

Maureen followed Alice Marble as the second of Teach Tennant's amazing prodigies. But history was to repeat itself in the cruelest way. Just as Teach and Alice achieved fame and glory together only to be followed by a bitter and irreconcilable parting, so, too, did Teach and Maureen.

Maureen, whose parents had separated when she was four, originally took to tennis because her mother could not afford her first kiddy passion, which was horse riding.

Maureen's mother was a church organist. She had desperately wanted to become a concert pianist, but she found her tiny hands could not span an octave. Having suffered the frustration of her own hopes, she centered her ambitions on a musical career for Maureen. But this was not to be. Hours of practice on the tennis court were one thing, but never, at any age, did Maureen see herself tolerating hours at the piano.

When Maureen had become the world's best tennis player, she piloted me on a nostalgic visit to the cracked, concrete San Diego courts where she had played her first tennis games because there was no cost involved.

As a promising twelve-year-old she had been noticed on these courts by a veteran player, Daisy Tree.

Daisy knew Teach Tennant by reputation. Mrs. Tree wanted lessons herself from Teach, but doubted Teach would accept her. It was a convenient passport for her to call Teach and draw her attention to this obviously talented kid. As it turned out, Mrs. Tree's inspiration was an act of destiny for Maureen and made her own hopes come true.

The passing years never softened Teach's idiom. When Daisy Tree first brought Teach and Maureen together, Teach's opening comments were as matter-of-fact as ever. "Right. Now let's hit a few and see what you can do." No how-do-you-dos. No pleased-to-meet-you. In Teach's opinion such refinements were a complete waste of time.

Teach was quietly impressed with Maureen, but not at all pleased with the fact the kid was left-handed at that time. There had never been a left-handed world beater among tennis women, and in Teach's logic Maureen would have to become right-handed if she were to interest herself in Daisy's "discovery."

o

But meanwhile Teach's solar plexus sent her the same message as it had about Alice Marble. Maureen could be a world champion.

So Teach agreed on a deal with Daisy Tree and began Maureen's training by spending countless hours making the youngster catch, not balls but racquets, with her right hand. What first appeared a reckless decision was soon acknowledged as a stroke of genius. In less time than some athletes need to get their first mention in sports columns, Maureen was already champion of the world.

Although I first met with Little Mo in Boston, the British press boys and the early postwar campaigners who came to the American circuit, had already given me exciting reports about her, very comparable to those one reads nowadays about Tracy Austin and Pam Shriver.

Betty Hilton, Britain's No. 1, returned to England after meeting with Maureen here and gave the English a totally revealing picture in two sentences. Meeting Maureen for the first time when she was fourteen, Betty, then aged thirty, introduced herself with her best British formality. "How do you do, Miss Connolly?" In reply, Little Mo had chirped, typically, "Hi, Betty!"

In the spring of '51 I was invited to make a personal appearance with my tennis designs at the Robert Simpson store in Toronto. In August I was invited back for a second week. On the way from London it was easy to stop off in Boston for the Wightman Cup matches.

America's leading player, Margaret Osborne, had recently married Willie duPont and was out of the team, but there were still four high-ranking Americans available right behind her, including the current Wimbledon champion, Doris Hart.

Hazel Wightman in person was captaining the American team. She always seemed to enjoy ruffling feathers, and on this occasion took the unprecedented step of selecting Maureen, ranked at the bottom of the American top ten, to play No. 3 spot in the Cup matches. Her gamble, in fact, paid off as Maureen scored a straightforward win over her British opponent, Kay Tuckey. This was the first explosion in her fireworks ascent to the top of the world.

I had not met with Teach Tennant since Alice Marble's triumphant night at the '39 Wimbledon Ball. At our Boston reunion Maureen rushed off to practice, and Teach was only too pleased to sit down with me and my business associate, Henry Turner, to fill us in on the details of her latest exciting find.

Teach was euphoric about the golden horizons she saw for Maureen. But she explained she also had problems. She was already thinking about Maureen's probable opponents in future years. She considered the world's leading players, Margaret duPont and Louise Brough past their best, and in Teach's mind, the ranking No. 3, Doris Hart, was already the one to beat for Little Mo.

At that time Little Mo was extremely cute with irresistible urchin-like appeal. Before she began beating the top players they all liked her. From Maureen's side, her idol was Doris Hart, but Teach was convinced that as long as this state of affairs endured, Maureen would never beat Doris.

Detailing her plans to make Maureen the world champion as quickly as possible, Teach startled Henry and me by telling us how she proposed to overcome Maureen's adulation for Doris. She was conceiving a number of cruel fabrications which she was about to represent to Maureen as Doris's opinion of her.

At the time, this strategy was successful, but in later years Maureen was to say that one of the major factors in her break with Teach was that Teach taught her only how to "win with hate," never for the love of the game.

Teach's unique success as a coach made her many enemies, but whatever was said about her in later years, she had an extraordinary instinct for strategic, psychological training of future champions.

Her forecast of Doris Hart's being the one to beat for Maureen took only two weeks to come true. The Boston hate campaign against Doris began in August. In early September Maureen found herself confronting Doris herself in the Forest Hills semifinal.

Throughout her life Maureen was (as Chris Evert is today) a fundamental baseliner. After five years domination by the trio of Brough, duPont, and Hart, the best serve-volleyers ever seen before Billie Jean King, it seemed inconceivable that any non-volleyer, let alone this tiny dynamo, could get her shots either past or over these Amazons.

But as Teach hoped, by the time Maureen took the court she aad come to despise Doris because of the things Teach had told her.

One important aspect of Maureen's breakthrough derived from her unique capacity to spoon-up precision lobs from what had been winning volleys to all the previous generation. Then Maureen would follow her lobs with devastating flat drives from both wings. It was these shots that showed all her newfound hatred for Doris. Her drives became arrows of destruction that could never have had the same damaging sting had she still considered Doris her idol.

In the windswept Forest Hills stadium Maureen shocked Doris and the world with a 6–4, 6–4 win.

That evening I wrote Jimmy Jones, editor of the magazine *British Lawn Tennis*, in whose columns I had so incensed Louis Greig. "I see

○

218   *Love & Faults*

J. Donald Budge, U.S.A., in play at Wimbledon, 1935. London News Agency photo

Eleanor "Teach" Tennant, a portrait.

Alice Marble winning Wimbledon, 1939. Fox Photos

Alice Marble (left), *with Tilden, Mary Harwick Hare, and Vincent Richards. Together they raised millions of dollars playing exhibitions in the United States during World War II.*

Alice Marble and Bobby Riggs dancing the "lap of honor" at the 1939 Wimbledon Ball after both had won all their events. Sport & General photo

Ted Tinling evening gown for Buckingham Palace presentation. Official regulations required a 12-inch train from the shoulders, the "Prince-of-Wales" (three white feathers) headpiece with white tulle veil, and 20-inch white kid gloves. Monica Merlin is seen here wearing diamonds by William Ogden worth $200,000 at today's value. This dress was chosen by five different London socialites at the 1938 palace presentation balls. From Ted Tinling's London Couture House, London, 1938. Copyright: Ted Tinling

The Duchess of York, subsequently Queen Elizabeth, now the "Queen Mum," and the Duke of York, subsequently King George VI, at Lady Crosfield's tennis garden party, 1924.

"The Way They Were," before Ted Tinling. Left: Joy Gannon (now Mrs. Tony Mottram, Buster Mottram's mother) with Mrs. Betty Hilton (now Mrs. Charles Harrison). Seen here in 1946.

A mannequin models the dress worn by Britain's No. 1 Betty Hilton. The shoulder and hem trim are sky blue. Mrs. Wightman successfully had the dress banned by the Wimbledon Committee after Mrs. Hilton had lost to Louise Brough in it in the Wightman Cup, 1948.

1949: "Gorgeous Gussy" Moran wearing the famous lace panties outfit. She added the color belt for the pic as all color was forbidden at Wimbledon that year.

←

"Gorgeous Gussy" returned to London for a store promotion to coincide with the first year of Open Tennis (1968). T.T. made this special outfit for her nineteen years after the original furor.

Beverly Baker of the United States is presented to Queen Elizabeth of England by Lady Crosfield (center). *Ted Tinling* (right) *waits to be presented.* Associated Press photo

Probably one of the most graceful players of all time: Maria Bueno of Brazil winning the Wimbledon final in 1960. London Sunday Telegraph photo

Queen's Club, London, 1952. Maureen Connolly had injured her shoulder that morning, 48 hours before the start of her first Wimbledon. Teach Tennant escorts her off the court after her win in the doubles final, which she had played very much against Teach's wishes.

Wimbledon, 1907. Left: Anthony Wilding (New Zealand) with Norman Brookes (Australia). Wilding, often referred to as an "Adonis," belonged to the Cambridge elite of an obsolescent society.

The Wimbledon Ball, 1952. Maureen Connolly, the champion, arrives unescorted. She had just split with Teach Tennant and was not on speaking terms with her mother. The T.T. ballgown is a mist-blue chiffon, with pink roses. News of the World photo

Maureen Connolly winning the 1953 Wimbledon final. The telltale strip of satin shows where T.T. tore the dress down the center at midnight the previous night.

June 11, 1955. Maureen Connolly becomes Mrs. Norman Brinker. T.T. made the nylon lace dress in London. TWA flew it to California in a special seat marked "Precious Cargo." Associated Press photo

Cleveland, Ohio, 1967. The last time I saw Maureen Connolly. Left to right: Ted Tinling, Maureen Connolly (in the taxi), Jesse Bell, Tony Moxham from England, and Mary Hardwick Hare.

Australia's winning Davis Cup Team, 1956. Left to right: Lew Hoad, Ken Rosewall, Harry Hopman (nonplaying captain), Ashley Cooper, and Neale Fraser.

Left: Lamar Hunt, the man who changed the face of men's tennis. Seen here with (left) Eddie Dibbs, runner-up and (right) Vitas Gerulaitis, winner, of the World Championship of Tennis, 1978. At center is Mrs. Lamar (Norma) Hunt.

Gladys Heldman, originator and organizer of women's independent tennis administration.

Nearly everything about Chris Evert is new to the '70s and was never seen in the first century of tennis: the two-fisted shot, the halter tennis dress, the purposely disarranged hairstyle. This picture combines them all. Russell/Kelly photo

Hotel Pierre, New York City, 1977. Left: Joseph F. Cullman II, chairman of the Board of Philip Morris Inc., presents a Virginia Slims trophy to Chris Evert.

The four who got it all together on the road. Left to right: John Granville, Peachy Kellmeyer, Ellen Merlo, and Ted Tinling. At extreme left is Mrs. Edy Ann McGoldrick, who originally worked in opposition to Virginia Slims. Russ Adams photo

Houston, 1973. Billi Jean King during h match against Bobb Riggs in Houston's A trodome. The T.T. dre is mint green. The bodi insert and her sneake are royal blue. T bodice embroidery forr the initials V.S. (Virginia Slims) in rhin stones and sequins. U photo

Billie Jean King in h early years at Wimbl don, wearing a Fre Perry "skirt and shir outfit of the '60s.

Vivian McGrath (Australia), 1933. The originator of the two-handed, sharpshooting shot from the left side. McGrath died in June, 1978.

Björn Borg (Sweden) holding the All England Lawn Tennis Club's silver-gilt trophy that he won in 1976, 1977, and 1978. Connors also won it in 1974, yet it is still inscribed "For the single-handed championship of the world (Gentlemen)." The trophy has been held by every men's singles winner of Wimbledon since the opening year (1877).

Wimbledon, 1972. The Wimbledon referee, Captain Michael Gibson, remonstrates with Rosie Casals over the design on her dress. She was sent off to change after the match had started, on the pretext that her dress "advertised" Virginia Slims. Syndication International photo

London, 1968. With the coming of Open Tennis in 1968, tennis stars could use their names to advertise for the first time in tennis history. Here Virginia Wade endorses a glamorous leotard. Terry O'Neill photo

ed Tinling's "star-studded stable" at a pre-Wimbledon showing of Tinling tennis designs. eft to right: Virginia Wade, Evonne Goolagong, Ted Tinling, Rosie Casals, and Billie ean King. Hyde Park, London, 1973.

Margaret Goatson Kirgin, ed Tinling's assistant for venty-one years, discusses creation for Billie Jean ing with Ted.

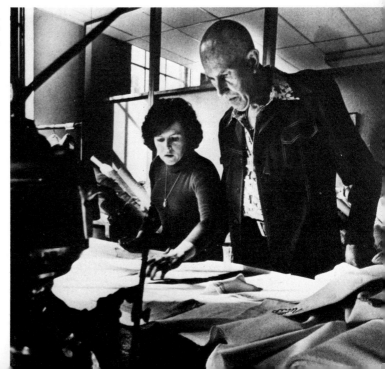

Martina Navratilova after inning the last Virginia lims championships (San rancisco, 1978). She is earing the "lucky dress" in hich she won seven Slims urnaments and the ampionship. She also ore it to win the Wimble- n 1978 final. It is the ress that has never yet been aten. Wide World photo

At one of Virginia Slims' memorable presentation banquets. Left to right: *Marilyn Fernberger, Ed Fernberger, Ted Tinling, and Nancy Jeffett.*

Tennis dress-designer's dream of the future. "Over 21" magazine photo

no reason why Maureen should lose a single in the next ten years," I told him.

After Maureen's shock victory Teach had tears of delight in her eyes. She was also excited because, in the final, Maureen had only to play Shirley Fry of whom Teach had a very mediocre opinion. On this subject, Teach and I had a heated argument. Having served my tennis apprenticeship in an era of incomparable baseliners, I have always known that a really sound baseliner much prefers playing a volleyer than someone of her own type of game.

Shirley Fry was a backboard, who ran and ran and returned everything. However, she rarely went for outright winners, and it was this defensive concept that made Teach derisive about her chances. "No one can win playing negative tennis," was her doctrine.

In fact, we were both right because Maureen, though she beat Shirley Fry in the final, had a marathon match and a very narrow escape. Marathons against Shirley Fry were to be repeated at intervals throughout Maureen's career.

On the surface Maureen's '51 Forest Hills victory as a mere sixteen-year-old was the start of a glorious rise to world fame. But underneath, she was quickly caught up in the treacherous emotional crosscurrents of stardom.

Her propulsion to sudden fame gave her a crash course in the facts of life. Almost within minutes of becoming the new American champion, Maureen, in the excitement of signing autographs, was tricked into signing a concealed check that was later cashed by a con man. This caused a lot of cynicism in her and made her very guarded against signing autographs for the rest of her life.

The dust had not even settled on her first major victory when she was shocked for a second time. Her mother, Jessamine, who had become Mrs. Bertse years before, reassumed overnight the name Connolly, obviously on the strength of her daughter's success.

Then came the third shock. As a result of Margaret Osborne's marriage, Teach arranged for Maureen to team up with Louise Brough. At the beginning Louise and Maureen were very friendly. However, at La Jolla in the spring of '52, the child prodigy with one major title had the temerity to beat Louise who had already won fourteen American and ten Wimbledon titles.

From then on Louise convinced herself that Maureen was her deadly rival. Maureen recounts that in their first hit together at Wimbledon a few months later, Louise was out to kill her, even in practice.

This sudden switch in Louise's attitude played right into Teach's

and accentuated her own plan of tempering Maureen into the
steel she knew would be needed for the road ahead.

Then the antagonism, which had been developing for some time
between Teach and Mrs. Connolly over Maureen's future, began to
assume problem proportions.

The two women's philosophies were polarized in that Teach clearly
saw in Maureen a repeat, if not an improvement, of her success with
Alice Marble. Mrs. Connolly, in absolute contradiction, saw her
daughter as a child being dragged out of her natural age group and
pushed relentlessly toward stardom.

The first major confrontation between Teach and Mrs. Connolly
arose over Maureen's initial trip to Europe in '52.

Because Maureen was still only seventeen years of age, Mrs. Connolly was still her legal guardian and was determined to use her right
to travel with Maureen to Wimbledon. She told Teach that if she did
not go along she would refuse permission for Maureen to go at all.

The familiar specter of tennis politics then appeared. Teach was
convinced that if Maureen was to follow the usual pattern of playing
the French championships before Wimbledon, she would most likely
lose both, so Teach ruled that Paris would be bypassed in Maureen's
first year in Europe.

As a result, both the USLTA and the French Federation filed
formal complaints that they were missing out on a valuable appearance of tennis's latest box-office star. Predictably, Teach held to her
theory, but only after bitter recriminations from all concerned.
Teach's determination to have the final say on Maureen's plans made
her as many new enemies among the establishment as it had in her
past association with Alice Marble.

Throughout the spring of '52 in London, I received letters regularly
from Teach explaining in great detail the schedule she was setting up
for Maureen's forthcoming visit. The prime reason for these letters
was that both Teach and Little Mo were determined I should take
care of her tennis clothes.

Teach always made her plans months in advance on the lines of a
military operation. So-and-so would happen on such-and-such a
date. Maureen's measurements were this-and-that and the parties
would arrive at the London airport on May 20 at 5:33 p.m.

A smiling photograph of Teach and Maureen leaving the plane at
London airport shows only the superficial happiness of anticipation.
Behind the smiles, many far-reaching problems were already
fermenting, and this photograph was, in fact, the last ever taken of
Teach and Maureen in harmony.

As Maureen came down the steps from the plane, a newsreel company asked me to pose with her. Remembering Teach's usual proprietary domination over her protégées, I said, "I hope Teach won't mind our doing this."

The effect was dramatic. From that moment on I was caught in the full force of the storm. Amazingly, the childish look left Maureen's face like a discarded mask, her eyes narrowed, and in a metallic voice I had not heard before but came to recognize later, she replied, "What I do is my own business." She was then seventeen and eight months.

Teach and Maureen's arrival at the London airport involved some rather unusual circumstances. Jimmy Jones was a prewar friend of Teach's and had also had letters from Teach about Maureen's forthcoming visit. Jimmy was an ex-British Davis Cup player, and we were good friends, having faced each other across the net at least half-a-dozen times on the tournament circuit.

On the night of Teach's arrival with the Connollys, there happened to be an important prizefight taking place in London, which Jimmy knew would attract at least ten thousand fans. Feeling this would be an opportune and complimentary way of introducing America's teenage champion to London, Jimmy arranged ringside seats for Teach, Maureen, her mother, and me.

I sat between Teach and Mrs. Connolly and instantly became involved in the obvious rivalry that had developed between them. Mrs. Connolly's suggestion that Maureen was tired after the long plane journey and should be in bed was the signal for immediate arguments from Teach over the relative importance of personal needs vis-à-vis public obligations.

Mrs. Connolly's hassle with Teach was becoming embarrassing, but was relieved by a brief moment of hilarity as Maureen was introduced to the audience. The MC, well on the way to being drunk, announced in his best fairground-barker's beery voice, "Laideez 'n Gennelmen, I wan year to meet a li'l lady 'ooze come all de way from de States for de Wimbledon tennis. Laideez 'n Gennelmen, I 'ave de pleasha of hinteroducin', Miss Maureen O'HARA."

Teach ordained that as Maureen's dress designer I should have preference the next day over all other business, and I was told to be at their London hotel for a 7 a.m. breakfast. When I arrived, a group of pressmen were already waiting in the lobby for the new celebrity to appear. As they pumped me for information, Teach swept Maureen past them with all the elegant disdain of a movie queen from the old school.

In the coffee shop it was immediately obvious that Teach was inadequately briefed about British postwar conditions. She ordered the traditional English breakfast of bacon and eggs for both herself and Maureen. At this distance it may seem remarkable that seven years after V-E Day bacon and eggs should not be obtainable in London, but they were not.

Helpfully, my manager rushed off to her apartment to collect some of her own egg ration for Maureen. Within minutes of returning she was off again to collect some towels. Teach wanted extra towels for Maureen's practice sessions, but with wartime restrictions still in force, none was available. These may seem trivial matters now, but Teach's unfamiliarity with the altered face of Britain was to have far deeper consequences before long.

Teach finally allowed the press boys their interviews with Maureen, and it was astonishing in those days to see so many well-known sportswriters focusing on an immature girl of seventeen. While everyone discussed and demanded every intimate detail of her past, her present, and her future intentions, Maureen would seem suspended in a cloud of oblivion. Her expression would denote meditation on faraway things, and one could have laid money on her not having kept abreast of the discussion.

Then, suddenly, something would be said that directly affected her or conflicted with her unerring instinct for what was right for Maureen, and she would spark instantly to life. Again the expression would change, the eyes narrow, and out would come some devastatingly relative appraisal in the metallic voice I first heard at the airport.

Maureen had a star's natural gift for dealing with the press. Her first practice hit at Surbiton, near London, attracted sixteen press photographers, and at one point she called to them, "Are you getting what you want, boys?" This instinct for what is now called Public Relations, disgusted the English purists, but her unexpected professionalism endeared her to the press.

Maureen's European debut at the Surbiton tournament produced another milestone in her career. After a long struggle she finally beat Pat Todd, her previous and ever-present stumbling block in America. I have always felt that had she not won this particular match she would not have won her first Wimbledon that same year.

During those early weeks in London I noticed signs of increasing unrest between Teach and Maureen. Naturally Little Mo was showered with all sorts of privileges and gifts. Teach obviously expected to share in these, but Maureen failed to see this, and friction quickly arose from these small details because of an already inflamed situation.

o

At the start, even the clothes I designed caused an embarrassment. My reputation had been built on properly styled garments. I made half-a-dozen outfits for Maureen that she and Teach appreciated with evident delight. Mrs. Connolly, however, was unenthusiastic and unconvinced. "It's odd," she said, "that when I made things like this for Maureen she would not wear them." I have never found it easy to reply to this kind of comment.

The Wightman Cup was scheduled for two weeks after Maureen's arrival. The American team of that year was probably the most disunited in history and split into three opposing camps.

In Margaret duPont's absence her close friend and partner Louise Brough maintained the keen rivalry they had always shown together toward anyone challenging their top-spot position. Doris Hart and Shirley Fry, a new team of young friends who had been nudging Margaret's and Louise's supremacy were also there. Into this already highly competitive situation came a third complication, Teach and Maureen. Under Teach's influence, Little Mo, the most junior of them all, quickly became the most dominating figure. With all six, and the nonplaying captain, Midge Buck, living in the same apartment block, antagonistic crosscurrents became as inevitable as the dawn.

Maureen's tennis worries began when the No. 1 English player, Jean Walker-Smith, suddenly soft-balled her with devastating effect in their opening cup match.

Once again I found myself pinioned between Teach and Mrs. Connolly, an error never to be repeated a third time. While Teach was grimly projecting graphic thought waves to her struggling protégée, Mrs. Connolly was constantly needling Teach. "I told you she shouldn't have come, she's too young," she kept repeating to Teach, and Teach no longer disguised her disgust.

Eventually Maureen won, but in the succeeding days the pressures on her and Teach, individually and combined, were enormous and aggravated at every point by Mrs. Connolly's refusal to accept the inevitable. Now at the heart of the maelstrom, Maureen found herself pulled in so many directions that she felt she was alone. Her loneliness was compounded by the bonds with her mother, who opposed Teach just as strongly as Teach opposed Mrs. Connolly.

With such emotional conflict between the three women, unity could not survive, and thereafter the cracks began to show very quickly. The train of events, which was to split Maureen and Teach irrevocably a few days later, was, in fact, already in motion.

The final, fateful blow, which would have submerged anyone with lesser spirit than Little Mo, came when she injured her shoulder in a practice hit with Louise Brough before the Queen's Club finals, only forty-eight hours before the opening of Wimbledon.

Teach called me at 11 a.m., completely distraught. "Do something, honey," she pleaded. "Something terrible has happened to Maureen's shoulder. She's in agony."

During Teach's London visits with Alice Marble in the late '30s, she had placed unshakable faith in a well-known chiropractor, Hugh Dempster.

Thirteen years had elapsed, but she asked me to alert him that Maureen needed immediate treatment. It was Saturday, and Dempster had already left for his country home, so I contacted Hugh Burt, the orthopedic director of one of London's top medical centers, the University College Hospital.

Maureen was rushed to Hugh Burt, and he diagnosed only a slight attack of fibrositis. He said this could easily be allayed by some weekend heat treatment. But by a curious and fatalistic coincidence, he was going on vacation that day and could not see Maureen again.

Meanwhile Hugh Dempster had been told on the golf course about my call and decided to sacrifice his Saturday so as not to miss the opportunity of including the new celebrity among his patients.

Teach was happy to take Maureen to see Dempster, but his diagnosis was the complete opposite of Hugh Burt's: a badly torn shoulder ligament. "The girl risks life injury if she plays again," Dempster warned Teach.

Maureen, exasperated by Dempster's diagnosis, wanted desperately to believe Hugh Burt, but Dempster's pronouncement terrified Teach who still had great belief in him. The question was: Which of the two Hughs was right?

Later, at Queen's Club, Teach was inundated with questions from an eager press.

Louise Brough was not reticent. "She's supposed to have hurt her shoulder," Louise was telling everyone inside the lounge, "but I can't help thinking what a great alibi she's got there."

Teach then made a serious tactical error. Instead of explaining the situation in detail and gaining press sympathy, Teach sat alone, outside on the terrace, her face with a thunder-cloud expression, muttering again and again, "I won't speak. I won't speak."

With Teach saying nothing and Maureen shut away in the locker room, reporters had little evidence to go on.

Louise's suggestion of an alibi was not completely outrageous. Maureen's narrow escape against Jean Walker-Smith had already brought hints that Little Mo's bubble could be burst.

Maureen defaulted the Queen's Club singles final, but then ap-

o

peared in the doubles final, validating Louise's suggestion as far as the press was concerned.

But through a fault in the main switchboard, as Maureen was dressing, she overheard a reporter calling in a story that she would not play Wimbledon at all.

Throwing a robe around her, Maureen rushed out of the locker room and threatened the reporter with dire circumstances if he did not cancel his story immediately. I doubt if he ever recovered from the shock of being confronted by a half-dressed teenager behaving like a bouncer ready to throw him out. Apart from illustrating the undercurrents of Maureen's character, this incident clearly demonstrated her determination to play Wimbledon, whatever Teach or any doctor might say.

The following day, Sunday, Maureen, Teach and Mrs. Connolly locked themselves in their apartment with the telephone ringing incessantly and half-a-dozen reporters camped outside their front door.

Maureen, who felt instinctively she did not have a severe injury, kept saying she was determined to play at all costs. Teach, terrified that Dempster's diagnosis might truly jeopardize Maureen's whole future, was nearly hysterical. Mrs. Connolly saw the whole situation as an opportunity to prove herself, repeating endlessly that their trip should never have taken place at all. Years later Maureen recalled that the events of this day brought her close to an emotional breakdown.

That Sunday night, on the very eve of Wimbledon, I had two phone calls within thirty minutes, the first from Teach, the second from Maureen.

"Against all advice," Teach told me, "this self-willed, headstrong, stupid girl will be playing Wimbledon. You must decide what she's to wear. Her shoulder is badly damaged. This will be her only appearance and probably her last match."

Maureen was next. It was midnight. In a remarkably calm voice she said, "When I play my Wimbledon match I shall need a warm jacket." I had to ask carefully, "Will this be your only match?" "Of course not," she said with scorching scorn in her voice. "But I thought you were badly injured?" I could picture the eyes narrowing. "That's what Teach thinks." The metallic tones were again unmistakable.

As I left the underground going to Wimbledon on Monday, the newsboys were all shouting "Little Mo doubtful!" I still believe that it was the newspapers, all declaring she was unlikely to play, which finally determined Maureen to compete.

Sometime previously Teach had already planned a few days' absence during the first days of Wimbledon to greet a close friend who was coming by ship from the United States, docking at Liverpool, a six-hour train journey from London.

In Teach's absence Maureen made her Wimbledon debut as planned. Against Mrs. Moeller on the grandstand court she won her match fairly easily and shortly afterwards decided on the action that was to change her whole life.

She marched alone to the secretary's office and said she wished to call a press conference.

In those days, this was an unheard-of thing for any player to do, let alone a junior. Even the most hardened journalists were startled when they heard of her summons.

They were startled even further when Maureen told them coldly that, henceforth, she would consider herself her own mistress and had no further intention of listening to Miss Tennant. "She does not represent my views," she added. "Anything she says is without my authority and I intend to play on through Wimbledon." All this was said in Teach's absence in Liverpool and without her prior knowledge. Mrs. Connolly was conspicuously absent from the whole scene.

Teach never really recovered from the shocks of those few days. On Saturday she had been aghast that the perfectly tuned machine she had built could break down. Now she realized that it could not only right itself but could go on without her. Little Mo, the "Automaton of Tennis," also proved to be automatic.

"I shall never understand why she could sell me short in this way," was Teach's heart cry. "Obviously I don't count any more. I have lost all affinity with her mental attitude."

Naturally I was deeply distressed by the course of events and embarrassed by not knowing the real depth of the chasm between them.

Would I still consult Teach about Maureen's clothes, or had Maureen also assumed authority in that department? All I knew was that they still shared the same apartment. I would have to wait and see how matters turned out before worrying about the following week's dresses.

Maureen's immediate future posed a more pressing problem for Wimbledon. The tournament director was besieged for answers by the press and the office staff inquisitioned hourly by the ticketholders.

Three of the top administrators of American tennis, Russell Kingman, Perry Jones, and Bill Kellogg, were at Wimbledon, but because of Teach's past belligerence toward all of them, they were too scared to speak to her in the early stages of the conflict. However,

○

immediately after Maureen disowned Teach, they approached Mrs. Connolly.

Maureen had already consulted two specialists. Perry Jones's proposal was that he would arrange a consultation with a third specialist, but with one condition: Maureen must agree in advance to abide by the decision of the consultant of his choice.

Little Mo's first reaction was expectable. She argued that she need not necessarily submit to anything or anybody. It took three hours of discussion to overcome Maureen's obstinancy, but her mother's pleadings and Perry Jones's reasoning finally won her over.

The third specialist was selected in conjunction with the Wimbledon committee. Maureen was taken "incognito"—in absolute and totally unnecessary secrecy—to see Dr. Knowland, the leading authority on physical medicine at King's College Hospital. The inevitable result of the secrecy was that, going to the hospital, she was shadowed and embarrassed by reporters in a convoy of cars who chased her right across London.

Maureen said later she felt her very life in the balance as she waited for the third specialist to pronounce judgment. Finally, his verdict was identical to Hugh Burt's. With the application of some intensive heat therapy she could play on at Wimbledon.

In her memoirs Maureen said she was already embracing Dr. Knowland before he finished his diagnosis. But being cleared to play Wimbledon was only the first obstacle. Now she had to climb over a series of difficult hurdles to survive.

In her third-round match Maureen came close to seeing her Wimbledon dream evaporate against the English international Susan Partridge.

Susan had carefully observed Jean Walker-Smith's near success in soft-balling Maureen two weeks earlier. Although the match was not played on the center court, Susan lost the first set easily from stage fright. But as soon as she recovered her composure she exploited Maureen's difficulties by slow-balling in exactly the same way. This plan enabled Susan to win the second set and lead 5–4 in the third set.

Maureen recounts that despite all the dramatics of her much-publicized split from Teach, from years of instinct she still looked for Teach's support and searched desperately for her in the stands. Instead, she saw only her mother.

It is widely accepted that minor injuries can be quite severely aggravated by nervous tension. At this point in the match Maureen seemed suddenly to become aware of her shoulder injury. In obvious pain she served double faults on both the first and third points of the tenth game. These brought her to within two points of defeat.

While all this was happening on court, there was a hilarious moment for me in the stands. After Maureen's second double fault a spectator directly behind me said: "What a silly girl. She obviously can't serve from the right court. Why doesn't she just serve every time from the left?"

In spite of this spectator's brilliant suggestion, at 15–30, Maureen served still another fault on her first serve. Somehow she managed to scramble the point for 30–all. A low moan rose from the gallery. The partisan crowd had eagerly anticipated the English girl reaching match point.

What then ensued can never be better described than by Maureen in her own story, *Forehand Drive*.

> For me, looking back on a brief span of star-rising, star-crossed tennis years, there is one dramatic moment when I knew this was my year, this was my hour, this was my time to become a champion. There could be no waiting. It was not the stuff of which headlines are made, but my heart knows a total stranger propelled me to the world championships at the age of seventeen.
>
> At 30–all, suddenly piercing the tense silence, a young voice rang out clear and bold: "Give 'em hell, Mo!" I stood stunned, paused, looked and saw a U.S. Air Force boy. His face was a flash of youth, shining and glowing with friendliness. I did not know him. I had never met him. But truly, in that second, I was lifted to the heights by a stranger. I smiled and said: "Thank you," in a fervent whisper.
>
> Truth can be stranger than fiction. If it seems incredible to believe one ringing cry of encouragement can turn the tide of a hopeless match, I say only: it happened!

Maureen's lifelong friend, newspaper columnist Nelson Fisher, originated the nickname "Little Mo," because he compared her "firing power" to that of the battleship "Big Mo," which frequently berthed at her hometown of San Diego.

In the Wimbledon semifinals, Little Mo had once again to face Shirley Fry. She was naturally apprehensive, and to make matters worse, the whole day's schedule was washed out by the rain. Nelson Fisher takes up the story of that day.

> The night before playing Shirley Fry, Maureen needed loosening-up after a long, rainy afternoon of tiresome stalling before a postponement was announced. Late in the evening Ted Tinling served as Little Mo's sparring-mate on the indoor wood courts of Queen's Club. Maureen vented a forty-five-minute stream of high-powered balls his way

but the man pounded them back on a continual run and also showed a dexterity of stroke which provided the American champion with a very good workout.

The result against Fry was devastating. Maureen won in straight sets, more easily than in any of their other encounters.

In the final Maureen faced Louise Brough, still her doubles partner but no longer a friend. Louise was out to regain the title she had won three times in succession in earlier years.

Maureen had never possessed a ballgown. In '52 it was inconceivable to attend the Wimbledon Ball in a short dress. Win or lose, Maureen intended to be there, so in the first week of Wimbledon she had asked me to create a special dress for her for the big night. To her delight I suggested a mist-blue silk chiffon that was to have a horseshoe spray of pink roses featured on a billowing skirt.

With the pressures of Wimbledon production in my workroom, the dress was only completed late on the morning of her final. In consequence, I had to take it myself to her hotel, and I arrived at 11:30, less than three hours before the start of her match.

In spite of the late hour I found no one in her suite. Apparently Mrs. Connolly had decided to take Maureen shopping with her. At noon Maureen and her mother returned together. Maureen snatched the dress from me, and in a matter of seconds both their characters were revealed to the utmost.

Maureen held the dress in front of her, inspecting it in the full-length closet mirror. She suddenly looked twenty years older. The eyes narrowed to slits and the voice became even more metallic than I had previously heard. "If I don't make the champion's speech in this dress tonight, " she said, "I SHALL TEAR IT TO PIECES."

I excused myself, saying, "I must leave you now. The car is already downstairs waiting to take you to Wimbledon."

There were less than two hours to go before Maureen's first Wimbledon final, the greatest opportunity of her life.

I never believed Mrs. Connolly had any comprehension of the situation surrounding her daughter. Even so, I was flabbergasted to hear her say to Maureen, "Honey, why don't we have a nice lunch here and go to Wimbledon later by cab?"

I did not wait for Maureen's reply.

Ninety minutes later she was on court against Louise, then playing her fifth singles-final at Wimbledon. Louise served for the first set, but Maureen managed to break back, and from then on she always looked a certain winner. The voice of the unknown stranger had projected her to the world championship!

For Teach, a moment of personal tragedy came at the Wimbledon Ball that same night.

A memory of the last Wimbledon Ball I had spent with Teach flooded into my mind. Alice, in her '39 champion's speech, then made a gracious and generous tribute to Teach, the woman who made her everything she was. This time the knife was twice twisted in the wound. In her speech Maureen made no reference whatever to Teach, and the added callousness of the praise she accorded to everyone else, down to the ballboys, was inescapable.

When the music started, Teach, sitting next to me, whispered, "Dance with me, honey."

As I made lame attempts at lighthearted conversation, Maureen and Frank Sedgman, the men's champion of the previous day, completing their lap of honor together, moved toward us. I saw a chance of breaking the intolerable tension, some hope that I could win Teach a friendly glance. Deftly, I piloted her to within inches of her erstwhile protégée. For a second their eyes met. Then Maureen turned coldly away.

Teach's irreconcilable break with Alice Marble had been shattering. Now she had to face another future alone. Twice she had given her all. Each time destiny, and her protégées, flung it back in her face.

[24]

Maureen

THE MORNING AFTER THE WIMBLEDON BALL MAUREEN WAS DUE to fly to Dublin for the Irish championships.

With her Catholic upbringing and her Irish ancestry she was very excited about this visit to her spiritual home. Within days in Dublin, she became such a favorite that most of the Monsignor Bishops and the Cardinal himself were keen to attend her matches.

Nancy Chaffee, an attractive and amusing American-ranked player, who often described herself as the "poor-man's Gussy Moran," was at Wimbledon in '52.

"Are you coming to Ireland?" Little Mo had asked her. "Are you crazy?" Nancy replied. "Do you think I'd play you where they'll put holy water on the balls?"

Before the tensions of the Wimbledon Ball, Henry Turner and I had already arranged to escort Maureen, Mrs. Connolly, and Teach to the airport for their flight to Ireland.

o

After Maureen's final snub to Teach the previous night, Teach had deep soul searchings about whether to make a break there and then, but she decided that for her "public face" she would go to Dublin with the Connollys. To avoid further publicity they maintained what Maureen later described as a "sham truce."

One of the most revealing insights into the complex contradictions of Little Mo's half-child, half-iron-willed-champion mentality, was revealed at the airport.

After winning Wimbledon the previous day, she had received her share of the official grant to the American team. This was fifty English pounds in cash, then the equivalent of two hundred and fifty U.S. dollars.

At the airport Maureen and I walked together toward the emigration booths. Henry was with Mrs. Connolly and Teach some twenty yards behind us.

Currency restrictions were then in full force, and as we reached the emigration officer, Maureen suddenly handed me, from her purse, the wad of ten five-pound notes she had received from Wimbledon.

"Please take these until we reach the aircraft," she said pleadingly. "If mother sees I have this money she will take it from me."

Once again the newsreel companies had obtained special permission for me to go with Maureen for final pictures near the plane (there were no "gates" in those days), so I was able to return her money unseen by either Mrs. Connolly or Teach.

In Ireland it was obvious that the scar had furrowed too deeply as the sham truce was terminated. Maureen and her mother came home to California, but Teach returned alone to London.

Although Maureen kept on winning, I believe she lost a little of her star quality after her parting from Teach. Though the supreme tennis skills were still there, the absolute confidence of stardom, which Teach infalliby imparted, seemed to have disappeared by the time she reached Forest Hills in '52.

Maureen's "kid-wonder" days were so focused on tennis she had no time or inclination to have playmates or to make friends of her own age.

For the first time in her life Maureen was playing the role of defending titleholder of a major championship. Yet instead of projecting the status she had earned from years of preparation and at great emotional cost, she looked more like a little girl lost. Without Teach's hour-to-hour counsel, she seemed disoriented and disconsolate. I remember she was so much alone she even passed the time helping out in a beauty shop.

o

Meanwhile Teach roamed around Forest Hills as aloof and alone as Maureen, avoiding conversations and greeting her few friends with only bluff, artificial joviality.

Nevertheless, in the second week of the tournament, and in spite of all that happened at Wimbledon two months before, Teach and Maureen had a momentary reunion. For a few fleeting minutes, the flame of success that illuminated their alliance for four years flared brightly once more. Maureen suddenly found herself facing defeat against Shirley Fry in the semifinal and in desperation turned again to her former friend.

The Fry-Connolly match was originally scheduled for the main stadium, but at the last minute was switched to the grandstand court. Shirley won the first set and was well on the way to winning the match when the tournament officials decided to move the girls to the stadium. They should have been there in the first place. It was one of those actions that tennis organizers decide upon without a moment's consideration for the players' feelings.

The switch unsettled Shirley's concentration. Once inside the stadium the match changed to a point-by-point struggle in which Maureen scraped the second set. Then in the ten-minute interval that was allowed in those days when women split sets, Maureen rushed straight to Teach's waiting arms in the locker room.

The ability to revitalize players and restore their confidence when in trouble, was always one of Teach's trump cards. In this moment of self-doubt Maureen found herself in dire need of Teach's magnetic influence and reassurance.

As soon as I saw this astonishing backtrack, I knew Maureen would make short work of Shirley Fry in the third set. In fact, she lost only one more game. To win the '52 American championships and retain her title, Maureen still needed Teach's help. I have always wondered if, at the time, Teach suspected this was to be their final moment of harmony.

Three weeks later Maureen and Shirley met again at Perry Jones's Los Angeles tournament. There, Shirley came closer to winning than ever before, taking the first set and having three successive match points at 8–7, 40–love, in the second.

I watched the match from a court-side box with my lifelong friend Elizabeth Ryan, and I remember saying to her, "The big season's over now, and if Maureen gets out of this on her own, she will never go back to Teach."

Elizabeth agreed with me. We were not being cynical, just acutely alert to the tennis facts of life. We were both convinced the Forest

Hills reunion was no more than a temporary expedient to overcome an emergency.

Maureen pulled the Los Angeles match out of the fire, beat Shirley Fry without Teach's help, and, unhappily, proved us correct.

Later that day a small gray-haired man walked up to Maureen and asked, "How is Jess?" Maureen, who thought she knew all her mother's friends, quickly forgot the incident.

After '52 I was one of only three or four people who managed to remain friends with both Teach and Maureen. Everyone declared themselves on one side or the other. I had known Teach through all her traumas with Alice Marble and could see she felt fate had again victimized her through Maureen.

But I was also able to follow Maureen's thinking. World tennis champions chasing world titles are lone, predatory hunters, and one should not expect them, at the same time, to be warm, loyal friends.

Yet two successive pages in my autograph book read as follows:

"Many thanks for all my lovely dresses. They inspire me to play better tennis. Always, 'Mo.'"

"After nineteen years it is still wonderful having old-home-week together whenever we meet. Love, 'Teach.'"

It was impossible not to admire the defiant, dominating spirit of both women. However, whatever Maureen's mental process in her actions toward Teach, I believe she could have achieved the same purpose with different methods.

The split with Teach left a vacuum in Maureen's life, and it was again Perry Jones who came up with a solution to her problem.

Jones was the czar of the Southern California Patrons Association that gave financial backing to Maureen's tennis. After Maureen finally beat Shirley Fry without Teach's help, Jones realized the hitherto implacable Connolly-Tennant association was finished once and for all.

But Maureen was still the top box-office attraction for the Patrons Association and an important source of its revenue, so Jones needed a new coach and a new chaperone for her without a moment's delay.

Harry Hopman, of Australian Davis Cup fame, had made repeated offers to help Maureen if she ever went to Australia.

Perry Jones had already planned a world tour for Maureen that would begin in Australia at the start of '53. He therefore decided that Hopman's wife, Nell, herself an international player, would be an ideal companion for Maureen. She would also be a reliable watchdog for the financial interests of the Patrons Association, so Jones set up a deal there and then with Nell Hopman.

In outlook, Nell was a striking contrast to Teach. Above all, she had a much softer, less professional, approach to life. Two years later Maureen confirmed this dramatically when she said Nell taught her to "win with love, not with hate."

At the start of '53 I received a cable from Maureen saying, "En route to Australia. Nothing to wear."

The coronation of Queen Elizabeth was approaching and I had already designed a Coronation Collection for New York Seventh Avenue reproduction. Inescapably this featured royal crowns, and when Maureen's summons came I still had crown trims on my mind. Almost automatically I put them on the dresses that were flown out to Maureen in Australia.

"Gee," Maureen said delightedly when she received the shipment. "Ted must think I'm a queen." The idea was only slightly premature. It was '53 when Maureen became Queen of Tennis by taking the Grand Slam of all the world's major titles. Seventeen years elapsed before Margaret Court became the only other woman to achieve this same feat.

After touring the Southern Hemisphere, Maureen and Nell made the Italian championships in Rome their first European stopover.

Nell was a compulsive sightseer. Her tour with Maureen took her to many famous places she had not previously visited, and in purposeful contrast to the manner in which Teach directed Little Mo's career, Nell arranged excursions, theaters, and a "dolce vita" in miniature to replace Teach's stern disciplines.

In Rome anyone could be excused for not concentrating on tennis.

For starters, Maureen was torn between her religion and her superstitions and could not decide whether to drop her coin in the Trevi Fountain before or after her audience at the Vatican.

The Feast of the Azaleas on the Spanish Steps usually coincides with tennis week. The Via Veneto and the Condotti are open invitations to spend money, and Roman evenings afterwards, at the Hostaria dell'Orso or Giggi Fazi, can be joys that have never been conducive to good tennis.

When Gussy first appeared in Rome in '50, the fans invaded her court for a closeup look, and a police guard had to be called.

When Maureen played her matches, Italian riot police were already positioned round the courts and sprinkled among the crowds to avoid a recurrence of such overenthusiasm.

The Italian championships are played in the famous Foro Italico—Mussolini's attempt to outdo the Caesars.

Fringed by cypresses, the dark terra-cotta of the arena contrasts magically with the royal blue of the sky. Marble terracing climbs toward almost constant sunshine, and the perimeter is watched over by twenty larger-than-life statues of civic dignitaries. Beyond the stadium the legendary hills of Rome zigzag in a blue haze, and the whole vista has a scented quality of romance only comparable with Provence.

The Foro Italico stadium court is the biggest in the world. It has also the slowest playing surface outside of Paris.

In setting up Maureen's '52 schedule, Teach showed her deep tennis insight by preventing Maureen from including Rome or Paris on her first trip. The contrast of unpredictable Wimbledon turf after hot sunshine and slow clay would be too great for any newcomer to absorb successfully at first try.

Whether because of the dolce vita distractions with Nell, or because of the unfamiliar, slow Roman courts, Maureen proved Teach's theory correct by losing the Italian championship to Doris Hart.

Henry and I met up with Maureen and Nell soon afterwards in Paris. We had long fashion conferences at the Hôtel Napoléon. At first these seemed strange without the constant presence of Teach. Nell, however, stepped readily into the role of friend and confidante. Henry and I took care to ensure that the subject of Teach was never raised in our conversations. Maureen gave no outward sign that Teach had ever played any part in her life.

In Rome, rumors were already buzzing that Maureen was in love. In Paris I certainly found her changed. Four national titles represented a tremendous fulfillment, and her previous brittle eagerness had blossomed into a glowing warmth. The transformation was accompanied by a mature and thoughtful interest in her clothes and new figure-consciousness. "I'm giving up chocolates and pastries to stay at one hundred and thirty pounds," she told me.

Although she denied being engaged, Maureen was wearing a square-cut amythest ring, the gift of Norman Brinker, the American Olympic equestrian whom she had met through her own passion for horses. In previous years Teach frequently complained that Maureen playing hooky to go horse-riding was damaging her tennis, though such pessimism was scarcely justified by her results.

As a motherly companion, Nell Hopman had all the qualifications needed to help a flowering teenager in the throes of her first love affair. As Maureen's business manager, on behalf of Perry Jones, she also kept a tight rein on the purse strings, sometimes to Maureen's

o

annoyance. The missing element was Teach's uncanny ability as a tennis coach, a quality Nell was never able to replace.

After losing the Rome final to Doris Hart, Maureen was very disturbed about her form and her inability to identify with the soft clay courts of Europe's mainland.

In desperation she recruited Fred Perry to advise her, and after hours of evening practice with Fred she would also come to me for long consultations, asking how the meteoric Suzanne Lenglen remained so supreme in these slow-motion conditions.

Maureen had good reason to be apprehensive because Doris Hart loomed between her and her first French national title. To reach the final she also had to beat Susan Partridge, the English girl who brought her to within a hairsbreadth of defeat ten months earlier.

Meanwhile, on St. Patrick's Day of that year, Susan had married the French charmer Philippe Chatrier, president of today's world-governing body of tennis.

Susan had an outstandingly beautiful figure, and I made her a very striking bridal for the ceremony at which nearly one thousand guests were present in England's Wolveringham Cathedral.

When Maureen met Susan in the French championships both girls were on cloud nine for their respective reasons; Susan just back from her honeymoon with Philippe Chatrier, Maureen at every mention of Norman Brinker.

Once again Maureen had a hard time, only beating Susan in a long three-set match.

Nevertheless the high drama and tension of the previous year were all gone. Maureen had already emerged from her youthful need for hate motivation. Little Mo was growing up fast and I doubt she would even have noticed, if, this time, an unknown voice in the crowd had cheered her to victory.

The confidence Maureen gained from beating Susan a second time carried her to an easy revenge over Doris Hart in the final and to the second leg of her historic Grand Slam.

After Rome and Paris, the tennis scene moved to England.

Maureen's youthful victory and her public confrontation with Teach the previous year aroused enormous press interest in her return, and I found myself inundated in advance with questions asking if her subsequent successes had changed her. "Had Maureen matured?" "Was she really in love?" "What would she wear?" So many journalists called me before her arrival, I decided on the unprecedented step of inviting all London's women editors to a special press reception to allow them to ask Maureen their questions in person.

More than a hundred writers, newsreel and television people, accepted the invitation. Many postwar journalists had never previously met a tennis star in the flesh. This was the beginning of the public's involvement in the real personality of sports performers instead of only their sensational aspects. In restrospect, it was the forerunner of today's accepted media routine.

With Maureen's incredible tennis record I was intensely conscious of having a queen on my hands.

Seeking a unique token of her supremacy, I devised a special logo symbolizing all Maureen's major championships in flowers: the rose of England, the Australian wattle, the American beauty rose, and the lily of France. Maureen had won the Irish championships in '52, so she insisted on the shamrock being included. I entwined the flowers around her initial "M," and partly because of its being coronation year in England, I surmounted the whole design with a crown.

The press reception was at London's socialite Empress Club, and I learned a hard lesson in what could happen on such occasions if each journalist does not get personal attention.

A girl cub-reporter was somehow squeezed out and had no contact with Maureen or me. The concept of such a press gathering was new, and if she complained to her editor she had not been able to speak to Maureen, I, as host, had only myself to blame.

The following day her paper, London's *Daily Sketch*, printed an irate front-page article headed: "Who Does She Think She Is?" Beneath Maureen's picture the caption said: "We call this disgraceful. The Crown is a symbol which should not be used to feed a star's conceit."

For days the usual flood of mail included several nasty anonymous letters. Naturally both Maureen and I were upset, and the dresses were instantly remade without the crowns.

After this initial upset, Maureen had warm and welcoming reports in the British press. I think all the journalists were relieved to find the metallic-voice tones and the unconcealed willfulness of the previous year had worn off.

Manchester in the north of England is one of the traditional run-in tournaments before Wimbledon, and soon we all found ourselves caught up there in the festive mood that pervaded England in that year of the Queen's coronation.

Nevertheless, we had one sad memory in Manchester.

Maureen and I were playing our matches on adjoining courts. Our matches happened to finish simultaneously, and we came off together laughing and happy, only to be greated at the entrance by reporters who told us of Bill Tilden's death.

Many of the young competitors in the tournament had never seen

o

Tilden, but such was their respect for his fame that only a handful of players turned out for the parties that evening.

Beginning in Rome, we had all been on the road for six weeks. The day after Manchester we converged as usual on London. In '53 there was the added excitement of the Coronation three days hence.

Nell and Maureen were given front-line seats on the coronation route from Buckingham Palace to Westminster Abbey, and remained starry-eyed from the spectacle all through Wimbledon.

Once back on the fast grass her tennis also seemed to fire, and in defending her Wimbledon title she lost only eight games in reaching the final.

Looking back, however, I think the '53 Wimbledon was probably one of the toughest I experienced. The pressures of my business were, fortunately, growing yearly. The aftermath of the press reception for Maureen also resulted in some new pressures.

With Perry Jones's financial backing, Nell was able to establish herself with Maureen in a comfortable suite in Grosvenor House. Life had never previously allowed Maureen a private sitting room in a hotel.

The anonymous letters she received about the crowns on her dress added to her sensitivity about her public image, and after discussions with Nell, it was decided Maureen would invite me to breakfast every morning in the suite. She would read her mail during breakfast. If there were any further problems in the mail I would at least be on hand to tackle these for her immediately.

Unfortunately my devoting so much time to Maureen sparked a flicker of jealousy from Nell, and for a time I thought I was back in '52 with Teach expecting to share in everything that was done for Maureen.

I reckoned that Maureen needed nine or ten outfits as she had nineteen possible matches at Wimbledon. Nell was unlikely to have more than six matches at most, yet she felt she needed a different dress for each match. As the likely champion-to-be, Maureen was naturally concerned about having a particularly beautiful ballgown in readiness for the champion's acceptance speech. As Maureen's official chaperone, Nell felt I should also provide her with an elaborate formal. Perhaps all chaperones are fundamentally alike, and my job again put me inescapably in the middle of an emotional tug of war.

For the third time in '53 Maureen faced Doris Hart in the final. Having regained her form on the fast grass, she was no longer having sleepless nights about playing Doris. This time it was my turn.

Maureen always chose new styles for each Wimbledon. By the time she reached the final she had invariably discovered one feature from

o

Maureen 239

each dress she particularly fancied. For the last day I would try to embody all her fancies in a single new design, which would not be made till the last moment.

In '53 we both decided on a high-necked design, but we reckoned without the weather. After a late practice on the eve of the final, Maureen came off sopping wet. "I just can't play in that high-neck dress tomorrow," she panted. "It's too hot, you've go to do something."

I realized it would be useless to argue, although the dress was already waiting delivery. It was Friday evening, and my staff, of course, had already gone home.

In a filthy temper I went back to my workrooms, hot and tired, and grabbed the dress. For speed, I ripped it right down the front. Only then did I realize there was not a scrap of the material left. By this time it was nearly midnight and I had nightmare visions of Maureen playing Doris in an old, soiled dress, and losing because of it.

Telling myself to keep calm, I tried to think. Eventually inspiration came. Finding an odd strip of white satin, I worked until dawn, stitching it to the torn edges and designing a low neckline.

That afternoon, when Maureen appeared for her final, a group of French journalist-friends who understood such things, rose to their feet and clapped. "*Bravo pour la robe!*" they chorused. It was very sweet music. Such near-disasters often made me wonder what the spectators would think if they knew all that goes on behind the outward facade.

Maureen beat Doris for the third leg of the Grand Slam in what many people still describe as one of the best-ever Wimbledon finals.

Then the two girls met once again, in the Forest Hills final in August. This time Maureen was unplayable. Her drives on both wings had tremendous power and seemed drawn, as if by a magnet, to the lines. I think this was the best match I ever saw Maureen play; so recently I was amazed on seeing a picture that revealed that there were less than three thousand spectators in the stands at the time.

This was Maureen's third American championship. She had won Wimbledon twice, the French and Australian titles once, but to be accorded the accolade of the Grand Slam, the news media required all these to be won in the same calendar year. Previously only Don Budge had achieved this. Now Maureen became the first woman to do so.

In the circumstances, I doubt if even the London press would have questioned the appropriateness of the crowns I had put on her dresses three months previously.

o

[25]

An Empire for a Horse

ALL HER YOUNG LIFE MAUREEN DREAMED OF OWNING A HORSE.

She had started regular horseback riding just as soon as her tennis brought in enough under-the-counter payments to pay for the expense. Teach, however, regarded all horses, and horseback riding, as a dangerous risk for her star protégée, and they would argue repeatedly about the whole subject.

In this respect Teach wasted her time. She could have realized, as she became familiar with Maureen's implacable obstinacy, that nothing she could do would keep Maureen away from horses. To Maureen, tennis was work. Riding was a relaxation that became a compulsive hobby. When I first came to know Maureen in '52, her greatest desire in life was to possess her very own golden palomino.

Teach's attempts to discourage Maureen's riding only resulted in Maureen's playing hooky from her tennis practices. The whole bitter

o

argument would begin again when she returned, and Teach would get very distraught.

But after Maureen won her first Wimbledon and retained her American title at the '52 Forest Hills championships, Teach was no longer a part of Maureen's life, and her good friends, the Nelson Fishers, arranged a wonderful surprise for her. Upon her return to San Diego, after Forest Hills, they, in collaboration with the local Junior Chamber of Commerce and another well-known horseback rider, Morley Golden, formally presented her with the thing she most wanted in life. Ironically, as it turned out, the golden palomino was called Colonel Merryboy.

Throughout the spring of '53, while Maureen was touring Europe with Nell Hopman and getting closer, title by title, to her eventual Grand Slam of that year, her mind was on other things: she was homesick for Colonel Merryboy and preoccupied almost daily about his welfare in her absence.

Neither Nell nor I had ever seen the horse, but Maureen chattered about it so incessantly we felt we knew every hair of its head. One day, at a dress fitting, even Nell was irritated into saying, "Maureen, why don't you skip Wimbledon, go back and take care of the goddam horse, because it seems like that's what you really want to do most." Nell's tart comment had the desired effect, and afterwards we were able to concentrate a bit more on the dress fittings.

Maureen's love affair with Norman Brinker was also blossoming at the same time, so it was remarkable, really, that with two distractions she was able to play the superlative tennis she did in completing her Grand Slam over Doris Hart in September.

However, once this was done, she had just one object in mind, to get back to Norman and Merryboy. Norman himself would probably be the first to agree that at that particular time no one was quite sure which of the two was uppermost in her mind.

I made the trip to California that fall, and almost within hours of my arrival, Maureen was calling to say that I had to come out and meet with "the Colonel."

We had lunch first at the Connolly home. I found Mrs. Connolly just as contentious as I remembered her from the '52 Wimbledon. There was even the usual embarrassing moment I had come to expect whenever Maureen and her mother were together. This time it was a Friday, and Mrs. Connolly was scandalized when Maureen helped herself from a casserole of meat that had been prepared specially for me.

Both Maureen and her mother were ardent Catholics, but Maureen had a special dispensation from the Pope to eat meat on Fridays before an important match.

Seeing Maureen help herself to the meat, Mrs. Connolly could not contain her indignation. "That's for Ted. You're not allowed to eat meat. You don't have an important match today," she remonstrated. Mother and daughter seemed just as polarized as ever, but Maureen just laughed. "Ted is my big match today," she said as she speared another sparerib.

After lunch Maureen drove me to Merryboy's stable. We did not even take the horse out, as she appeared overwhelmed with delight at just seeing her beloved pet. Moreover, the horse showed no particular delight at seeing her for as she went lovingly to feed Merryboy he tried to bite her. Again Maureen laughed off the incident saying, "He's just in a bad mood today."

In fact, nothing could really disturb her happiness at that time. She and Nell Hopman had just completed the first year of their association. Maureen had won every major title in the world except Rome, and Nell had been able to put in a very satisfying financial report to Perry Jones for his Patrons Association. A few weeks later Maureen announced her engagement to Norman Brinker.

Everything seemed idyllic, until, without warning, a stormy engagement period followed between Maureen and Norman. In that '53–'54 winter, Maureen's tennis enthusiasm suddenly lapsed alarmingly. Without Teach to insist on the daily practices both Shirley Fry and Beverly Baker finally broke Maureen's long winning spell.

But these upsets all disappeared with the spring. Perry Jones reappointed Nell as chaperone for Maureen's '54 tour. I was summoned to Paris as usual to discuss her new outfits, and in May the British journalists asked me to arrange a repeat of the previous year's press reception in London. There was only one problem. Harry Hopman had succeeded Fred Perry as Maureen's coach, so between them the two Hopmans now had complete control over Maureen's movements. When I met with them all in Paris, I became perturbed over Maureen's tennis attitude, and this led me to a head-on clash with Nell.

During the first four months of '54 Maureen's tennis had been in the doldrums. She was bored, listless, and worried over her lovers' quarrels with Norman. She had spent a lot of her time just out riding or drooling over her horse. So I decided to speak to Maureen myself. About tennis, for a change, and not just about dresses.

Between Paris and Wimbledon there were competing tournaments, in Berlin and Manchester. Nell had entered Maureen for

Berlin where there was no suitable opposition for her at all. All the top names were going to Manchester to familiarize themselves in good time with England's wet turf.

I reminded Maureen of her lack of match practice. I told her that if she went to Berlin she could conceivably find herself playing Louise Brough or Doris Hart for the first time that year in an important Wimbledon match. Without any proper preparation she might have a bad time and no chance of recovery.

Maureen's reply was immediate and forceful. "I'm playing Manchester." Nell had never been to Berlin and made no secret of her disgust at my intervention.

What happened later completely vindicated my contention. In Manchester, Maureen met and beat both Louise and Doris. In the '54 Wimbledon final, the exact situation I had imagined occurred. Suddenly Maureen found herself 2–5 down in the second set to Louise, but with the Manchester tests successfully behind her, she was able to come back and win without the anxieties of a third set.

Within fifteen minutes, she came to tell me she felt she owed her ability to win that match to my advice. As this final became the last championship match she was ever to play in her life, I was glad I had spoken up.

Maureen was still only nineteen. Yet within seventeen days of her third Wimbledon title, her whole tennis career would be terminated by an accident involving Merryboy.

On July 20, out riding with a party, Merryboy was frightened by a speeding truck and threw her against it, breaking her right leg and severing all the muscles in her calf. Maureen was in the operating room for four hours and under heavy sedation for four days. Teach had been right about so many things, and so often Maureen had been unwilling to listen.

Maureen sued the trucking company for damages. Her comeback was long and painful, but, as always, Maureen refused to acknowledge defeat.

Her recovery began with such simple exercises as picking up marbles with her foot, then progressed to ballet class and eventually to some minor tennis hits. Her mind was always fixed on her future. She said she planned to defend all her titles in '55 and, in '56, would turn professional.

In January '55 I heard from Nell that she was meeting with Maureen as usual in April, and they expected me to meet with them again in Rome or Paris to discuss Maureen's dresses.

Later Nell recounted her full horror on receiving a late-night call in

Australia, from Perry Jones in Los Angeles, telling her that Maureen would never play tennis again. She had experienced a total setback in her recuperation.

In the subsequent court case it was said the accident prevented Maureen from earning substantial sums of money as a professional. Eventually, after years of legal argument, the trucking company was ordered to pay her $100,000. By today's reckoning this would be closer to $500,000.

In March '55 I received a letter from Maureen telling me she expected to marry Norman Brinker within three months and asking me to send some sketches for her wedding dress. She also told me of a strange incident that occurred while she was in hospital. A visitor was announced, and she was surprised to see that this was the same man who had asked about her mother two years previously. A few words revealed him as Martin Connolly, ex-U.S. Navy boxer, her father. All her life she had been told he was dead.

Maureen's marriage took place on June 11. Meanwhile in London I made her what I still think of as one of the most beautiful bridals of my career. The fact that she invited me, from six thousand miles away, to make the dress for the biggest day of her life, aroused so much interest that Trans World Airlines offered to fly the dress to California. The huge box, marked "Precious Cargo," was even given a special seat.

After the stormy beginnings of Maureen's engagement to Norman, their marriage developed into a life of complete happiness. Their first home was in San Diego. Later they moved to Arizona and eventually to Dallas. While Maureen was rearing two lovely daughters Brenda and Cindy, Norman was establishing a nationwide restaurant chain. Today, his Willow Bend Polo stud, near Dallas, has taken him to even greater success.

The damages awarded to Maureen in the court case were eventually agreed on, and the settlement brought the final contact between Maureen and Teach. Teach's summing up of the incident reflected the five years of pent-up bitterness she has experienced. "A brief phone call, a brief visit, and a check for a small sum left on my dining-room table." To many of us this was a tragic last happening in the interplay of two forceful characters, both raised by each other to the highest peaks of success by their onetime mutual respect.

In Dallas Maureen resumed short sessions of tennis and eventually became a much sought-after coach. Dallas also brought her a new partnership of lasting significance. There she met with Nancy Jeffett, a former nationally ranked junior from St. Louis. Together they organized clinics and exhibitions—anything that would help the development of junior tennis. Their aims became so closely identified they decided to work together, and as a result the Maureen Connolly Brinker Foundation was formed.

In the years between '63 and '71 the Wightman Cup matches alternated between Wimbledon and Cleveland, Ohio. When Britain's Ann Jones became captain of the British team, one of her first actions was to induce Maureen to become the official coach to the British girls.

In '65 in Cleveland I was honored with the Marlboro Award and was particularly pleased to meet with Maureen again on a day-to-day basis, after a ten-year lapse. We discussed old times, of course, but without ever mentioning Teach. Maureen was as bubbling and effervescent as ever, and she was still wearing the square-cut amethyst ring which had told us so much about her first blossoming way back in '53.

However, at the '67 Cleveland matches, I thought I detected some loss of Maureen's customary bright eagerness. The following day Ann Jones confided the news that Maureen had cancer. Two more years were to elapse while she conducted a gallant but losing struggle against a terminal illness. She died on June 21, '69, two days before the beginning of the Wimbledon championships she was expecting to attend as a writer.

In recent years I have met regularly in Dallas with Cindy and Brenda Brinker. Both girls only know from hearsay about Maureen at the height of her fame, and they question me about her relentlessly.

How to sum up a child who hit the tennis world with such blinding brilliance, so young and for so short a time?

The compelling human angle was the transformation of her psychological make-up, which took place when she switched from Teach's to Nell Hopman's influence. Maureen's early story paints an angry picture of her success years with Teach, when every shot was an assassin's dart, and she was taught to hate, loathe, and destroy.

This may well be true, but I do not believe any deal in life can be altogether one sided. Maureen would never have submitted to Teach's doctrine had she not also believed in it herself, however subconsciously.

There is no doubt that Teach's methods, however distasteful they seem in retrospect, took Maureen to her initial successes. Nell taught her to love. Simultaneously destiny provided in Norman Brinker the ideal partner for a more adult approach to life.

At my first meeting with "Little Mo," when she gave the inescapable impression of being an automated toy, she was sixteen.

How to explain that underneath the childish, giggling facade, there was a tough, iron-willed, and ruthless prodigy?

o

Designing her tennis wear, I decided to focus entirely on all the kiddy features that were appropriate to the lovable side of her. The inner ruthlessness and the iron will could best be illustrated, I thought, by the results on the scoreboard.

Alison Adburgham, one of London's best-known women editors at the time, perceived all this with great insight when writing about Little Mo's dresses in her Grand Slam year: *"It is touching, reassuring, that this teenage girl, already at the pinnacle of world fame, should find delight in little things, in little cats with smiles, in furry poodles with sequin eyes, in dainty birds with fly-away wings which quiver as she runs."*

These were the kiddy trims I chose with deliberate care to show the world that Maureen was, at least in part, a lovable young person regardless of her merciless dismissal of Teach and her determination to crush all opposition.

But all this is long ago, and with confidence acquired through an idyllic marriage to Norman, Maureen became a loving and warm person.

There could be no more fitting memorial to her than Nancy Jeffett's devoted work for the Maureen Connolly Brinker Foundation. Maureen would be proud of its achievements.

[26]

Southern Cross

FROM 1900 TO THE PRESENT DAY A SILVER TROPHY KNOWN AS THE Davis Cup has been the supreme award in international tennis. Each round of the annual competition is composed of four men's singles and a men's double.

At the time of writing only seven countries have won the Davis Cup in the seventy-seven years of its history. For fifty of those years the trophy has been proudly shared exactly twenty-five times each by the United States and Australia. Britain has won it nine times and France six. South Africa, Sweden, and Italy have one victory apiece. The campaigns were halted for nine years by the interruptions of the two world wars.

The Davis Cup, in its original state, was an elaborate rose bowl boasting a content of 217 troy ounces of sterling silver. It was the brainchild of Dwight Filley Davis who donated it for the purpose of

○

bringing the nations of the world together on a tennis court. I met with Davis frequently.

As a young man in St. Louis, Missouri, Dwight Davis, who was born on July 5, 1879, had the conviction that of all the sports, tennis could be played universally and be the best medium for the spread of goodwill among nations.

At the age of twenty-one he quantified his beliefs by offering the Cup to the USLTA. It soon became popularly known as the Davis Cup. Today more than fifty nations campaign annually in quest of his Cup. It is the most widespread annual event in any sport.

In the sixty-eight playing years of the Cup, eighty-nine men have represented America and fifty-four Australians have crusaded against them.

From this long procession of talent, the most outstanding role on the courts was undoubtedly played by Tilden. Big Bill figured in every Davis Cup final, or Challenge Round as it was called in those days, for a decade. Out of twenty-eight individual matches he won twenty-one for the United States.

Big Bill's story is covered earlier in this book. But what of the great Australians?

The panorama of Australia's Cup battles has been dominated by two men, Norman Brookes and Harry Hopman.

By an extraordinary coincidence, my life and the lives of these two masters of Australia's tennis fate, all came together on the same day. This was at the Easter tournament in Monte Carlo in '28. I was in charge of the tournament because my boss, George Simond, was sick.

In '28 Brookes was already fifty-one and no longer on the selectors' list. He was traveling as adviser to the official Australian team. Harry Hopman was making his first tour as a team member. He was twenty-one at the time.

That particular Australian crusade brought the historic overlap of these two men's dynamic careers and a memorable moment for me, meeting with them both simultaneously. Brookes was a legend; Hopman was to become one.

In 1907 Brookes had been the first overseas visitor ever to win the Wimbledon men's singles championship. I had heard my parents mention his name a hundred times.

The newcomers to the '28 Australian team in Monte Carlo were Harry Hopman and Jack Crawford. They had still to earn their spurs, and their names were almost unknown outside Australia.

I have often wondered what crossed the minds of these five tough

Aussies when confronted with a tournament director still in his teens. But whatever their initial thoughts, the week ran smoothly and began a long and happy association for me with countless future Australian friends.

Norman Brookes was the father of Australian tennis, and many years my senior. Those whose experiences I have shared were his successors. The list is a long one—inevitably so, because it records exactly half a century of happy memories.

Chronologically I recall Brookes, Patterson, Hopman, Crawford, Quist, Bromwich, McGrath, Pails, Brown, Sidwell, Sedgman, Hoad, Rosewall, Cooper, Fraser, Emerson, Newcombe and, probably the greatest of them all, Rod Laver.

Perhaps my longest association was with the Brookes family.

Sir Norman and Lady Brookes originated in the "Upstairs" era of tennis. Their house was one of Melbourne's most beautiful residences. They frequented all the palace hotels of the Lenglen coastline and, in the late '20s, spent the whole summer season at Le Touquet with their three daughters, Cynthia, Hersey, and Elaine, who were my contemporaries.

I shared in a few fun tennis games with Sir Norman at Le Touquet and remember him as dour and serious outwardly, but with a sense of humor as sharp as his left-handed angled volleys.

At times he would regale us with accounts of his early campaigns in Europe when the long journey from Australia took six or seven weeks by steamship, and Lady Brookes would go in search of Pacific pearls at every port of call.

In the '30s Hersey and Elaine Brookes both married Londoners, and it seemed natural that on being presented at the Court of St. James's, Elaine should ask me to design her dress for Buckingham Palace.

My association with the Brookes family continued when Lady Brookes lent her all-important patronage to the charity showings of my collections in Melbourne in '53.

In pre-World War I days, Brookes's regular partner was another legendary player of my parents' time, young Tony Wilding, of New Zealand, who was killed in Flanders.

Along with Brookes, young Wilding had captivated Edwardian tennis. At Wimbledon they won the men's singles title six times between them from 1907 to 1914. The Beautiful People were first represented on a tennis court, when Wilding, described by many contemporaries as an "Adonis," reached the 1914 Wimbledon mixed-doubles final with Marguerite Broquedis, so often described as a "Goddess."

o

Wilding's good looks, his charm, and his premature death on the battlefield have made him a part of lawn tennis folklore and link him inescapably with the hero of British Edwardian poetry, Rupert Brooke.

Both Wilding and the poet Brooke were revered graduates of Cambridge University, an elite flowering of fin-de-siècle sophistication. Wilding was Brooke's senior by four years, but both died as soldiers within sixteen days of each other in the spring of 1915.

A Young Apollo golden haired, stands trembling on the brink of
    strife,
Magnificently unprepared for the long littleness of life.

In 1918 my family and I lived for a while in a beautiful residence in Cambridge while my brother, Collingwood, was at Jesus College there. The house belonged to the British poetess Frances Cornford. Her epitaph for Rupert Brooke, which I recall here, seems an apt eulogy for both Brooke and Wilding, a tragic glance at an already obsolescent society.

At Wimbledon's reopening after World War I, Norman Brookes lost his title to another Australian, Gerald Patterson, who was to become enamored of Suzanne Lenglen and won the mixed-doubles championship with her.

To sufferers of tennis elbow, it may be some consolation to know that in talking to Gerald Patterson in Melbourne in '53, he told me that even at the peak of his playing career he had never played a match without being in pain. At the time we were watching the masterly ease of Ken Rosewall's backhand. No doubt Patterson was remembering the brute strength of his own ungainly cannon-ball technique and the price paid by those early players for their lack of instruction and proven techniques to emulate.

Jack Crawford was another tennis sufferer. He was a chronic asthma case, and during his center-court matches at Wimbledon would always ask me to take a pot of tea on a tray to the umpire's chair after the third set of a five-set match.

Jack was also an anachronism in appearance. Even winning Wimbledon in '33 he still favored the old square-topped racquet of Victorian days and never rolled the long sleeves of the cream flannel cricket shirt he wore for tennis, until the going got really tough.

Nowadays I can never watch Jimmy Connors, Chris Evert, or Bjorn Borg, without remembering the originator of the two-handed game, young Vivian McGrath from Sydney. He was seventeen when he first startled Europe in '33 with his two-handed stroke.

o

Probably Adrian Quist's greatest claim to fame was his long partnership with John Bromwich. Together, Quist and Bromwich won their own Australian championships no fewer than eight successive times and won the American championships in '39.

Together, they won the Davis Cup for Australia that same year. The match was in my home city of Philadelphia and finished on September 5, two days after Britain and Germany were at war.

By another coincidence, Australia was also playing in Pennsylvania when World War I was declared. On that occasion the circumstances were even stranger because the Australians were playing the Imperial German team, and the two countries formally declared war against each other while their Davis Cup match was still in progress.

Before '39 Brookes was the dominating force in Australian tennis. Hopman was appointed captain of the Australians in '38. The Australian Davis Cup victory over the United States in '39 marked the switch from Brookes's to Hopman's reign. Hopman picked up the scepter overnight and ruled as a dictator for the next twenty-nine years.

At the first postwar Wimbledon in '46 I resumed my Call-Boy duties, although I was still to be in uniform for another year. Physical reminders of World War II could be seen on all sides. Sixteen bombs had been dropped on the Wimbledon Club while Norah Cleather was in charge and living in the secretary's cottage on the grounds.

The men's locker room still bore a warning notice that read: "Gas Casualties—Men."

In '50 Harry brought the Australian Davis Cup team to Wimbledon.

In the Brookes era the atmosphere of the team resembled that of a gentlemanly cricket eleven on their way to a Saturday afternoon match in an English village. Harry's spartan approach went to the other extreme. He demanded long hours of preliminary workouts, tactical talks, rigid codes of behavior, and instituted a system of fines for any team member breaking his rules.

In the public relations area, all journalists were refused direct access to any of Harry's players. All his team members were instructed to reply "No comment, see Hop," to a point where this became a joke answer throughout the tennis community.

Harry seemed to have modeled himself on Field Marshal Montgomery in charge of the Desert Army. As for Montgomery, I can speak with experience. When he was appointed commander of the Army formation in which I was serving in '41, we were immediately ordered on a hundred-mile forced march in full combat equipment, and I often felt Harry would have found this same torture suitable for his tennis team.

o

Even in '50 it was almost impossible to obtain proper tennis shorts. Many players resorted to surplus Navy issue, and quite a few asked me to help out with their problems.

In England fabrics were still rationed, and restrictions on the manufacture of all garments were still in force. Both these problems disappeared on my '51 trip to America, when I had a New York tailor make up some shorts in a new fabric by American Celanese, which seemed ideal for the purpose.

Harry was always very concerned about the appearance of his team. In fact, legend has it that in the days of the long steamship journeys, when evening dress was de rigueur in the dining saloon, Harry had one junior member of his team locked in his cabin for refusing to wear his tuxedo for the dinner ritual.

In '51 Frank Sedgman became the first-ever Australian to win the American championships in the seventy years of its history. He became the golden boy of that era, and in '52 Harry asked if I could make Frank some tennis shorts that would fit him properly.

In May '52 I was playing a match on the court next to Frank's in one of the British circuit tournaments. Our matches finished together, and I thought it an appropriate moment to ask if he would like to have my shorts for the forthcoming Wimbledon. His answer was expectable. "No comment, see Hop."

The following week I was drawn in a mixed doubles against Frank and his lovely wife, Jean, and I repeated the question.

Frank quickly disappeared into the shower, but on emerging, and without further preamble, he signified his agreement with one simple question: "Gotta tape?" he asked. I often thought that two nude men going through a measuring routine in the locker room would have been a prize picture for any photographer.

This incident actually made history for me because Frank won the '52 Wimbledon, twenty-four hours before Little Mo, and thus became the first of the twenty-one singles champions I have dressed there.

The year '53 brought the advent of the first drip-dry fabrics to England. The idea of having no more worries with laundries was immensely appealing to the globe-trotting Aussie boys, and I made nylon shorts for the four Wimbledon doubles finalists of that year, Hoad, Rosewall, Hartwig, and Rose.

However, the Wimbledon corridors still echoed with the accusations of transparency suffered by Beverly Baker, and Harry developed a sudden fear that the nylon shorts might be transparent.

Fifteen minutes before the doubles final of that year, Harry gave a good imitation of Hazel Wightman by ordering all four players to change from their shorts to something more "decent." Only Mervyn Rose, always a maverick and eventually to be the first rebel against Harry's spartan regime, refused. I must record that Rose's nylon shorts did not cause the slightest criticism.

A few months later I was in Melbourne for the famous Davis Cup match when the two eighteen-year-olds Hoad and Rosewall were selected—the youngest team ever to be given this honor.

I knew they would like some new shorts for the great day, so I cabled my London office and four pairs were specially flown out to Melbourne.

I collected these myself from Essendon airport, and after obtaining at least three permissions from Harry to visit with the boys at the Australia Hotel, and three more before being allowed to speak to them, I delivered the shorts to Ken and Lew personally. They were delighted and romped around the room like kids with new toys.

Tony Trabert captained the American team. His after-match speech was appropriate: "We were beaten by two babes and a fox."

It was this reputation that enabled Harry and his teams to win the Davis Cup for Australia fifteen times in the next nineteen years.

In '26 I played Toto Brugnon, and in '30 I played Bill Tilden. In '48–'52 I played Sedgman, Bromwich, Brown, and Sidwell, but I still hoped for the opportunity of playing the current Wimbledon champion Lew Hoad.

The chance came in '57 in the second round of the Manchester tournament before Wimbledon. The men's singles had a 64–draw, and from the whole total, fate had given me the only unknown player, the one man I was sure to beat.

So much for being overconfident. My opponent turned out to be a dark horse, and before long I found myself 3–6, 0–5, 15–40 down. I remember my feelings of rage, mixed with frustration and despair, at missing the long-awaited opportunity of playing Lew. But somehow a miracle happened. My guy's game suddenly fell apart, and I scrambled home in the third set.

I was already forty-seven. Britain's young squad, Michael Davies, Tony Pickard, and Billy Knight, were all buddies who looked on me as their Dutch uncle and were laughing their heads off at the prospect of my arena court match with Hoad.

The whole affair was wild. Lew, of course, toyed with me at will. But at 1–1 in the second set I managed to break Lew's serve with a lucky net cord on game point. Thereupon Tony Pickard leaped to his feet in the stands shouting, "Come on, fella, you've got the break. You've got him now!" There were about 2,000 spectators. Including mine, there were 2,001 good laughs.

o

Lew was always an easygoing tennis phenomenon. Worldwide success did nothing to disturb his disarming simplicity.

After winning Wimbledon for the second time in '57, he wrestled all night with the decision whether or not to turn pro.

Then from Wimbledon's sacred and still strict amateur precincts he called Jack Kramer in Los Angeles. "Is the pro option still O.K.?" he asked.

"Yes," said Jake.

"Right, I'll fly tomorrow."

Late that night I left the celebration party at his apartment only to return early the following morning to deliver the dress his wife, Jenny, had ordered from me for the Wimbledon ball.

Jenny was up and about, but shadowy forms from the night before were still huddled on couches around the room.

After a time Lew emerged from the bedroom, wearing only a towel, a picture of idealized, blond athleticism. "You've had a wonderful press, Lew," I said enthusiastically. "Everyone's said you played the greatest . . ."

He cut me short. "What's Peanuts doing today?" he asked. Grabbing the papers, he ignored all the reports of his win and settled down to his favorite comic strip.

In those days Hopman seemed to have call on an inexhaustible well of tennis talent. Perhaps he created it, because no sooner had Hoad and Rosewall turned pro than the young generation of Cooper and Fraser emerged. Fortunately for me, they emerged as my clients, carrying on my association with Australia, which dated back to 1928.

Even Harry's already marvelous array of talent was leading to a climax of supremacy in the '60s with the coming of Laver, Emerson, Stolle, Newcombe, and Roche.

Consequently, it was always a source of amazement to me that Harry fought tooth-and-nail against open tennis. Had it been the old, gentlemanly world of Norman Brookes, his attitude would have been altogether consistent.

But Harry had no pretense to being from the privileged Brookes background. At heart he was a tough, hard-hitting, hard-working pro himself, and it was an uncomfortable paradox for him to resent anyone else exhibiting the same qualities.

With the coming of open tennis in '68, Harry seemed to lose interest in his long crusades for the Davis Cup. By a strange turnabout, Harry has now joined the professional ranks in the United States. As a teaching pro, he conducts one of the most successful tennis camps in this country.

Coincidentally, many of the later characters in this panorama have responded, like myself, to the glitter of the Star-Spangled Banner.

Laver, Newcombe, Hopman, Emerson, Stolle, and I now live in the United States. Our happy association still continues. When Larry and Billie Jean King launched World Team Tennis in '74, Fred Stolle was the coach, and for first night of the new tennis format Dick Butera, the owner of the "Philadelphia Freedoms" team, invited me to design their uniforms.

In '77 Fred Stolle, then the coach of the New York Apples, piloted his team to victory, and for two years the uniforms of all the women team members were my responsibility.

Destiny seems determined that I should never be in an "Auld Lang Syne" relationship with Australian tennis stars. In '76 and '77 Australia's TV Channel 7 invited me to join them for nationally televised tournaments in Sydney and Melbourne, and I found myself on the same commentary teams as Neale Fraser and John Newcombe.

The year '78 was the fiftieth anniversary of my simultaneous meeting with Norman Brookes and Harry Hopman.

However contrasting their personalities, these two inspired a glorious era of Australian tennis. Without their sixty-one years of crusades for the Davis Cup, the history of tennis would not be the same.

[27]

You Came
a Long Way, Baby (1)

IN 1879 A MEMBER OF THE ALL-POWERFUL, ALL-MALE TENNIS CLUB at Wimbledon, England, offered a trophy for a ladies' championship event.

The club committee rejected his proposal. Stunned by the rebuff, the member responded in the best Victorian English. His words were prophetic: "I cannot but think the committee ungallant in passing by the ladies. They will, I think, come in time."

History may one day decide whether the first-ever lawn tennis tournament took place in Nahant, near Boston, Massachusetts, or in the Birmingham area of the English Midlands. There is evidence for both cases.

But it is not contested that, in 1877, Wimbledon staged the first championship in the world. It was for men only, and the all-male committee of the day intended to keep it that way.

○

In 1879, the year of the Wimbledon members' proposal that a ladies' event be included there, the first Irish championships were arranged.

The spirited Irish ladies, much less passive than their English counterparts, frightened their men into submission and were permitted a singles championship of their own.

Accordingly, the first tennis championships ever to include women took place in Dublin. The women were even granted a doubles event with the men. This was considered so strange it needed the program to explain that "mixed doubles is an event where a Gentleman is partnered by a Lady."

Shamed by the success of the Dublin innovation and taking five years to absorb the shock, Wimbledon eventually capitulated and allowed ladies in their championships in 1884.

But after this initial breakthrough, successive Victorian and Edwardian women asked no more of their men than permission to compete. They were even flattered if a man deigned to call one of their matches.

Even forty years later, in the '20s, when Suzanne Lenglen dared question the conduct and administration of the game, she was indignantly rebuffed by both the French and British establishments. In the '30s Helen Wills sometimes had difficulty in finding the finance necessary to achieve her all-time Wimbledon singles record. The blazing confrontations between Mike Myrick and Teach Tennant, in defense of Alice Marble, have become a part of tennis history.

The end product of this chauvinism was that for ninety-one years the administration of women's tennis was dominated by men, and they consistently gave the women players a raw deal.

So September 23, 1970, could justifiably be called "H-day," because it was then that Gladys Heldman at last achieved women's tennis independence. In her Houston home she assembled ten women rebels, and that very afternoon, at the local Racquet Club, began the first-ever professional tournament organized by women and for women.

Inspired by Gladys Heldman, championed by Billie Jean King, and with the powerful backing of Joseph F. Cullman II, chairman of the board of Philip Morris Inc., the women professionals that day braved an action which was to change forever the history of women's tennis.

Marching behind the Virginia Slims banner, with its appropriate slogan "You've Come a Long Way, Baby," the women thereafter moved rapidly up a stairway to the stars. As prophesied ninety-one years earlier, the ladies had indeed *come in time.*

Until the eruption of Gladys Heldman, women never had an effective voice in tennis politics. Wimbledon, while still priding itself on staging the world's leading championships, had not, at the end of its first century, admitted a woman to its committee.

The record of plots, intrigue, threats, and traps, instigated by the establishment to prevent the professional women's progress toward independence, has ensured that Gladys's visionary breakaway will rank on level terms with the best of traditional revolutions.

Gladys's background and education prepared her ideally for the campaign struggles ahead. Her father was George Z. Medalie, a judge of the New York Court of Appeals, president of the New York City Bar Association, and legal counsel to, among others, Louis B. Mayer of MGM fame. So she was brought up in law.

After graduating from Stanford with straight A's, the highest grades in the university's history at that time, she married into tennis. Her husband, Julius, was junior champion of the United States in '36, following immediately behind the great names of Frank Parker, Donald Budge, Gene Mako, and Bobby Riggs.

After the birth of their two daughters, Carrie and Julie M., Gladys persuaded Julius to teach her tennis. It is a tribute to her application and natural ability that, within a year, she won her first trophy and, within two years, was ranked No. 9 in Northern California. Later she was ranked No. 1 in Texas. She played the Wimbledon championships in '54 and the U.S. championships five times.

Julius had a Ph.D. in physical chemistry and won a National Research Fellowship. While Julius was teaching at the University of California in Berkeley, Gladys achieved her master's degree in medieval history at the same college, reading Latin scrolls. Later at Berkeley, she became a professor of mathematics at the Williams Institute.

In '49 Julius joined the Shell Oil Company, and the family moved to Houston.

Julius was soon elected president of the Houston Tennis Association. This, Gladys points out amusingly, brought the total membership to twelve. To attract more members, Gladys produced a one-page mimeographed newssheet. It was called *The Houston Tennis News*, and was handed out at all the public parks courts.

In '53 Gladys decided to launch the magazine *World Tennis*, soon to be well known to tennis lovers around the world. Shortly afterwards, *World Tennis* incorporated the sport's previous bible, the magazine *American Lawn Tennis*, which Wallis Merrihew had edited with loving care since 1909.

So at last there was a woman's voice in tennis. It was not an official voice, but a powerful one.

Gladys was always strictly fair in her editorial comment, but in the

o

'60s she saw the game needed a desperate reassessment and aligned herself with its critics. Her bold and provocative opinions were always expressed with the confidence of logic and hence achieved maximum credibility with businessmen.

In fact, by the middle '60s she had instilled so much fear in the amateur establishment that on one occasion the president of the USLTA imagined she was planning to destroy the national association and asked me personally what I knew of her "plot." Thereafter every issue of *World Tennis* became a prospective nightmare to the administration.

The Heldmans moved to New York in July '53. I first met Gladys when she came to Wimbledon in '54.

In the late '50s an event of inestimable significance to the future of all tennis occurred: Gladys met Joe Cullman.

More than a decade before tennis opened its doors to professionals, Gladys already foresaw that for any renaissance of its former glories the game would depend on a marriage with big business.

In the early '60s the once-powerful U.S. championships at Forest Hills were fast withering. Fewer overseas players were entering, and the tournament was becoming a prestige event in name only.

In '62, stirred by the failure of the establishment to recognize the signs of decay, Gladys opened a salvaging campaign with a proposition to Forest Hills president Augie Millang. "Charter a plane," she suggested, "and airlift eighty-five of the world's best men and women players from overseas."

Gladys calculated this would cost $18,000 at that time. Millang and USLTA president Ed Turville were agreeable, so she contacted a group of her business associates. She launched the necessary fund with her personal $1,800 check and asked $1,800 from each of nine other friends. Such were her powers of persuasion she received an affirmative from all but one of the first calls she made. It was agreed that if the championships made a profit, these advances would be repaid.

Gladys's next problem concerned the subsistence of the eighty-five players during their stay in New York. She calculated this at $125 a player and wrote 130 letters asking other personal friends each to sponsor one player for the duration of the championships.

Gladys also sold marquees and boxes at Forest Hills to corporations for $450 each, a revolutionary concept in those days. This provided free meals, boat trips, movie outings, and parties where the players could meet up with their sponsors. Finally, Gladys herself financed a monster farewell ball.

○

All this was new and exciting. For the first time in years the U.S. championships were a resounding success. In fact the '62 championships took in $100,000 more than in any previous year.

Joe Cullman, whose corporation had been the first to sponsor professional football in this country, confirms that he owes his original interest in tennis to Gladys Heldman. "She stimulated me with the opportunities she foresaw for the game and tempted me to get involved in a much wider sense," he told me.

Joe and Gladys met for the first time at the socialite Century Club in Purchase, New York. Their initial friendship, which included fiercely competitive singles against each other, led directly to Joe Cullman's involvement in tennis and revolutionary changes he has brought about in the historic face of the game.

At the time Joe Cullman was president and chief executive officer of Philip Morris Incorporated. He had left the Navy after four and a half years of World War II service with the rank of commander and a Commendation Ribbon bearing seven stars.

After becoming chairman of the board of Philip Morris in '66, Joe Cullman was named "One of the Ten Outstanding Chief Executive Officers in American Business and Industry" in '76, and "Most Outstanding Chief Executive Officer of the Year" in '77. He is a current commissioner of the Port Authority of New York and New Jersey. He is also a director of IBM, Bankers Trust, Ford Motors, and Levi Strauss.

In a recent discussion with Joe Cullman, he told me, "When I first met Gladys, the game was handled by a relatively small group of people. Their thinking was more in the traditional country-club attitude and they did not envisage the wider opportunities Gladys foresaw for the game. She deserves all the credit for realizing the great potential of tennis and the interest it could develop if properly exposed to the public."

When tennis finally went "open," Joe Cullman was the first to make a move in this country. It was Joe who persuaded the board of Philip Morris to sponsor the '68 U.S. Open championships.

All this was a victory for Gladys's vision and initiative, but she was still not satisfied, and the following year her influence and connections resulted in Joe Cullman being asked to be tournament director at Forest Hills.

So it was the financial commitment of Joe's corporation that enabled the championships to be nationally televised for the first time. Philip Morris, contributing large sums of money and its own uniquely successful promotional techniques, firmly established the

U.S. Open championships on its present road to ever-expanding prosperity.

But worldwide, the growing pains were only just starting. The coming of open tennis had, in monetary terms, spotlighted the inequality between the sexes that had been fostered by the all-male administrators since the origins of the game.

English men pioneered the beginnings of championship tennis in 1877. Their successors also introduced open tennis in 1968. But even with this ninety-year span, they still demonstrated the same disregard for the appeal of women's tennis by allocating the new prize fund on a two-to-one basis, or worse, against women.

The first-ever open tournament was at Bournemouth, England, in April '68. Ken Rosewall, winning the men's singles, received $4,000. Virginia Wade, winning the comparable women's event, received $1,200. At the first open Wimbledon, Rod Laver, the men's singles champion, received $8,000. The woman champion, Billie Jean, received less than $3,000.

"Insult To Our Sex," screamed one newspaper headline. "I don't suggest equality, just a fairer assessment. I think the women are more popular than the men," said Angela Mortimer Barrett, winner of the '61 women's title. One of the most telling protests came from the late Lady Spencer Churchill, Sir Winston's widow. The London *Times* gave prominence to her letter, condemning the disparity in the prize money.

In the locker rooms tempers were simmering. Billie Jean, of course, spoke out vehemently, but words alone availed no one.

Finally in '70 the dam burst. The direction of Perry Jones's famous Los Angeles tournament had been assumed by Jack Kramer, and he announced that the winner of the men's singles would receive twelve times the amount allocated to the winner of the women's event.

It seems natural that Billie Jean and Rosie Casals were the first to protest. Knowing that Gladys would sympathize, it was also natural they should turn to her for support.

At least a dozen top women players were finalizing their fall schedule at that time. Indignation about the Los Angeles prize money ratio spread through their ranks like a forest fire. Gladys is considerably younger than I, but all of us who remember the great days of Perry Jones's tournament were shocked that Jack's well-known chauvinism might damage its popularity. "Someone had to do the dirty work and talk to Jack Kramer," recalls Billie Jean. "So we asked Gladys Heldman."

Gladys has recorded that she did so on two occasions.

Thereafter began the double-talk, double-dealing, and double-

o

crossing that involved the USLTA and characterized the whole women's tennis scene for the ensuing three years.

After drawing a blank on any collaboration with Kramer, Gladys decided to "go it alone." She would help out the women by arranging a tournament in Houston where the prize money would at least give them the chance of recouping their expenses on transportation and living.

At that time Gladys and Julius had resided for some years in a luxurious penthouse overlooking New York's Gracie Mansion, the official residence of the mayor of New York. The Heldmans' Manhattan apartment was traditionally a "home-away-from-home" for visiting players. I was privileged on many occasions to be their houseguest.

But coincidentally with the fruitless Heldman-Kramer meetings, the Shell Company was moving its organization from New York to Houston. Julius Heldman was by then a vice-president of the company, so, naturally, this also involved a change of headquarters for the Heldman household.

Momentous decisions are often made in unlikely circumstances. The decision by ten of the world's leading players to boycott the Los Angeles tournament was certainly no exception.

The Heldmans were leaving for Houston by charter plane forty-eight hours after the finals of the '70 U.S. nationals.

For the last night of the championships Gladys had planned her customary farewell party for the players. But the furniture movers had already been in action, and the apartment was bare.

About a hundred players of both sexes milled around the empty apartment, but we were all so fond of Gladys that no one thought of the discomfort.

In the middle of this extraordinary scene, Gladys suddenly stood, framed in a doorway, beckoning certain figures to her side. The Pied Piper effect was dramatic, and we saw the elite of women's tennis disappear with her through the door to the dark bareness beyond.

In less than fifteen minutes they reemerged smiling. Gladys had revealed to them her plan for a tournament in her new hometown of Houston, and the ten leading women players decided this would be greatly preferable to the demeaning Kramer proposal.

Kramer was naturally furious, and it is generally agreed that he was not slow in enlisting the support of the USLTA in reprisals against Gladys.

On arrival in Houston, Gladys found herself involved in a barrage of double-talk with the USLTA. By the rules, she was required to obtain their authority for her plan.

Her goal of "going it alone" had not included breaking rules. However, three days before the Houston tournament began, Gladys was informed that the authority of the national association would be withheld from her event.

She was also told that if she proceeded with her plan, any players involved, the officials, and also the Houston Racquet Club, could all be disbarred from future national affiliation.

As a solution one USLTA official suggested that Gladys pay the prize money sub rosa. The players declined, considering such action dishonest, but a loophole was found in the rules that would allow the players to sign with Gladys as bona-fide professionals for a nominal sum.

It was at this point Gladys turned to Joe Cullman. She said that if her tournament was not authorized by the national association she needed the alternative status of his personal backing. Once again her theory that tennis must have big-business support came into play.

Joe agreed to involve Virginia Slims, the Philip Morris brand specially addressed to women. As a result, the Houston prize purse was increased from $5,000 to $7,500.

Gladys then announced the first-ever Virginia Slims Women's Pro Tournament. September 23, 1970, was the historic day when nine women signed one-week, one-dollar contracts with Gladys, and the since-famous Virginia Slims Circuit was born.

The makers of this piece of tennis history were the American players, Peaches Bartkowicz, Rosie Casals, Julie M. Heldman, Billie Jean King, Kristy Pigeon, Nancy Richey, and Val Zeigenfuss, plus the Australians, Judy Dalton and Kerry Melville Reid. Patti Hogan was originally involved, but a last-minute change of heart precludes her a place in this record.

The following day all the American women who had signed with Gladys were formally notified by telegrams from the USLTA president that they were suspended forthwith from national affiliation.

This meant they were no longer eligible for national ranking, nor for selection in official matches such as the Wightman and Federation cups. In addition, they were no longer eligible to compete in the "big four" tournaments of Wimbledon, Forest Hills, France, and Australia.

It was an ironic twist that by the deletion of the top players from the national ranking list, Patti Hogan assumed the No. 1 spot and temporarily became America's top-ranking player.

For the record, Julie M. Heldman made only a token appearance in the tournament because of an arm injury. Rosie Casals won the first prize of $1,500 in Gladys's brave venture, beating Judy Dalton in the final.

But that week there was more activity off court than on. All the players, even Gladys herself, were hit by "after-birth blues." They had cut loose from all accepted routines, and the question was "Where would they go next?" Besides being formally suspended by the USLTA, the women endured derisive remarks from the men players, many of whom told them they had destroyed themselves and had no chance whatever of lasting success.

Billie Jean explains that the women really took a big chance. "For us the Virginia Slims Circuit in '70 was a real risk," she still says. "We would have looked pretty silly had we failed. If nobody came to see us play we would have been dead. But they did come. The timing was right."

Gladys's office was soon a scene of more feverish activity than usual. Within days she arranged further tournaments in San Francisco, and Richmond, Virginia.

The women gladly voted to sign a second one-dollar contract to legalize their position with Gladys until the end of '70. Gladys made alternative financial arrangements for San Francisco, but for the Richmond tournament Joe Cullman again came forward with backing from Virginia Slims.

Gladys was at last able to sit back for a brief respite before facing the upcoming problems of '71.

Public response to women playing tennis without men had been favorable. She had crashed all the barriers that had confined women's tennis for the past century. By infusing the interest and financial backing of one of the nation's most successful business operations, she had saved the game from near-bankruptcy. Thanks to her efforts, tennis as a whole had bounced back off the floor. She had a justifiable smile on her face. Whatever difficulties the future might bring, she had already achieved a virtual miracle.

Inevitably, Gladys's next step took her back to the Philip Morris offices on New York's Park Avenue.

She had discussed the possibilities for '71 at great length with the women players and proposed a circuit of twenty-four tournaments in the winter-spring and summer-fall periods.

From safari in Africa Joe Cullman authorized the continuation of Virginia Slims sponsorship, and Gladys was prepared to fill in herself any holes that might appear in the promising package she had put together.

"By November I had twenty-four tournaments lined up for '71, and

I guaranteed $10,000 minimum prize money for each," Gladys told me. "To our great surprise and delight," she added, "the public adored the women. They still enjoy the longer rallies, the greater variation and consistency of the women's matches compared with the men's."

Another surprise was that in February '71 the USLTA realized they had made a big mistake in banning the women. They backtracked, at least temporarily, and the suspensions were lifted, though Gladys never really believed in this sham truce.

Her suspicions were well founded because, very soon after, turbulent relations with the USLTA resumed with increased bitterness.

The establishment planned to continue their traditional circuit as before. "And they went around telling all the players to boycott my tournaments," says Gladys, "even though my tournaments were offering up to $40,000 in prizes, while the USLTA women's events could not make it above $2,000."

Eventually the year '71 became one long succession of threats and counterthreats between Gladys and the USLTA. And the USLTA held one trump card. The international prestige events of Paris, Wimbledon, and Forest Hills were now soon ahead. Had Gladys again resorted to her private contract arrangements of '70, the international establishment would have had the weapon of precluding any woman signing with Gladys from competing in these forthcoming major events.

Joe Cullman takes up the story:

"It took a long time before the establishment recognized that personalities like Gladys Heldman, Lamar Hunt, etc., were here to stay. The USLTA tried doggedly to impose its will on the players and resist the emergence of bigger prize-money scales. We had some classic confrontations with successive USLTA presidents. They had the tournaments, we had the chips, and Gladys could deliver the players. But the USLTA didn't want to pay the price the players and sponsors were entitled to. They couldn't understand why Gladys wouldn't just go away."

Gladys had introduced me to Joe Cullman five years before, in the days of their fierce singles battles at Century.

In '70 Joe invited me to the Forest Hills championships as his personal guest. At the time I could not know that my entire life-style would be changed by the relationship I would develop with Joe in the coming years.

In August '71 the Virginia Slims first birthday tournament offered a top prize of $10,000, at that time the largest single prize ever offered to

○

266   *Love & Faults*

a tennis woman. Billie Jean won it and, three tournaments later, became the first woman athlete ever to win $100,000 in one year.

The birthday tournament took place at the Hofheinz Pavilion of Houston University. Presumably, because of the prominence and success it achieved, the event became the ultimate target of USLTA fury.

Everything possible was done to prevent the tournament from getting off the ground. Threats were even made to disenfranchise the university. The fee asked by the USLTA for the national authorization, which was necessary if the women were not to be banned again, was increased week by week. Finally, to ensure the fulfillment of the promises made to the women, Joe Cullman intervened and paid the USLTA demands.

Yet despite all the double-dealing and the hassles, the week proved a happy one.

For my part I was making daily appearances with a collection of tennis wear I had made for Neiman-Marcus. In the evenings Gladys's houseguests migrated en masse to the Hofheinz Pavilion. Amazingly, Gladys showed no outward signs of the traumatic pressures the making of tennis history had imposed on her in the preceding twelve months.

Joe Cullman, with an entourage of his top aides, came to Houston to celebrate the occasion.

With bittersweet appropriateness, Virginia Slims, still unfamiliar with the machinations of the tennis community, made a framed scroll presentation to Gladys.

It read: "What Kind Of Game Can Tennis Be Where Love Is Nothing?"

[28]

You Came
a Long Way, Baby (2)

IN THE EARLY '60S GLADYS HELDMAN'S EDITORIALS REPEATEDLY expressed the conviction that American amateur tennis was slipping steadily into a decline, and the statistics were on her side.

American players had virtually ruled the tennis world from the late '30s to the '50s. Yet for twelve years, from '56 through '67, no American managed to win the U.S. national title. Neither did any American woman achieve this distinction from '62 through '66. America managed only once to win the Davis Cup between the years '59 and '68, and in six of the eight losing years the United States team could not even reach the final round.

The already long-overdue proposal to end the definition between amateur and professional players had been turned down by the world governing body in '60. Amateurs could still not be paid for their playing skills and were barred from competing in any events that

o

included professionals. Shamateurism reached its peak, yet the majority of the clubs refused permission to the pros to stage exhibitions on their courts.

A mood of discouragement pervaded the whole scene. Gladys attributed this to an administration that dragged its feet and was incapable of leading the world into the new age. Most players now wanted to be paid honestly for their performances, and large sums of money would be needed for this purpose.

It was not Gladys's job to devise a cure for these ills, but by now she was totally dedicated to tennis through her magazine. She saw the tennis world as rife with inefficiency and became determined to improve matters.

In search of an effective formula Gladys convinced herself the time had come to transfer the leadership of the game from volunteers to professional businessmen. Her mental process was direct. The best businessman she knew was Joe Cullman. Henceforth, her preoccupation would be to find a way of involving Joe in the direction of American tennis.

It was probably inevitable that the establishment should regard Gladys as an outsider with uncomfortable, innovative ideas, many of which opposed a century of tradition. Certainly it was not long before all the official hierarchies came to think of her as a positive threat to their authority.

However, in '67, a welcome light dawned on the horizon. Lamar Hunt, the Dallas-based oil millionaire, unexpectedly became interested in tennis, and big business was on the scene. It was not yet, of course, on the official scene, but very much a force of influence demanding immediate recognition.

Gladys had already stimulated Joe Cullman's interest to a point where he had recruited four world stars, headed by the Australian Roy Emerson, to the promotions staff of Philip Morris.

With the new competitive interest of tycoon Lamar Hunt at the top of professional tennis, Gladys was able to give real meaning to a warning she had already given in *World Tennis*: "If the establishment refuses any longer to learn from professional business methods they are signing their own death warrant."

In Europe, the main body of the international administration was still adamantly opposed to professional tennis. But in late '66 we heard strong rumors that the Wimbledon Club was seriously thinking of taking matters into its own hands. With Lamar Hunt now a declared rebel tempting away the top players to the professional ranks, the unbelievable was being openly discussed. Wimbledon might soon allow professionals on its sacred turf, whatever the international administrators had to say. If this happened, there could be no doubt the U.S. championships at Forest Hills would be obliged to follow suit. Gladys had waited for this situation for a decade.

In the spring of '67 I was sitting with Gladys in the patrons' lounge of the Ellis Park Club in Johannesburg when she told me the good news.

"The professionals are probably being allowed a trial match at Wimbledon this fall. With Lamar Hunt in the race, open tennis has got to come next year," said Gladys. "If this happens, Joe has promised that one of his Philip Morris products will tie in with Forest Hills and his business brain will be the salvation of the U.S. nationals."

In August '67 the trial professional tournament duly took place at Wimbledon. Eight pros were allowed, for the first time ever, on the center court.

From then on it was clear that a bona-fide Wimbledon championship, open to all players, had to come soon. Nevertheless the world-governing body continued to turn a blind eye to the inevitable, so Wimbledon used its century of power to take unilateral action.

A few weeks later the British national association was forced to give Wimbledon its blessing. In March '68 the International Federation, at an emergency meeting, was faced with a fait accompli.

January '68 was the month when Lamar Hunt changed the whole course of men's tennis history. The first salvo of his revolution was to present, in Australia, eight of the most handsome top tennis professionals in a completely new ambiance of razzmatazz and show biz.

Lamar's scenario included such novelties as players in different colored shirts competing against time clocks, artificial turf, sudden-death scoring, and even audience participation with giveaways for lucky forecasts—and the spectators loved it. Men's tennis, as it had been conceived for the past hundred years, was never to be the same again.

Later in '68 this revolutionary concept of Lamar's was preached throughout the United States by his able lieutenants Al Hill and Michael Davies.

To compete against Lamar, and with the inevitability of open tennis in Europe, the forthcoming U.S. Nationals would clearly need much more money and better presentation than ever before. This situation was tailor-made for all Gladys's aspirations.

Nevertheless, the first U.S. Open, won by Arthur Ashe and Virginia Wade in '68, still fell short of Gladys's farseeing concept.

Another powerful editorial in the October issue of Gladys's magazine called for big improvements the following year. She asked specifically for an electronic scoreboard on the arena court, a sponsor's minimum guarantee of $100,000 for television, and the scheduling of the matches by a professional referee.

Gladys must have had it in mind that she could tempt Joe Cullman into underwriting a high proportion of these items on behalf of Philip Morris. She obviously succeeded because I remember a press conference at New York's '21 Club in the spring of '69, at which Joe Cullman announced, not only that most of Gladys's suggestions would be put into effect but that Joe himself had agreed to be chairman of the '69 championships.

Spectators arriving at Forest Hills in August of that year were amazed to see the modernization of the scene brought about by Joe with the help of his right-hand tennis man Billy Talbert.

One of the most impressive illustrations of the contemporary big-business image was the imposing 30-by-20 foot electronic scoreboard that Gladys had asked for.

An even more outstanding milestone was the achievement by Joe Cullman of a five-year contract with CBS Television. Not only did this ensure that, for the first time, the world's top players could be seen by the whole nation with some consistency, but the fees paid by the network enabled Forest Hills and the national tennis administration to increase the players' prize fund to levels in keeping with their ever-increasing status.

Today it only remains remarkable that it took two long years of delicate negotiations, of bargaining and counterbargaining, the sending of TV crews to Wimbledon for special indoctrination, of countless aspects of public relations expertise, all meticulously guided for Joe and Philip Morris by Jim Bowling, to bring about these improvements.

Jim Bowling recalls that when he first proposed nationally televised tennis to America's top TV hierarchy, one head of programs told him, "We'd get more viewers watching a test pattern than watching tennis." It took every ounce of Jim's charm and New York's respect for his reputation to overcome the obstacles that were raised in those first years of open tennis.

Following the success of the improved '69 U.S. nationals, the eyes of many other big-business interests turned enviously toward tennis.

One of the pioneer promoters, Jack Kramer, finding himself without a piece of the action in any of the new camps, surprisingly aligned himself with the establishment—in the opposite camp to Lamar Hunt. It was the ensuing rivalry between the two camps that

pushed the value of the men players to hitherto astronomical proportions.

Meanwhile, the reigning women stars of the day, Billie Jean King,
Margaret Court and Ann Jones, considered themselves as having
quite as much box-office appeal as the men. They thought the three-
to-one ratio of prize money, which had been allocated to the men
since '68, an ongoing unfairness.

The success of the '69–'70 Marlboro-sponsored, nationally televised championships began what the press in this country described
as the "tennis explosion." It was then the women began thinking the
time had come for their own explosion.

Destiny played a part by chosing this particular moment to move
Gladys and Julius Heldman from New York, the geographical heart of
the affair, to Houston.

Before leaving, Gladys had achieved the main objective of her past
decade by salvaging American tennis from its failures. Under Joe
Cullman's helmsmanship, she had set the game on a fair course to
success. Now she had a new life to build a new and throbbing Houston, unrecognizable from her earlier days. Gladys was ready for a new
cause, and the cause of the women players' independence exactly
fitted her psychological need at the time.

The previous chapter recounts the birth pangs of the Virginia Slims
Circuit. From '68 and through '70 the men also encountered problems inevitably brought by the millions of dollars infused so fast and
unexpectedly into their game.

This was the peak period in the struggle for international control of
tennis and its newly found riches. There were even internal disputes
within the brotherhood of administrators.

As early as '62 a modest indoor tournament was organized in the
field house of St. Joseph's College in Philadelphia.

This was the brainchild of a local ménage, Ed and Marilyn
Fernberger, who have since become the famous promoters of what is
today the most important indoor men's championship in the world,
the INA U.S. Pro Indoors in the Philadelphia Spectrum. Through
their untiring efforts for over sixteen years, the Fernbergers have
raised more than one million dollars for the cause of junior development in the Philadelphia area.

In '70 their innovative spirit decided to update their event by
introducing Jimmy van Alen's sudden-death, nine-point tie-breaker.
This was condoned by the American national association, but the
world governing body was outraged and actually imposed a fine on
the American administration for not having "controlled the
Fernbergers."

o

Later in '70 the success of Lamar Hunt's circuit was such that his forceful aide, Michael Davies, felt strong enough to threaten a boycott by Hunt's players of the '71 Wimbledon championships. At first the establishment treated this as an unbelievable impertinence, but it was later seen to be a threat that could become very real.

In November '70 I was brought unwittingly into this troubled scene. I had known Michael Davies since his boyhood. As Britain's top-ranked player in '60 he had joined Jack Kramer's professional circus. Mike's memoirs, appropriately called *Tennis Rebel*, describe his feelings. "As soon as I turned professional I needed someone to look after my affairs. The only person possible was Ted Tinling, who for so long had been like an extra parent to me."

At the time I was familiar not only with Britain's tennis administrators who were in the camp opposing Davies, but in my playing days I had known most of their fathers before them.

Negotiations between Davies, the British establishment, and the international authorities, had dragged fruitlessly for months. "The situation has reached an impasse and there seems no way out," wrote London's Lance Tingay, describing the conflict.

Lamar Hunt's pro circuit was now a business concern and on a time-study basis (which had never before been considered in tennis), Davies had a good case for saying the three weeks required for competing at Wimbledon were a financial loss for his players.

The British Tennis Association had recently hired Gerald Williams, a well-known sports journalist, to take care of their public relations, and it was Williams who first made a suggestion that I found almost comic. "The establishment all know you and you are the one man who can talk sense to Davies. Do you think you could get the two sides to sit down together?" Williams asked me.

In a subsequent report on what occurred, J. L. Manning, London's *Daily Mail* sports-feature writer, commented, "How sick can a sport be when it requires a dressmaker to solve its problems." I did not exactly agree with him, but quite a few people thought he made an amusing point.

Eventually, the improbable, not to say the impossible, was achieved, and we all sat down in London for days and nights of secret and difficult discussion.

This particular anecdote should not be prolonged. Suffice to say, the thirty-two players controlled by Lamar Hunt and Davies, all played the '71 Wimbledon, and I shall always be proud of this achievement.

However, at this same Wimbledon, Lamar and Al Hill themselves decided to discuss with the establishment their future plans arising from the temporary truce I had arranged. Thereupon, tact, diplomacy, even common courtesy, went right out the window. Many of Lamar's quite logical points of discussion were misunderstood and deliberately misinterpreted.

The end of the whole sorry dialogue was that all Lamar's players were banned from participation in any establishment tournament from 1972 on. At times I was ashamed myself and felt it necessary to apologize to Lamar for the demeanor of some of the English sports press and the administrators.

Subsequently a meeting of the world-governing body of amateur tennis, at Stresa, Italy, in July '71, effectively outlawed most of the world's leading men players from any of the major tournaments the following year.

The decisions taken at this meeting must surely rank as the blindest, most retrogressive and destructive in the game's history. It was indeed fortunate for the future of tennis that Lamar Hunt and Joe Cullman now had the interest and involvement to fight the whole issue.

In August I went to Houston for the Virginia Slims first birthday tournament, still depressed by the mauling Lamar and Al Hill had received at Wimbledon. I was equally depressed by the myopic obstinacy of the world-governing body and certainly in the right mood to identify with Gladys in the trials and treacherous dealings that lay ahead for her in the women's game.

Two weeks after the Houston tournament, all the fears Gladys, Joe, and Lamar had aroused among the volunteer administrators erupted into open hostility.

Self-inflated by its so-called "show of strength" at the Stresa meeting, the world-governing body issued an ultimatum to the Virginia Slims Circuit. Four of its points were so phrased as to be totally impracticable. The fifth made a condition of Gladys's resignation for the price of official acceptance of the Virginia Slims circuit in the future.

This time it was not Gladys who complained. Typically, Joe assumed the leadership.

The five-year TV contract between the CBS network and Philip Morris also enjoined the USTLA. The contract committed the USLTA to use "its best efforts" in having the world's most outstanding players appear in its championships whatever their status.

The decisions of the Stresa meeting had disillusioned many of the top players. Although the forthcoming ban on them was not yet in effect, such leading stars as Rod Laver and Ken Rosewall did not enter

o

the '71 Forest Hills championships from sheer discouragement with the whole situation.

This was already an obvious letdown for Joe Cullman. There would be two other deterrents to the participation of the best players the following year: first, the ban on Lamar Hunt's pro players, and second, the threatened suspension of the Virginia Slims women.

Joe rightly interpreted these possibilities as a potential breach of the USLTA's undertakings to Philip Morris and the CBS network. His conclusion led to two strong and dramatic statements.

In the first, Joe Cullman wrote to Frank Smith, then a director of CBS, saying, "In the event the USLTA should bar the Virginia Slims women as well as uphold the International Federation's ban on the men players, we shall consider our commitment to CBS to sponsor future telecasts of the U.S. Open Championships as terminated."

Philip Morris had been indirectly contributing more than $100,000 annually to the USLTA. At a press conference relative to Joe's letter to Frank Smith, a reporter asked what would be done with the money in the event of the USLTA and the ILTF confirming their intentions in defiance of Joe's ultimatum. "It will all be put into the Virginia Slims Circuit," Joe replied.

Need one say that after a very few days the USLTA backtracked again and voted not to ban the women players? The ILTF ban on the men was also lifted in time for them to compete at Forest Hills.

In September '71 Joe appointed me official designer to the Virginia Slims Circuit.

The first showing of my Virginia Slims tennis wear took place at the Fairmont Hotel in San Francisco to coincide with the opening tournament of the '72 Virginia Slims tour. At the time I was still working out of London, and the airline mistakenly shipped the collection of thirty-eight specially designed outfits to Atlanta instead of San Francisco. The shipment was lost for more than a week and retrieved only a few hours before my grand opening.

For Gladys, the '72 San Francisco tournament also came close to disaster. In '71 the USLTA had asked the customary $480 fee to grant its authority for the tournament. In '72 the fee was raised to $1,000.

When the local organizers refused this inflated demand, all the participants in the tournament were told they would automatically be banned. The threat was ignored by all but one player. Three days later the USLTA lifted the suspensions.

Following these unending skirmishes and Pyrrhic victories, it seemed that a temporary come-home, all-is-forgiven atmosphere took over. In February '72 Gladys Heldman was surprisingly invited to become the USLTA coordinator of American women's tennis and official director of the women's tour.

In April an uneasy peace was arranged in the men's game when Lamar Hunt and his attorneys (and, astonishingly, Jack Kramer) journeyed to England and extracted most of the terms they wanted from the world-governing body.

As a result, Joe Cullman announced on May 8, 1972, that telecasts of the U.S. nationals would continue and that the Miller Brewing company, of which Philip Morris is the parent group, would be the principal TV sponsor at the '72 U.S. championships.

Some years later Gladys was to recall, with justifiable bitterness, that the women's peace "did not last as long as the Munich Agreement."

The story of the '68–'73 period in tennis was so complex it was sometimes difficult, even for those long experienced in the turbulence of tennis politics, to comprehend the power plays, the conflicts of interest, and the bitter personal antagonisms that arose.

In June '72 a new and significant character joined the cast of this tragicomedy when Mrs. Edy Ann McGoldrick of Boston, Massachusetts, was appointed by the USLTA to captain the American Wightman Cup team. In recent years her influence has been greater than that of any other person in the women's game.

In the fall of '72 the USLTA shocked Gladys, supposedly their own official director of women's tennis, by announcing an independent women's circuit. This would be in direct competition with the Virginia Slims Circuit and also scheduled on many of the same dates.

Gladys, of course, immediately resigned from the USLTA. Then, for the seventh time, the national administration announced that any woman player participating in the forthcoming Virginia Slims Circuit would be banned from all official tournaments.

In January '73 Gladys countered by forming what she then called the "Women's International Tennis Federation." The women of the Virginia Slims Circuit had talked her into staying as their leader. This initial federation of women players was the direct forerunner of today's democratic Women's Tennis Association.

The rival women's circuits, organized respectively by Gladys Heldman and Edy Ann McGoldrick, revealed deep-seated differences of thought between the world's leading players. On the one hand, Mrs. McGoldrick secured Evonne Goolagong, Virginia Wade, and the new rising star Chris Evert. On the other, the Virginia Slims banner still flourished with the support of Billie Jean King, Margaret Court, Kerry Melville Reid, and Rosie Casals.

o

Unhappily the whole year 1973 was a sad history of litigation and cross-litigation between the USLTA and Gladys, joined on one occasion by Billie Jean King on the side of Gladys Heldman.

The head of the Virginia Slims division of Philip Morris at that time was John Granville. Reflecting recently on these events, Granville said, "In effect, Gladys lost the battle but won the war," because an armistice between the warring parties was eventually negotiated by John Granville and made possible by some of the points that had been made in the courts.

It was a short-lived truce, for soon afterwards the world-governing body made a final effort to rid itself of Gladys. John Granville and Gladys journeyed specially to London with the hope of reaching a friendly agreement, but the then president of the International Federation, an expatriate, power-conscious Dane, Allan Hayman, was so intent on Gladys's removal as an unwanted influence in the women's game that they were met with only a blank wall of hostility.

Throughout the winter–spring '72–'73 seasons, most of the women players, having had to choose between the two rival circuits, were subjected to threats and ominous warnings of the consequences that would befall them if they took part in Gladys's Virginia Slims tournaments. Finally, Allan Hayman gave them the deadline of April 30, 1973, to sign undertakings that they would all submit to the authority of their national associations. I have always felt that only bad sheepdogs frighten the sheep.

However, with their international reputations at stake, stars like Margaret Court and Billie Jean King were unable to resist this pistol pointed directly at their heads.

By now Gladys had spent twenty years and a good part of her personal fortune to achieve what was, in many opinions, the salvation of American tennis from its ultimate decline. Even more particularly, she achieved an administration of women's tennis independent of men and able to govern its own destiny.

The USLTA and Forest Hills were still unwilling to give equal prize money to the men and the women. However, that year, Billy Talbert, who had succeeded Joe Cullman as chairman of the championships, persuaded an additional sponsor to make up the difference.

Having finally achieved her main purpose, Gladys then withdrew from the Virginia Slims Circuit. "I am leaving for the peace of the game," she said cryptically. Her finest hour induced her greatest dignity.

On September 20, 1973, the memorable night of the Billy Jean King-Bobby Riggs encounter, Joe Cullman, with many of the top executives of Philip Morris, bade farewell to Gladys from their immediate midst, hosting an appropriate party in Houston's Astro Club in her honor.

Afterwards, we all went down to the floor of the vast Astrodome to see Billie Jean beat Bobby Riggs.

For my part I had the good fortune to remain the official designer to the Virginia Slims Circuit for seven years, from '72 through '78.

From the days of Gussy Moran I had always foreseen that if top tennis was to be viable in the modern era it would need the new element of spectacle added increasingly to the old element of sport.

At the time of my first two Virginia Slims collections, tennis dresses the world over had still mandatorily to be all white. The first solid pastel dresses ever allowed in a national championship were worn at Forest Hills in '72.

For the next two years the women played inside or outside, by sunshine or artificial light, at breakfast time or at midnight. I had to be ready for all these contrasting circumstances, many of which I had never before encountered.

My associations with Joe Cullman, with successive brand managers of the Virginia Slims division of Philip Morris, notably with Ellen Merlo whose contribution to today's glamor image of women's professional tennis has probably been the most outstanding of all, have given me some of my most gratifying moments.

For centuries outside patronage of creative artists has been an accepted necessity to which the world owes many of its artistic pleasures. Patronage is not just relative to financing experimentation. It implies, far beyond this, the constant imparting of confidence and encouragement. Virginia Slims gave me all these things. Meanwhile the expertise of Frank Saunders, Philip Morris's chief of press relations, enthused the press critics to support me at all times.

For the last Virginia Slims season of '78, I designed no fewer than ninety-five dresses for the individual stars, no two alike.

For contractual reasons I have not dressed Evonne Goolagong since '73. It is a great personal disappointment to me never to have had the opportunity to design for the ever-gracious Chris Evert.

These two stars shared the ultimate Virginia Slims Championship title from '72 through '77. A player wearing one of my designs had won every other major championship in the world, so it was gratifying that in the ultimate match of eight years of the Virginia Slims circuit, the "final final," in '78, was won by Martina Navratilova, giving me the missing title I most wanted.

The '74 to '78 Virginia Slims tours can best be described as exercises in progressive professionalism and a continuing tribute to Joe

o

Cullman's enthusiasm. Each year brought more prize money, better management, new venues, above all, more spectators. The tournament director for six years, Peachy Kellmeyer, should be credited with many of the improvements.

Lamar Hunt must feel gratified at having been first in accurately forecasting the spectators' taste, at having the financial and organizational ability to assemble his star-studded cast, and giving his players their annual goal in World Championship Tennis.

How to qualify the instigator of it all, Gladys Heldman?

Perhaps her greatest gratification could be in the comparative prize-funds and the attendances of the U.S. National Championships during her peak thrust for improvement. The stark figures need no comment:

Prize-fund U.S. National Championships:

1963	NIL
1968	$100,000
1973	$558,130
1978	$550,000

Total paid attendances:

1963	52,000
1968	97,294
1973	137,488
1978	275,300

Joe Cullman must also think of these figures with pride, but meanwhile he has more time now to devote to his particular love of Super-Senior tennis in which he is nationally ranked in both singles and doubles.

At one of the recent Robert Kennedy Celebrity Tournament days, which are supported by Philip Morris, I particularly enjoyed seeing Joe on the Forest Hills stadium court partnered by Don Budge. At times it seemed that Joe was more industrious on the court than even the redheaded immortal of Grand Slam tennis.

These last two chapters tell a story of dedication, attrition, of ambitions and goals achieved and frustrations surmounted.

Sadly, however, the Virginia Slims account closes with a curt press release from Jerry Diamond, executive director of the Women's Tennis Association, which appeared unexpectedly on April 22, 1978, coincidentally ten years to the day from the beginning of open tennis.

The release read: "Due to a difference in philosophies with the

Virginia Slims Circuit concept, the contract between the Women's Tennis Association and Virginia Slims will not be renewed."*

Perhaps with the presentation scroll made to Gladys Heldman at the '72 Slims first birthday tournament, the fates were really trying to warn us all for it asked, almost prophetically, *"What Kind Of Game Can Tennis Be Where Love Is Nothing?"*

---

*The 1977–79 president of the world-governing body (The International Tennis Federation) is Philippe Chatrier. In '78 he initiated an Annual Review of the work of his International Federation, which comprises no fewer than 104 nation members. The '78 report included the following paragraph:

> "It is also important to say something about the end of the Virginia Slims circuit. This was one of the game's pioneering ventures. Virginia Slims showed, to the surprise of many of those who were promoting the game at the start of the decade, that women could draw large crowds and attract the same kind of sponsorship as the men in the United States. Virginia Slims, with their flair for publicity, their energy and enthusiasm, won converts everywhere. Among those converts were, it must be said, the leaders of the International Federation who had been skeptical and chauvinistic at the start but finished as admirers. It is a great pity that such good sponsors should depart from the game."

It is ironic that the visionary achievements of Gladys Heldman and Joe Cullman should finally be granted formal acknowledgment by the establishment in the obituary for the Virginia Slims Circuit, but I would like to pay personal tribute to the fine work on international administration and international relations currently being done by president Chatrier and his Federation secretary, David Gray.

○

[29]

Madam Superstar

BILLIE JEAN LEANED BACK IN HER PLUSHY DESK CHAIR. WE WERE
in the executive suite of Kingdom, Inc., her sixteen-office complex in
San Mateo, California.

"Tennis is really what I know," she began slowly. "I love the gray
locker-rooms, the smell of liniment, the waiting crowds, the intensity
of the game. I love banging away at a ball."

There was a long pause. She gazed up at the ceiling lights as if they
recalled all the sunlit matches she had won.

"There's something about the whole bit that's right for me." Now
her eyes sparkled behind the lilac-tinted glasses. "I've learned what it
means to be what I am." Her voice tensed at the mental re-creation of
her successes.

Suddenly she bared her soul in four passionate sentences:

"I've suffered pain for tennis."

"I feel I'm tennis."

"Now I know I'm tennis."

"I don't just play tennis, I AM tennis."

I agreed completely.

Yet even this dramatic self-analysis seemed an oversimplification of her complex and probing character. In reality, Billie Jean is a fascinating amalgam of many things, many causes, all of which transcend the restrictive dimensions of a tennis court.

As a player and a champion, Billie Jean has unquestionably earned her place among the greatest.

In addition, she has been a fearless agitator against the hypocrisy of shamateurism; the quantifier of Gladys Heldman's and Joe Cullman's inspired vision of the first Women's Pro Circuit; the originator with her husband, Larry, of the multi-million-dollar Team Tennis concept, and, throughout, a firebrand debater of women's rights.

Fittingly, recognition of her campaigns has been forthcoming from all sides. In the last decade she has been named outstanding woman personality of the year in at least a dozen categories. Perhaps the most appropriate have been *Time*'s "Woman of the Year" award in '76, and being listed with *Harper's Bazaar*'s "Ten Most Powerful Women in America" in '77. Meanwhile, *Sports Illustrated* assessed her as "probably the most influential athlete of her time."

Beyond these accolades, Billie Jean's putdown of the interloper Bobby Riggs, in defense of women's place in today's sports, is the crowning crusade of her career to date. Her victory focused the eyes of the world not only on women's tennis but all tennis. It gave the upper echelons of the game, once and for all, the glittering status of big-money entertainment.

Like prophetic priestesses of the Oracle, both Marguerite Broquedis and Suzanne Lenglen, foresaw all this when tennis was still adolescent.

Bill Tilden was Lenglen's self-appointed enemy, but very much a soulmate in their joint pioneering in the '20s.

In the post-World War II tennis explosion, Gussy Moran was first in attracting the essential interest of the media. Gladys Heldman for the women, Lamar Hunt for the men, and Joe Cullman for both sexes set today's stage by successfully marrying American big-business to tennis.

Billie Jean's stardom as a world personality has come later than her stardom in tennis. In a sense, her tennis has been the vehicle in which she has traveled to world fame in a much wider scene.

Throughout the inevitable conflict of the game's development,

Billie Jean has played the Joan of Arc role, responding to her own inner call and to those from outside whenever public attack or defense was needed to help the sport's evolution.

When I talked to Billie Jean in San Mateo she was wearing a perfectly cut green-velvet pants suit, a tailored silk shirt from Dior, and two hair-fine gold necklaces. Physically, she is not the girl in the ads for *Cosmo* magazine, but exactly the image of the top woman-executive men would like at their business conferences.

The immaculate appearance of today's Billie Jean in the understated comfort of her executive sanctum forced my mind back seventeen years to my first sight of her. This was in her opening singles match at '61 Wimbledon.

In those days she gave England the impression of an irrepressible tomboy with a loud mouth and a myopic gaze through owlish glasses.

In our years of friendship I have never told Billie Jean I was instrumental in bringing about her defeat in her Wimbledon debut.

Billie Jean was playing a very close friend and faithful client of mine, Mexico's Yola Ramirez. That year Yola was seeded fifth at Wimbledon, but was having a lot of problems with the brash and talented Californian newcomer.

Billie Jean and Yola had split sets when bad light stopped play.

The third set was postponed until the next day, and I remember Billie Jean, who had settled into her rhythm before the interruption, remonstrated strongly with the umpire. There was no argument because Yola, too cagy to be caught up in any hassle, had quickly picked up her gear and left for the locker room.

As she passed me, Yola muttered in an undertone of broken English, "Tonight we eat dinner. Tonight I speak with you." Later we went to a small restaurant, and Yola asked my advice on how to play the final set the next day.

The interrupted match had been my first sight of Billie Jean, but it was obvious she had a vulnerable forehand. In strong contrast she had an attacking, well-controlled backhand. "If you put one single shot on her backhand tomorrow you will lose," I told Yola.

Fifteen years later Billie Jean gave an account of the match in her autobiography. "When Yola and I resumed," she wrote, "it was obvious she had my game figured out because in that last set she hit everything to my forehand. My forehand was vulnerable in those days. I'd kept that little fact hidden from her the day before, but I couldn't now. I didn't see one backhand the rest of the match and I lost badly."

Afterwards a delighted Yola told me to join her for a celebration with strawberries and cream. She was right-handed, but in the competitors' room I noticed her eating her strawberries and drinking her tea in full southpaw fashion. Then the joke became clear. Every time she picked up her fork or her cup with her left hand, she giggled infectiously. "Look. No forehand! Look. No forehand!" she laughed.

I certainly had no affinity with Billie Jean's image, her gamesmanship, nor her Fred Perry tennis gear during those early years of the '60s.

In those days Billie Jean, with her whoops and yowls and tough, aggressive behavior on court, lost no time in polarizing the spectators everywhere.

But, as the years went by, no one could deny her progress toward stardom. She set herself the goal of being the world's No. 1, and reached that milestone in '66 when she beat Margaret Court and Maria Bueno for the first of her six singles championships at Wimbledon.

Meanwhile she married Larry King, a boyfriend from college days. The resulting responsibility soon began to have an effect on her personality. She had an unhappy incident with Ann Jones in the '66 Wightman Cup, and with the winning of her first singles title at Wimbledon, Billie Jean realized her projection on court was damaging to her overall image. She recounts in her story that she began to work hard on improving the earlier impressions she had given. To my mind, this decision ended the first stage of her career.

The transition years of the late '60s were the second stage. This was the period of her awakening as a professional tennis player. Later came her consciousness of her role as a leader and a celebrity.

I had asked to meet with Billie Jean in San Mateo to bring myself up-to-date with the new ideas that constantly ferment in her brain. But the fervor and dedication she expressed at the beginning of our interview made it essential to ask where it all began.

Ironically, it was Perry Jones who unknowingly aroused Billie Jean's rebellious fervor during the '55 Junior Championships at his Los Angeles club. Billie Jean was eleven years old at the time.

As a kid, Billie Jean was a carbon copy of Alice Marble, kicking footballs, running track, playing softball, and throwing baseballs with her young brother Randy. For a short time she was even coached by Alice.

Billie Jean told me that although her family were not poor, they always felt they came from the wrong side of the tracks. Eventually it was her father, a local fireman, who told her she must become more "ladylike." For this purpose he suggested golf, swimming, or tennis.

o

She chose tennis and spent the next months working odd jobs to buy her first racquet.

Less than a year after her first game, on the Long Beach public courts, Billie Jean entered Perry Jones's junior championships. She was beaten in the second round, but what embarrassed her more was the uneasiness she felt in the class-conscious Los Angeles club.

She says she took her lunch in a brown bag while most other kids ate in the clubhouse. Her parents were uncomfortable because they could not afford drinks at the bar with other parents. It was all this that lit the flame in her soul.

The first flaring came when Perry Jones refused to include Billie Jean in a group photograph of the juniors because she was wearing shorts and not a dress.

"By that time I was really hooked on tennis. I loved tennis, I just dreamed about it, I lived it. When I went to bed I took my racquet with me and looked at it. I saw myself playing at Wimbledon, the red carpet, the whole bit."

"So when this guy told me I couldn't be in the photograph, I said to myself: 'Who cares? It's small time. I'll show you anyway.' That immediately sparked something inside me that said: 'Hey, I'm going to change all this.' " In San Mateo, Billie Jean was reliving the episode as if it were yesterday.

A flashing signal on her desk caused another long pause. When she came back to her subject indignation was already simmering in her voice.

"I came to despise the system as a junior, but at that age I wasn't sure how to change it," she said.

"The USLTA and other establishments around the world made you feel obligated because THEY gave YOU the opportunity to play. They thought they owned you body and soul."

"Well, eventually, I did play a part in changing the system and today it gives me total gratification to know this."

I felt I could not let Billie Jean get too far into tennis politics without asking her again about the milestones of her tennis achievement.

"It's quite a long story now," she said, "and it relates mostly to Margaret Court."

"I beat Margaret, the No. 1 seed, at the '62 Wimbledon the first time I played her. After that she beat me fourteen straight times. The fourteenth time was the final of '65 Forest Hills. I led 5–3 in both sets, but she won 8–6, 7–5. During the presentation to Margaret I realized I could beat her. I began to sense what it meant to have her killer instinct, what it meant to 'go for the jugular.' Suddenly I knew I would

o

Madam Superstar 285

beat Margaret the next time I played her."

Billie Jean's instinct was unerring. She lost only eleven games in her next two meetings with Margaret and, with these victories, began her three successive years of Wimbledon domination.

In the course of a decade, Wimbledon, the subject of her childhood dreams, became a stage for her best performances. She piled title upon title to reach the co-record of nineteen with Elizabeth Ryan, and became such a part of Wimbledon that her friend and partner Rosie Casals, who always calls her the "Old Lady," describes Wimbledon's center court as the "Old Lady's House."

By '67 Billie Jean was clearly the best player in the world. If proof were needed, winning the elusive triple of all three events at both Wimbledon and Forest Hills is undeniable evidence. In terms of performance, that year must surely be the crowning glory of her career. In terms of significance, her winning of the Riggs Astrodome match in '73 was probably more important.

Today her major target is to become the all-time Wimbledon recordholder with twenty titles. In this respect, statistical comparisons between Billie Jean and Elizabeth Ryan are astonishing. Both have played eighteen Wimbledon championships. At the conclusion of the '78 championships, Billie Jean had actually played in 223 matches as compared with Elizabeth's 221. In total, Billie Jean has had 29 losses at Wimbledon, exactly the same number as Elizabeth, although Billie Jean has won six singles titles and thirteen doubles as opposed to Elizabeth's nineteen doubles titles. As a final coincidence, both Billie Jean and Elizabeth have benefited exactly four times each from opponents' defaults. Billie Jean has herself been forced to default once, and Elizabeth twice. Elizabeth lost five times to Lenglen in the seven years Lenglen played Wimbledon. She also suffered the four years' interruption of World War I. Billie Jean played against doctor's orders, with heavy bronchitis in '74, and had knee surgery in '68, '72, and '76, from which she has shown her marvelous powers of "recycling." To use her own words, she is still "banging away at a ball," and very much a challenger for further world crowns.

In my fifty-one Wimbledons I have never seen two more indomitable and "gutsier" competitors than Elizabeth Ryan and Billie Jean King. "Records are made to be broken," Elizabeth has always said. "If mine is to go, I would like Billie Jean to have it because she has so much guts."

As Billie Jean's fervor and dedication erupted periodically during our conversation, I felt more and more conscious of the Joan of Arc role she has played in tennis.

Throughout the '60s tennis was in an increasing state of ferment.

o

Open competition for professionals and amateurs alike was being demanded on all sides, but was being consistently blocked by the outdated necessity for a two-thirds majority vote at the council table of the world-governing body.

The system was heavily weighted in favor of men, and the women's locker rooms were places of vented anger. The women looked to Billie Jean for leadership, and like Joan of Arc, she felt destined to take up their cause.

In '67 her supremacy gave her the platform to express the women's complaints. She became a fierce campaigner and shouted her opinions from the rooftops. Officials in this country became more and more agitated as Billie Jean made outspoken statements about their malhandling of the game.

The situation reached boiling point after she won the '67 Forest Hills triple. Her press conference was one long attack on the establishment, and her statements so stirred the USLTA that the president, Bob Kelleher, personally threatened her with suspension.

Finally, in '68, Wimbledon itself took the historic step of opening its championship to both amateurs and professionals. It was only fitting that after years of condemning shamateurism, Billie Jean should become the first professional champion of Wimbledon and the world.

But Billie Jean may well have thought she won only a hollow crown.

The first big prize money ever allocated in tennis was allocated by men, in favor of men, on a two-against-one ratio. Henceforth, Billie Jean had a bigger-than-ever cause on her hands. It needed another two years for the Virginia Slims breakaway and another three years of Billie Jean's fire-and-brimstone campaigning before women were given an equal share of the prize money at a major championship.

In '71 Billie Jean's name appeared among the fifty-three signatures under a bold headline in Ms. magazine: "We Have Had Abortions."

Pioneers often shock, not least from a tennis court. Just as Suzanne Lenglen's little pleated frocks were said to "brazen" and "indecent" in 1919, the idea of the world's top tennis star letting it be known she had had an abortion, caused shock waves around the world in '71.

Billie Jean had to withstand a torrent of criticism from all sides, open attacks in the newspapers, and private letters of abuse.

Her tennis started to suffer badly and she decided to take a break. It was her moment of truth. For once Billie Jean all but succumbed to the pressure. She details in her memoirs her agonizing indecision. Should she continue her tennis or retire?

While she and her husband, Larry, were having a hit together in San Francisco, Billie Jean changed her mind half-a-dozen times.

"I'm going to retire. No, I can't. I'm quitting. No, I've got to play."

Finally she told Larry it was all over. She was definitely giving up tennis. They walked back to their apartment, and Larry was about to call the organizers of the Dallas tournament, due to start the next day, when she stopped him.

I asked if she remembered her exact words. "I can't cop out any more. I'm gonna play," she told Larry. "I don't care if I lose the first round. I've got to turn myself around and Dallas is gonna be the start."

Billie Jean did turn around.

Chris Evert had had her first major successes a few months previously, and Dallas was to be Evonne Goolagong's first-ever tournament in the United States.

Nancy Jeffett, the queen of Dallas tennis, was predicting an Evert-Goolagong semifinal. This was to be the first meeting of these two young and favorite stars, and Nancy had arranged a black-tie evening for the occasion.

Even to me a tennis audience in evening clothes was a novelty. At the time I was dressing Evonne Goolagong, but not Chris and not yet Billie Jean.

I forecast accurately that there would be millions of dollars in jewels in Nancy's courtside boxes. So it was for this occasion that I first used large rhinestones on a tennis dress and spread these on the special wardrobe I made for Evonne's American debut.

But, like Nancy Jeffett, I underestimated the Old Lady. Billie Jean certainly turned around. She had an amazing comeback win over Chris Evert after trailing by a set and 1–4 and, the following night, repeated her performance against Evonne. This was less than seven days after she told Larry she was retiring.

In the tennis dress area, the end of '72 brought a big switch in my clientele. Evonne Goolagong left me for a king-size American contract. Billie Jean gave up an even bigger contract to come to me.

In the years '71 and '72 the Virginia Slims Circuit had faced, and overcome, threats from every area of the American and international establishments. Yet still another threat to the overall appeal of women's tennis came from an unexpected source, Bobby Riggs.

In '71, during a practice hit at Forest Hills, Riggs jumped the fence of Billie Jean's court, challenging her to beat him in a public confrontation. At the time Billie Jean ignored him because to win would prove nothing more than the predictable fact she could beat a man twenty-five years her senior.

Bobby's idea was that he could beat Billie Jean and, in so doing, would create rewarding publicity for himself by inflicting a huge

○

put-down on the newfound popularity of the women's circuit.

Bobby was not to be turned aside lightly. In January '73 we were all in Miami when Bobby renewed his attack. This time his target was Margaret Court.

Margaret always found big-time exposure and money appealing. The combination of both proved irresistible. She soon told me she would be playing Riggs in a nationally televised challenge match in California in May and asked me for a specially designed outfit for the occasion.

I think Margaret interpreted Riggs's challenge as something personal to her. She was a very self-centered person, and the responsibility she had to the whole cause of women's tennis may not even have occurred to her.

Billie Jean was furious when she heard Margaret had swallowed Riggs's bait. Her passion for defending causes close to her heart was instantly aroused. All her instincts warned of the risks to women's tennis if Riggs won.

The relationship between Billie Jean and Margaret became even more tense than usual. Margaret's reaction was expectable. She interpreted as personal jealousy Billie Jean's opposition to her acceptance of Riggs's challenge. Meanwhile Billie Jean could do nothing but wait and pray that Margaret would win.

The Mother's Day Court–Riggs match at Ramona, California, proved a triumph for Riggs's hopes and ambitions. Margaret was a nervous wreck throughout the match and won only three games.

The San Vincente Club is located at 1,200 feet, near Ramona, hidden away among the Cuyamaca mountains behind San Diego. Margaret was quite unprepared for this altitude. She was also unprepared for Riggs's prematch propaganda. All in all she succumbed totally to Riggs's psychological warfare. For the final ironic twist, just before the match, her little boy, Danny, drowned her favorite sneakers in the toilet.

The press described Margaret's performance as a "Mother's Day Massacre."

The preceding week, Billie Jean, Rosie Casals, and I were in Tokyo. I was so determined to see Margaret's match, I left Japan before the end of the tournament. But Billie Jean and Rosie were in the finals and could not make the plane. Billie Jean had just reached Honolulu when she caught the end of the game on Rosie's radio.

In San Mateo, Billie Jean recalled her reaction. "I went BANANAS. When I heard those scores, 6–2, 6–1, I knew I had to play Bobby Riggs."

Billie Jean felt Margaret had betrayed the women's cause at a crucial moment in the development of the Virginia Slims' tour. Her inner call obliged her to recoup the situation.

"Margaret had opened the door," she said. "Things had gotten out of control. I had to play Riggs. It was only a matter of time and place, and the money."

I had the job of designing the all-important dress for the Great Challenge. I was particularly delighted because, that year, every major championship in the world had already been won by a player wearing a T.T. design. I thought Billie Jean would beat Riggs and this would be MY Grand Slam.

The match was set for September 20, only eleven days after the finals of the U.S. nationals at Forest Hills. August 28 was the day I was told. I realized I had no time at all and everything would have to be decided, at latest, during the first week of Forest Hills. Even so, I would have to return to Europe to supervise the final touches of the dress in London and be back in Houston by September 15.

Understanding as always, Virginia Slims suggested my chief seamstress, Mrs. Rose Stevens, come to New York to save time in this crisis. Billie Jean and her secretary, Marilyn Barnett, were staying at New York's La Guardia Sheraton.

When the date of the match was announced, Marilyn told me she had no fewer than 112 well-known sportswriters lined up for personal interviews with Billie Jean. I had to discuss fabric and designs with Billie Jean as a matter of urgency, so Marilyn put me at the top of the list. Mrs. Stevens and I were allocated one hour at the Sheraton, at 9 p.m. on September 2.

I took Mrs. Stevens in a cab from Manhattan. America was new to her, and she was dazzled all through the ride by the glittering Manhattan skyline.

However, as we turned the last bend to the La Guardia Sheraton, the entire area blacked out and we just made it in total darkness to the hotel entrance. In the chaos of the hotel, we were lucky to be guided with one candle to Billie Jean's room by Kris Kemmer.

Even in the near-darkness I could see Billie Jean's room was a bower of red roses and other bouquets already sent by fans who expected her to win Forest Hills.

In Paris I had found a length of truly beautiful and unusual fabric, which was composed of opalescent cellophane stitched in wavy stripes onto thin nylon net. By candlelight all its rainbow shades shimmered like an oil slick in the sun. Billie Jean was ecstatic. "I love it. I love it," she cried.

Then she retired to the bathroom with our one candle in a vain attempt to see how the fabric looked in the mirror.

o

Like the lights, the air-conditioning had failed. Marilyn had opened the windows, the temperature outside was ninety plus. Awaiting Billie Jean's second verdict, Marilyn, Mrs. Stevens, and I sat in total darkness, almost stifled by the scent of the massed roses. In such strange circumstances creations for big occasions can be conceived.

The following morning I dispatched Mrs. Stevens back to London. She was caught up in Billie Jean's enthusiasm, but my long years had taught me to be ready for anything. "We must have a standby dress 'just in case,' " I told Mrs. Stevens.

On our way together in a cab to JFK airport, with so little time to do anything, we decided on a remake of the dress Billie Jean had worn winning Wimbledon. In retrospect, this was one of my luckiest decisions because it was the standby dress she eventually wore.

On September 15 I arrived in Houston with the two dresses. Mrs. Stevens had done a good job, but Billie Jean, Larry, and Marilyn Barnett were hidden away so well that I could not find them. I was Gladys Heldman's houseguest for the week. Eventually Larry called Gladys's home to say the *New York Times* wanted a picture of Billie Jean with me.

Billie Jean had not seen either dress. The big match was forty-eight hours away, yet nothing whatever had been said about the fit or the chance the dresses could be wrong. At the top level of dress design there is always this possibility.

Larry met me and took me to Billie Jean's hideaway. After the photographer had left she at last said she wanted to try the two dresses. I had made her a simple button-down in the exotic Paris fabric. She looked great in it, and we were both delighted when her expression changed suddenly.

"I can't wear this dress," she said. In less than a moment all the excitement was gone from her suite. By the looking glass she had done a routine of her usual tennis gestures, which included wiping the palm of her hand on her dress. "I have never felt anything like this before," she said. "I could not risk upsetting my concentration with this strange sensation on my hand."

We had silk-lined the inside of the dress throughout, but Billie Jean is extremely responsive to the feel of all fabrics, and I had failed to foresee that the outside surface of the cellophane might upset her, no matter how beautiful to the eye. I thanked all my lucky stars for the standby dress.

Nevertheless my face must have shown the disappointment I felt.

"I won Wimbledon in this style. It has 'great vibes,' " Billie Jean said. The Wimbledon dress had been white trimmed with lilac. The standby replica was mint green with royal blue, and I think Billie Jean was concerned about bringing a smile back to my face as she expressed enthusiasm over the soft colors.

I had one more problem. The previous night I had made a point of visiting the vast Astrodome for the first time and realized that from many of the high balconies the performers would be almost indiscernible. The cellophane dress would have sparkled and shimmered. The detail of the standby dress could be appreciated only a few yards away.

On the day of the match, Ron Bookman, currently editor of *World Tennis*, was lunching with Gladys Heldman. We discussed my predicament, and with only six hours to go, Ron took me on a wild chase through Houston in search of some sequins and rhinestones.

The motorcade of Gladys's houseguests was leaving for the Astrodome at 4 p.m. At 3:55 I finished sewing, in my bedroom, about two hundred rhinestones and almost as many sequins. After that I felt Cinderella Standby could really go to the ball.

Billie Jean's triumph was bounced from the stratosphere to an approximated 200-million color TV screens around the world.

In later months I received letters from four continents. Each one was different. "How clever of you to put her in bright red," said the first. "I am surprised you chose lilac," said another. At least all my friends in this country saw the dress in its true green and blue and agreed with Billie Jean's appreciation of its subtlety. I am told the glittering rhinestones that outlined the Virginia Slims motif and entwined it with embroidered flowers, showed clearly all over the world.

At the Astrodome match, Gladys Heldman gave her guests the privilege of an entire row of gold-ticketed courtside seats. Joe Cullman and Lee Iacocca, the top men of Philip Morris and Ford respectively, together with the chairmen of two other great conglomerates, sat with us and their aides.

Joe Cullman had been the lone pioneer. Now Big Business was dotted all around the arena. The total number of spectators in the Astrodome was close to 35,000. This was the night tennis grew up and came of age.

I think the significance of the King-Riggs match, and Billie Jean's victory, will endure for at least fifty years.

Small related events began the very next morning. At one bank where fifty women were employed, the entire female staff showed up for work on September 21 wearing tennis gear. The match was so widely discussed across the country the head of one nationwide sales group sent all his men to Houston just to prepare them for the prime

o

topic of conversation in the ensuing days.

As the months went by, the tide of discussion swelled and swelled. People who had never previously given a thought to a tennis racquet were heatedly arguing the merits and demerits of a man losing to a woman, or a woman beating a man, according to their personal philosophies.

By playing Riggs in response to her inner call, Billie Jean made tennis an instrument of world communication as far reaching as the TV image of her match. She bounced tennis itself off the stratosphere.

Billie Jean and I are rarely in the same city at the same time, so most of the necessary dialogue about her dresses is done through the extensive business network she has built.

Currently, Kingdom, Inc. controls twenty-six separate companies. Her office complex has the activity of an ant heap. Competent-looking people carrying the inevitable sheaths of business documents bustle down the corridors. During our interview, long-distance calls for Billie Jean made an aurora borealis of flashing lights on her desk.

Billie Jean can be aggressive, abrasive, and comically self-deriding in rapid succession. I once said to her, "I do take it as a compliment I rarely hear from you personally and all our work is done through your secretaries."

"Bet your life," she laughed. "If there was any reason for having a real bitch, I wouldn't miss the opportunity for any money."

But at all times Billie Jean is a tomorrow's woman.

In our conversation it was obvious that tennis is now only her short-term occupation.

I asked where she hoped to go beyond tennis. Her eyes sparkled again. "Larry's always telling me, 'Go ahead and see if you can become the first woman president of the United States.' Can you imagine that?" She laughed.

"Maybe I will go into politics, television, something in public life, or continue to be just a business executive. Maybe it will be a combination of all these things. Sometime, someplace, the answer will come, and I will certainly do something more to change today's systems."

I asked if she would confine her leadership to women's causes, and my question prompted another rapid fire of machine-gun sentences.

"People put me in the women's slot because I happen to be a woman. But I feel that men as well as women are affected by what I have done. Men come up to me more often than women. Men have said to me: 'You have made my life better by beating Riggs.' Others have said: 'You have made my life worse.' Either way people are not

o

Madam Superstar   293

indifferent. I hate people who are indifferent. The thing that makes me go is being a perfectionist."

In the tennis community it is widely said that Billie Jean talks too much. Locker-room gossip paints lonely pictures of her expounding passionately long after the last writer has left her press conferences.

But creative thinking and the expression of her thoughts are the very essence of Billie Jean. And the essence is not sweet vanilla.

Billie Jean of the late '70s is a STAR. Years ago I nicknamed her "Madam Superstar" because this implies the full gamut of her emotions, from great loyalty, great professionalism, and warm affection, all the way to deceit, bitchery, and at times, self-destruction.

I was a young man in '33 in Hollywood when Hedda Hopper gave me her personal dictum: "If you want the girl next door, go next door." I have never wanted to "go next door." Which is probably why I have had so much happiness in my life among the stars of this world!

The brightness of Billie Jean's stardom rubs off on her surroundings. When I have been with her I always come away thinking I must do better work. Most times she is a warm human person. In '73 my staff and I made our first dresses for her. She won Wimbledon and, the following day, arrived loaded with gifts of flowers and plants for my workers. This was no sudden emotion, but a typical illustration of her thoughtfulness for those who collaborate with her.

In her bad moods Billie Jean can convey the contention and turbulence of the barricades. Sometimes the locker rooms see only this side of her.

In my lifetime, two players, through the sheer force of their skill and outstanding personalities, have expanded the importance of tennis in everyday life to hitherto unthought-of proportions. By a strange coincidence both have been women: Suzanne Lenglen and Billie Jean King. It is no coincidence that both emerged as world trend-setters at the exact moment when women around the world were themselves emerging from a chrysalis.

For ten years before 1918, British suffragettes campaigned to a point of violence for the right to vote. Concurrently, Lenglen dared the world to refuse women the choice of their own style of behavior.

In 1919, within months, both causes were won. In 1920 American women won their own battle when the Nineteenth Amendment gave them, for the first time, a true voice in the nation's government.

Fifty years later the multifaceted women's lib gained more momentum. Just as in 1919 women worshipped Lenglen for daring to live their secret dreams, in the '60s and '70s, Billie Jean blazed trails that were previously unthinkable and far beyond the realms of tennis.

○

Both women came unsuspectingly into a simple pastime. For both, tennis became a platform for their inspired leadership. Even the exposure of their human frailties on the center courts of the world has served to forge essential bonds of communication with their followers.

As I took leave of Madam Superstar in her San Mateo office, my mind wandered back to my visit with Marguerite Broquedis in Orléans, France, after the '77 Wimbledon Centennial.

In the smaller parameters of tennis at the start of this century, Marguerite Broquedis used her skill, her brains, and her beauty, to emerge as its first leader toward progress.

Waiting for my appointment with Madame Broquedis, I sat in a café in the town square, dominated by a twenty-foot statue of the city's greatest heroine, Joan of Arc, the Maid of Orléans.

The association with Billie Jean was inescapable. That evening my memories made a rainbow bridge across fifty years of tennis evolution, from Broquedis to Lenglen to King.

I had a feeling that for the next half century, Billie Jean could be known as the "Maid of Long Beach."

[30]

The Sharpshooters

BILLIE JEAN KING CHANGED THE FACE OF TENNIS AT THE HEIGHT of her career, the decade from '65 to '75. "Madam Superstar" threw brick after brick in the pond, and the outer ripples may well be visible for the next fifty years.

More recently two other Americans and a Swede, Chris Evert, Jimmy Connors, and Björn Borg, have held the popularity of tennis in their hands. More specifically, they exercise that popularity with two hands. And both of them on the backhand side.

Evert, Connors, and Borg emerged at the precise moment in time when the world was hungry for a basic change in the conventional playing styles of tennis of the first hundred years. They were the sharpshooters who arrived on the scene and promoted a trend that lifted the horizons of the game, particularly for the young.

Yet tennis played with two hands is not new.

○

In the '30s Australian teenager Vivian McGrath, was the first player to reach international status with a two-fisted style. He was followed by three more Australians, John Bromwich, the American men's doubles champion in '39, '49, and '50; Geoff Brown, the Wimbledon finalist in '46; Bob Howe, the Wimbledon mixed titlist in '58. Finally, everybody's friend, Pancho Segura. As I write *Love and Faults*, Björn Borg sits at the very summit of two-fisted tennis.

Among the women, Jan Lehane, yet another Australian, and a faithful client of mine in the '60s, was the first woman to achieve the upper reaches of tennis using two hands on the backhand side.

In my lifetime there have been other isolated cases of unconventional techniques at the top levels: Georgio di Stefani in the '30s and Beverly Baker in the '50s. Both were completely ambidextrous, changing hands during rallies, but playing perfect tennis with either hand.

I remember Bill Tilden asking Georgio which hand he used for shaving. "Sometimes I can't remember," replied Georgio. "I shall probably end up slitting my throat in the center."

But before the '70s the world was not quite ready to accept such revolutions. Equally, none of the pioneers of the two-handed game had the world exposure, the explosive power, and the target-shooting precision of Evert, Connors, and Borg.

American youth, in particular, identifies with the new trend. Connors projects a belligerence of nature in his playing style that attracts many young people. The less emotional or more studious types are deeply attracted to Björn Borg.

On the other hand, Chris has communicated, to an extraordinary degree, an idealized image of today's young womanhood.

Billie Jean in her younger days was the darling of the campus, with her neat skirts and shirts, her boyish hairstyle, and effusive language.

By the time Chris emerged, the sought-after image had softened considerably. Chris has epitomized American Pie and the fresh Outdoor Girl, much more copied by today's decade.

Except in a tiny minority of cases, women's backhands have, traditionally, been a defensive stroke. To a lesser degree, this has also been true of the men's.

In today's idiom, "defensive" has become a word the young frequently associate derisively with their parents' philosophies.

The two-handed backhand, personified by Evert, Connors, and Borg, has taken the word "defense" right out of tennis terminology and has given more power to the game—in every sense. Their sharpshooting tennis made it clear to young people they were not being asked to pick up the country-club pastime of their fathers.

They have also provided an antidote to the anti-establishment feeling many teenagers have had since the '60s. They hit the scene when the kids felt the need for an element in tennis that was not in the game they had spurned in the past. The bottom line is that this extraordinarily gifted trio have been recruiting agents for millions of teenagers.

Chris first came to international notice when, at the age of fifteen, she beat Margaret Court. At that time, Margaret had won close to eighty world titles.

I have always been fascinated by the arrival of any outstanding newcomer in my panorama, so Ed and Marilyn Fernberger arranged for me to make a special journey to Philadelphia to see Chris win the Under-18 National Girls' title over Janet Newberry in '71.

That Philadelphia victory became a part of several long-winning sequences for which she has since become renowned. The first winning run of forty-six matches was already a long one. Nowadays 100–0 winning records are regarded as normal for Chris Evert.

It was from Pancho Gonzalez that I first heard of Jimmy Connors. During the pro tours of the late '60s, Pancho was often in London, and I remember the enthusiasm he expressed about the latest boy-wonder with the two-handed game. He was even proposing to play doubles with "Jimbo" at Wimbledon, a big compliment from a world-famous star to a relatively unknown teenager.

When Connors went to England, Pancho asked me, through some mutual friends, the London tennis-playing Prenns, to tell Jimmy hello and give him a kind welcome.

Jimmy Connors was born on September 2, 1952, in East St. Louis, Missouri, and grew up in Belleville, Illinois. His father, also James Connors, managed the toll bridge that links St. Louis with Belleville. His mother, Gloria, and his grandmother, Bertha, to whom he still refers as "Mom" and "Two-Mom," were however, the driving forces behind his eventual stardom in tennis.

In the '60s Gloria Connors had been the No. 1 ranked player of the Missouri Valley. Mom and Two-Mom set up a commando course for Jimmy's development which emulated the training techniques of Harry Hopman and Papa Lenglen.

Jimmy was always small for his age and just did "what came naturally" when he started hitting balls on public courts in Belleville, using two hands to hold his racquet for the more difficult strokes on the backhand side.

Mom was coach and Two-Mom the taskmaster. Friends have

recalled that in Jimmy's early days at the St. Louis Armory, Mom would watch with an eagle eye over three sets of tennis practice. Two-Mom would then take over, enforcing rope-jumping drills and a daily mile of running up and down the armory stairs.

The "Two Panchos," Gonzalez and Segura, first noticed Jimbo during one of their whistle-stop pro tour matches in the late '60s. Connors's Mom had been Segura's partner in mixed doubles in her playing days. She realized the affinity between her son's backhand and Segura's two-handed style and asked if Segura would coach Jimmy.

Segura was quick to take up the challenge. He arranged for Jimbo to move to California, where he and his own son, Spencer, could go to the same school. Segura also arranged for Connors to have access to the Beverly Hills Country Club.

Then Mom and Two-Mom, both anxious to maintain the strict guidance over Jimmy's career, which Gloria Connors maintains to this day, both traveled to California to oversee Jimmy's progress.

Meanwhile, for long years already, fifteen-year-old Chris Evert had been trading metronome rallies with her dad, Jimmy Evert, the well-known teaching pro at Fort Lauderdale.

I saw Chris for the second time in '72. By then sportswriter Bob Getz was already reporting: "If the day ever comes when Chris meets someone who plays the baseline as well as she, the game will go on indefinitely, its winner only being determined by whoever lives longest."

Jimmy Evert's tennis philosophy is to "get the ball back at all costs." It has been his determination on this point that has brought about Chris's marvelous footwork and mechanical ability, sometimes taking precedence over more imaginative tactics.

The added dimension, which comes from Chris's own star personality, is her ability to keep her finger patiently on the trigger, to fire her pistol shots at the first available opportunity, and her capacity to do so with lethal effect.

Chris's development into a match winner of implacable resilience was demonstrated in '71 in her first Forest Hills championship.

At this time Chris, who was born on December 21, 1954, was playing America's No. 4 ranking Wightman Cup player Mary Ann Eisel, eight years her senior. In this match she saved six match points. It was the forty-fourth of her forty-six successive wins. Her final victims in that first golden spell were Françoise Durr and Lesley Hunt. In the Forest Hills semifinal she then ran into Billie Jean King.

The next day London's ace tennis writer David Gray told British

readers, *"The Demon King put an end to the fairytale of Chris Evert."*
But there were more pages to come in the fairy story.

For the next six years, Billie Jean King and Evonne Goolagong
were to be Chris's major opponents.

In '72 a strange coincidence occurred when Evonne Goolagong
made her first appearance in this country, and three months later,
Chris made her first journey to England.

I was involved in both events because, at the time, I was still
dressing Evonne.

For Evonne's American debut everyone converged on Nancy Jeffett's tournament in Dallas in March. We all sensed the dawning of a
new era in women's tennis.

For years past Margaret Court and Billie Jean King had dominated
all the big finals. Even the expectation of a first meeting between
Chris and Evonne in Dallas brought a breath of spring to the whole
women's scene.

I have described in a previous chapter how the Demon King delayed the first meeting of the new prodigies. This was to come in the
Wimbledon semifinals on July 5. Mary Hardwick Hare relates part of
the story of these two emotion-charged matches.

> Three Americans, Billie Jean King, Rosie Casals and Chris Evert,
> plus one Australian, Evonne Goolagong, were involved. Billie Jean
> appeared in the required white costume, but little Rosie startled the
> crowd by her choice of outfits, a dress specially designed for her by Ted
> Tinling for the Virginia Slims Indoor Circuit. It was dramatic, with a
> pattern of purple squiggles back and front, which suggested the initials
> "V.S." Ted had advised her not to wear it at Wimbledon, but Rosie is
> Rosie and was going to do it "her way."

In the second semifinal, Evonne beat Chris in one of the most
exciting and emotional matches of the decade.

In defeat, Chris was as gracious and charming as she has been ever
since.

"I look forward to meeting Evonne many more times," she said
afterwards. At the time of writing, the two girls' win-loss record is
18–13 in Chris's favor.

The next day Rosie and Wimbledon referee Captain Mike Gibson
had a head-on confrontation that resulted in Rosie becoming an
immortal in tennis history. Captain Gibson appeared on the court,
took exception to her dress, and she became the only player ever to be
sent back to the Wimbledon locker room to change in the course of a
match.

In '73 Connors earned this country's joint No. 1 spot with Stan

Smith. Chris Evert reached the Wimbledon final and the semifinal at Forest Hills for the second time.

In the first five years of open tennis the main subject of discussion among teenagers and young hopefuls centered on how much money they might earn from their tennis. Henceforth, it was all Chris, Björn, and Jimmy and the two-handed backhand.

The year '74 was the year of the famous "Love Double," so called because both Chris and Jimmy won the Wimbledon singles championships, and also because Chris embarked on another of her long golden spells while Jimmy lost only four out of the 102 matches that he played.

Until the '78 U.S. Nationals Jimmy found it harder to hit the bull's-eye with such total accuracy, although in '76 he won 106 matches and lost only 12. The distractions of world stardom no doubt had an effect on his play. He had also to cope with the enormous publicity given to his temporary engagement to Chris; his huge financial successes; the usual attendant litigation of fast-rising stars with their managers; and the ascendancy of another sharpshooting, two-hander, Björn Borg.

I have personally seen more than half of Chris's thirty-one matches with Evonne and most of her now-famous encounters with Billie Jean King, Virginia Wade, and the "Czech that bounces," Martina Navritilova.

Besides Chris's many victories, which are becoming a legend in her lifetime, I have seen her beaten three times by Virginia, five times by Martina, and four times by Billie Jean.

In a remarkably sensitive interview for Philadelphia's *Inquirer*, Bill Lyon wrote: "Ice Maiden. Machine. Robot. Cold and calculating." Something, in short, not quite human. That is how Chris is presented.

Chris told Bill Lyon: "Behind closed doors I am a totally different person. Of all the things my father said, what stuck with me most was this: 'Be a lady on court!' I think the spectators now respect me for what I have achieved, I guess I'm somewhere between Billie Jean King, who is a legend, and Tracy Austin, who is a novelty."

"A Lady on Court" is the heart and soul of Chris Evert. I can say, with total sincerity, that in fifty years I have never seen a more gracious and sporting world champion.

Since my first sight of Chris Evert, innumerable people have told me how strikingly she compares with Maureen Connolly. I have always refuted this. To me, Chris has a much deeper resemblance to Helen Wills, though I think today's life-styles will distract her from tennis well before she has time to equal Helen Wills's record.

Talking to Will Grimsley in late '77, Helen Wills said: "I don't like the two-fisted shot, except with Chris Evert. She has a way of making it look beautiful. She is a lovely person, so well-mannered. I am flattered when they sometimes compare her with me."

Today, in this country alone, many thousands of young players are using the two-handed, sharpshooter backhand. Many thousands more have been attracted to tennis by the examples of Chris Evert, Jimmy Connors, and Björn Borg.

Tracy Austin's two-handed successes and charming manners are already perpetuating their example. She will certainly recruit thousands more to the contemporary delights of sharpshooting tennis.

And there is no doubt the marvelous fire power of Björn Borg would have been a delight to the late "Mr. G.," His Majesty King Gustav of Sweden.

I really wonder whether if in my fifty-plus years of tennis watching I have ever seen anyone play better tennis than Borg in the '78 Wimbledon men's singles final.

Yet the All England Lawn Tennis Club's silver-gilt trophy, first won by S. W. Gore at the 1877 inaugural championships and awarded annually ever since, is still inscribed "For the Single-handed Championships of the World (Gentlemen)."

Epilogue

Scattered Pictures

FOR OVER FIFTY YEARS I HAVE LIVED IN THE MAIN SETTLEMENTS
of the community of tennis players.

All of us have shared to some degree in one another's successes and
frustrations. Our hopes and fears have related to a common cause.
Thousands of players from our community have given immeasurable
pleasure to a century of spectators.

The main endeavor of *Love and Faults* has been to sketch, from
the lake of time, the reflections of eighteen personalities, who by their
beliefs and strength of character have changed the face of tennis in
my lifetime and who have led our community, in successive eras, to
promised lands of new and improved circumstances.

I have particularly selected Suzanne Lenglen, Elizabeth Ryan,
Helen Wills, Alice Marble, "Gorgeous Gussy" Moran, "Little Mo"
(and the Maureen Connolly Brinker Foundation she inspired),

Gladys Heldman, Billie Jean King, and Chris Evert, and on the men's side, "Big Bill" Tilden, the four "French Musketeers," Perry Jones, Fred Perry, Harry Hopman for his Davis Cup successes, Lamar Hunt, Joe Cullman, and Jimmy Connors.

These were the leaders. Many other personalities helped them, of course, toward their respective goals. Destiny has allowed me my part.

The long years, and the experiences shared in our community have inevitably created a legacy of scattered pictures.

Recalled at random, I would like to record this assortment:

* * * *

My first-ever game of tennis. With my governess on a public park court at Hastings, England, in 1919, with my mother's 1896 racquet from her trousseau.

*

Sports Illustrated's cover picture showing "Sportswoman of the Year" '76, Chris Evert, wearing my Victorian repro tennis dress and holding the self-same racquet—then eighty years old.

*

Gene Scott, legal counsel to the USLTA '72, telling me, as a throwaway comment, that for the first time in all tennis history, colored tennis dresses would be allowed at Forest Hills four weeks later. I'd been waiting for ten years.

*

The radiantly sunny morning when Betty Stove and Françoise Durr won the '72 Forest Hills doubles, the first women ever to win an international tennis title in colored dresses.

*

Evelyn Dewhurst, playing forty exhibition matches against Suzanne Lenglen in Britain '27. "Facially, she was frighteningly ugly," Evelyn said, "but her magnetism was so compelling one forgot this."

*

General Eisenhower's memo saying "No. This is a man's war and tennis is a woman's game," when I had asked permission to stage an exhibition match for the Red Cross in Algiers '43.

*

Simonne Mathieu saying "Even the bloody nets are English," after her English opponent had scored three winning net-cord shots against her.

*

Shirley Bloomer, world-ranked No. 3, snapping the waistband of a blue tennis underskirt I had made her. It fell to the ground during a

Wightman Cup match on Wimbledon's grandstand court. Five thousand male spectators shouted "More, more," as she calmly stepped out of it.

*

Making the first tropically flowered tennis dresses to cheer Martina Navratilova after her defection from Czechoslovakia in '75, "They'er wild," someone said to Martina. "Yes, like my personality," she said.

*

Marilyn Fernberger's comment on seeing Martina in the flowered dresses at Forest Hills: "So we're into shower-curtains, now!"

*

Peter Bodo's wonderful report on Virginia Wade's Wimbledon '77 Centennial title that quotes the comments of a London cab driver speaking in genuine Cockney idiom, for *Tennis* magazine: "Wimbledon? 'Ats right, mate. Get yer there in no time. Mind yer 'ead gettin' in. Goin' to the tennis are yer then? Big to-do there, I reckon, centenary an' all. I'm a football man meself, but I seen a bit o' tennis on the box I did. Reckon all o' bleddin' England did wi' Virginia Wade in the final. Picked a right un to win, didn't she? Wasn't a sane man in London picked 'er to win this one. But she 'ad us bang to rights. Bad afternoon for us cabbies, it was. They were queued up watchin' 'er on the box by every shop window. She was smashin' tho', wasn't she, that Virginia Wade?"

*

Queen Elizabeth saying to me "I had no idea tennis girls could look so pretty."

*

Gladys Heldman's wickedly ironic remark when asked by a reporter if it was really she who started the Virginia Slims Women's Circuit. "No," she replied, "it was Jack Kramer."

*

When a girl from the Communist bloc played Nancy Jeffett's Dallas tournament with no panties at all. "They do not have the right type behind the Iron Curtain," she explained innocently.

*

Evonne Goolagong bringing "instant spring" into '71 tennis. After making a peerless winner she would give little lonely smiles to herself like a child who has spied a pretty flower in the grass.

*

Bobby Riggs saying, before playing Billie Jean King in the Houston Astrodome, "I shall probably turn up in black so as to be correctly dressed for her funeral."

*

My telling Wimbledon '47 finalists Jack Kramer and Tom Brown indignantly "The King and Queen of England are never late." They were. Jack and Tom had to hold the start of their final for ten minutes.

*

Diddie Vlasto's absolute horror in '26 on learning that Suzanne Lenglen proposed to let herself be massaged by a man.

*

Karen Susman playing Lea Pericoli in Rome with two thousand Romans cheering Lea's every shot. Karen questioning the fourth ghastly line call given against her. "I always play to the umpire's decision," said Lea, with an angelic smile. "Have you no eyes, no conscience?" said Karen. Lea won the match.

*

My receiving a letter from Karen Krantzcke a week before her death, saying how much she was enjoying life and how she loved playing tennis.

*

My enjoying all the conversations I have ever had with *World Tennis* statistician Steve Flink.

*

Chris Evert and Virginia Wade, finalists in Washington's vast Capital Center in '76. Chris in bright sunshine yellow, Virginia shimmering in rose pink lamé, both looking divine. 14.000 excited spectators. At courtside, Jack Ford, the President's son, surrounded by bored security men, all looking like Hollywood extras. Jack drooling over Chris.

*

Peachy Kellmeyer arranging a memorable visit to the White House for me with a personal greeting from President Gerald Ford. A proud moment for an immigrant.

*

The cub reporter who said to me "What a pity you didn't design Gussy's panties. Now, that would really have given you some good publicity."

*

Helen Wills and Karol Fageros, the two most beautiful women I ever saw in championship tennis.

*

Alison Adburgham writing about Karol Fageros: "Her smile blazes from a cloudless face. She poses against the privet hedge as though it were a palm tree. She mounts the steps to the players' lounge as if they were the gangway to a yacht."

*

o
306 *Epilogue*

The "wages of sin" for Lew Hoad. While on Army service in Australia he rolled his shirt-sleeves, contrary to all Army instructions. Lew was promptly bitten on the elbow by a lethal spider and was unconscious for two days. "Death occurs on the fifth day," all the medical manuals say about this particular spider bite. "I always knew Lew had a thick skin," said his wife, Jenny.

*

Dick Savitt, Wimbledon and Australian '51 Singles champion, climbing on the Forest Hills locker-room table to see if the crotch of the shorts I made him was high enough. He pronounced it "too low."

*

Fitting Gladys Heldman at Ellis Park, Johannesburg, in the men's locker room by mistake. "Dahling, the crotch is too high, it's killing me," she was saying while a man flushed the toilet four times in back before we understood his embarrassment.

*

Arthur Ashe's wonderful mental triumph over Jimmy Connors at '75 Wimbledon.

*

The 18-karat gold Virginia Slims logo and neck chain specially made for me at London's Asprey's, a gift from Billie Jean King, Rosie Casals, and Vicki Berner.

*

Christine Truman, on being told in a Rome restaurant that her order of spring chicken would take thirty minutes, saying "All right, bring me an older one!"

*

The incandescent English of Herbert Warren Wind's tennis and golf reports for *The New Yorker*.

*

The "Pavlova" dessert to end all Pavlovas, cooked up by Australia's Mary Hawton for all the visiting stars at her beautiful Sydney home.

*

The amazing improvement in Margaret Court's previously twisted back after being "called to the Lord," through her spiritual healer, Mary Rogers.

*

Mary Rogers "seeing" Suzanne Lenglen standing beside me in Melbourne '76, thirty-eight years after Lenglen's death.

*

Maria Bueno borrowing a bra five minutes before an important Wimbledon center-court match and my having to sew a strip torn off my handkerchief in the neckline of her dress before she could play.

o

Maria Bueno and Alex Olmedo winning '59 Wimbledon simultaneously, the first Latins to do so. The Wimbledon Ball lap of honor had been a waltz for fifty years. That night it was switched to a cha-cha-cha. The coming of the laughing Latins put champagne into tennis.

*

Prudence Glynn, woman's editor of the London *Times*, cutting roses for me in her garden after Billie Jean King won her first Wimbledon wearing one of my dresses. The first day Billie Jean saw that particular dress she said it had "good vibes."

*

Ellen Merlo in *Newsweek*: "We figured that to be important women's tennis had to look important, so we hired noted designer, Ted Tinling, to make the girls look glamorous when they were normally playing in T-shirts."

*

David Gray's description in London's *Guardian*: "Virginia Wade, a mixture of Sarah Bernhardt and Maria Callas playing Medea."

*

Bridget Byrne, reporting a Virginia Wade-Julie Heldman match for the *Los Angeles Herald Examiner*: "Two cats fighting in a psychiatric ward. Wade, the jewelled puma, won."

*

Margaret Goatson Kirgin working for me for twenty-two years and hand-cutting every tennis dress worn by every T.T. star from 1937 to this day.

*

Martina Navratilova saying, after losing to JoAnne Russell, "I like your new hairstyle and glasses." JoAnne saying "They're not new. It's just that before I beat you you never bothered to look at me."

*

Jean Rook, women's editor of London's *Daily Express*, headlining, on my immigration to the United States, "Who's for England now that Ted Tinling has served his notice?"

*

Briefly away from tennis, the ten years' happiness I experienced in tenpin bowling when I gave up playing tennis. Particularly with my league buddies in our "Green Arrows" team. We "tore a few jerseys," as the Rugby footballers say when they win.

*

My enormous admiration for Alberta Crowe, the beneficient president W.I.B.C. of more than 4,200,000 American women bowlers.

o

Being at the heart of the American/British Intelligence Service for five years in World War II.

My Connecticut socialite client Audrey Lamont, instructing that she be buried in one of her T.T. tennis dresses. "They have been my happy clothes," she explained to her attorneys.

*

Always carrying a tennis-action pic of Lamar Hunt's lovely wife, Norma, in my wallet. "On my heart," I told Lamar. He looked surprised.

*

Watching Sue Cullman complete the world's most difficult crossword in ten minutes flat.

*

Remembering the pretty South African "twins" Sandra Reynolds and Renée Schuurman, who always wore identical dresses. They could have met in the '61 Wimbledon final as they were simultaneously in the semis. "What shall we do?" Margaret Kirgin asked me. "Look at their horoscopes in the newspaper," I told her. "This time they cannot wear the same dresses." "Disappointment in the afternoon," was predicted for Sandra. "So we have no problem," I told Margaret. That afternoon, Sandra lost.

*

Back to America. The many happy visits I have made to Cleveland, Ohio, when the Wightman Cup marches were played there. Finalizing the details of Christine Truman's wedding dress at courtside between her matches.

*

With Pip and Ann Jones, happy days in at least half dozen countries.

*

The very moving medal presentation ceremony at centennial Wimbledon with forty-one of the fifty-two living champions on center court. The greatest names from more than fifty years of tennis history, united for a few transient moments of incomparable nostalgia.

*

The four "French Musketeers" being inducted into Jimmy Van Alen's Newport Hall of Fame in '76, the first overseas players included there. Lacoste, the youngest at 72, Brugnon the eldest at 81. All four still radiating the same Gallic charm and humor as in their golden era of the '20s.

○

Jean Borotra flying from Paris to Wimbledon and back three times in one week, a pioneer of air travel in the early '20s. Toto Brugnon refusing all his life to go in an airplane but finally being induced to come to Newport by Concorde. "If I'd known flying was like this, I'd have flown thirty years ago," he said, quite seriously.

A thousand happy experiences shared with Flo Blanchard, Lee Jackson, and Mike Blanchard. They have to be the world's best umpires.

Simonne Mathieu, after winning the '33 Wimbledon Doubles with Elizabeth Ryan, saying "When I was first brought to see Elizabeth *in my pram*, I didn't think we should be winning Wimbledon together."

Elizabeth missing two "sitters" and Simonne bitching at her for doing so. Elizabeth, wanting to say in her limited French "Let's forget what's past," said *"Oubliez mon derrière."* Translated literally, this means "Forget my ass."

The outstandingly pretty girls who don't make daily headlines but get their men: Helen Gourlay Cawley and Julie Anthony Butera.

Barbara Kahn, tennis girl, realtor and decorator-in-chief to Philadelphia's smart fund-raising set.

Nell Hopman, finding the name of her next-seat neighbor on British Airways was "Jesus," asking if he would like to look through her Bible.

Tracy Austin's mother, Jeanne, the most helpful "Tennis Mom" I have ever worked with.

My Margaret Kirgin always having to remember that Dianne Fromholtz and Ann Jones, both obstinate southpaws, want their zippers on the right-hand side of their dresses.

My remembering that girls with Leo horoscope signs often win. Lesley Turner Bowery and Evonne Goolagong, both good examples, with long lists of titles.

Olga Morozova, making my dresses seem part of the Bolshoi.

Breaking my toe in "Jude" and David Dalton's Sydney swimming pool on Christmas Day '75.

Lesley Hunt, originally the complete shorts-and-shirts tomboy, now the very feminine wife on perennial honeymoon with Jim Hambueschen.

Terry Holladay, crossing the international dateline going to Australia in '76, jumped from November 27 to 29. November 28 was her twenty-first birthday. It took us quite a time to explain "the one that got away."

Ed and Marilyn Fernberger's wonderful airport greeting to me when I immigrated to America: "Welcome to the second half of your youth."

Marilyn Fernberger ordering an exact copy of the tennis outfit I had just delivered to Farah Diba, the Empress of Iran.

Headlines in London '68: "19 years after, Gussy still gorgeous." She was.

Wallis Myers about my Wimbledon Call-Boy job: "Tinling is the man who conducts the stars from the wings onto the stage. A moment as intimate as those some people spend upon their knees."

My being taken in by the Santa Monica police in '33 for swimming in trunks only. I should have asked the rules.

My being taken in in Brisbane, Australia, in '53 because my swim trunks had no belt. I should have read the rules.

My being presented with a beautiful pearl necklace in Japan. The interpreter saying "We hope humble gift suitable for honorable new mistress."

On center court, Wimbledon, June 20, '77. The band of the Queen's Royal Guards, a scarlet splash of spit-and-shine on the green turf, playing Vera Lynn's famous World War II weepie: "I'll See You Again, Don't Know Where, Don't Know When." An inspired choice.

On center court also, forty-one top stars, some of whom were not exactly friendly with one other at the peak of their careers, all kissing, crossing hands, and singing "Auld Lang Syne."

Barry Lorge's sensitive and evocative reports for the *Washington Post*. Many of his accounts are tennis gems.

o

Epilogue 311

The most classic continental forehands ever seen in the game: Lennart Bergelin from Sweden, Simonne Mathieu and Maude Galtier from France.

*

The frustrated woman who said to me "No wonder Maria Bueno is so popular in England. She has a boy's legs and most Englishmen are fags anyway."

*

The good fortune we have that the Italian star writers Gianni Clerici and Rino Tommasi are sent so often by their respective, and respected, newspapers to be with us in the United States.

*

Jack Kramer's match being delayed by a long women's single. "Women should never be allowed on center court," he said.

*

Vice-President Mondale saying recently how much the United States is indebted to Italian-Americans. In many ways American tennis is indebted to Mike Lupica.

*

Queen Elizabeth of England seldom honors a tennis match with her interest, but she was present at '77 Wimbledon long enough to congratulate her subject Virginia Wade on the crowning achievement of Virginia's life. The Queen even removed her white gloves, which was an unusual compliment.

*

Rex Bellamy, the perennial "Writer of the Year" award winner from players of both sexes.

*

Six happy months as consultant to beautiful people Jesse and Julie Bell when they launched the Bonne Bell Cup, now contested between under-18 American and Australian girls.

*

My wisest counselors during my difficult '71 mediation between World Championship Tennis and the International Federation: Richard Evans, John Barrett, and David Gray.

*

Judith Elian, the ultracosmopolitan Rumanian-Italian-Spanish-Turkish tennis writer, always bringing a breath of Parisian charm to every tournament she reports for France's leading sports newspaper L'Equipe.

*

Suzanne Lenglen at a Nice thé-dansant with Rudolph Valentino.

○

"He danced very sensually," Suzanne said afterwards (as if we hadn't already noticed).

*

Neil Amdur's unfailing generosity to me at the *New York Times*.

*

The powerful: Washington's tennis wheeler-dealer Donald Dell and Women's Tennis Association Executive Director Jerry Diamond. The beautiful: Dell's wife Carole and Diamond's wife Barbara. The powerful and beautiful: Colgate Palmolive Vice-President Tina Santi.

*

Alfonso Smith, the super of the Super-Seniors.

*

Mrs Ivy Wightwick, a cozy English grand-mum who worked for me for twenty-three years, hand-knitting in her lunch break, the mint-green cardigan worn by Billie Jean King against Bobby Riggs. We had searched England and the United States unsuccessfully for a ready-to-wear garment in the exact shade. "We can't have her getting chilled in that drafty Astroplace," said Ivy.

*

Charles Pomeranz, Milton Weiss, and Eddy Jo Bernal, the Hollywood triplets handling all my Californian presentations. Eddy Jo, Ellen Merlo, and I traveled eleven cities, from Seattle to Miami, in thirteen days, and were still speaking.

*

Martina Navratilova asking me, in May '78 for a duplicate of the gold pin-striped, navy-collared, white dress I first made her in December '77. Wearing the original, she won seven straight Virginia Slims finals plus the Virginia Slims championship. Wearing the duplicate for the first time at Eastbourne '78, she beat Chris Evert. At Wimbledon '78, she wore the duplicate to beat Tracy Austin, Julie Anthony, and Evonne Goolagong. Then she returned to the original to win the final against Chris Evert.

*

Bud Collins, NBC/TV's star commentator and the *Boston Globe*'s star columnist, is addicted to wearing strident colors. Interviewing Pam Shriver at '78 Wimbledon he wore glaring canary-yellow trousers. "First turn off those pants," said Pam before answering his opening question.

*

The amazement expressed by DD Eisenberg, Philadelphia's star sports columnist, when I told her that among the five-hundred-plus championship tennis players I have dressed none have had a waist measurement of less than 27 inches. DD's own glamor silhouette boasts a 23-inch waist.

*

London *Times*'s Geoffrey Green, the tennis writer whose glamor touches always make one wish one had been present at the matches he reports.

*

Onetime top-money golfer Sandra Haynie, now managing Martina Navratilova. Always practical, always sporting, always positive. The best manager I have worked with.

*

My two favorite tennis reports, particularly when picturing the full surrounding circumstances:

A Paris newspaper reporting a French provincial tournament that said: "The ladies' final did not take place as one participant, Mlle Joinville, brought with her a brand of tennis balls not acceptable to her opponent. In turn, Mme Landru, the opposing finalist, was insistent on a brand of balls not acceptable to Mlle Joinville. Unfortunately, the trophies became damaged in the discussion and the committee decided they could not be awarded on this occasion."

A German newspaper reporting an international match in the Mittel Europa Cup between two communist nations, which said: "At one point play was interrupted because the crowds had become noisy and partisan. However, after the guards had fired machine guns over the heads of the spectators, play was resumed in a normal manner."

*

Slew Hester's miracle in raising the Flushing Meadow complex, literally out of the bare ground in less than fifty-two weeks. Vicki Berner, Mike Burns, and Ed Fabricius, executive assistants to Slew and the USLTA, lifting the prestige of his association to levels hitherto unthought of.

*

October 18, 1977, Martina was twenty-one years old. On July 12, 1978, the Women's Tennis Association computer ranking made her No. 1 in the world. "I have waited since I was seven for this moment," said Martina.

*

Love and Faults mostly recounts the stories of star performers and high-level administrators. The British invented tennis, but today's tennis embraces no less than 104 nations.

I close these chapters respectfully saluting the 200 million hackers from these nations who have brought the game to its present level of popularity and prosperity.

o